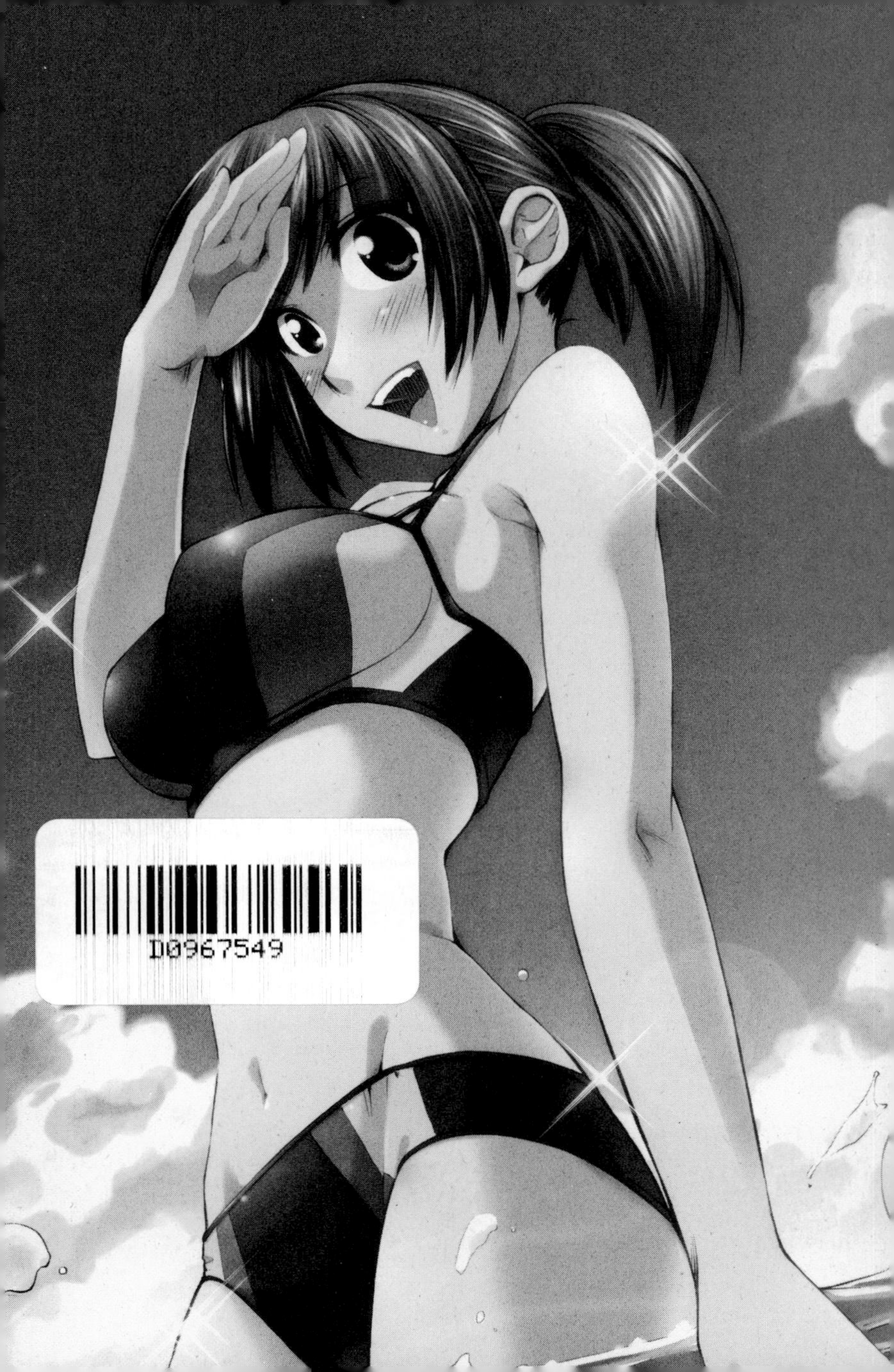

KimiKiss Volume 2
Art by Taro Shinonome
Story by ENTERBRAIN, INC.

Translation - Alexis Kirsch
English Adaptation - Katherine Schilling
Retouch and Lettering - Star Print Brokers
Production Artist - J. Doe
Graphic Designer - Chelsea Windlinger

Editor - Alexis Kirsch
Print Production Manager - Lucas Rivera
Managing Editor - Vy Nguyen
Senior Designer - Louis Csontos
Director of Sales and Manufacturing - Allyson De Simone
Associate Publisher - Marco F. Pavia
President and C.O.O. - John Parker
C.E.O. and Chief Creative Officer - Stu Levy

A  Manga

TOKYOPOP and  are trademarks or registered trademarks of TOKYOPOP Inc.

TOKYOPOP Inc.
5900 Wilshire Blvd. Suite 2000
Los Angeles, CA 90036

E-mail: info@TOKYOPOP.com
Come visit us online at www.TOKYOPOP.com

ISBN: 978-1-4278-1582-8

First TOKYOPOP printing: October 2009
10 9 8 7 6 5 4 3 2
Printed in the USA

KIMIKISS

VOLUME 2

Art by Taro Shinonome
Story by Enterbrain, Inc.

HAMBURG // LONDON // LOS ANGELES // TOKYO

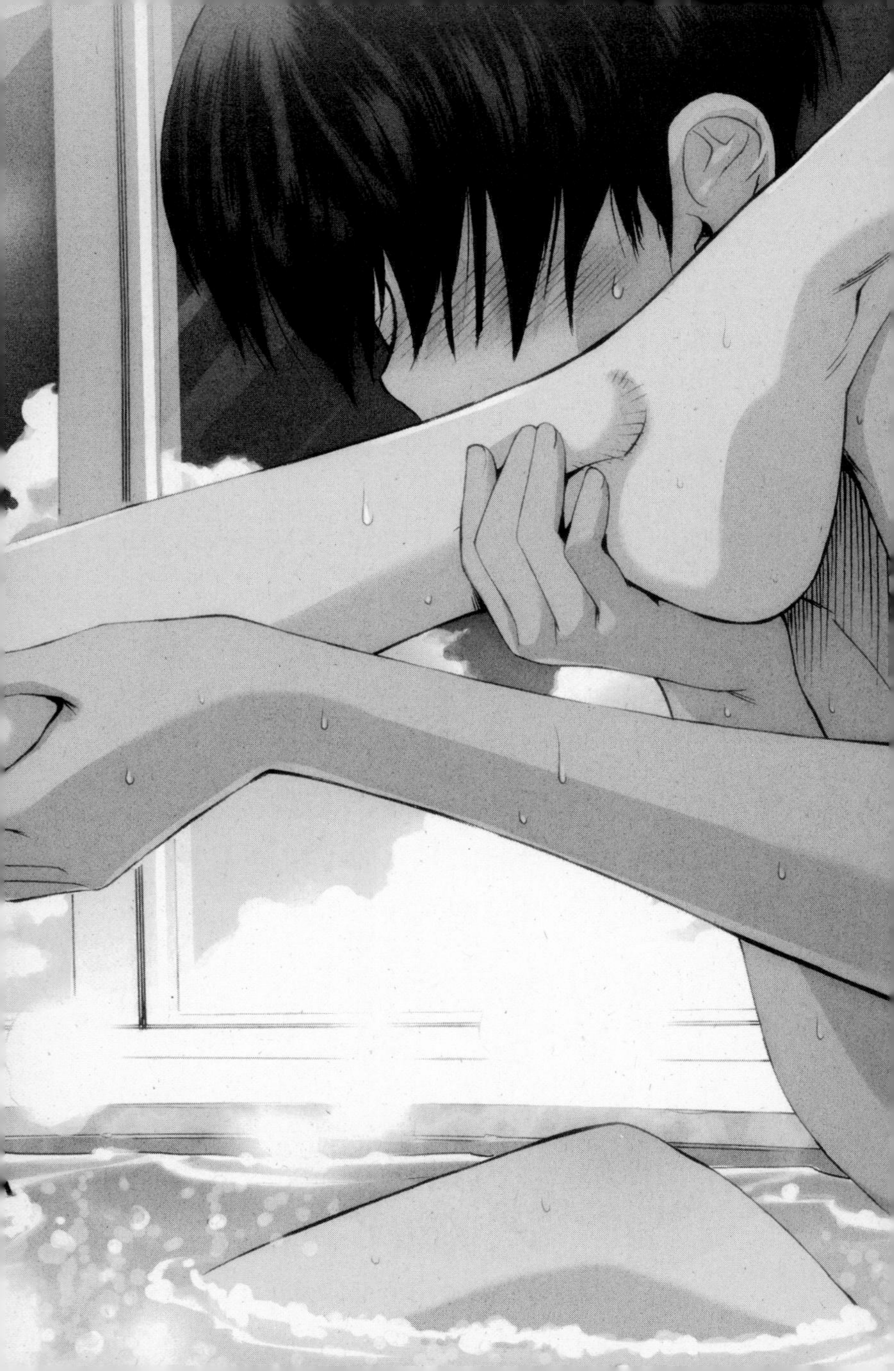

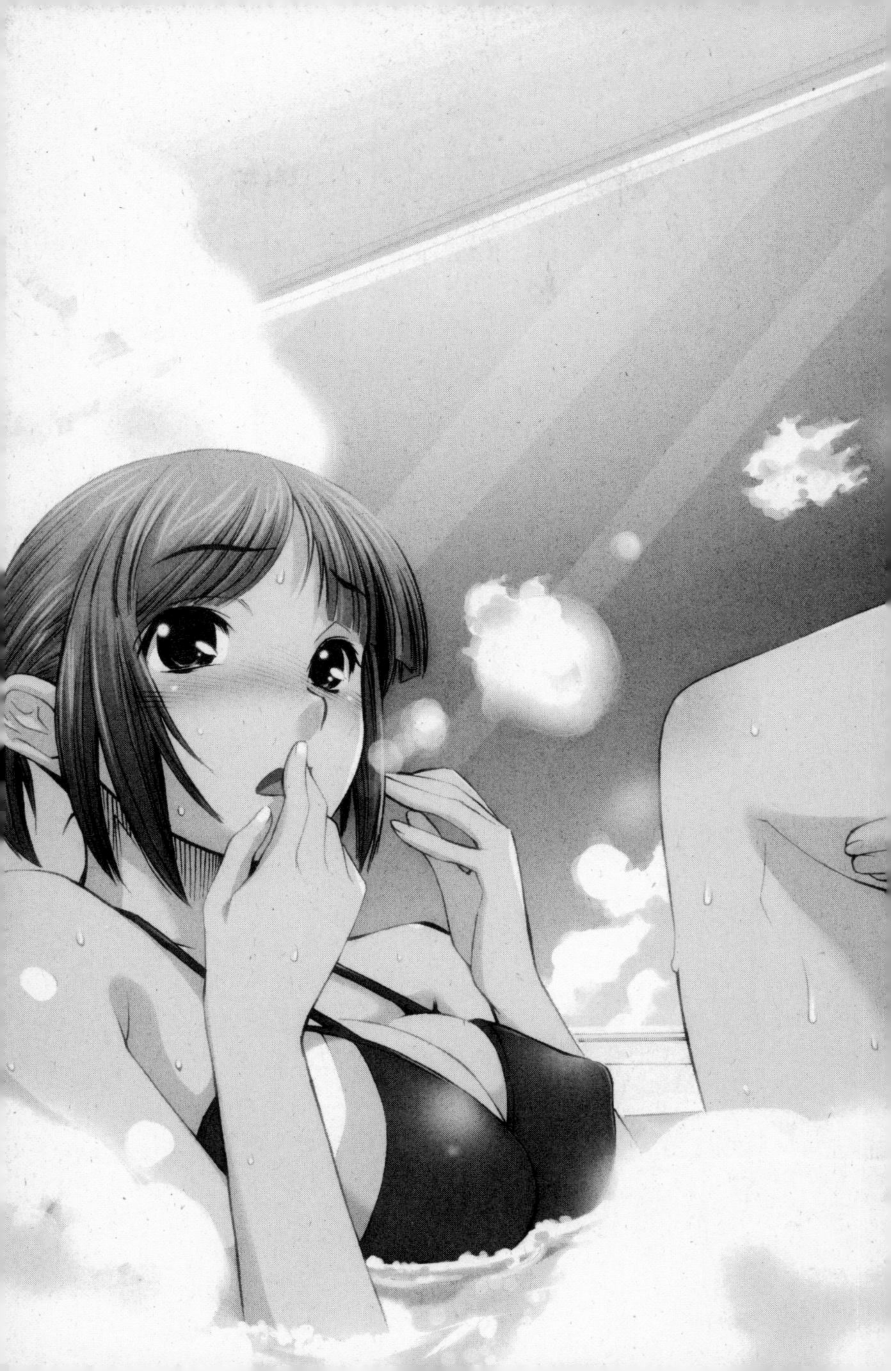

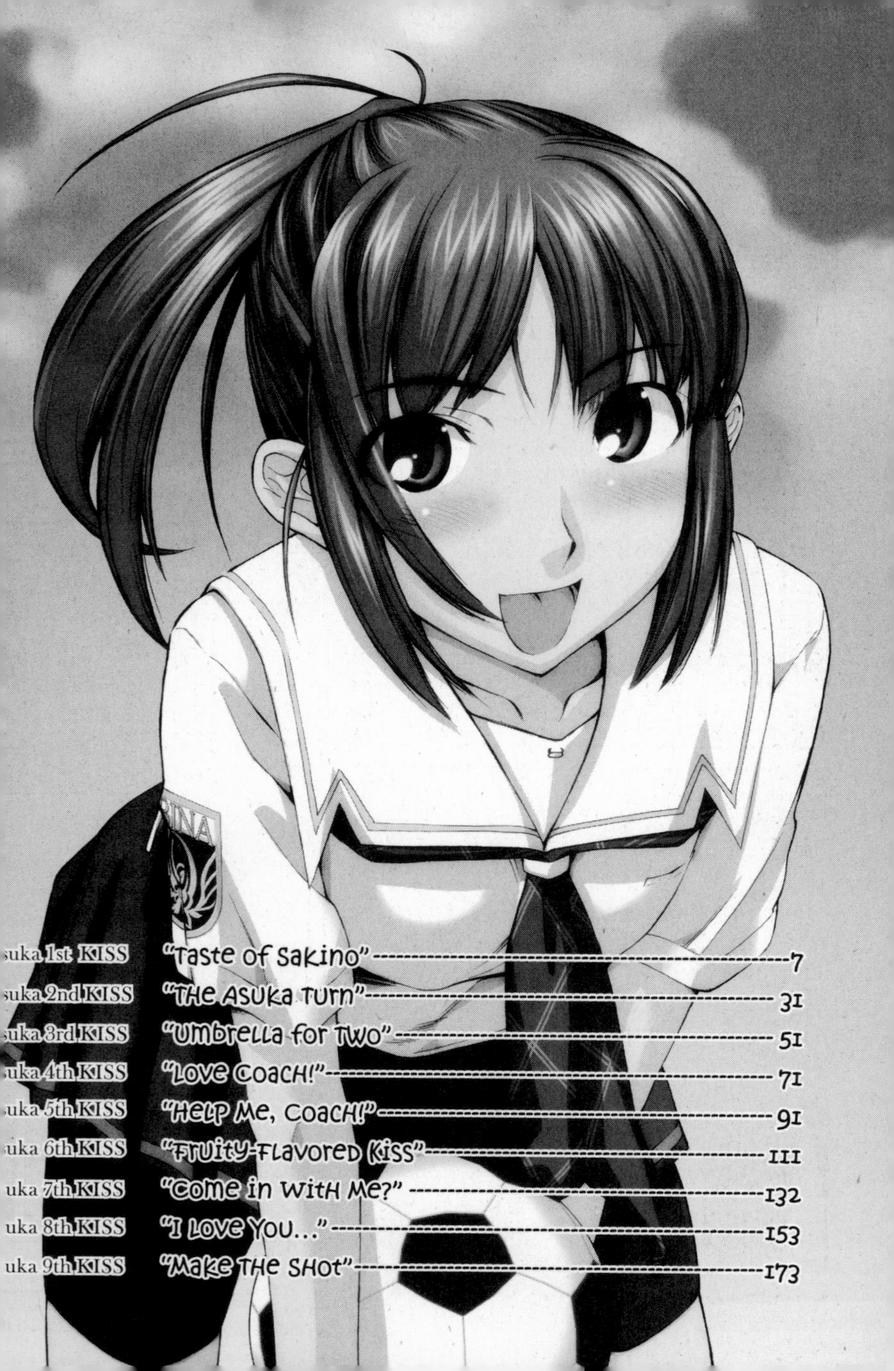

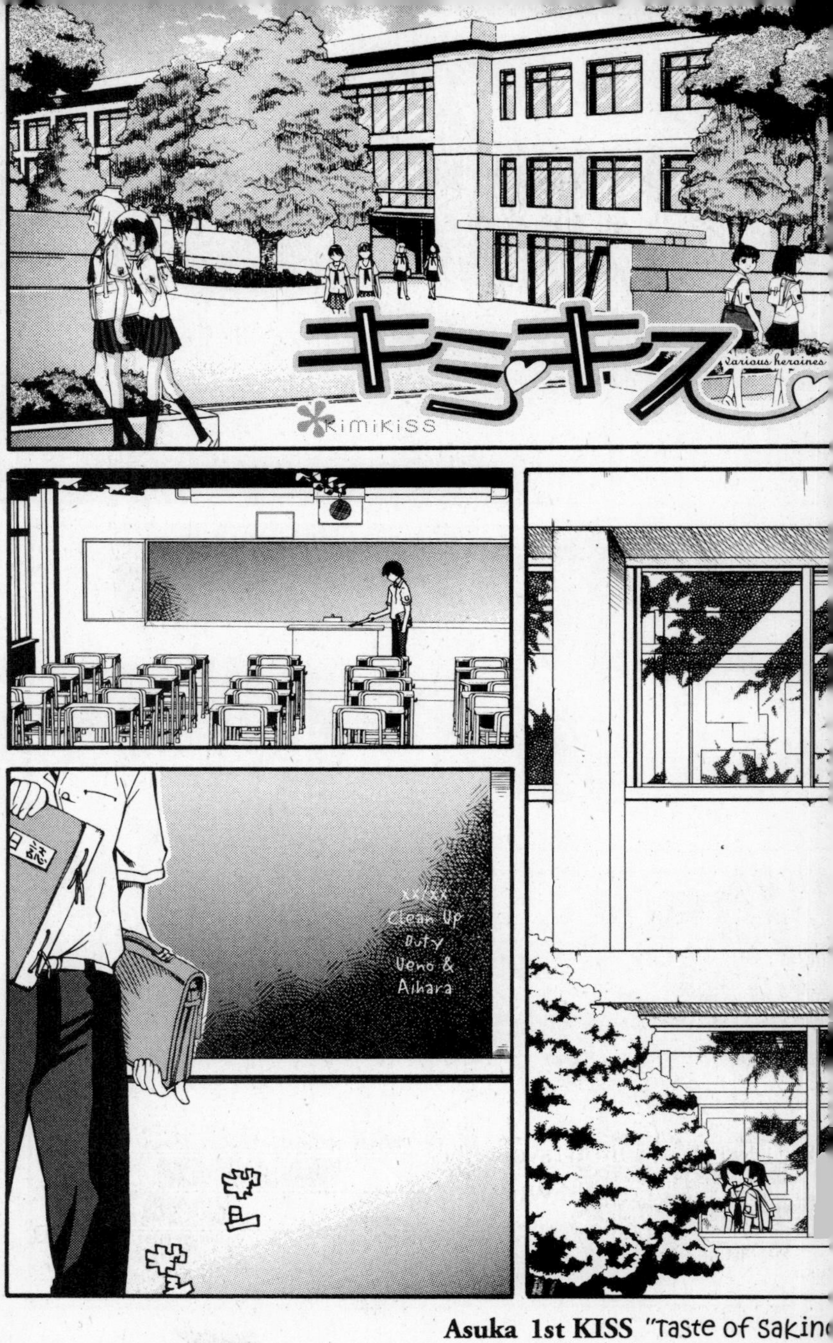
キミキス
various heroines
KimiKiSS
XX/XX
Clean Up
Duty
Ueno &
Aihara

Asuka 1st KISS "Taste of Sakin

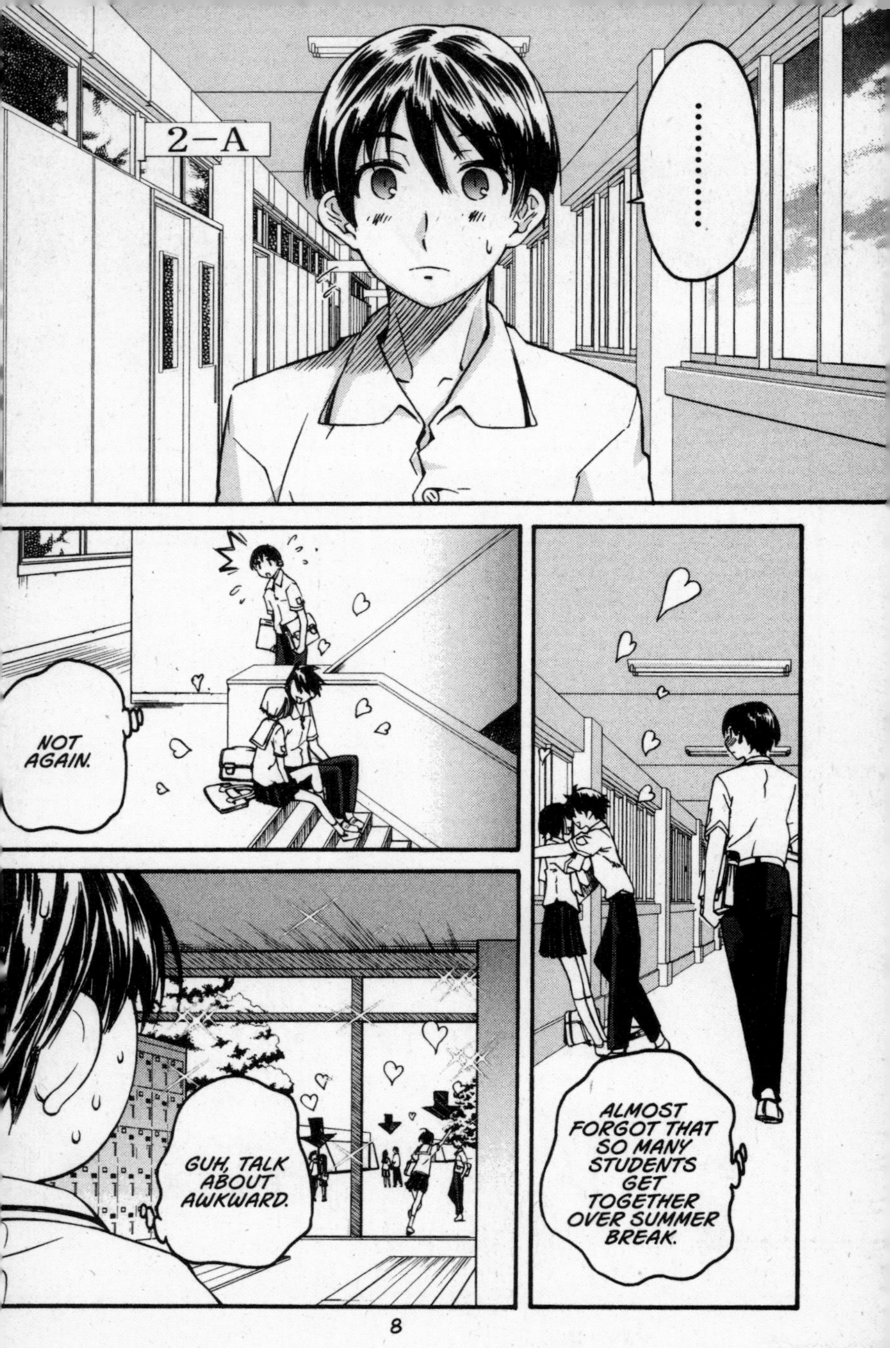
2-A
....
ALMOST FORGOT THAT SO MANY STUDENTS GET TOGETHER OVER SUMMER BREAK.
NOT AGAIN.
GUH, TALK ABOUT AWKWARD.

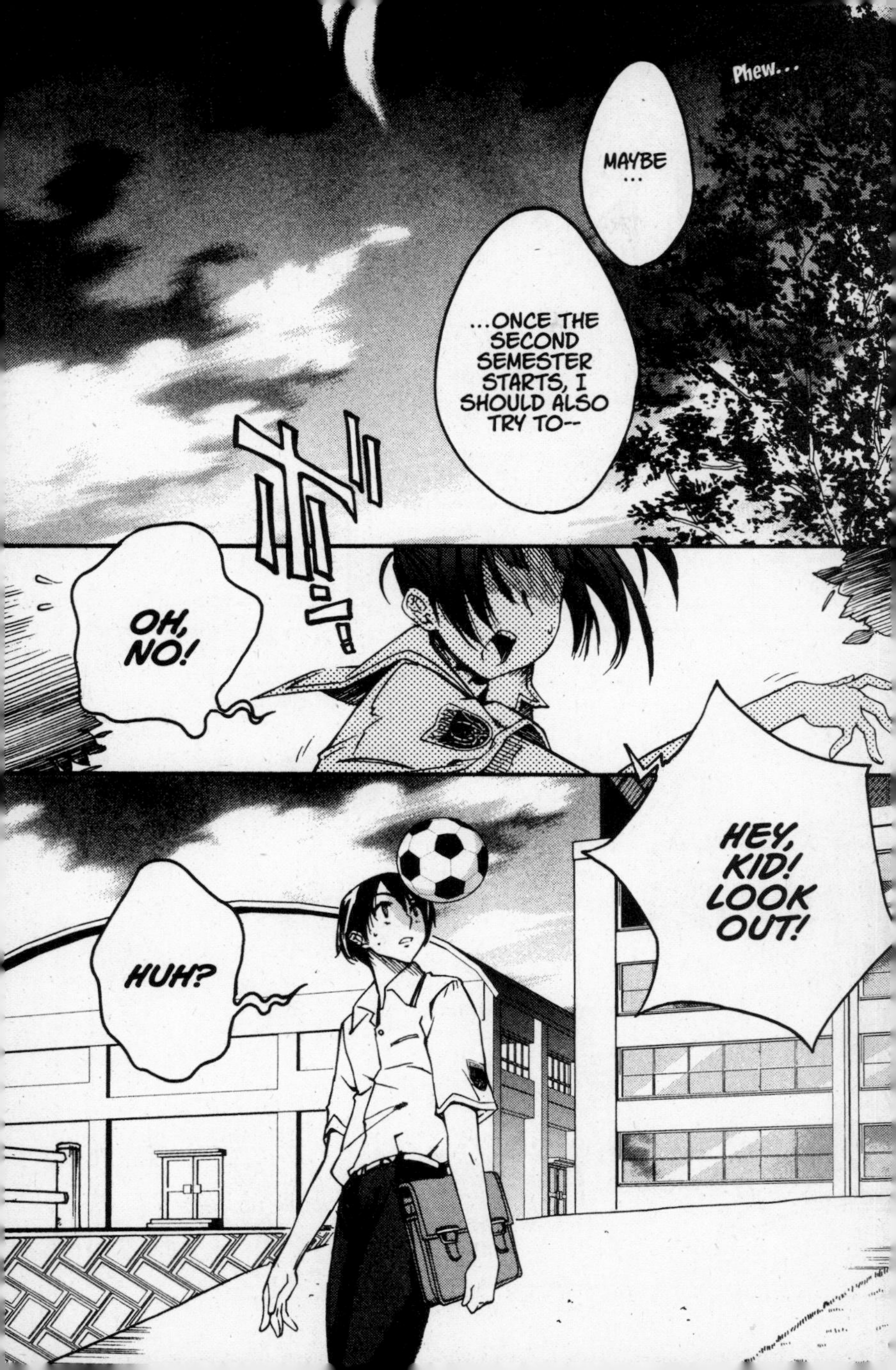
Phew...
MAYBE ...
...ONCE THE SECOND SEMESTER STARTS, I SHOULD ALSO TRY TO--
OH, NO!
HEY, KID! LOOK OUT!
HUH?

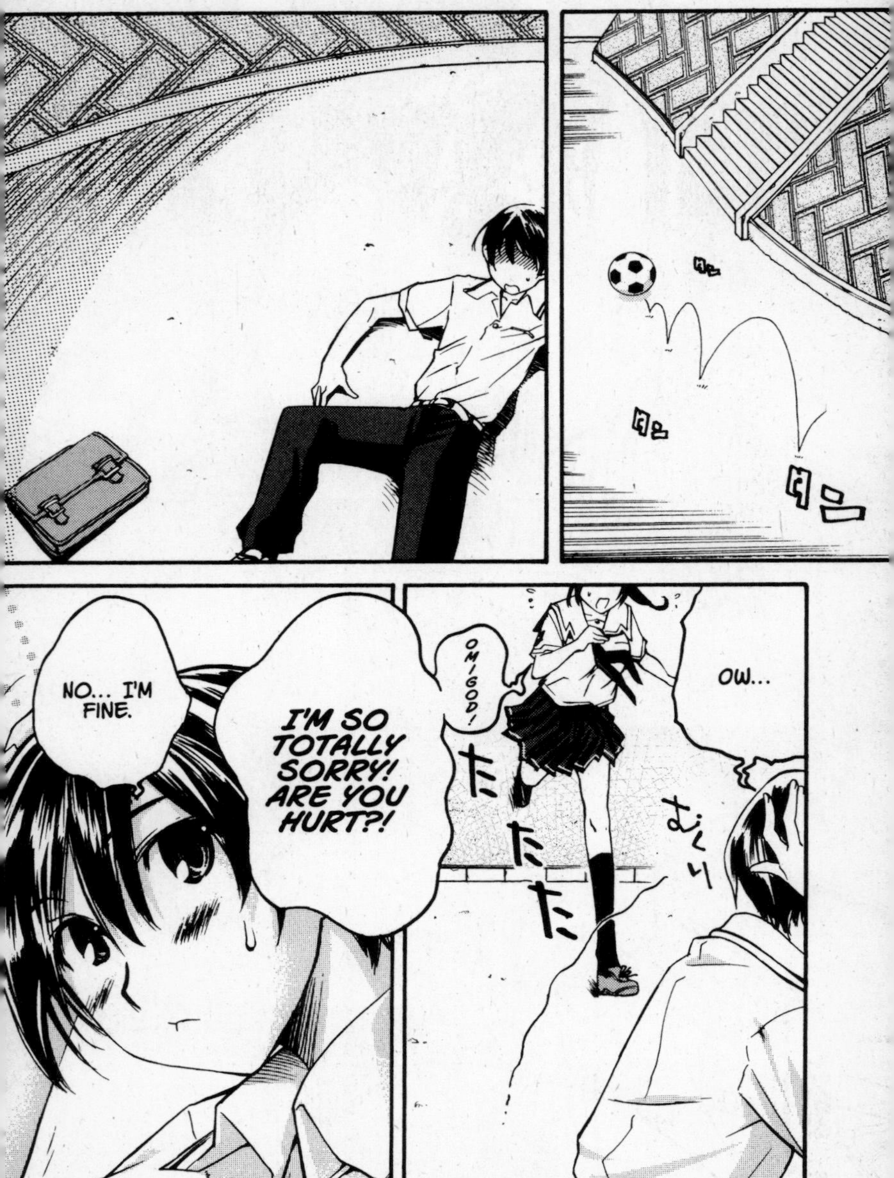
OW...
OMIGOD!
たたた
むくり
I'M SO TOTALLY SORRY! ARE YOU HURT?!
NO... I'M FINE.

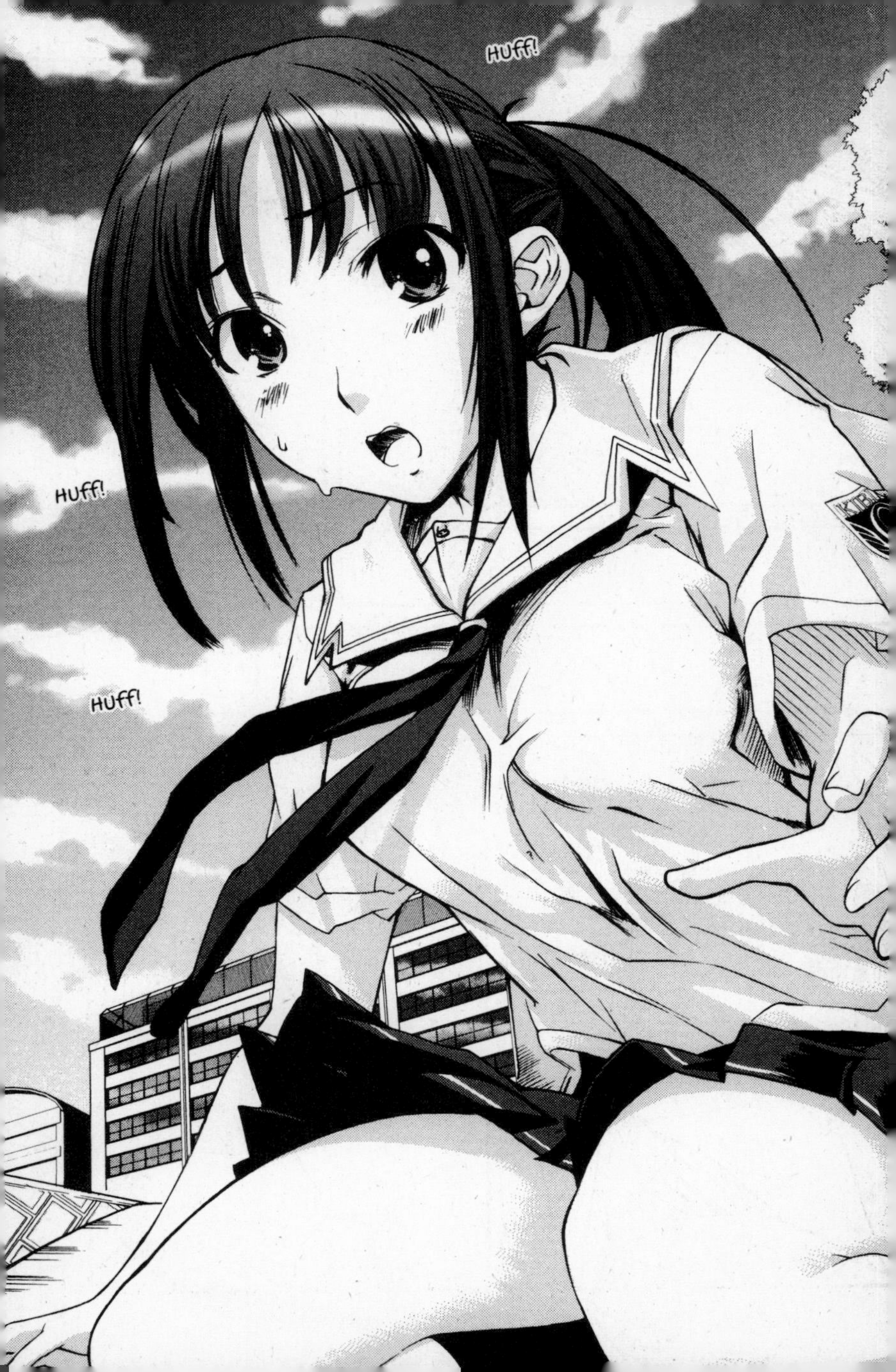
HUFF!
HUFF!
HUFF!

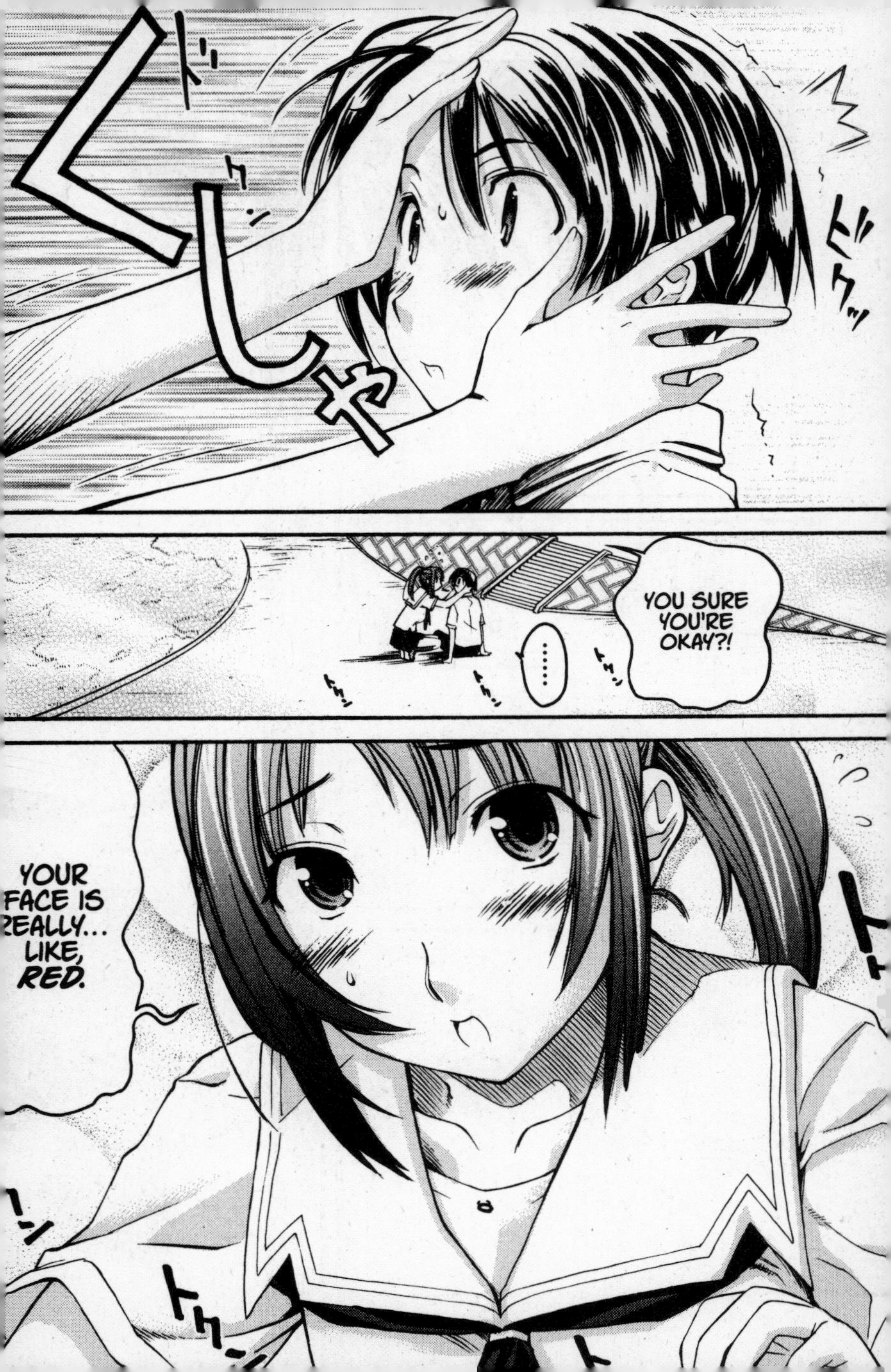
ビクッ
ぐしゃ
YOU SURE YOU'RE OKAY?!
......
YOUR FACE IS REALLY... LIKE, RED.

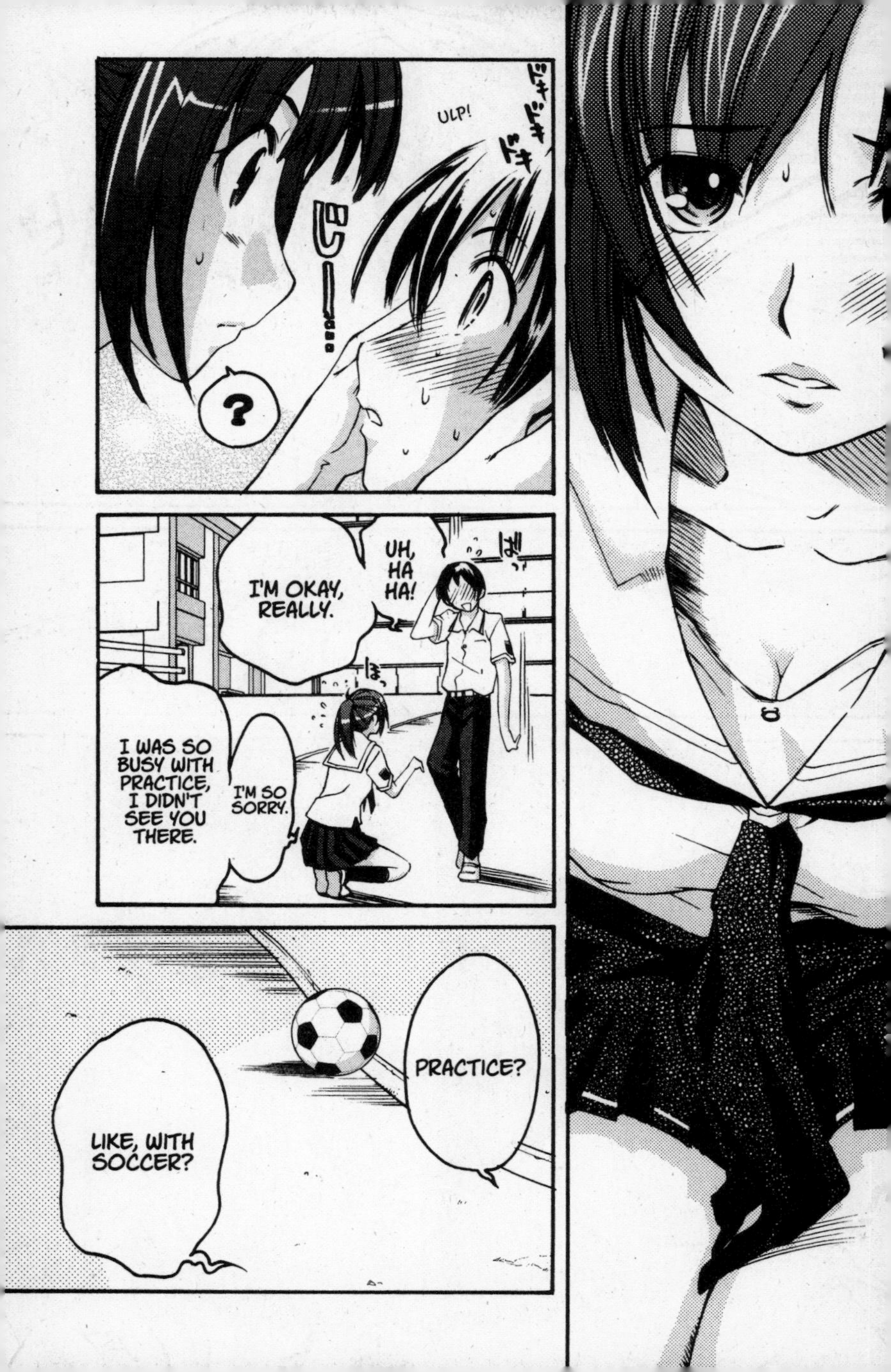
ドキドキドキ
ULP!
じー…
?
UH, HA HA!
ぱっ
I'M OKAY, REALLY.
ほっ
I'M SO SORRY.
I WAS SO BUSY WITH PRACTICE, I DIDN'T SEE YOU THERE.
PRACTICE?
LIKE, WITH SOCCER?

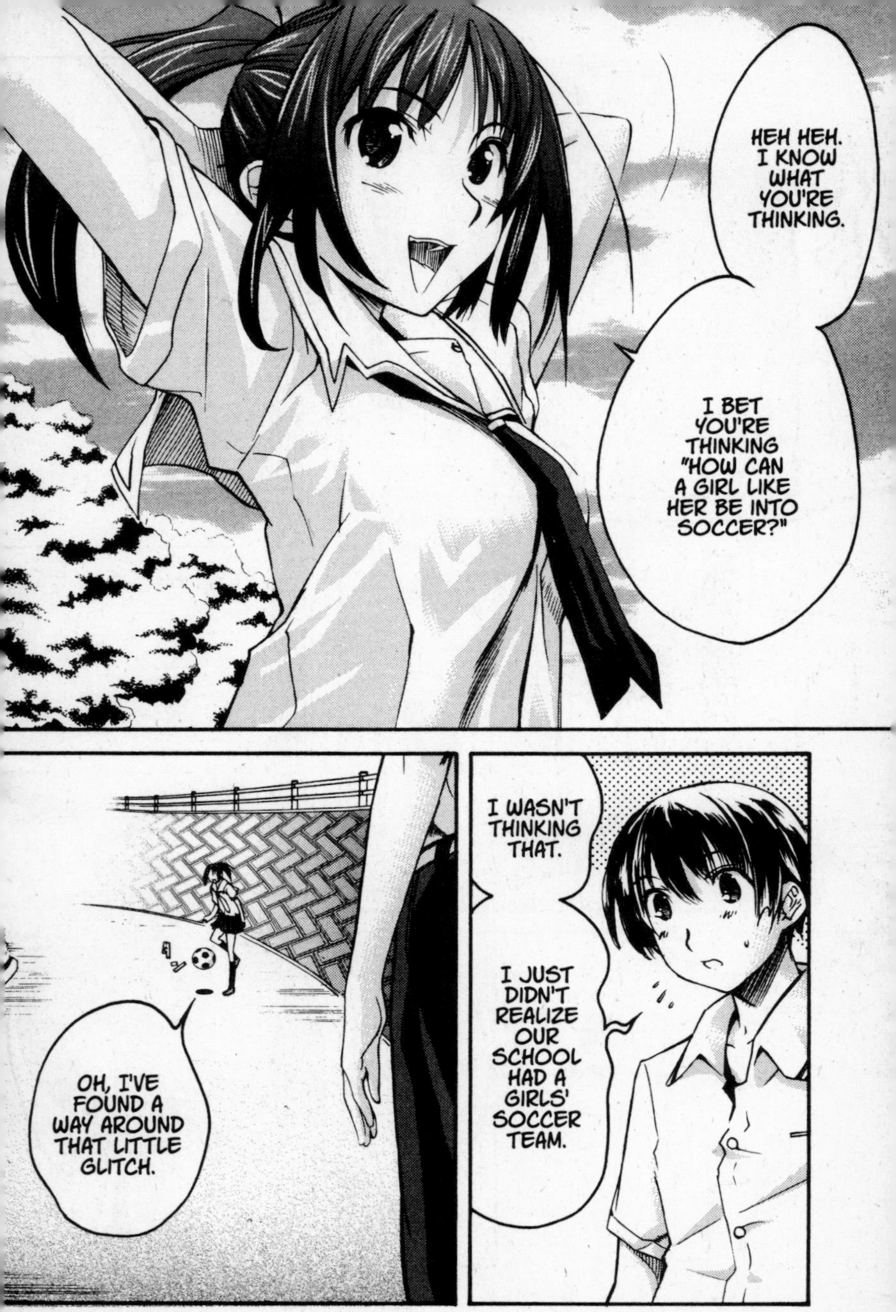
HEH HEH. I KNOW WHAT YOU'RE THINKING.
I BET YOU'RE THINKING "HOW CAN A GIRL LIKE HER BE INTO SOCCER?"
I WASN'T THINKING THAT.
I JUST DIDN'T REALIZE OUR SCHOOL HAD A GIRLS' SOCCER TEAM.
OH, I'VE FOUND A WAY AROUND THAT LITTLE GLITCH.

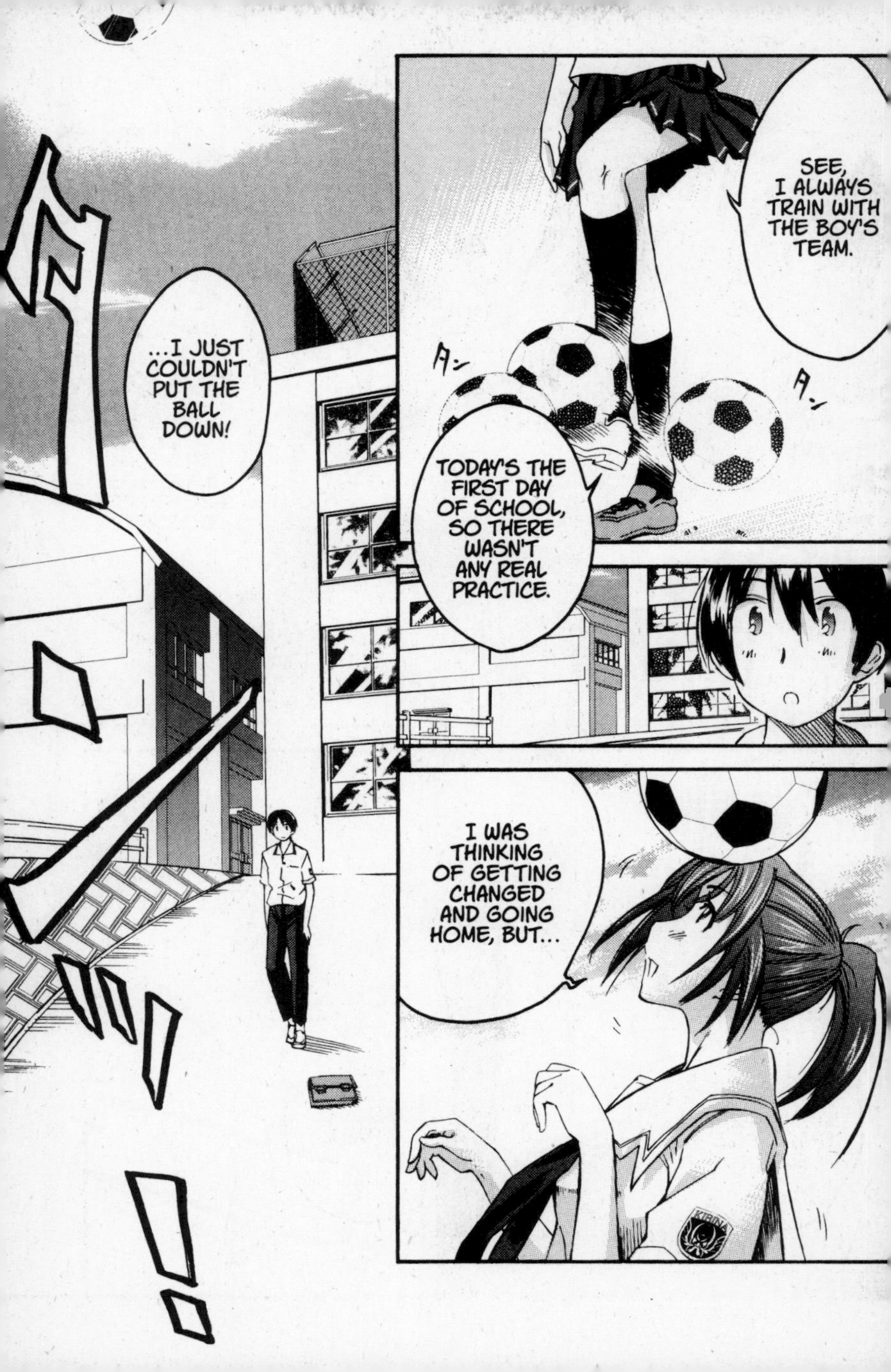
SEE, I ALWAYS TRAIN WITH THE BOY'S TEAM.
TODAY'S THE FIRST DAY OF SCHOOL, SO THERE WASN'T ANY REAL PRACTICE.
I WAS THINKING OF GETTING CHANGED AND GOING HOME, BUT...
...I JUST COULDN'T PUT THE BALL DOWN!
!

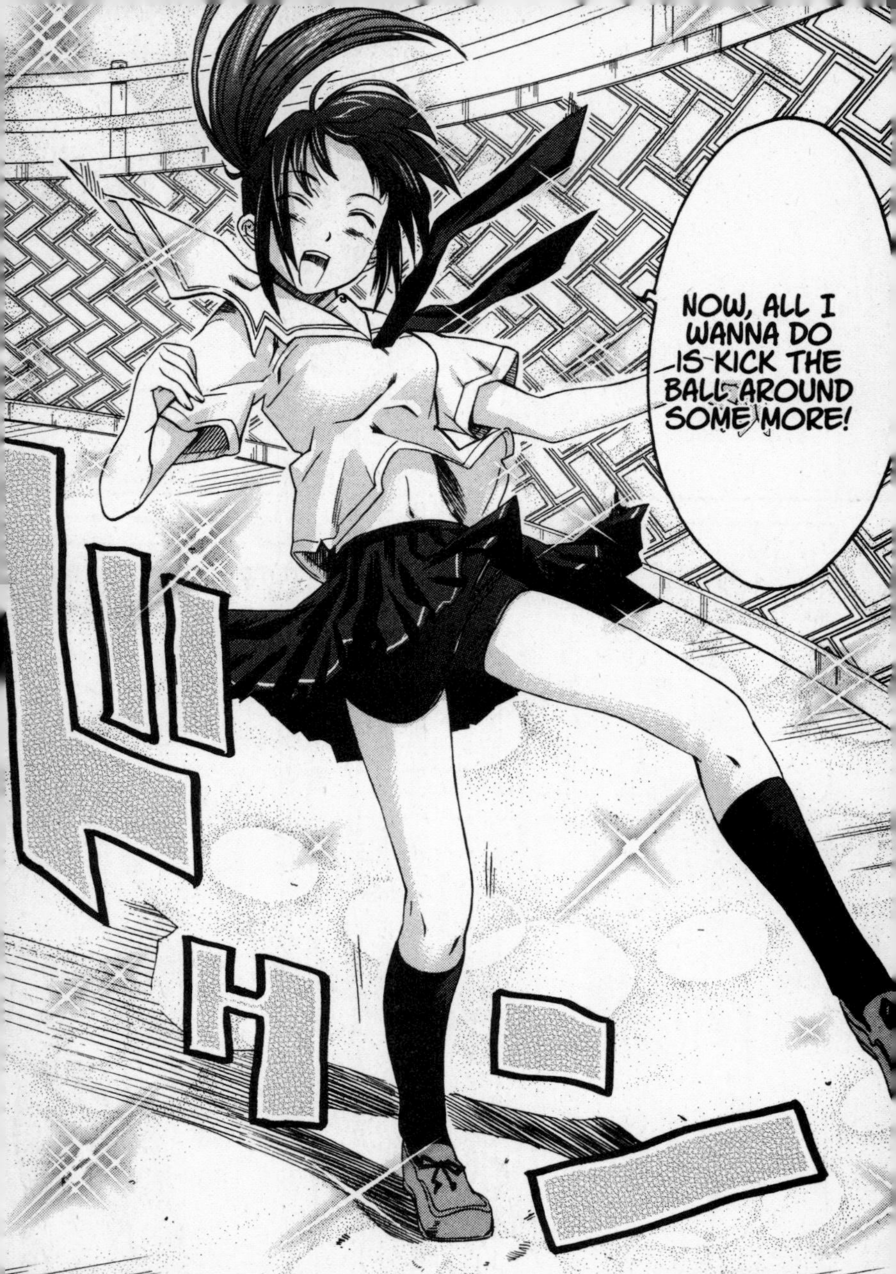
NOW, ALL I WANNA DO IS KICK THE BALL AROUND SOME MORE!

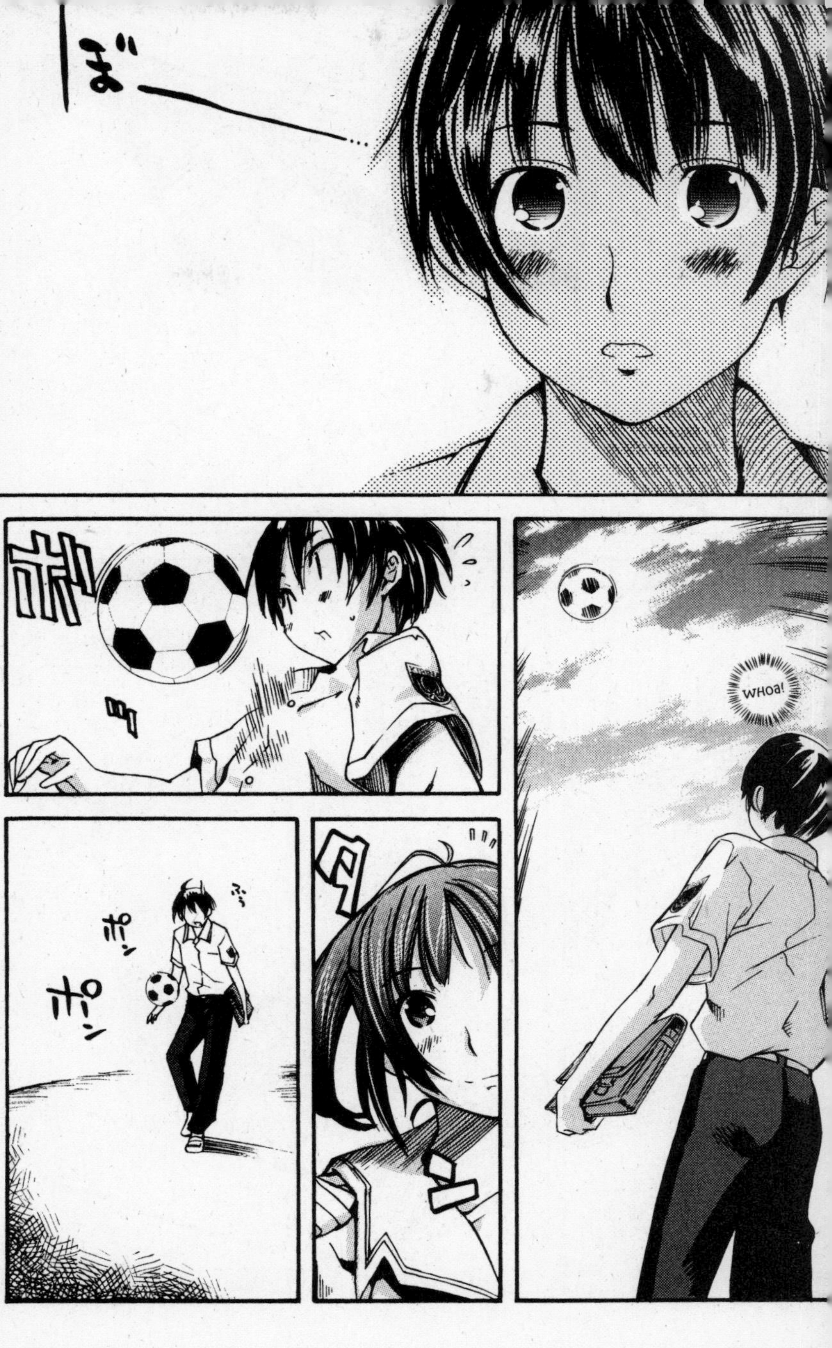
ぼー……
WHOA!
ふぅ
ポン
ポン

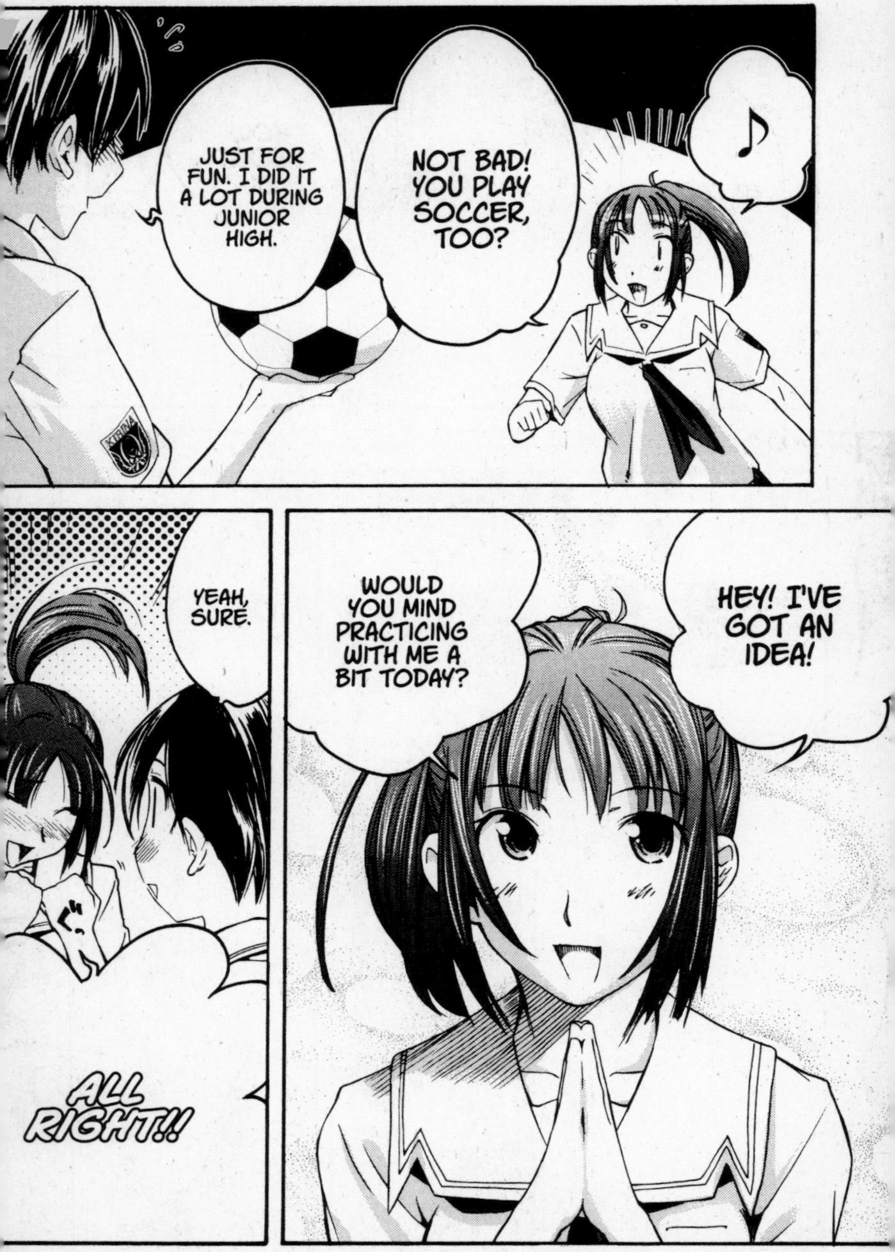
♪
NOT BAD! YOU PLAY SOCCER, TOO?
JUST FOR FUN. I DID IT A LOT DURING JUNIOR HIGH.
HEY! I'VE GOT AN IDEA!
WOULD YOU MIND PRACTICING WITH ME A BIT TODAY?
YEAH, SURE.
ALL RIGHT!!

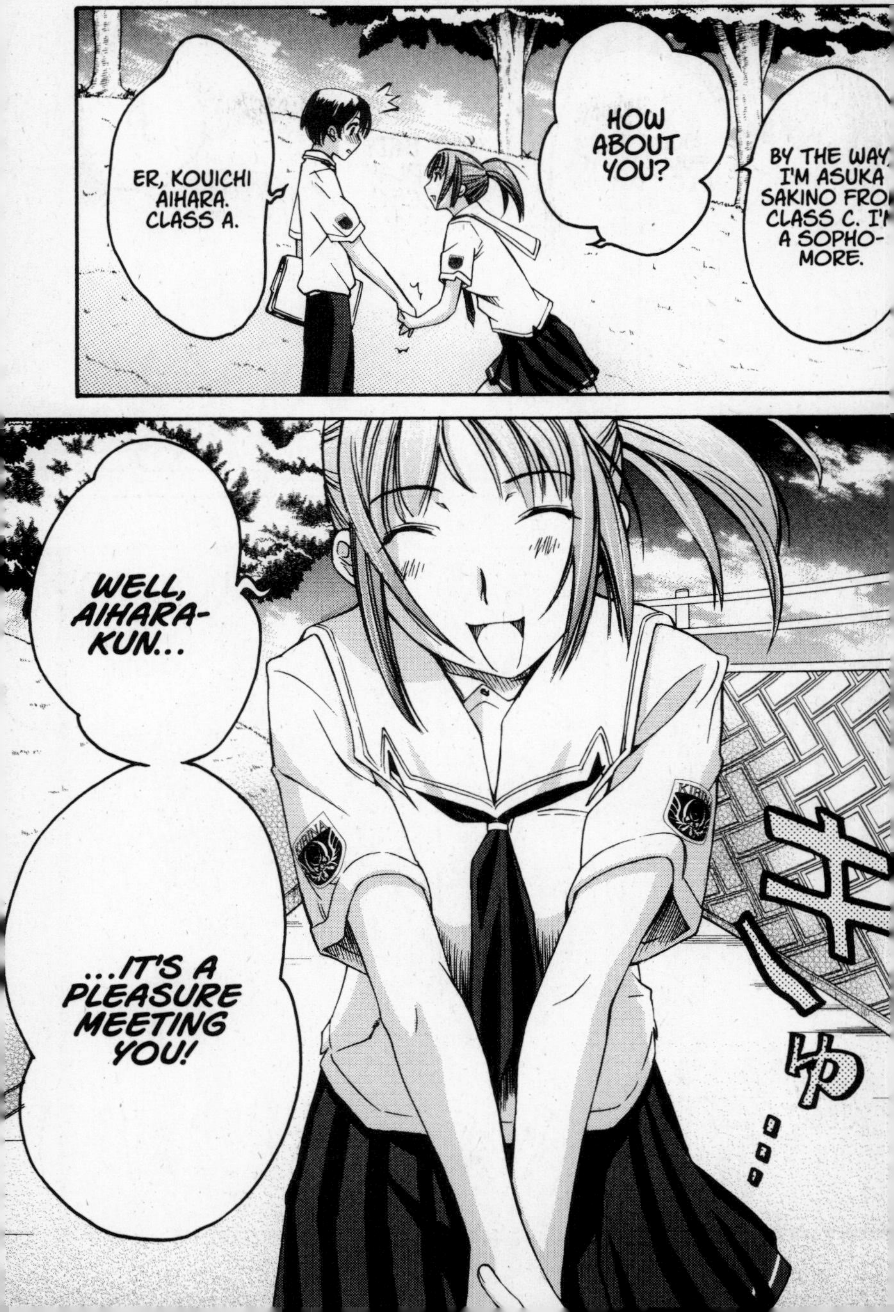
BY THE WAY, I'M ASUKA SAKINO FROM CLASS C. I'M A SOPHOMORE.
HOW ABOUT YOU?
ER, KOUICHI AIHARA. CLASS A.
WELL, AIHARA-KUN...
...IT'S A PLEASURE MEETING YOU!

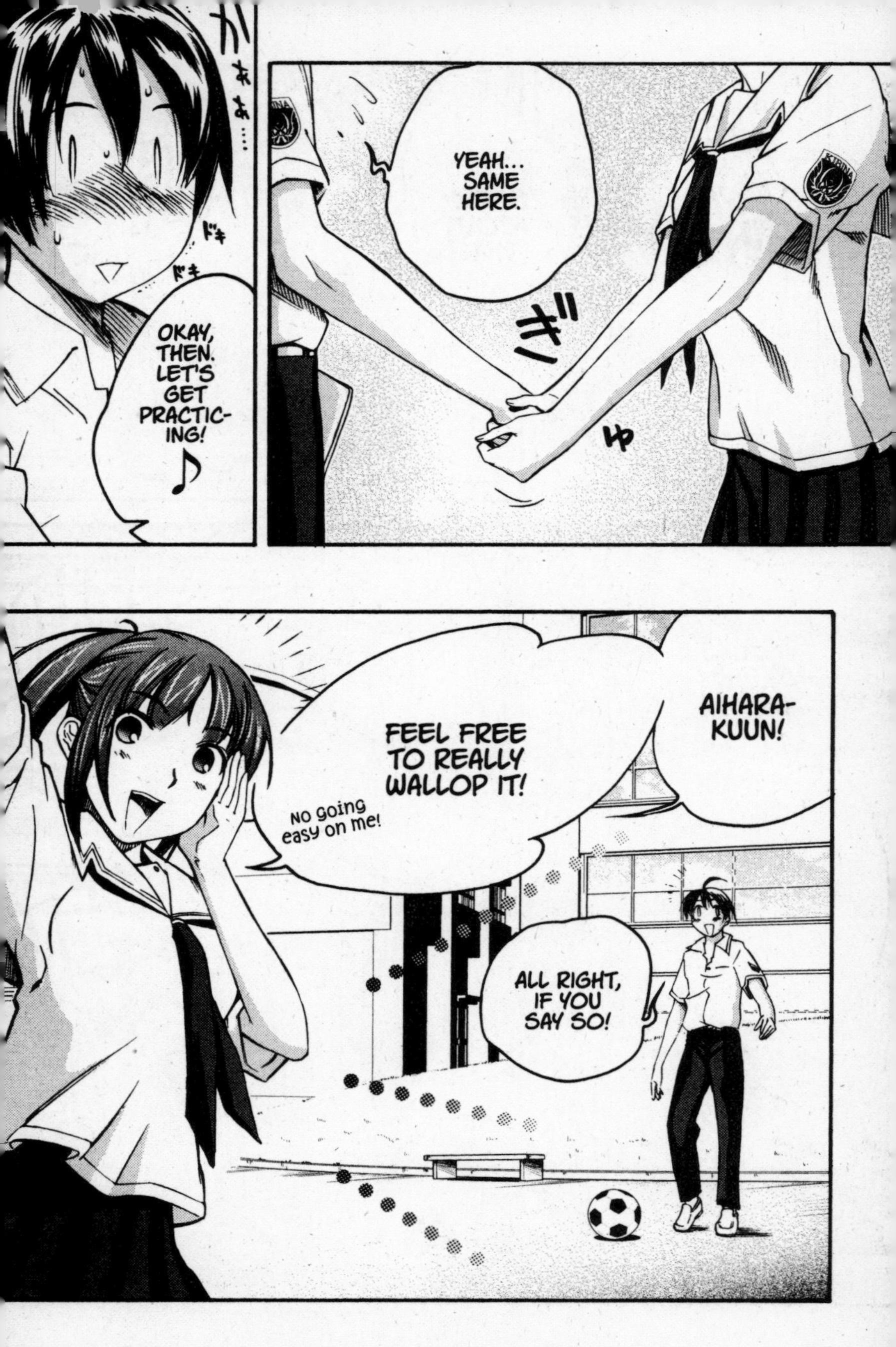
YEAH... SAME HERE.
ギ
ゅ
かぁぁ……
ドキ
ドキ
OKAY, THEN. LET'S GET PRACTIC-ING! ♪
AIHARA-KUUN!
FEEL FREE TO REALLY WALLOP IT!
No going easy on me!
ALL RIGHT, IF YOU SAY SO!

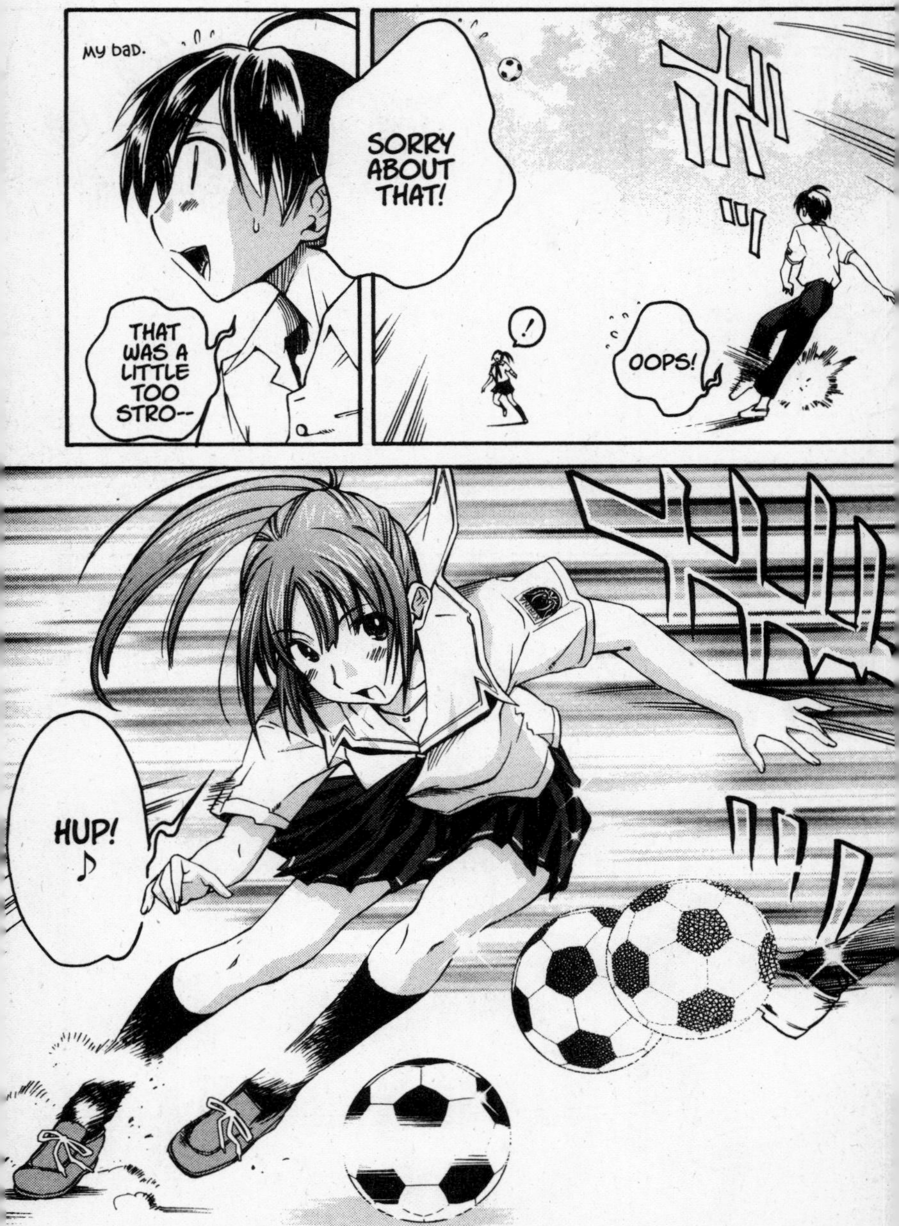
OOPS!
SORRY ABOUT THAT!
My bad.
THAT WAS A LITTLE TOO STRO--
HUP! ♪

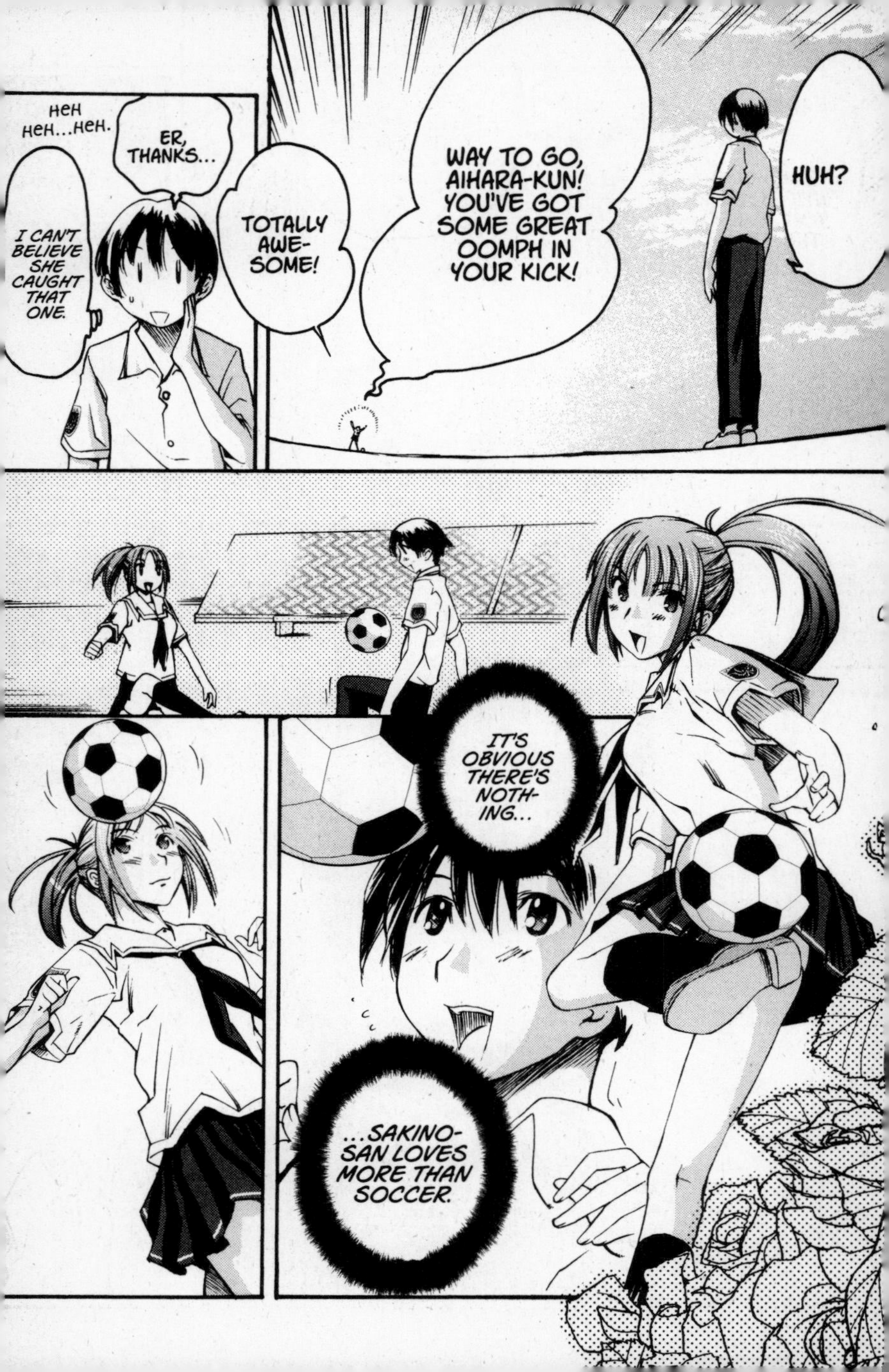
HUH?
WAY TO GO, AIHARA-KUN! YOU'VE GOT SOME GREAT OOMPH IN YOUR KICK!
TOTALLY AWE-SOME!
ER, THANKS...
HEH HEH...HEH.
I CAN'T BELIEVE SHE CAUGHT THAT ONE.
IT'S OBVIOUS THERE'S NOTH-ING...
...SAKINO-SAN LOVES MORE THAN SOCCER.

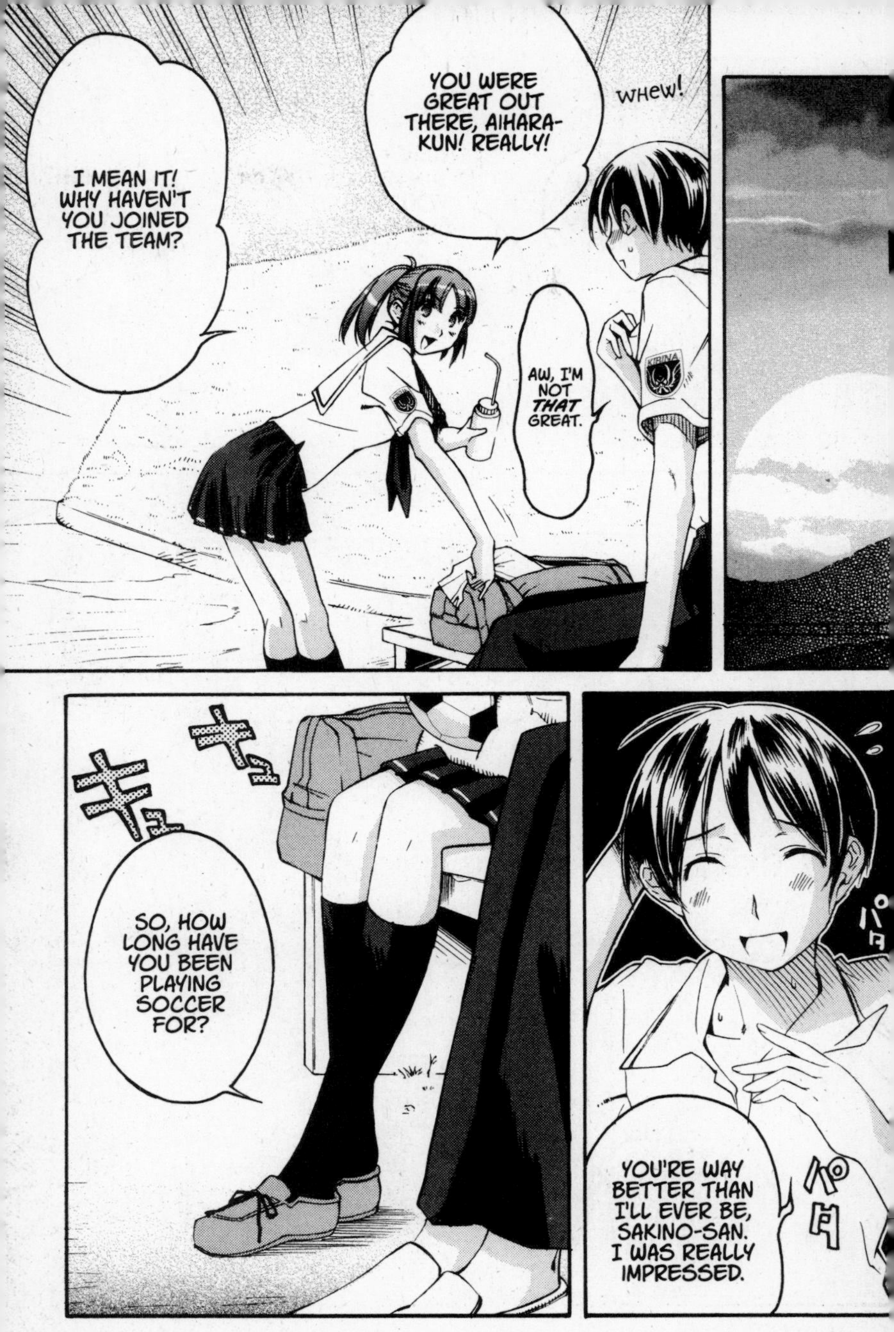

WHEW!
YOU WERE GREAT OUT THERE, AIHARA-KUN! REALLY!
I MEAN IT! WHY HAVEN'T YOU JOINED THE TEAM?
AW, I'M NOT *THAT* GREAT.
KIRINA
パタ
パタ
YOU'RE WAY BETTER THAN I'LL EVER BE, SAKINO-SAN. I WAS REALLY IMPRESSED.
キュ
キュ
SO, HOW LONG HAVE YOU BEEN PLAYING SOCCER FOR?

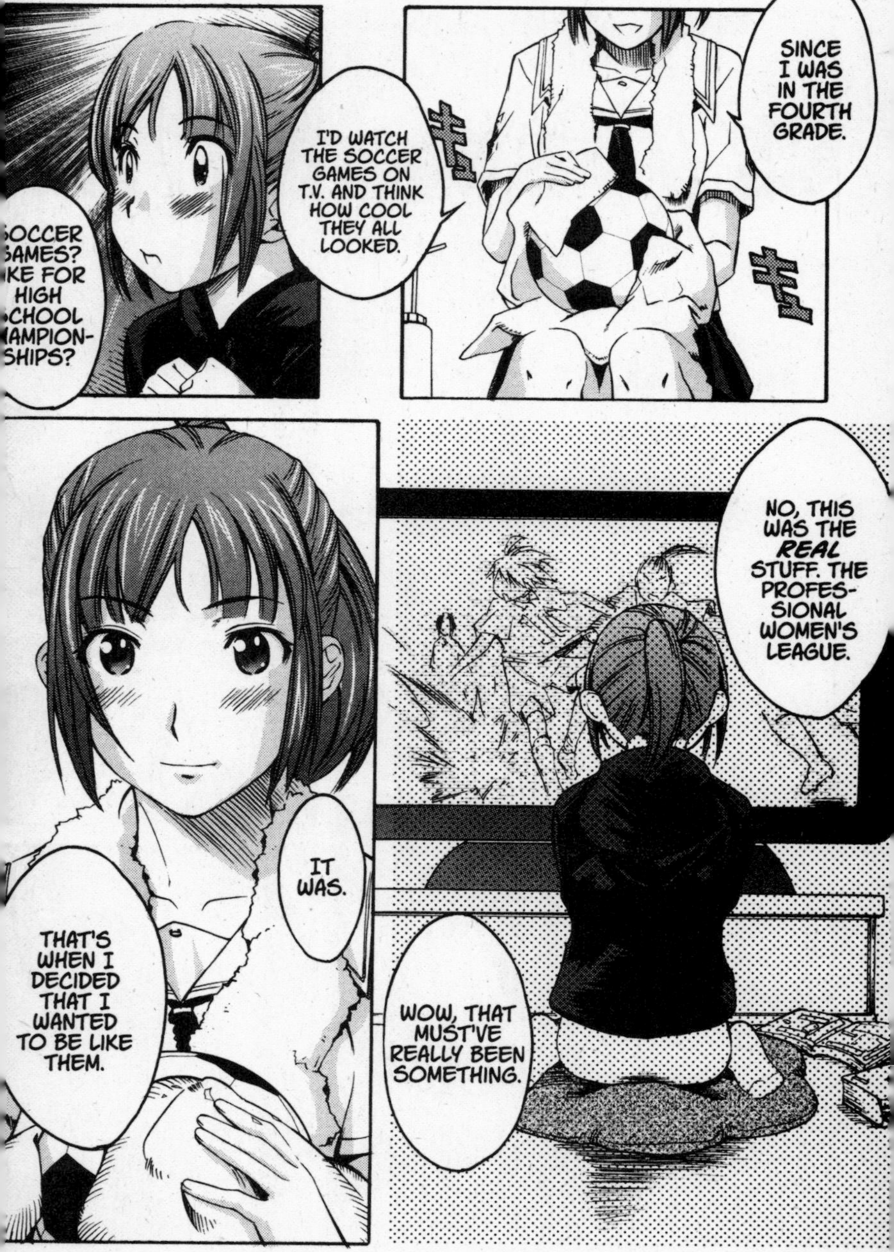
SINCE I WAS IN THE FOURTH GRADE.
I'D WATCH THE SOCCER GAMES ON T.V. AND THINK HOW COOL THEY ALL LOOKED.
SOCCER GAMES? LIKE FOR HIGH SCHOOL CHAMPIONSHIPS?
NO, THIS WAS THE *REAL* STUFF. THE PROFESSIONAL WOMEN'S LEAGUE.
WOW, THAT MUST'VE REALLY BEEN SOMETHING.
IT WAS.
THAT'S WHEN I DECIDED THAT I WANTED TO BE LIKE THEM.

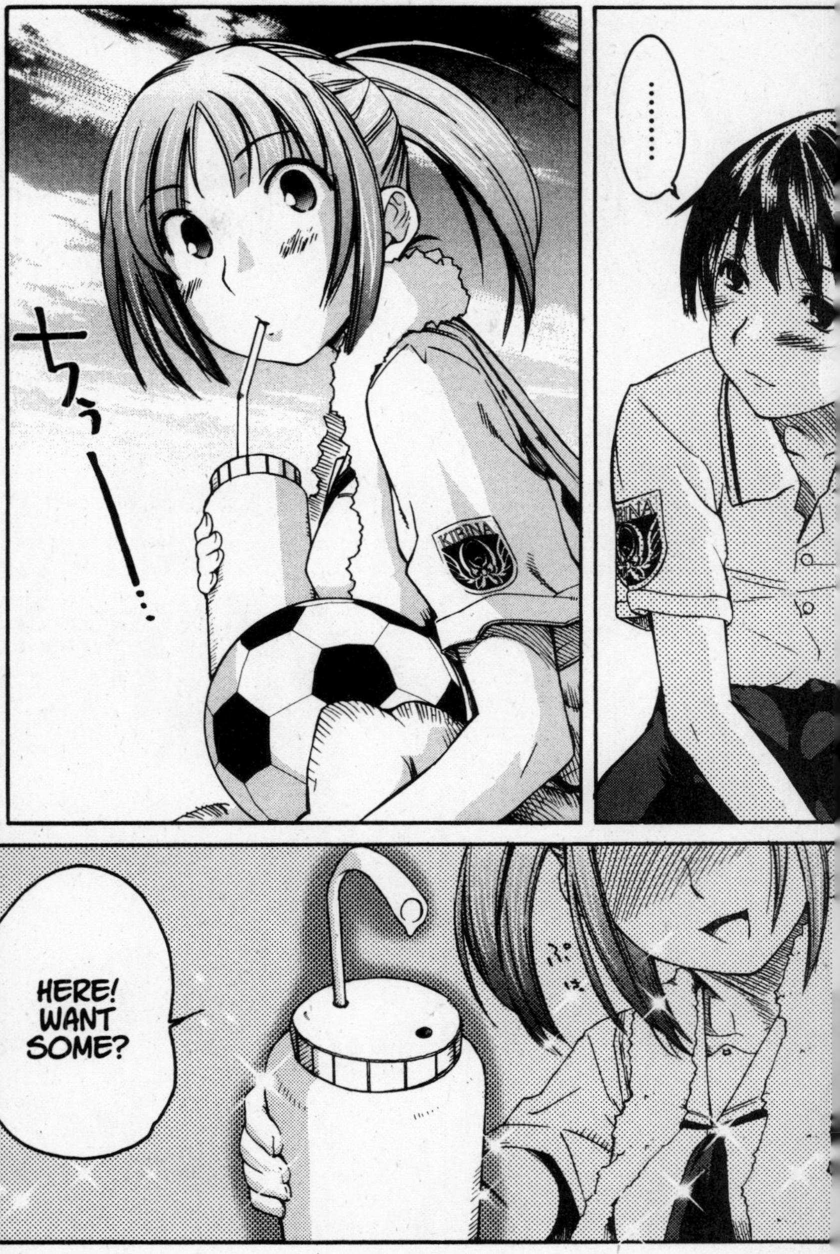

......
KIBINA
ちぅー…
KIBINA
HERE! WANT SOME?
ぷは

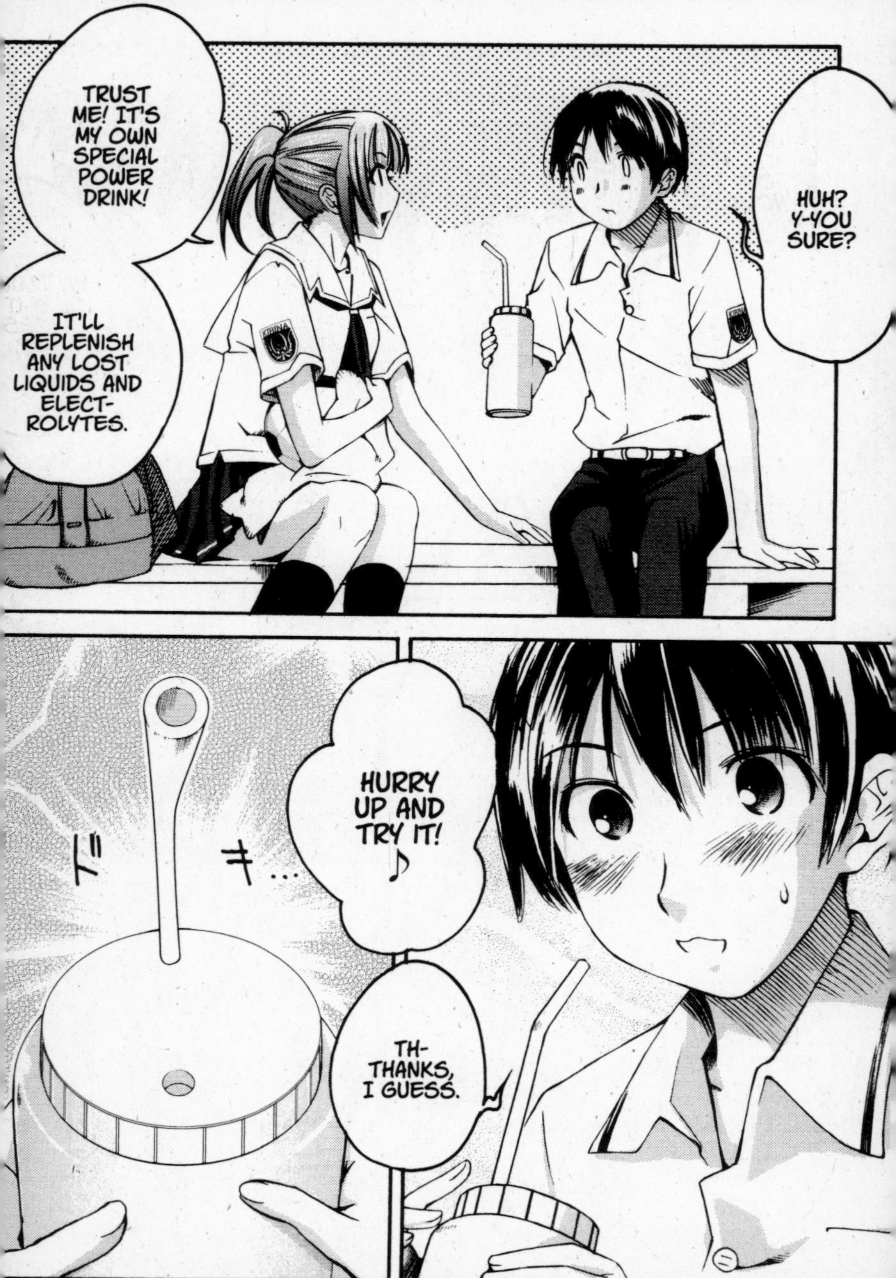
HUH? Y-YOU SURE?
TRUST ME! IT'S MY OWN SPECIAL POWER DRINK!
IT'LL REPLENISH ANY LOST LIQUIDS AND ELECT-ROLYTES.
HURRY UP AND TRY IT! ♪
TH-THANKS, I GUESS.
ドキ…

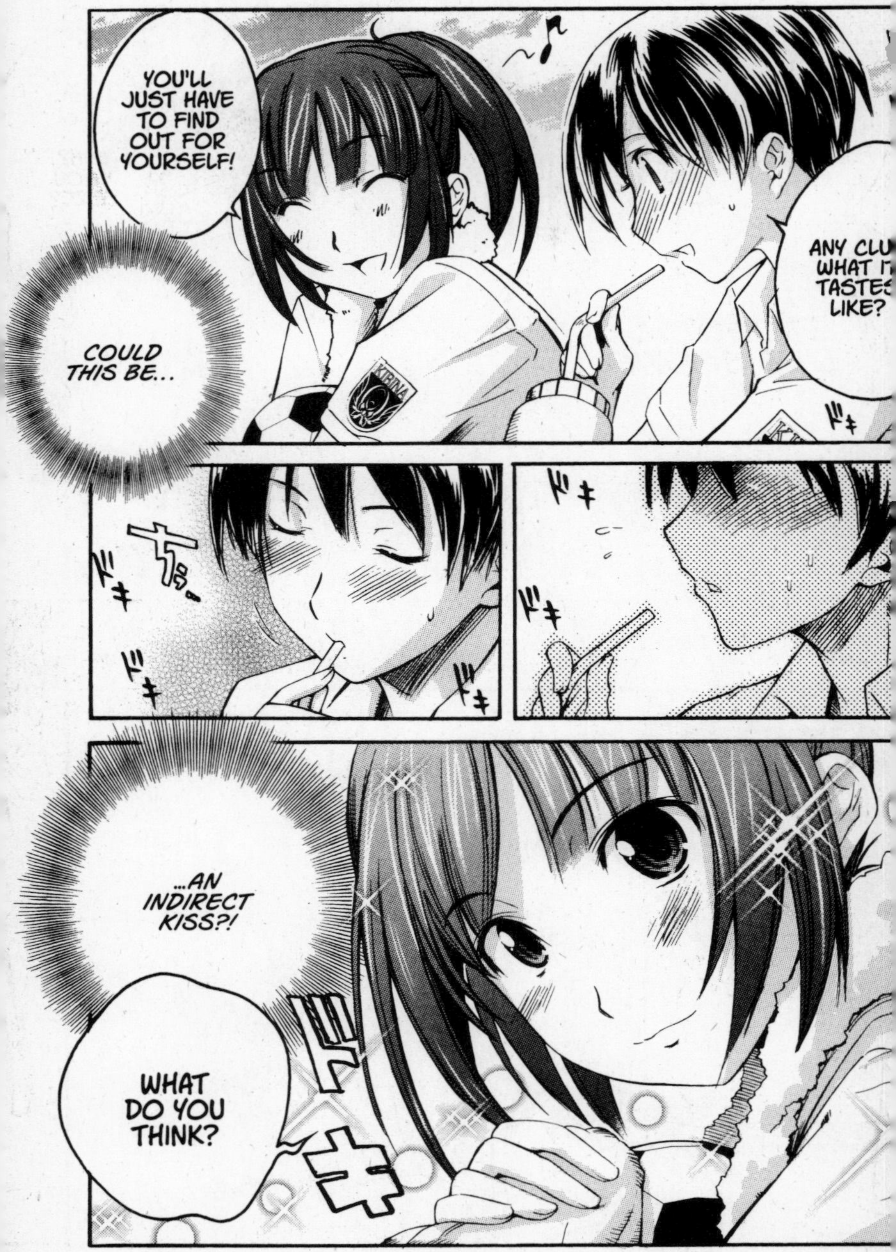

ANY CLU WHAT IT TASTES LIKE?
ドキ
YOU'LL JUST HAVE TO FIND OUT FOR YOURSELF!
COULD THIS BE...
ドキ
ドキ
ドキ
ドキ
ドキ
...AN INDIRECT KISS?!
ドキ
WHAT DO YOU THINK?

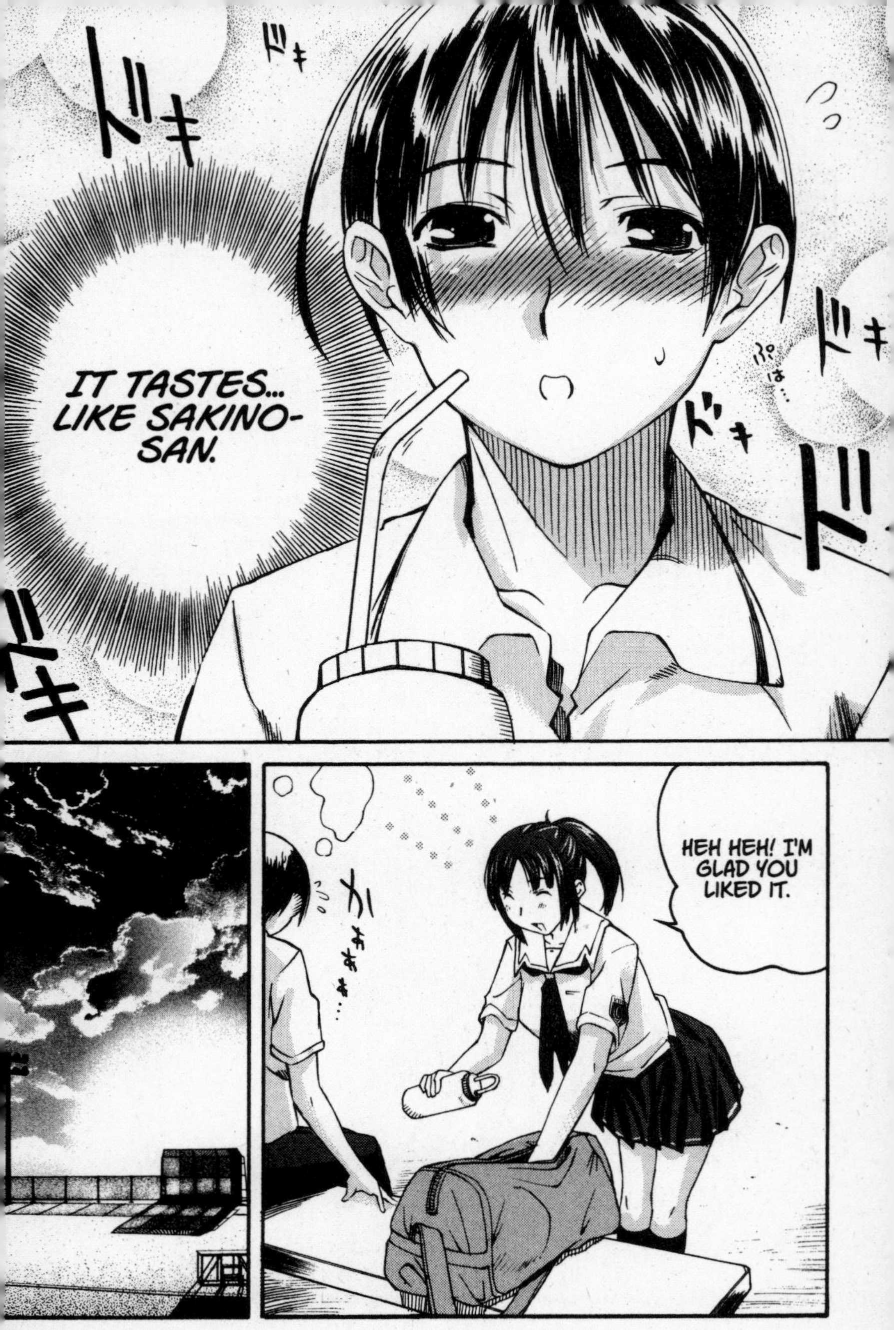
ドキ
ドキ
IT TASTES... LIKE SAKINO-SAN.
ぷは…
ドキ
ドキ
ドキ
ドキ
HEH HEH! I'M GLAD YOU LIKED IT.
かあああ…

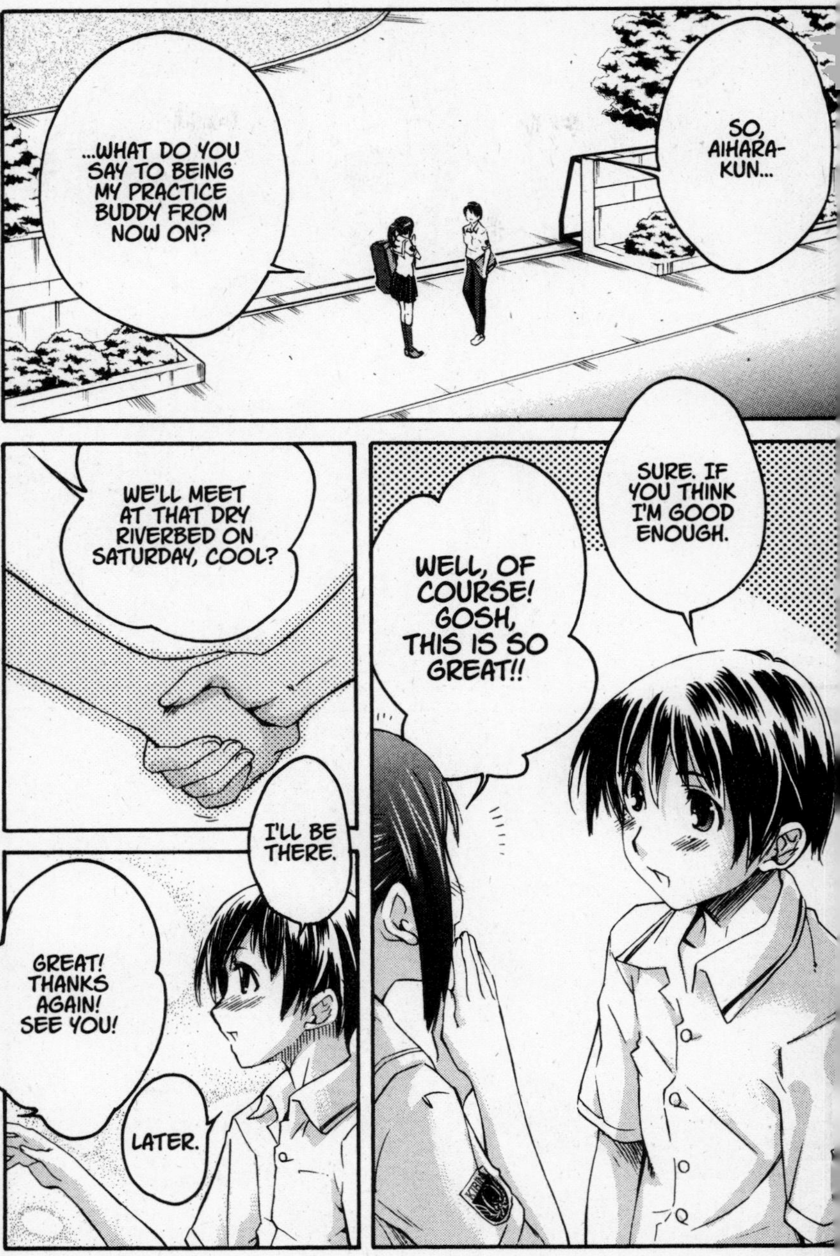
SO, AIHARA-KUN...
...WHAT DO YOU SAY TO BEING MY PRACTICE BUDDY FROM NOW ON?
SURE. IF YOU THINK I'M GOOD ENOUGH.
WELL, OF COURSE! GOSH, THIS IS SO GREAT!!
WE'LL MEET AT THAT DRY RIVERBED ON SATURDAY, COOL?
I'LL BE THERE.
GREAT! THANKS AGAIN! SEE YOU!
LATER.

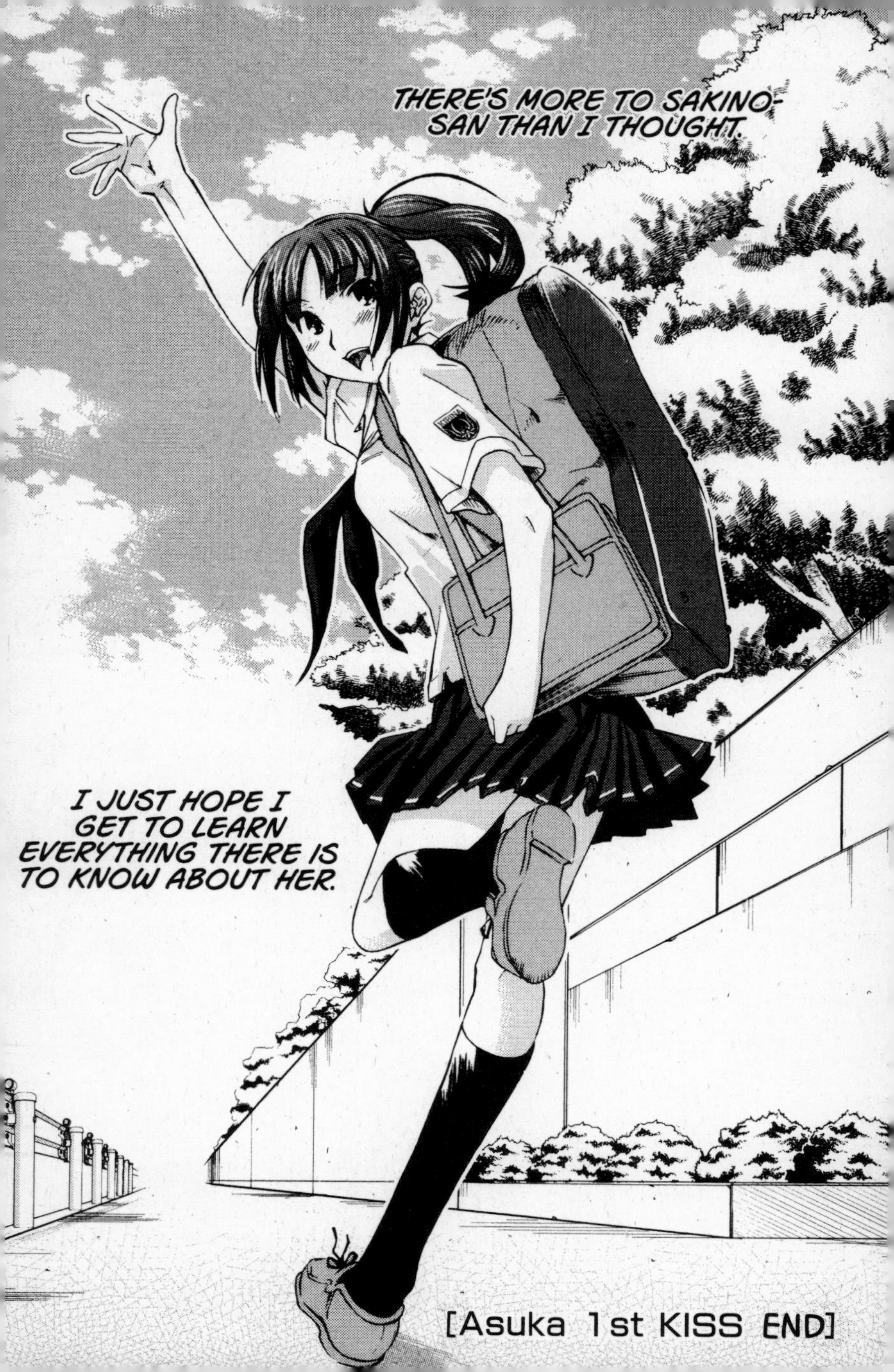
THERE'S MORE TO SAKINO-SAN THAN I THOUGHT.
I JUST HOPE I GET TO LEARN EVERYTHING THERE IS TO KNOW ABOUT HER.
[Asuka 1st KISS END]

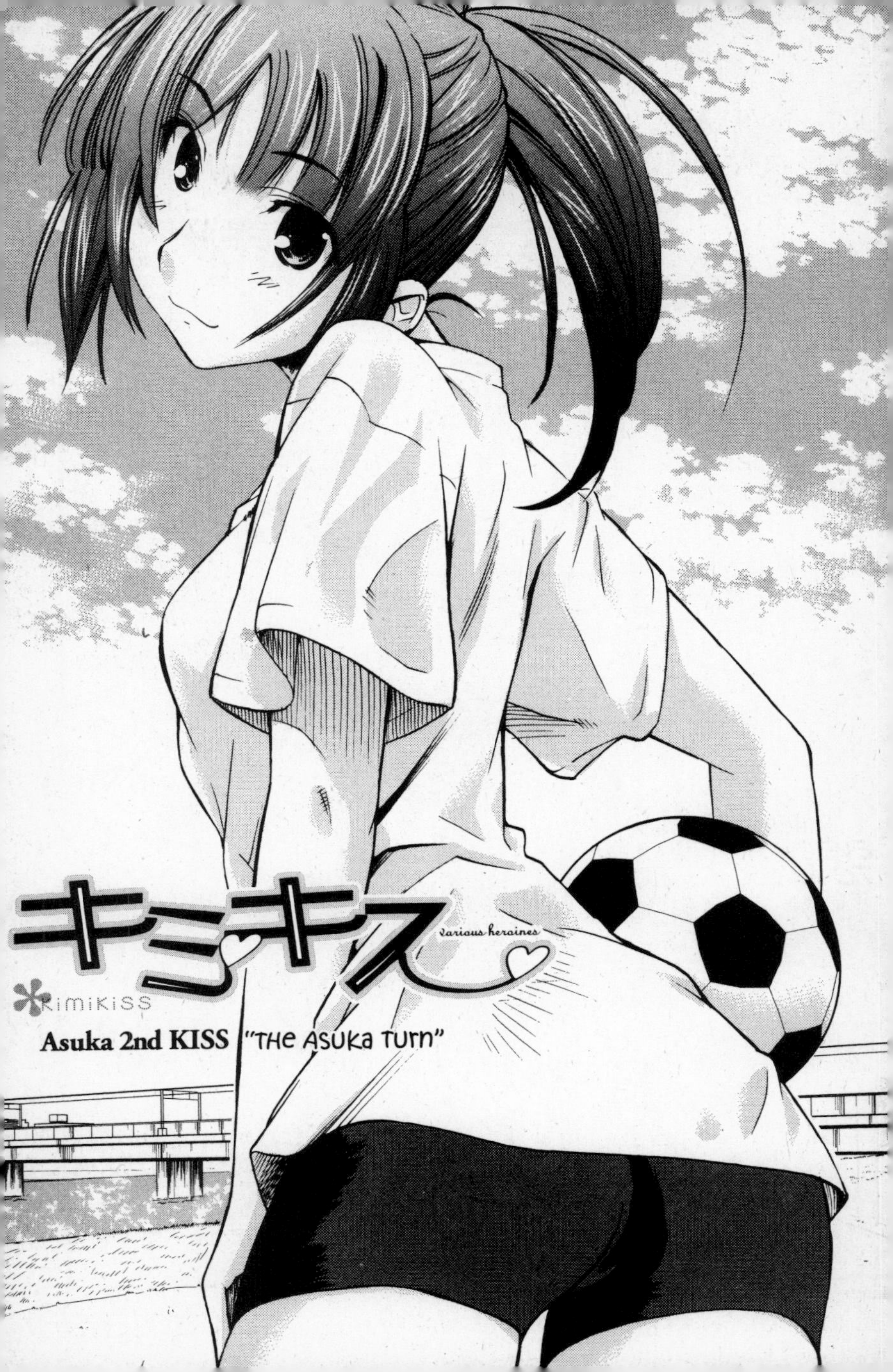
キミキス
various heroines
KimiKiss
Asuka 2nd KISS "The Asuka Turn"

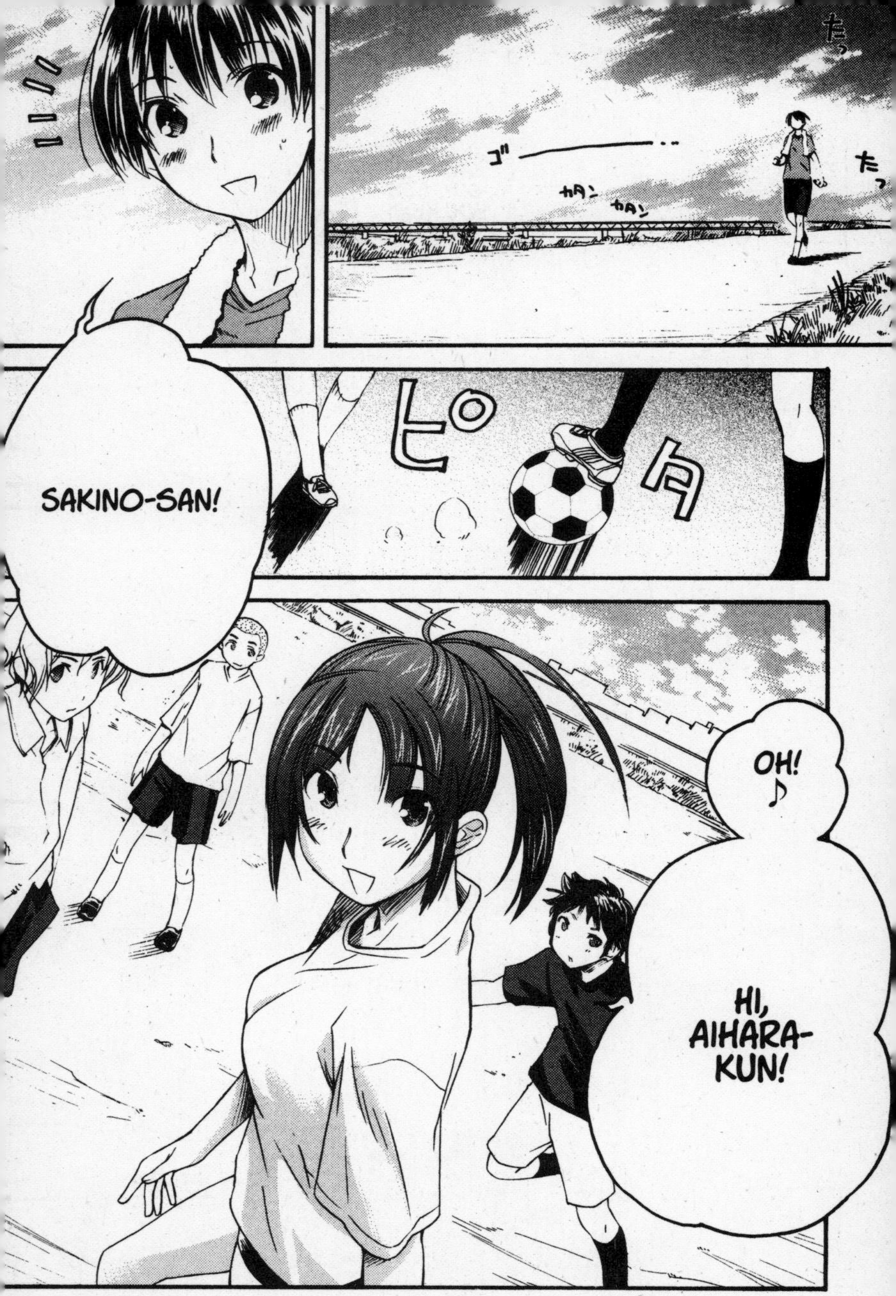
たっ
ゴーーー…
カタン
カタン
たっ
SAKINO-SAN!
ピタ
OH! ♪
HI, AIHARA-KUN!

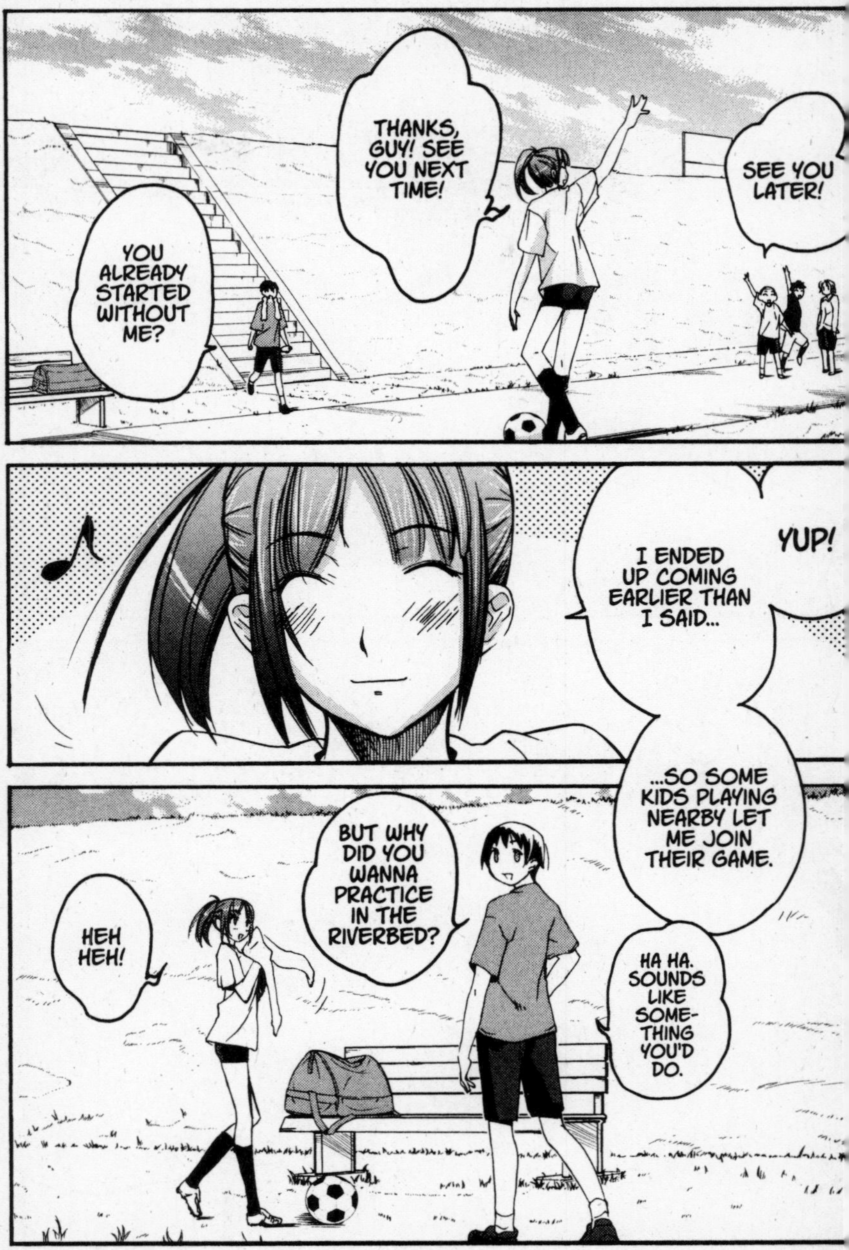

SEE YOU LATER!
THANKS, GUY! SEE YOU NEXT TIME!
YOU ALREADY STARTED WITHOUT ME?
YUP!
I ENDED UP COMING EARLIER THAN I SAID...
...SO SOME KIDS PLAYING NEARBY LET ME JOIN THEIR GAME.
HA HA. SOUNDS LIKE SOME-THING YOU'D DO.
BUT WHY DID YOU WANNA PRACTICE IN THE RIVERBED?
HEH HEH!

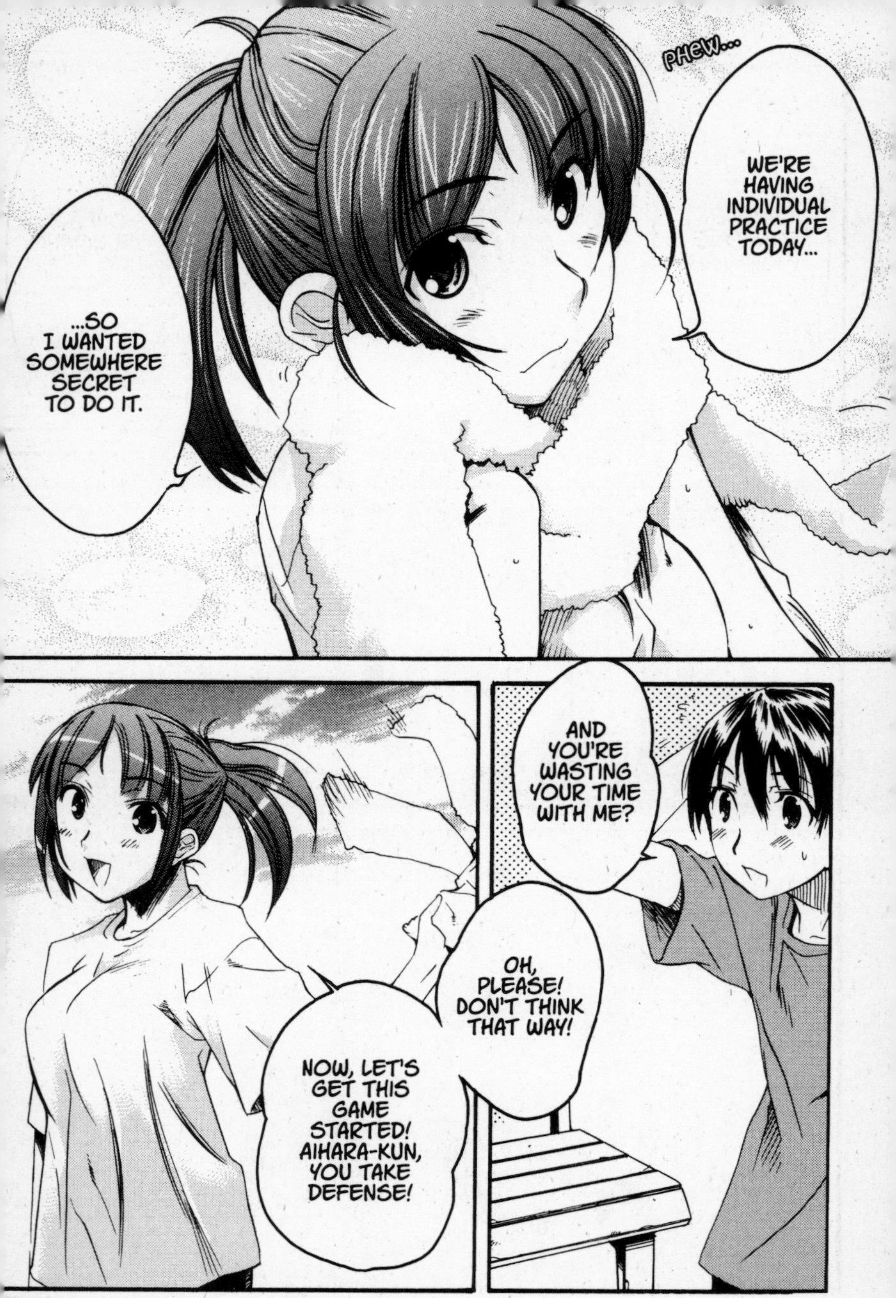
PHEW...
WE'RE HAVING INDIVIDUAL PRACTICE TODAY...
...SO I WANTED SOMEWHERE SECRET TO DO IT.
AND YOU'RE WASTING YOUR TIME WITH ME?
OH, PLEASE! DON'T THINK THAT WAY!
NOW, LET'S GET THIS GAME STARTED! AIHARA-KUN, YOU TAKE DEFENSE!

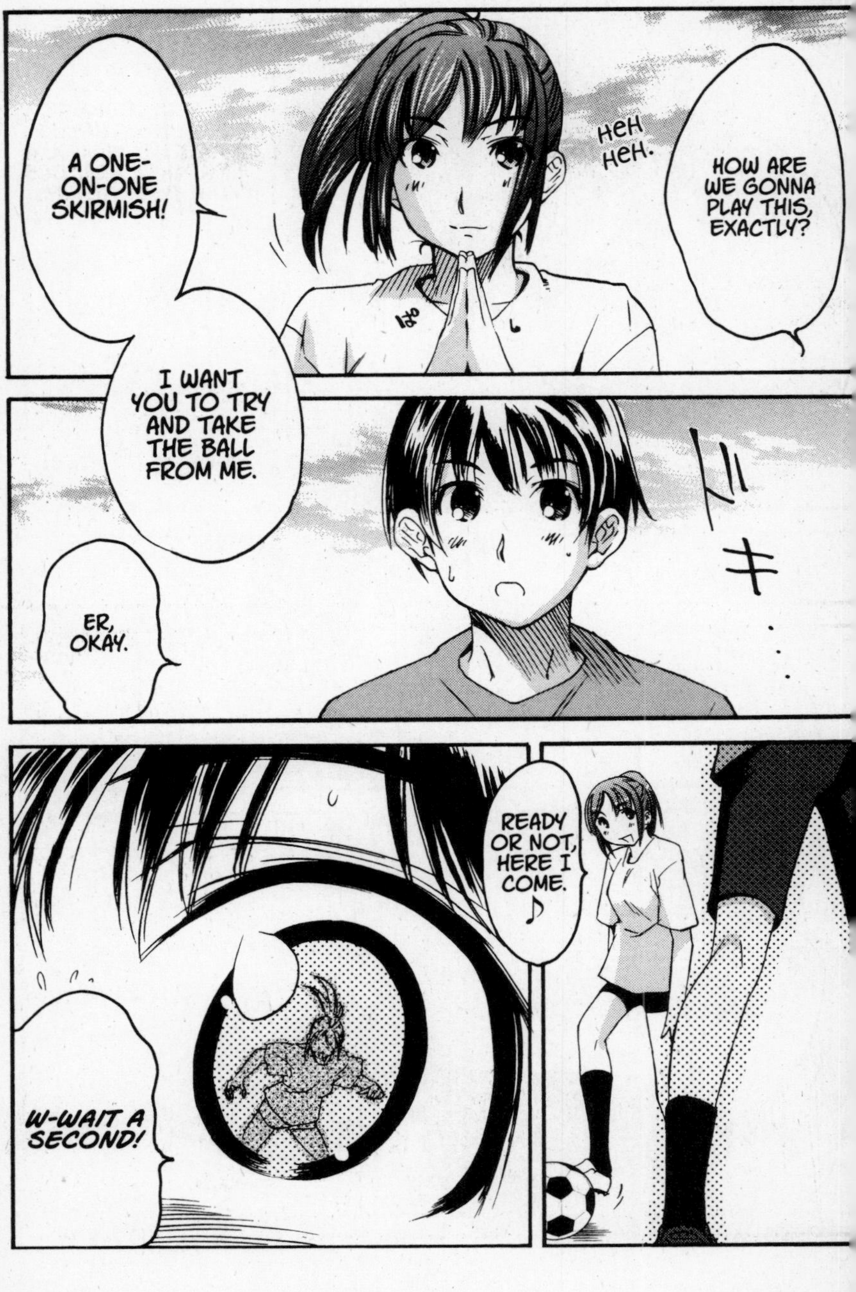
HOW ARE WE GONNA PLAY THIS, EXACTLY?
HEH HEH.
A ONE-ON-ONE SKIRMISH!
ぱし
I WANT YOU TO TRY AND TAKE THE BALL FROM ME.
ドキ
ER, OKAY.
READY OR NOT, HERE I COME. ♪
W-WAIT A SECOND!

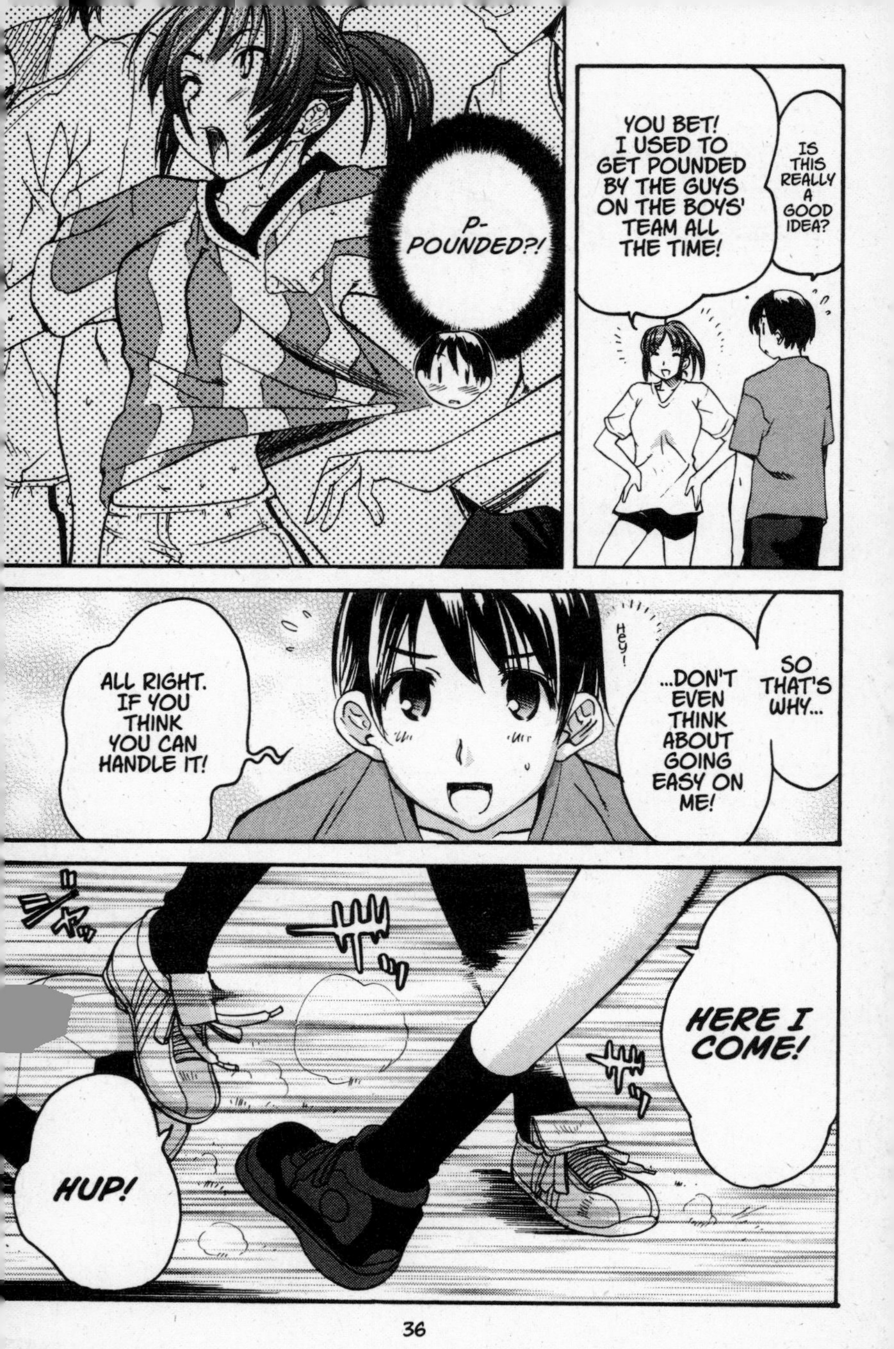
IS THIS REALLY A GOOD IDEA?
YOU BET! I USED TO GET POUNDED BY THE GUYS ON THE BOYS' TEAM ALL THE TIME!
P-POUNDED?!
SO THAT'S WHY...
...DON'T EVEN THINK ABOUT GOING EASY ON ME!
Hey!
ALL RIGHT. IF YOU THINK YOU CAN HANDLE IT!
HERE I COME!
HUP!

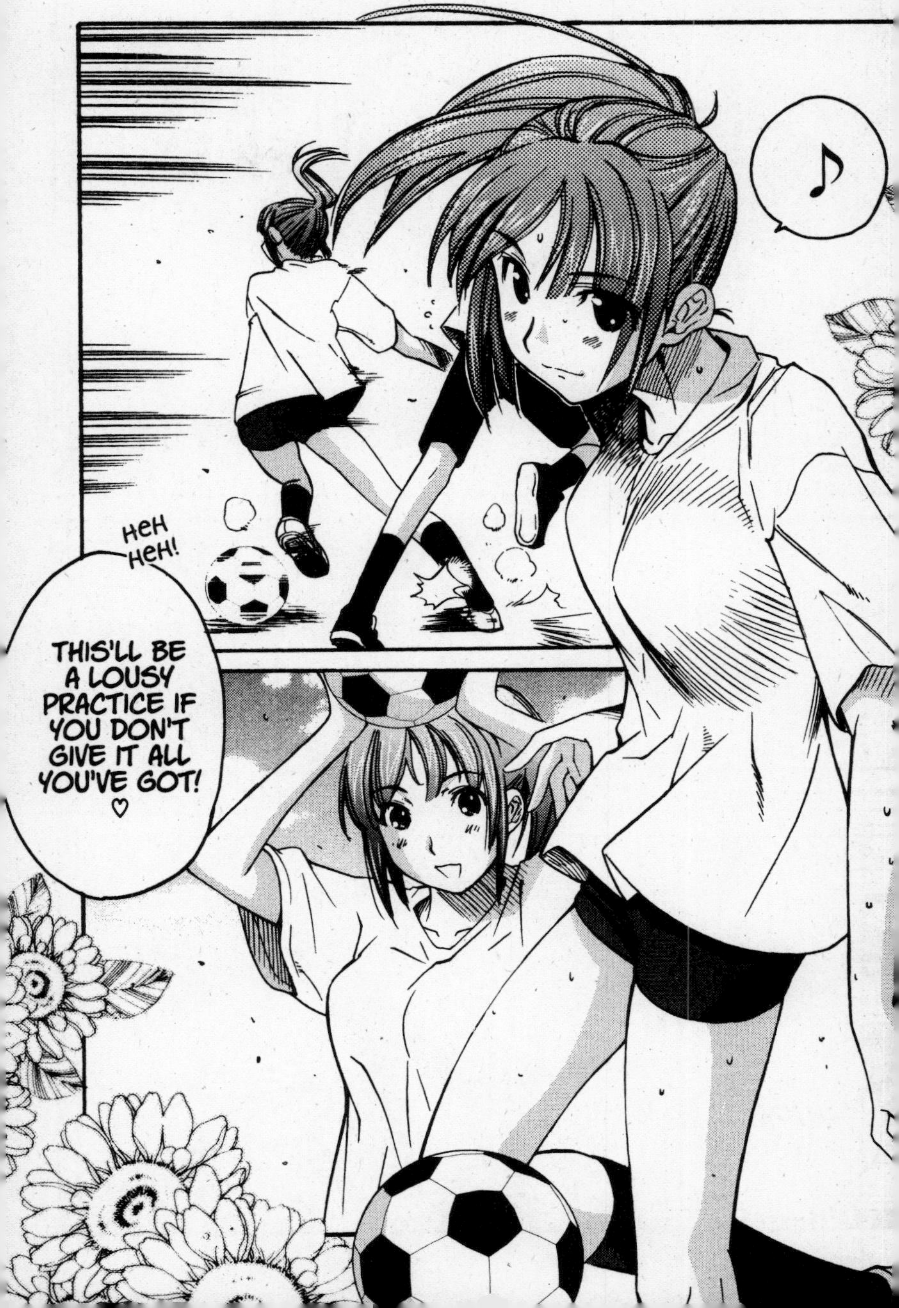
♪
HEH HEH!
THIS'LL BE A LOUSY PRACTICE IF YOU DON'T GIVE IT ALL YOU'VE GOT! ♡

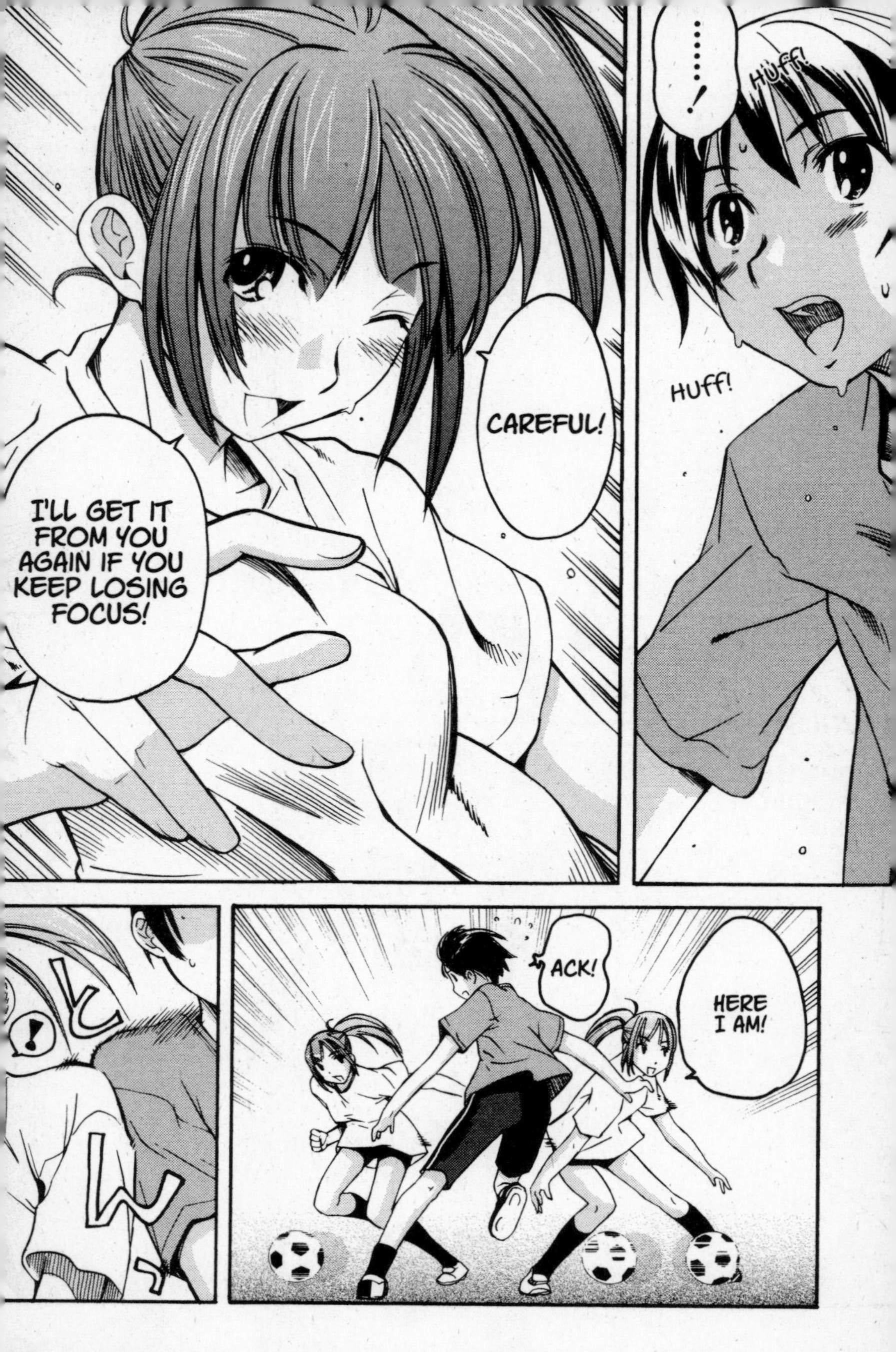
HUFF!
......!
HUFF!
CAREFUL!
I'LL GET IT FROM YOU AGAIN IF YOU KEEP LOSING FOCUS!
HERE I AM!
ACK!
!

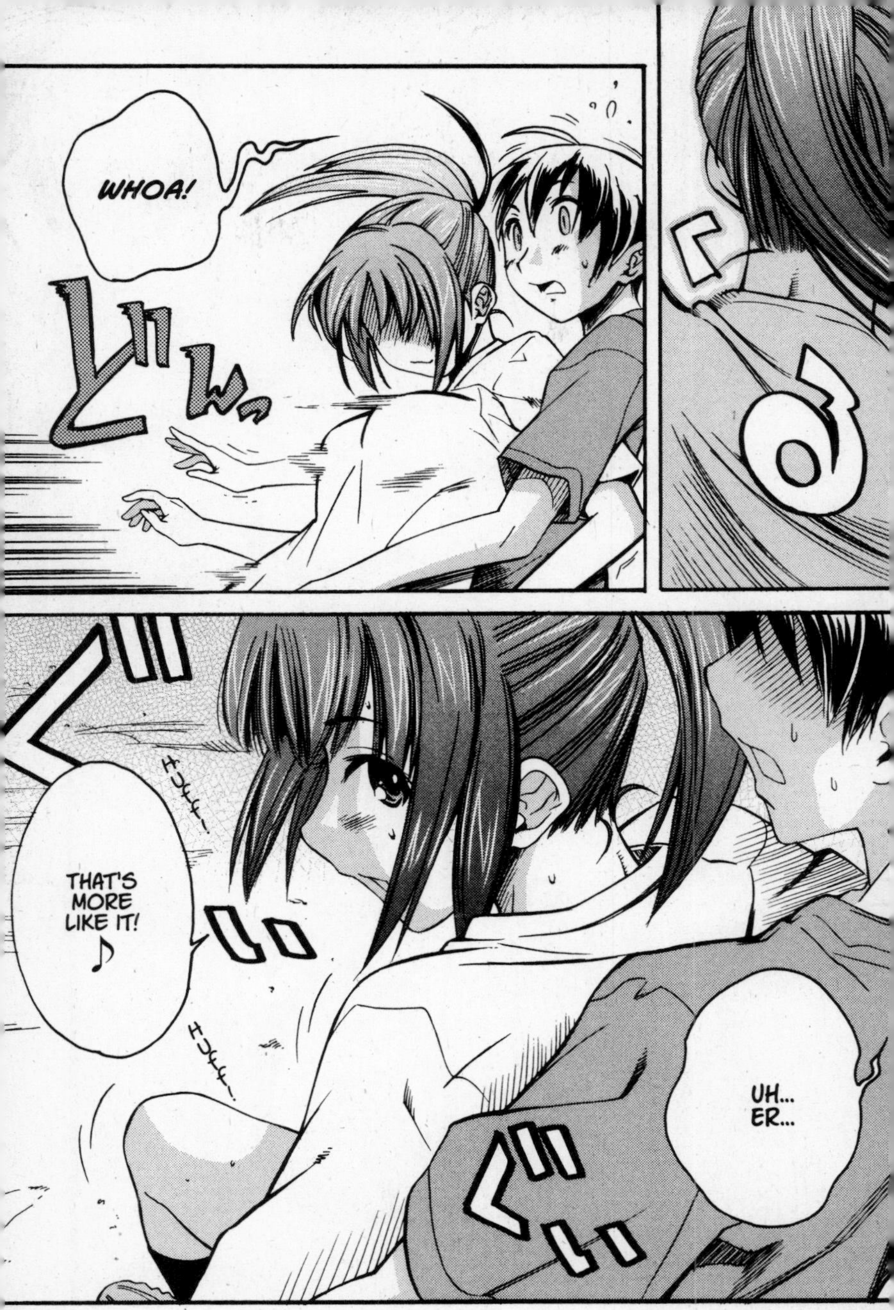
WHOA!
HUFF!
THAT'S MORE LIKE IT! ♪
HUFF!
UH... ER...

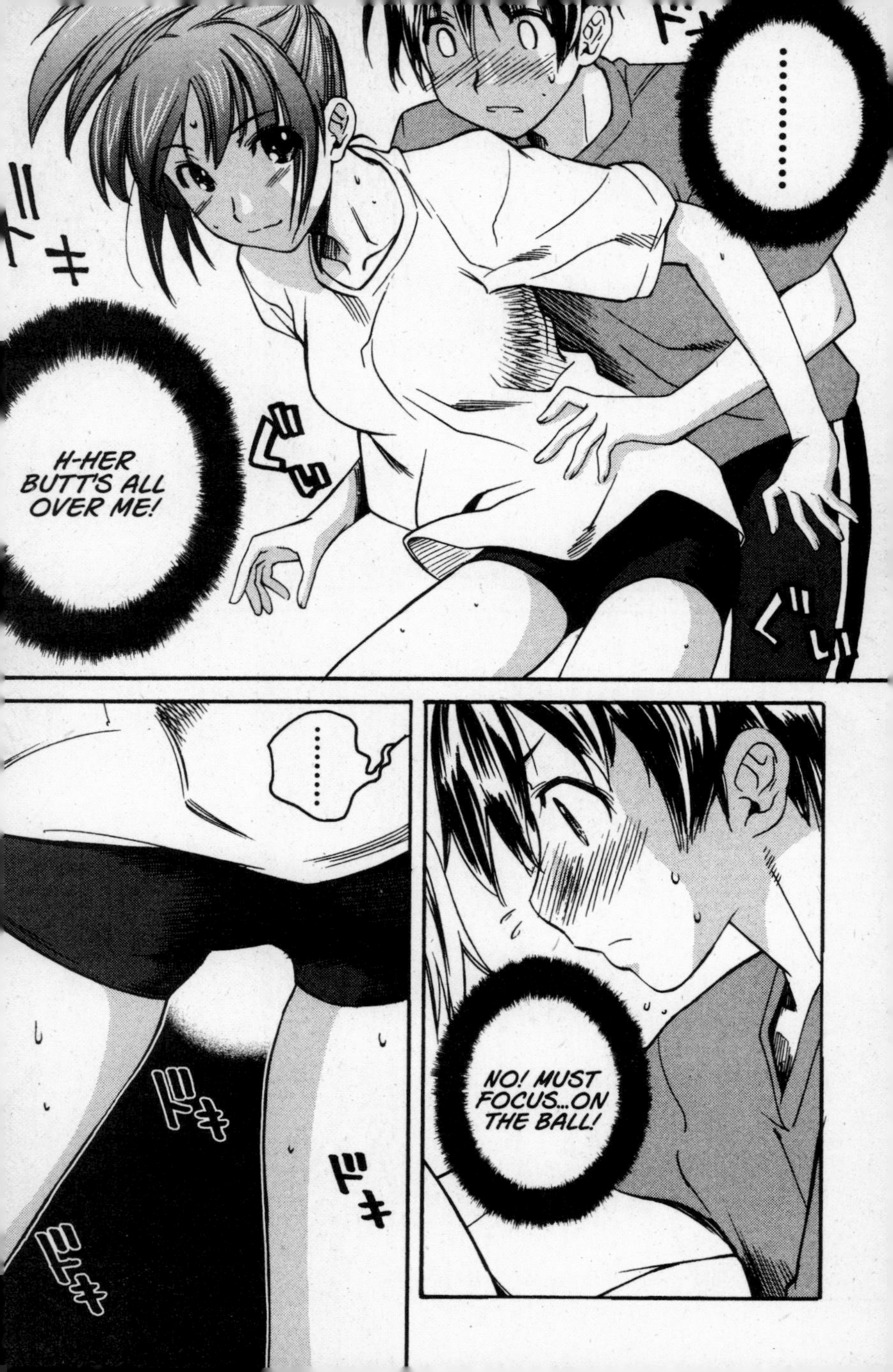
……
H-HER BUTT'S ALL OVER ME!
NO! MUST FOCUS...ON THE BALL!
……
ドキ
ドキ

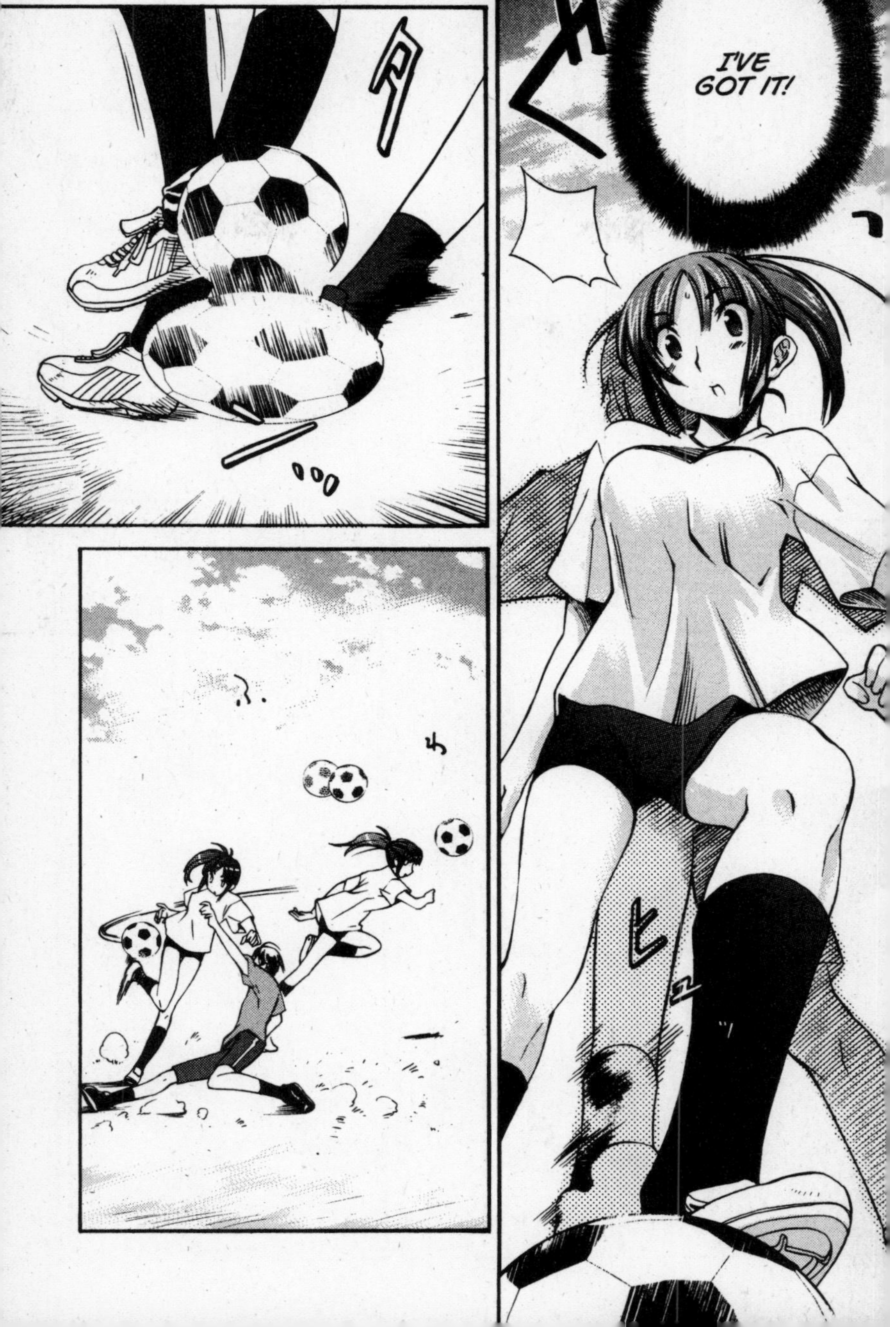
I'VE GOT IT!

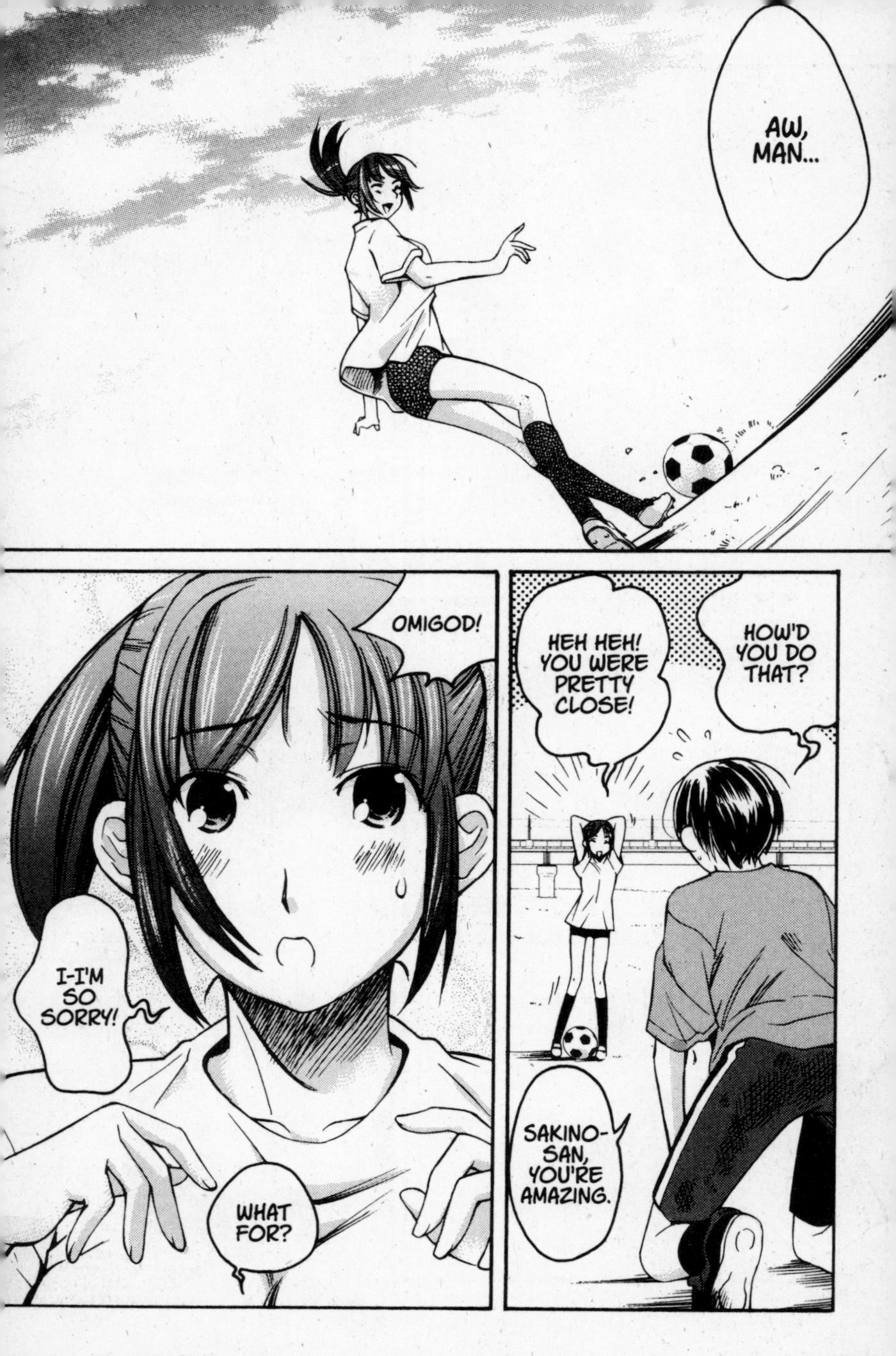
AW, MAN...
HOW'D YOU DO THAT?
HEH HEH! YOU WERE PRETTY CLOSE!
SAKINO-SAN, YOU'RE AMAZING.
OMIGOD!
I-I'M SO SORRY!
WHAT FOR?

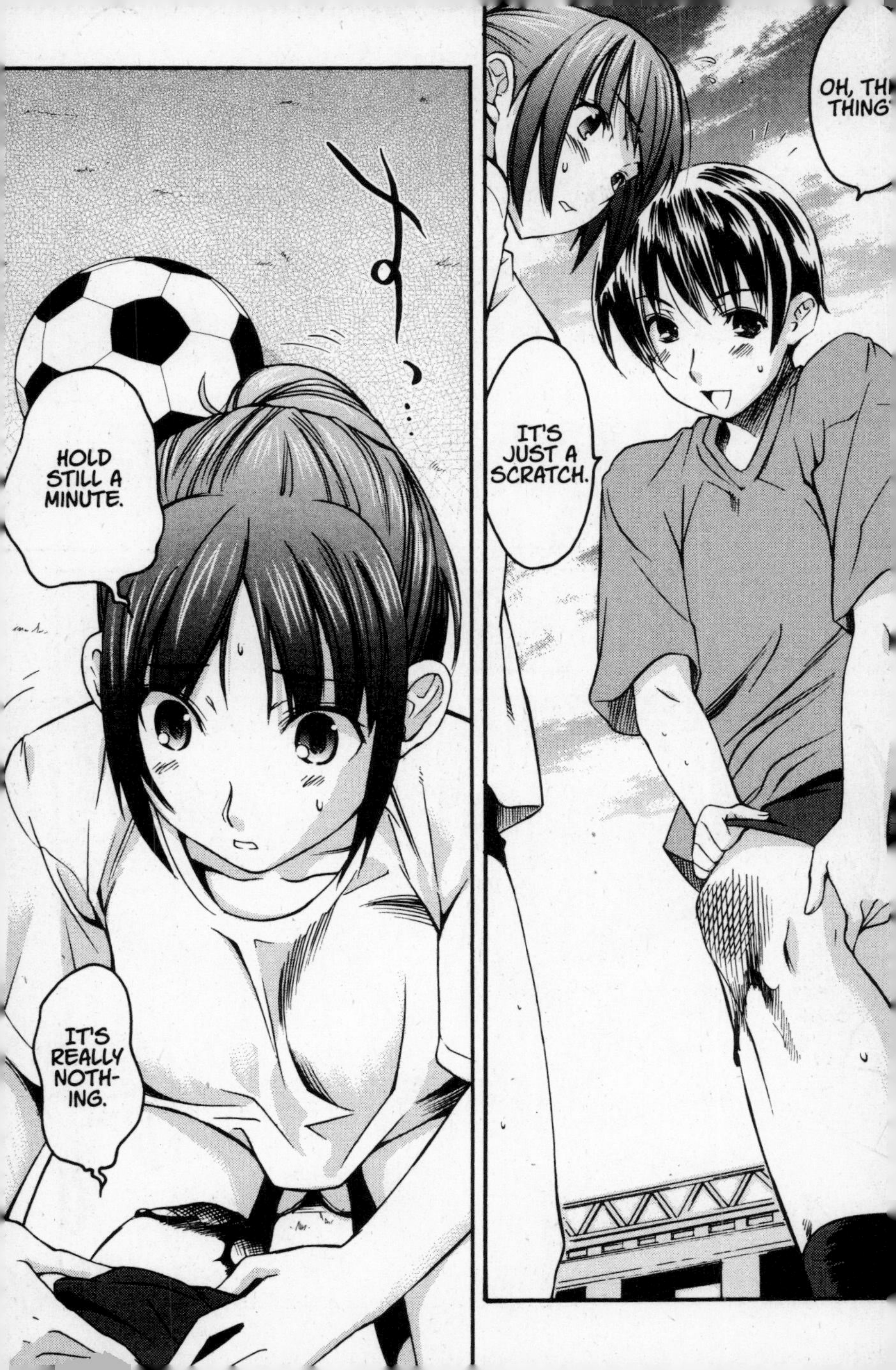
OH, THI THING'
IT'S JUST A SCRATCH.
HOLD STILL A MINUTE.
IT'S REALLY NOTH-ING.

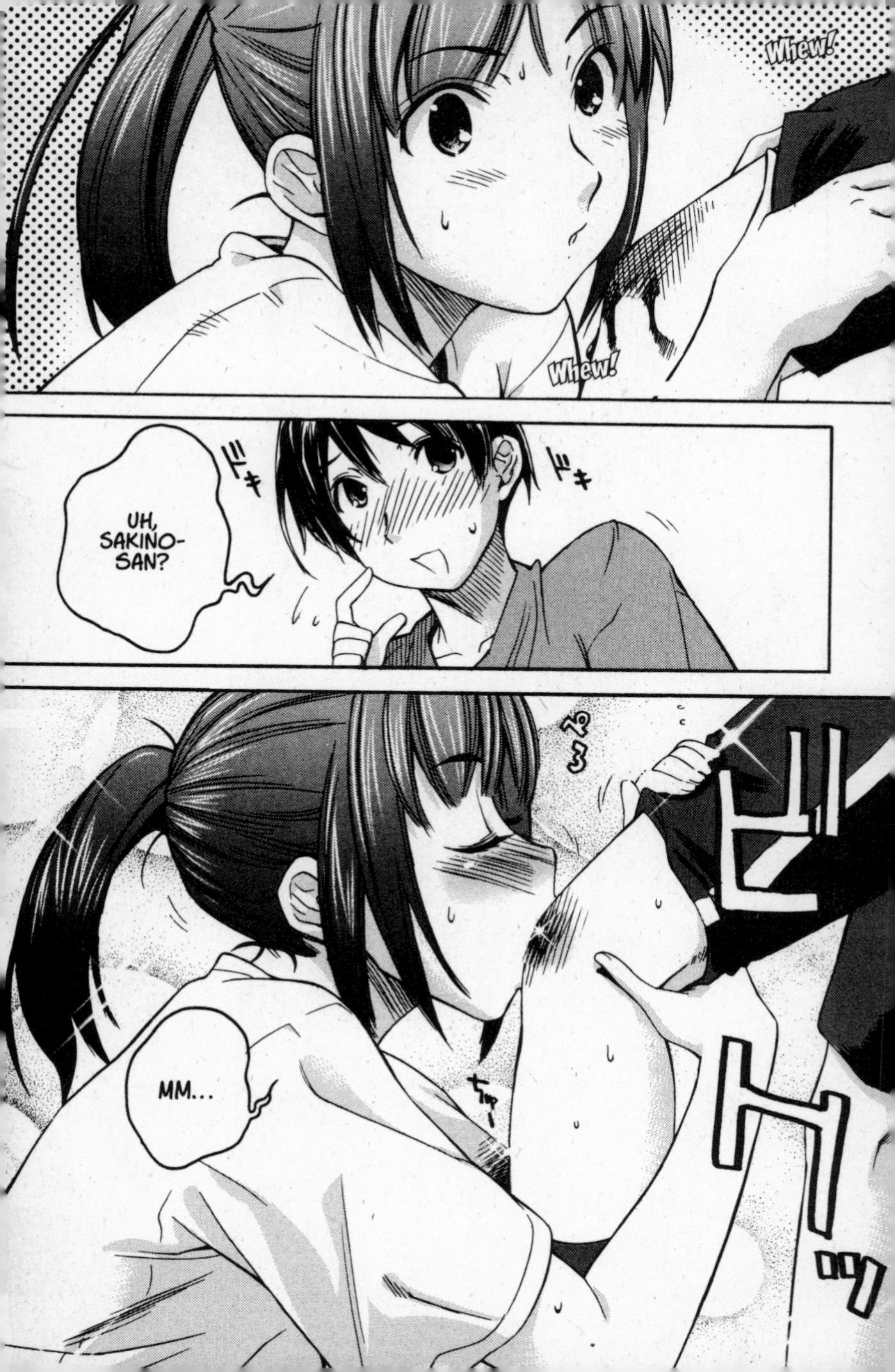
Whew!
Whew!
ドキ
ドキ
UH, SAKINO-SAN?
MM...

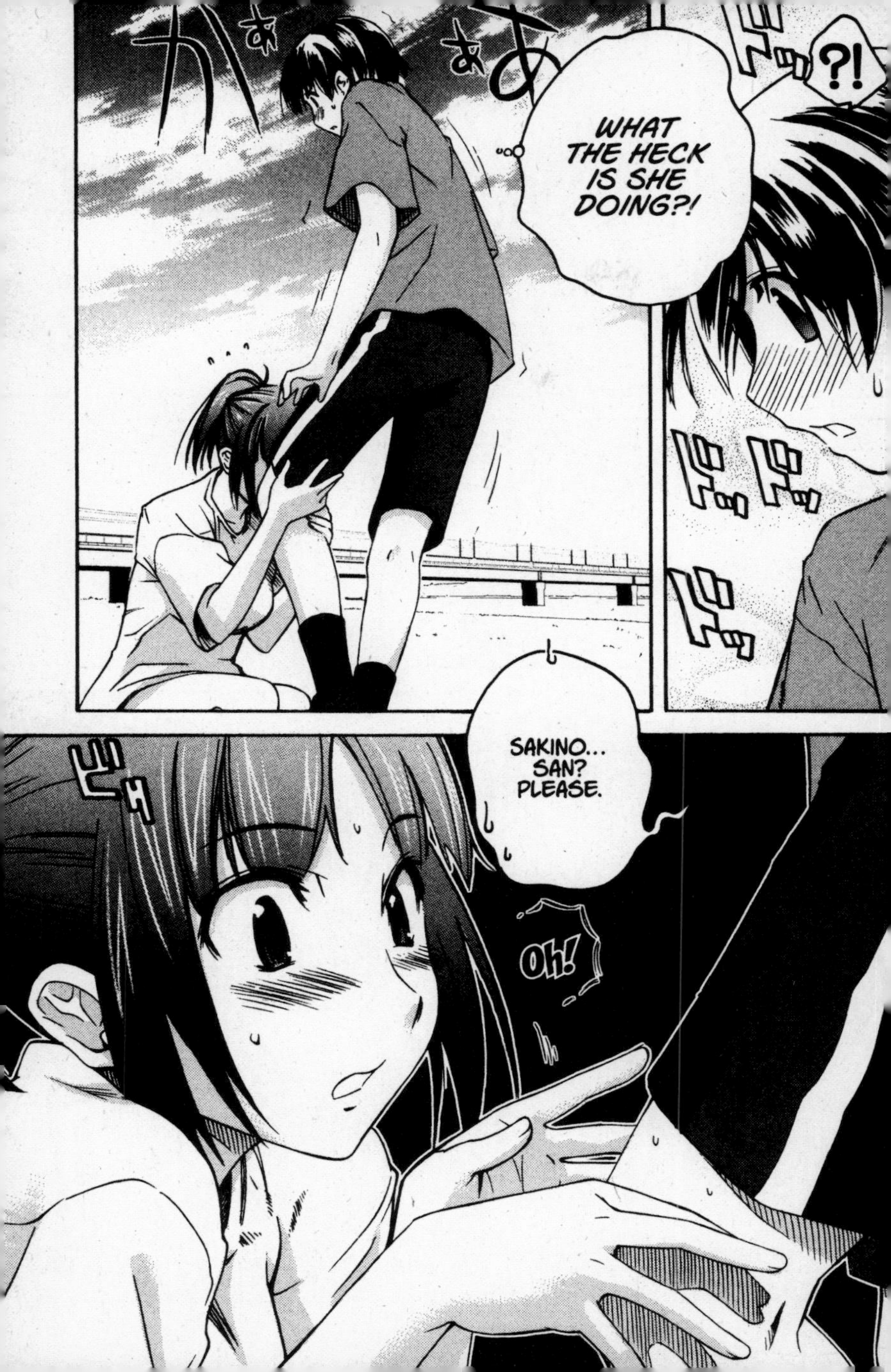
?!
WHAT THE HECK IS SHE DOING?!
SAKINO... SAN? PLEASE.
Oh!

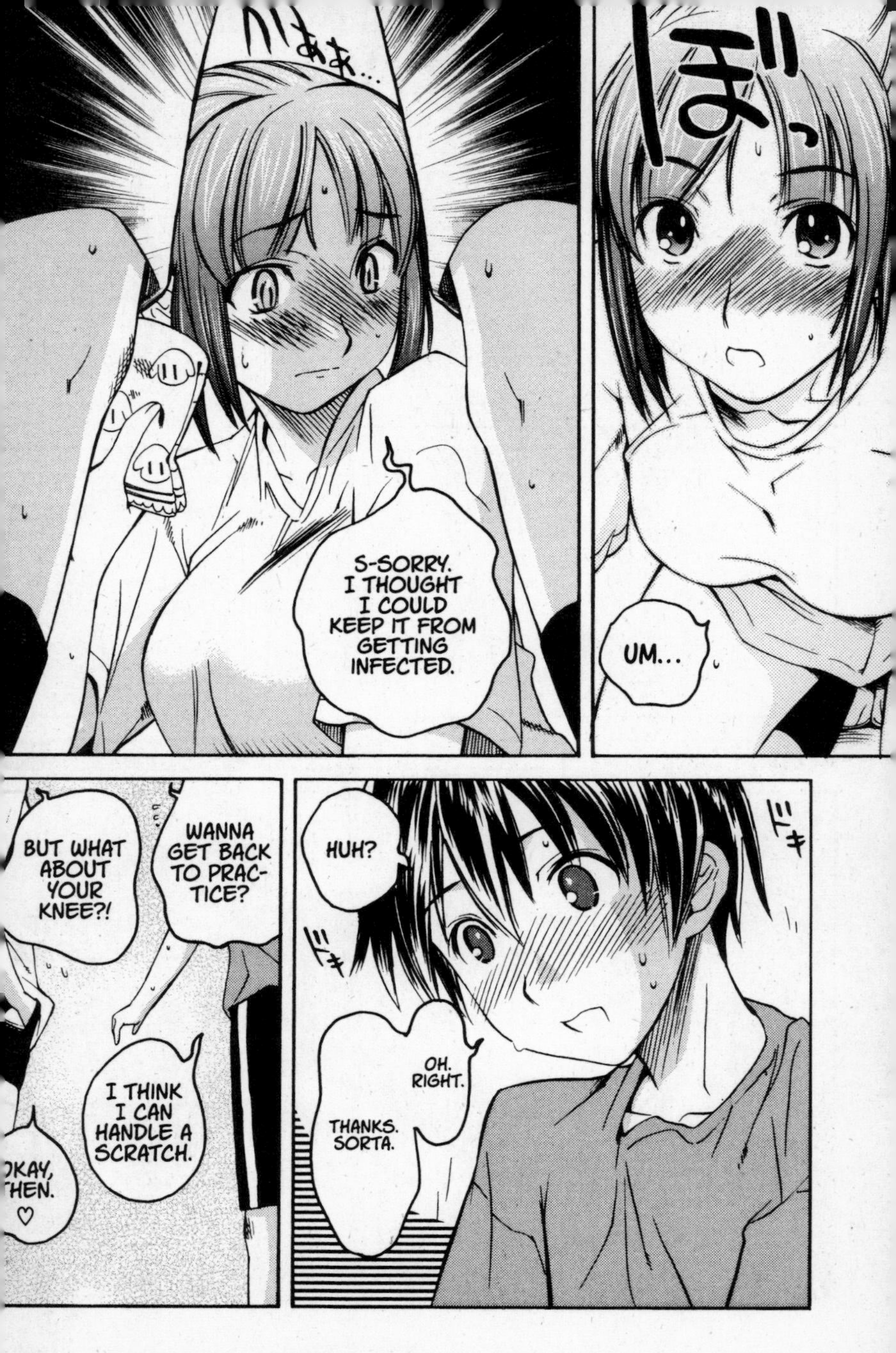
ぼっ
UM...
へあぁ…
S-SORRY. I THOUGHT I COULD KEEP IT FROM GETTING INFECTED.
HUH?
ドキ
ドキ
OH. RIGHT.
THANKS. SORTA.
WANNA GET BACK TO PRAC-TICE?
BUT WHAT ABOUT YOUR KNEE?!
I THINK I CAN HANDLE A SCRATCH.
OKAY, THEN. ♡

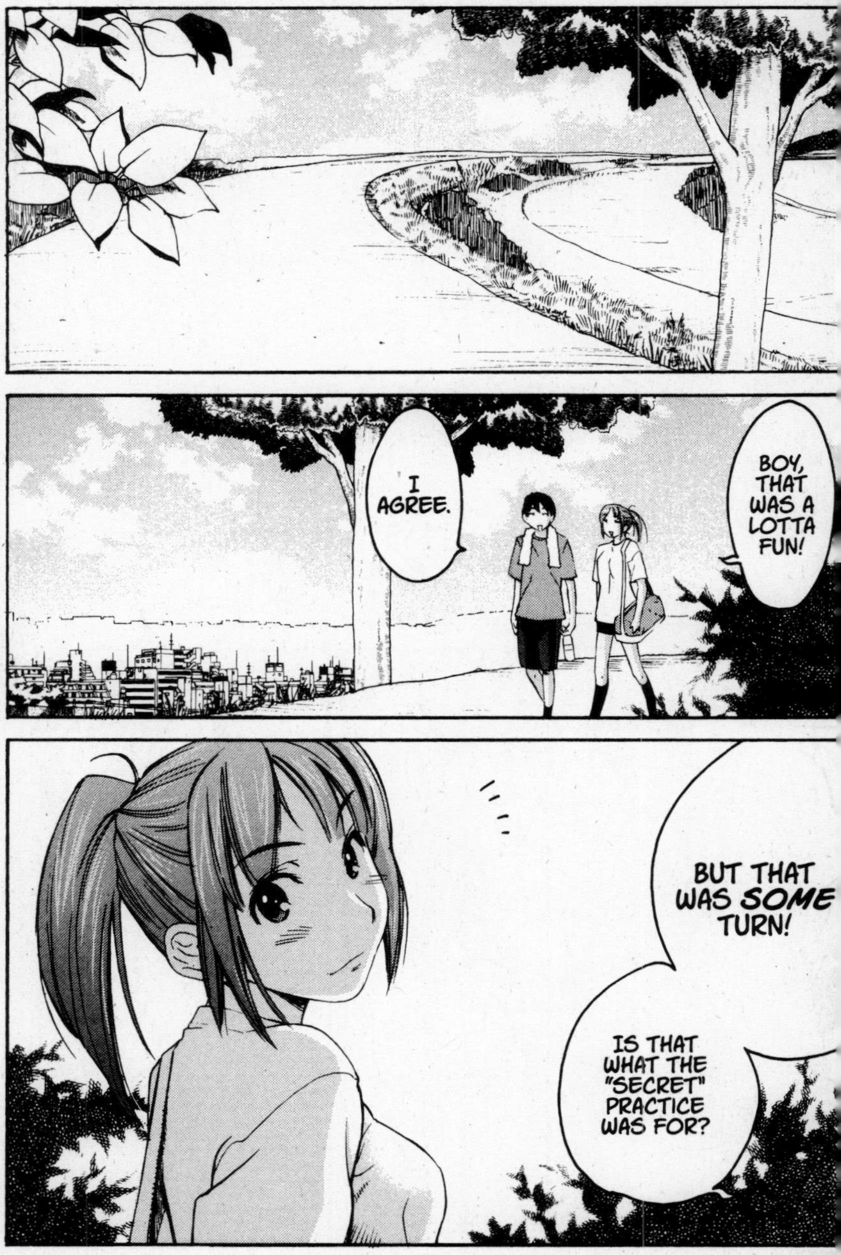
BOY, THAT WAS A LOTTA FUN!
I AGREE.
BUT THAT WAS *SOME* TURN!
IS THAT WHAT THE "SECRET" PRACTICE WAS FOR?

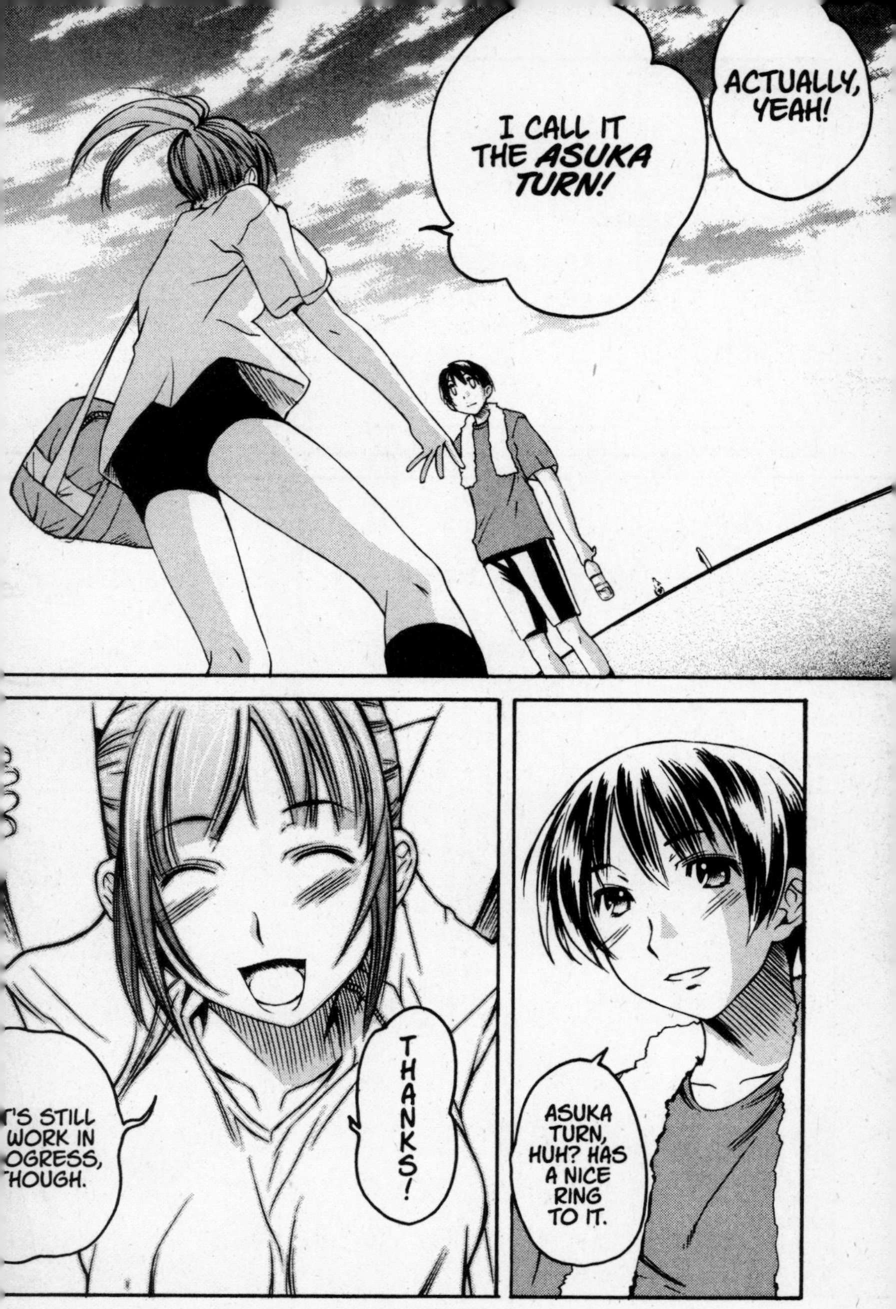
ACTUALLY, YEAH!
I CALL IT THE *ASUKA TURN!*
ASUKA TURN, HUH? HAS A NICE RING TO IT.
THANKS!
T'S STILL WORK IN OGRESS, THOUGH.

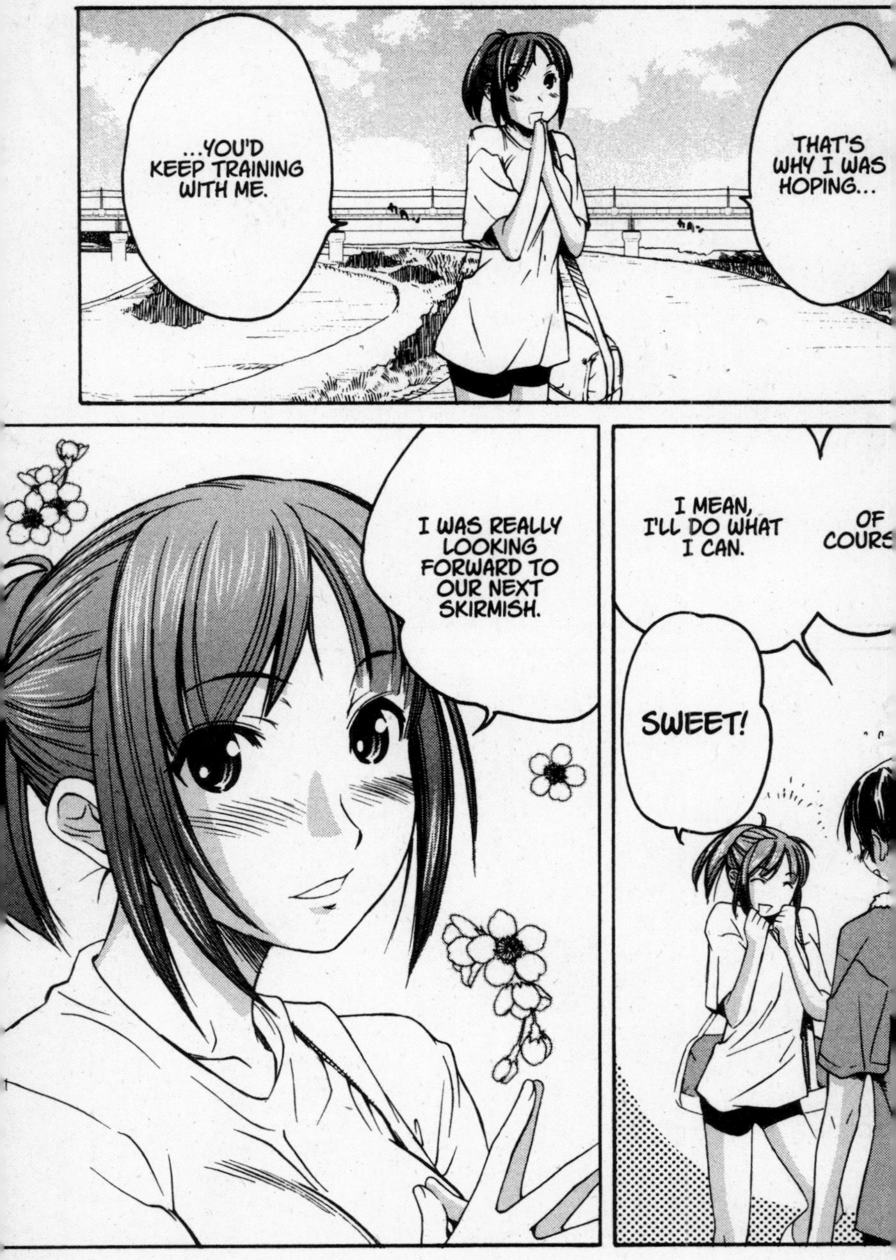
THAT'S WHY I WAS HOPING...
...YOU'D KEEP TRAINING WITH ME.
OF COURS
I MEAN, I'LL DO WHAT I CAN.
SWEET!
I WAS REALLY LOOKING FORWARD TO OUR NEXT SKIRMISH.

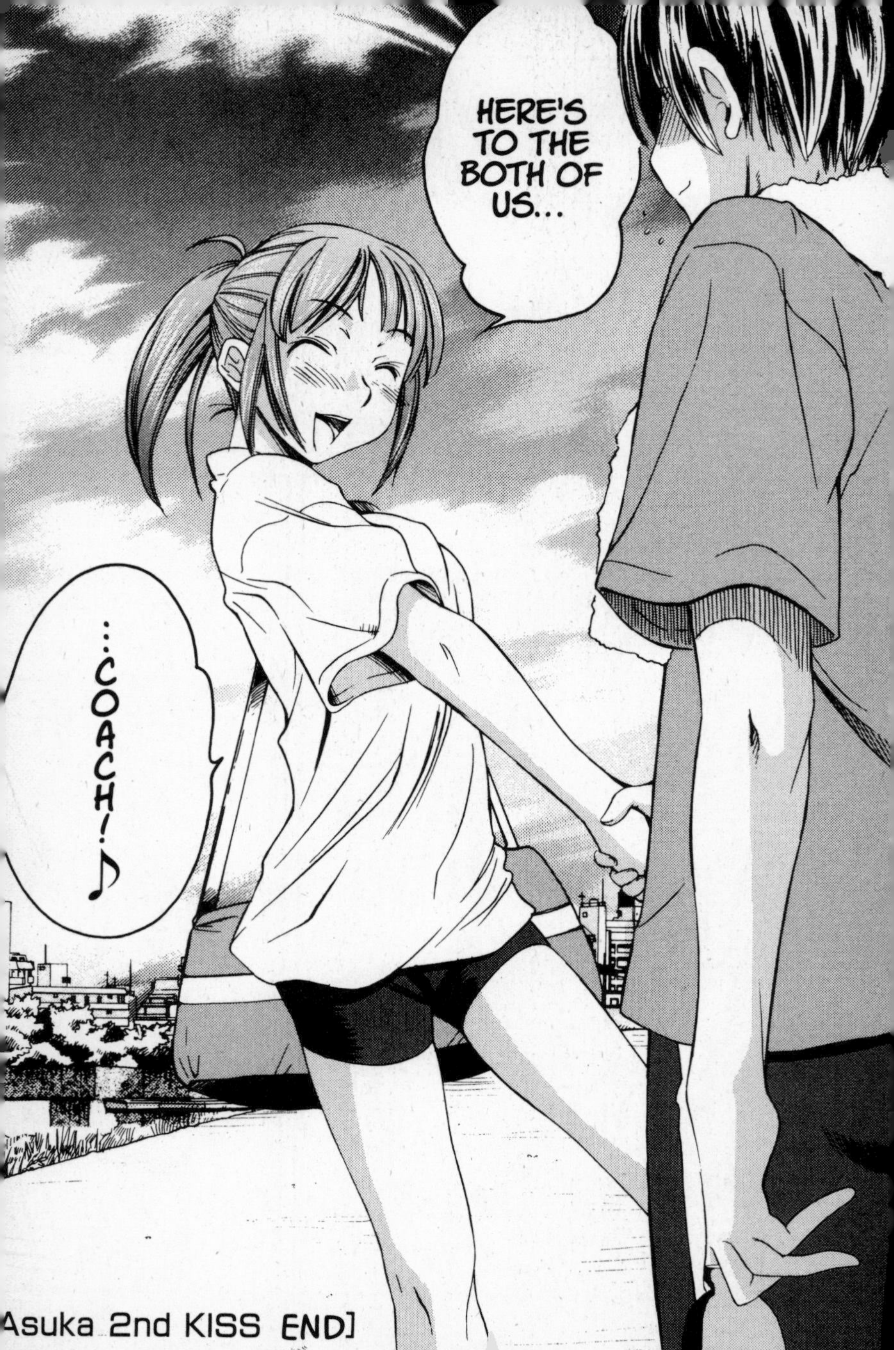
HERE'S TO THE BOTH OF US...
...COACH!♪

[Asuka 2nd KISS END]

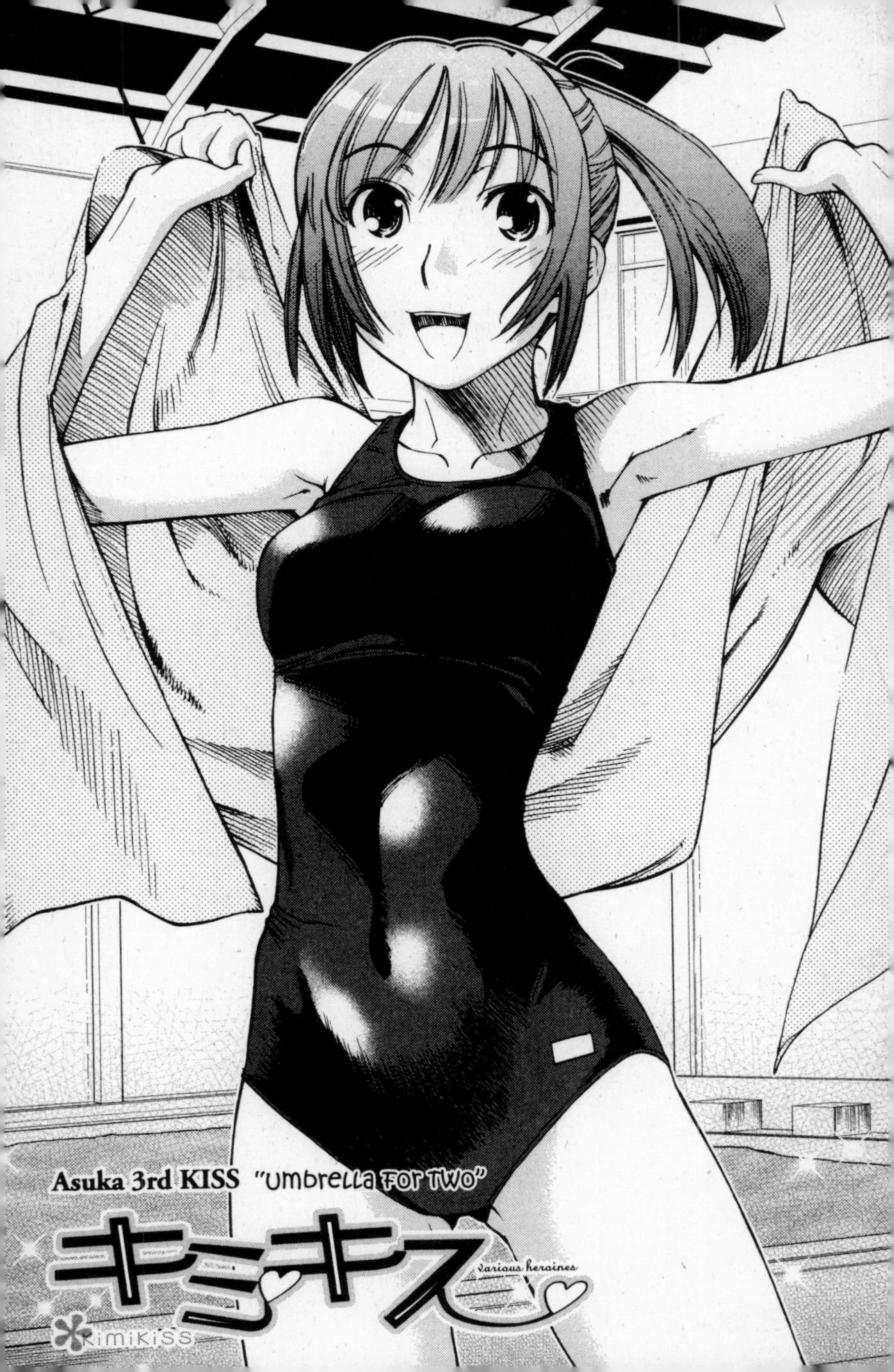
Asuka 3rd KISS "Umbrella For Two"
キミキス
various heroines
KimiKiss

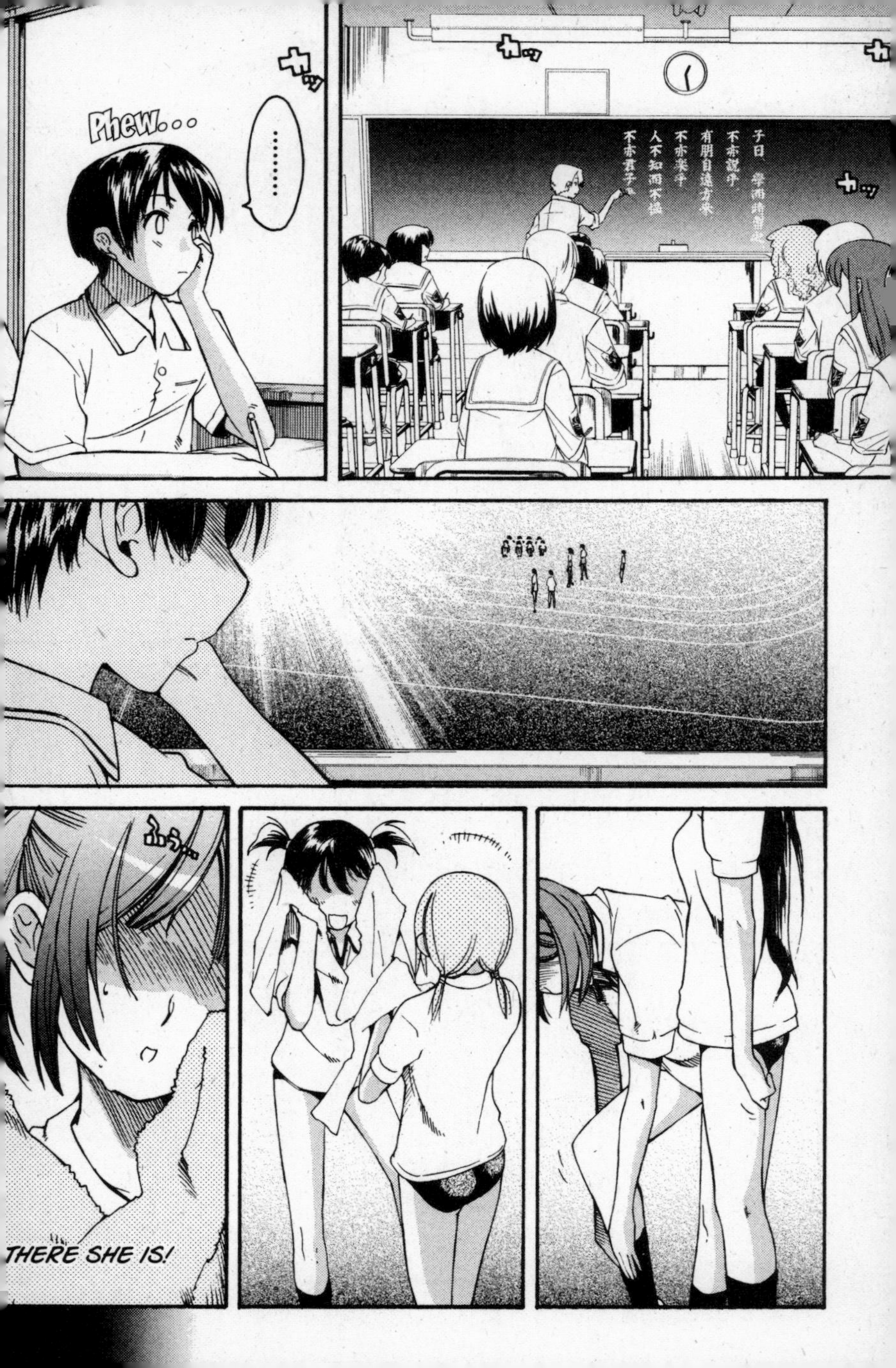
カッ
カッ
カッ
カッ
......
Phew...
ふぅ...
THERE SHE IS!

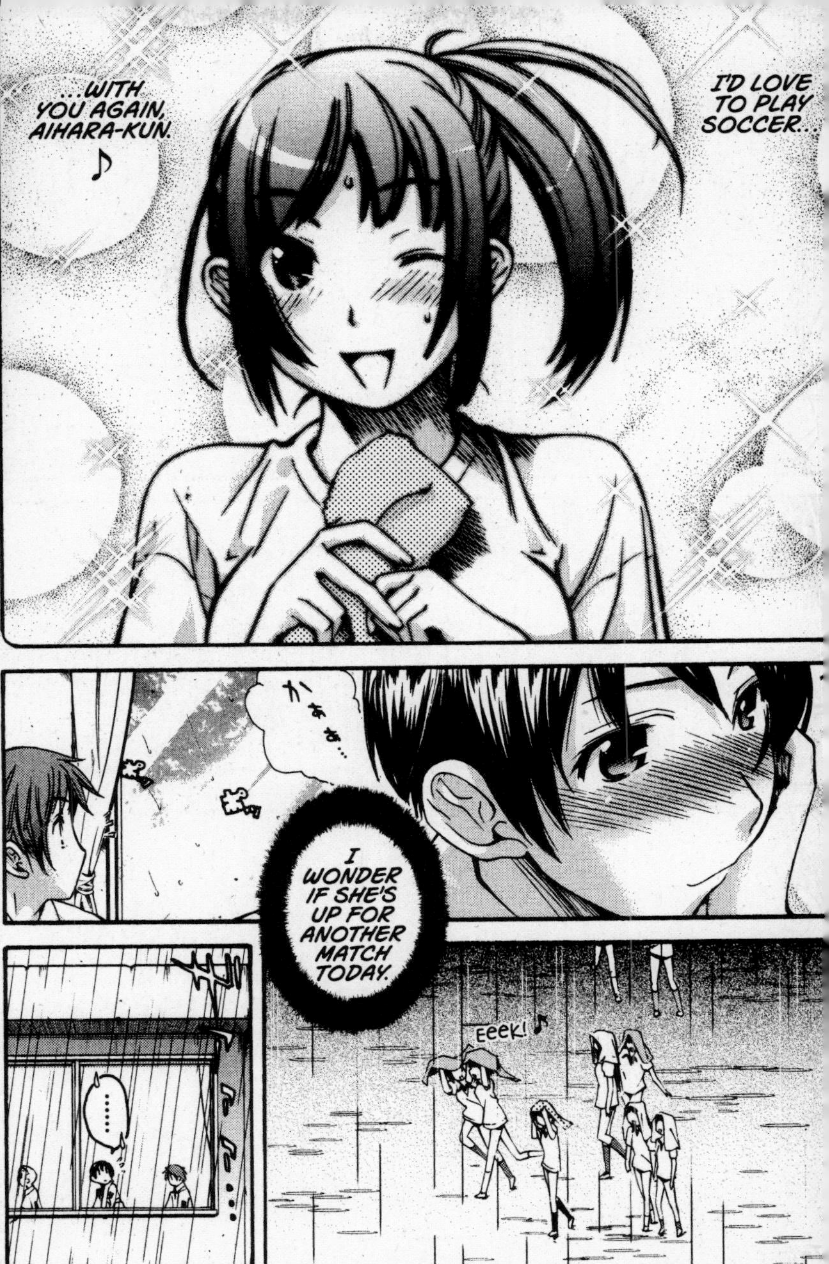
I'D LOVE TO PLAY SOCCER...
...WITH YOU AGAIN, AIHARA-KUN. ♪
かぁぁ…
I WONDER IF SHE'S UP FOR ANOTHER MATCH TODAY.
Eeek! ♪
……

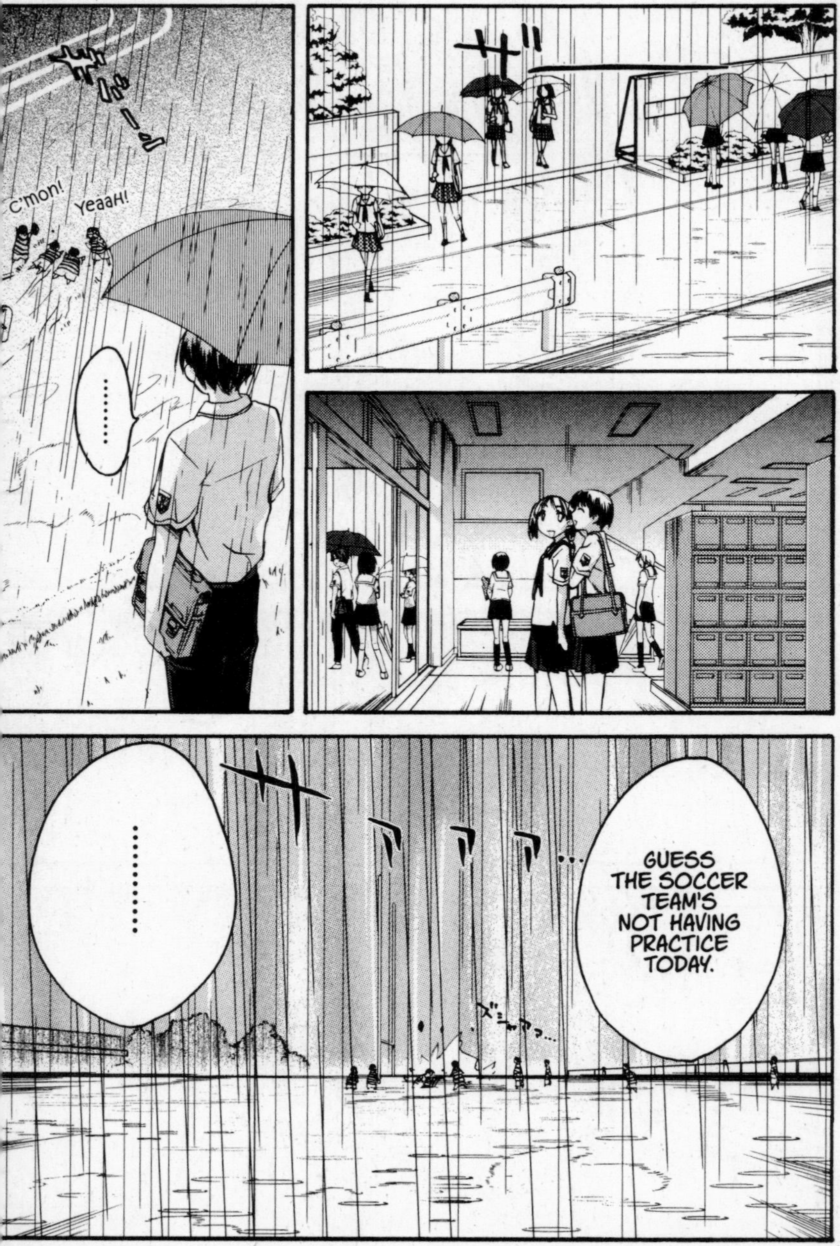
C'mon!
Yeaah!
......
GUESS THE SOCCER TEAM'S NOT HAVING PRACTICE TODAY.
....

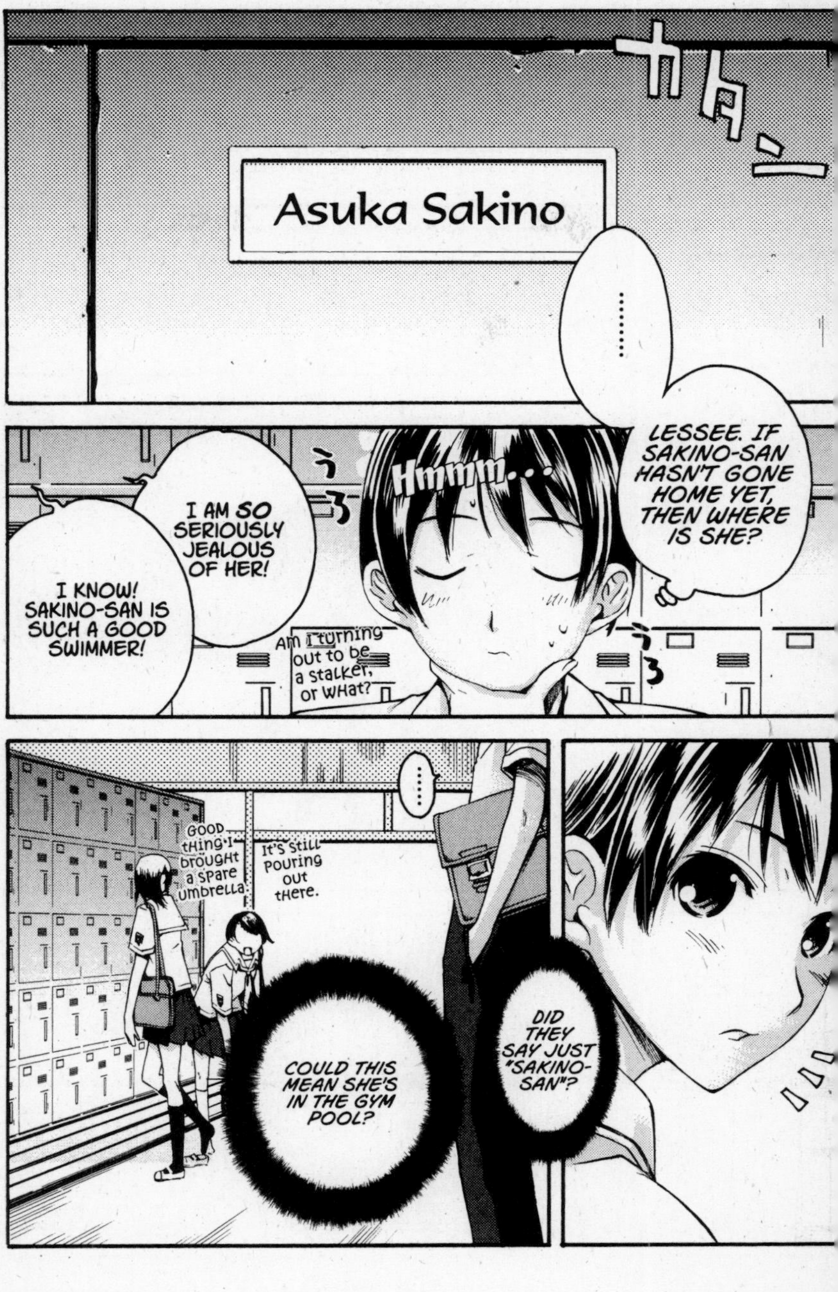

カタン
Asuka Sakino
……
LESSEE. IF SAKINO-SAN HASN'T GONE HOME YET, THEN WHERE IS SHE?
Hmmm...
うろ
うろ
Am I turning out to be a stalker, or WHAt?
I AM SO SERIOUSLY JEALOUS OF HER!
I KNOW! SAKINO-SAN IS SUCH A GOOD SWIMMER!
DID THEY SAY JUST "SAKINO-SAN"?
……
It's Still Pouring out tHere.
GOOD tHing I brought a Spare umbrella.
COULD THIS MEAN SHE'S IN THE GYM POOL?

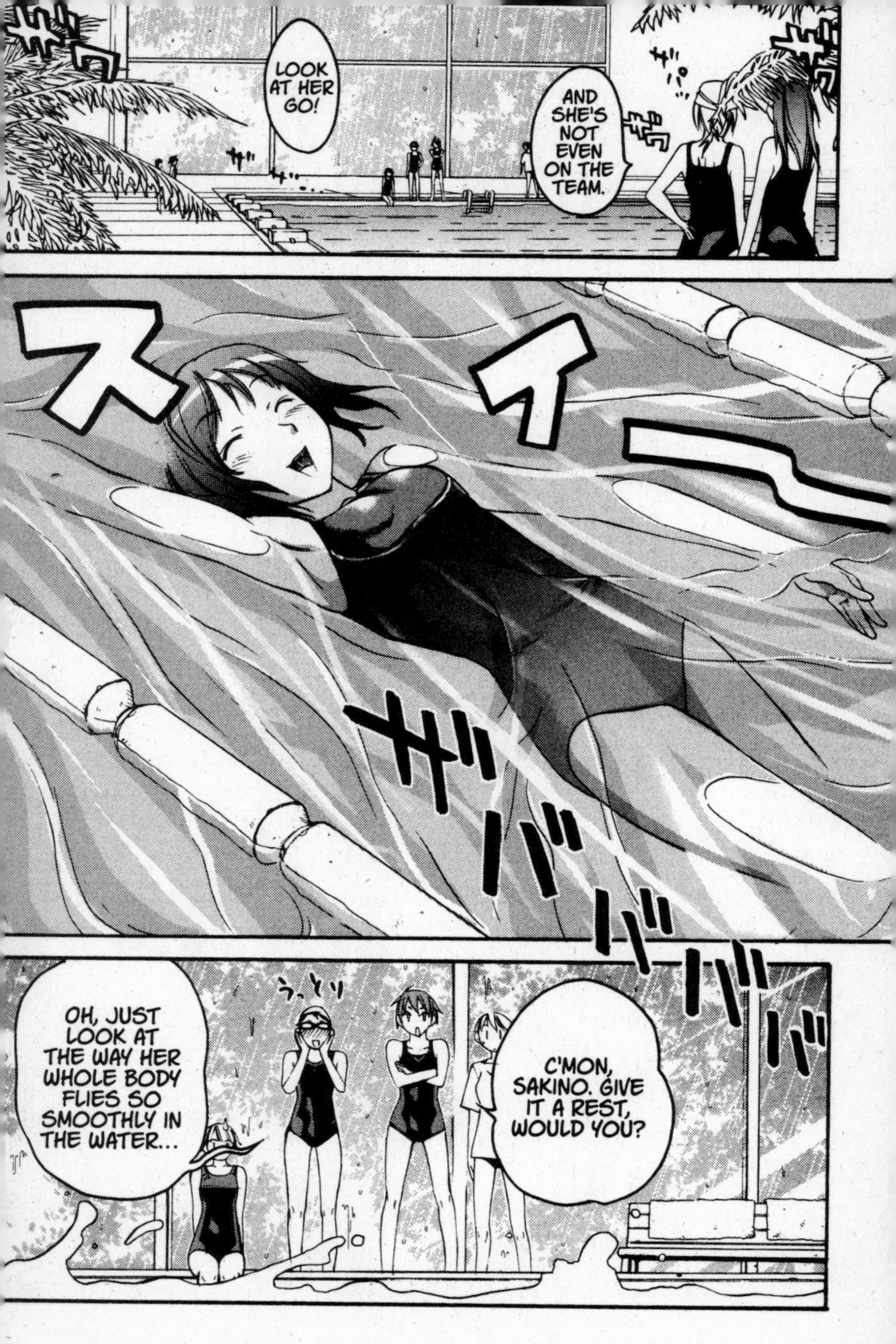
LOOK AT HER GO!
AND SHE'S NOT EVEN ON THE TEAM.
OH, JUST LOOK AT THE WAY HER WHOLE BODY FLIES SO SMOOTHLY IN THE WATER...
C'MON, SAKINO. GIVE IT A REST, WOULD YOU?

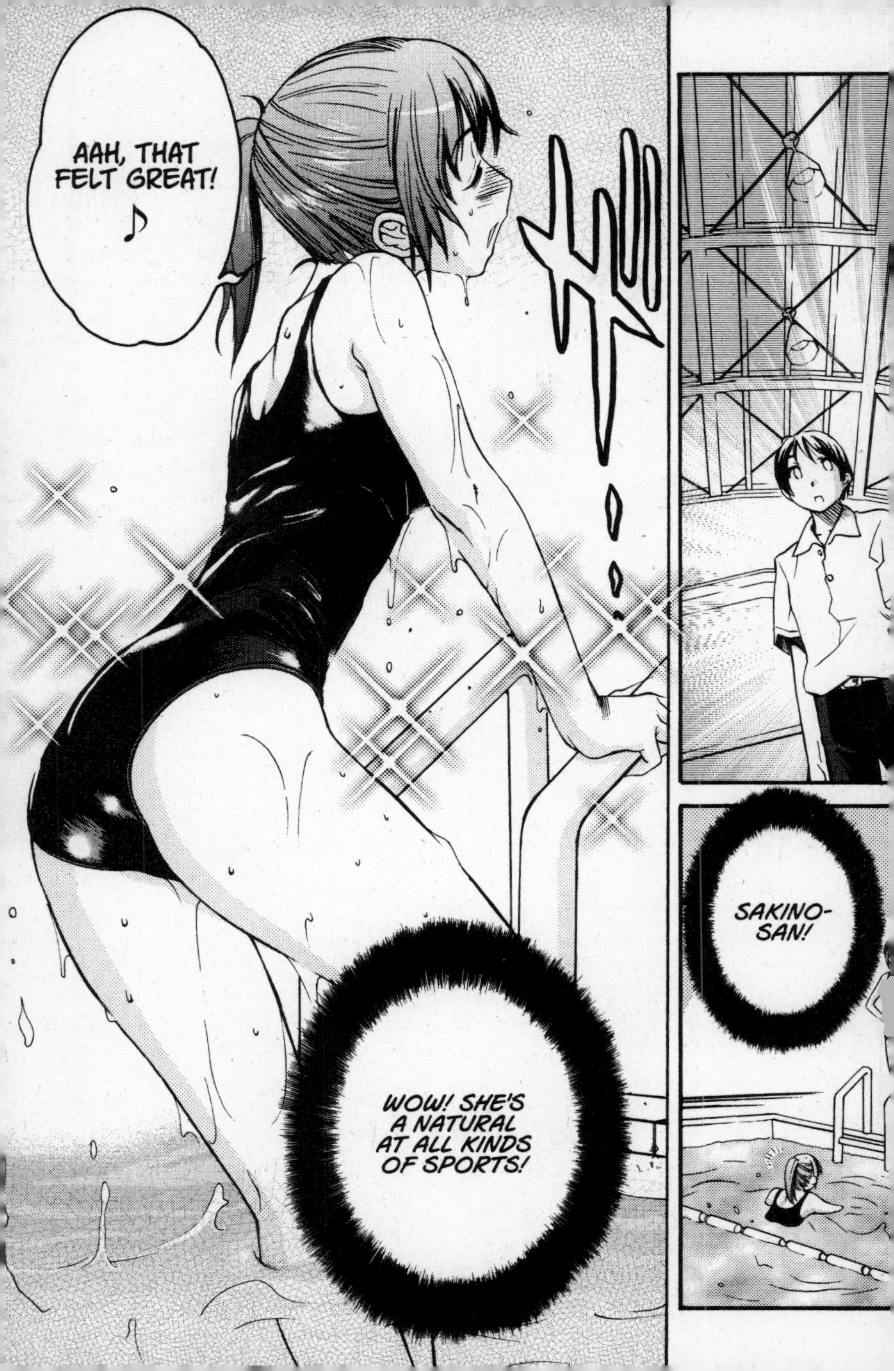
SAKINO-SAN!
AAH, THAT FELT GREAT! ♪
WOW! SHE'S A NATURAL AT ALL KINDS OF SPORTS!

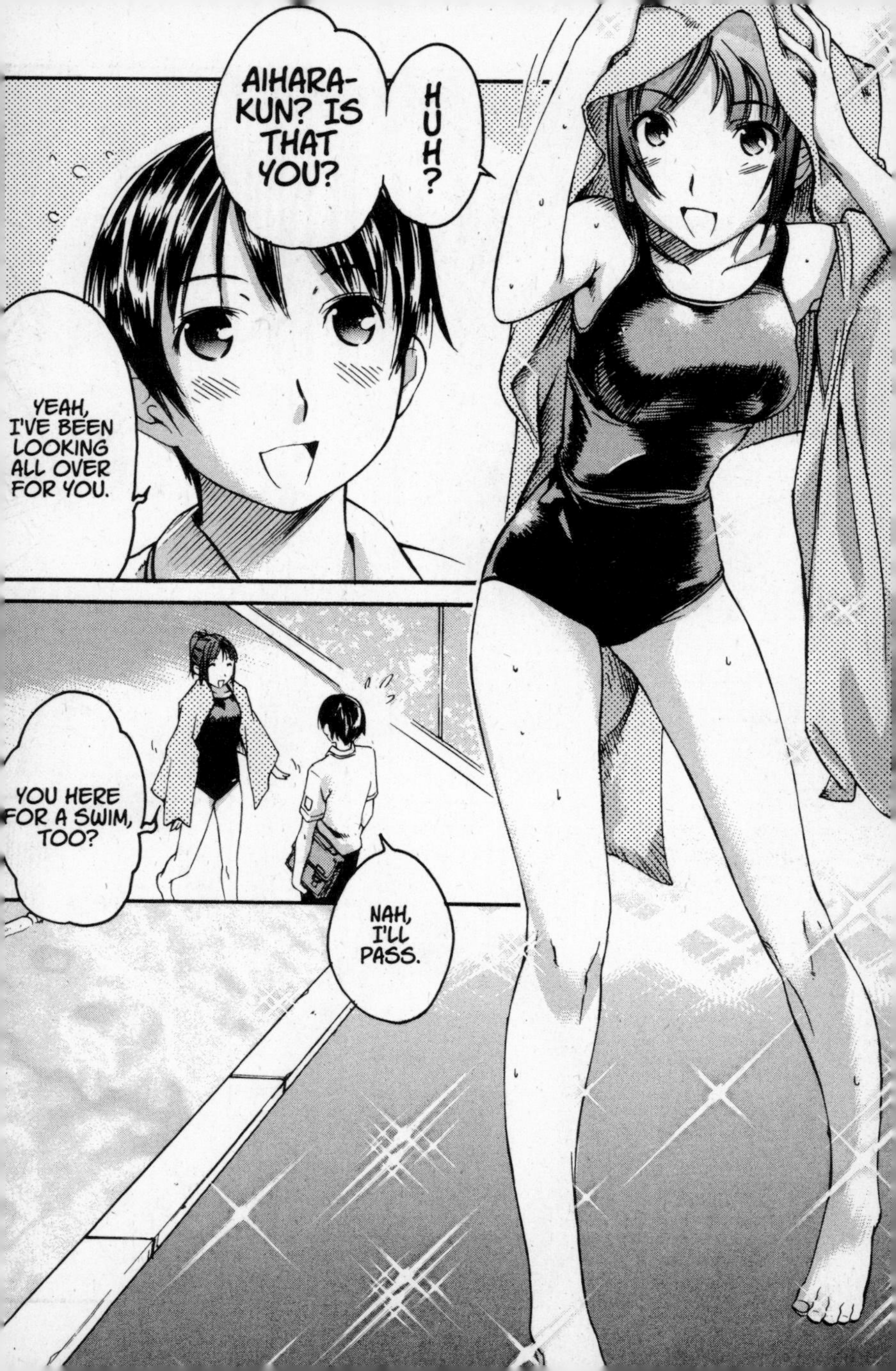
HUH?
AIHARA-KUN? IS THAT YOU?
YEAH, I'VE BEEN LOOKING ALL OVER FOR YOU.
YOU HERE FOR A SWIM, TOO?
NAH, I'LL PASS.

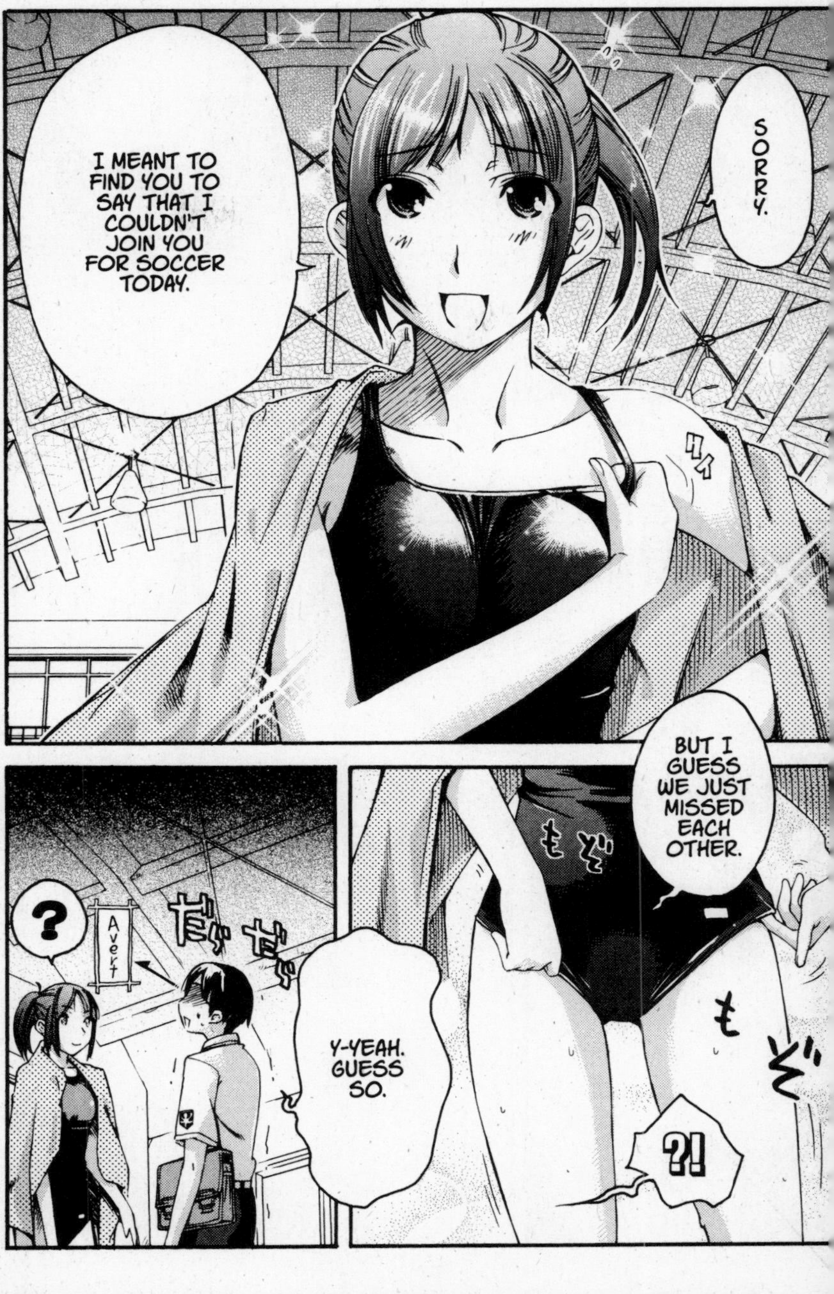
SORRY.
I MEANT TO FIND YOU TO SAY THAT I COULDN'T JOIN YOU FOR SOCCER TODAY.
BUT I GUESS WE JUST MISSED EACH OTHER.
もぞ
もぞ
?!
Y-YEAH. GUESS SO.
?
Avert

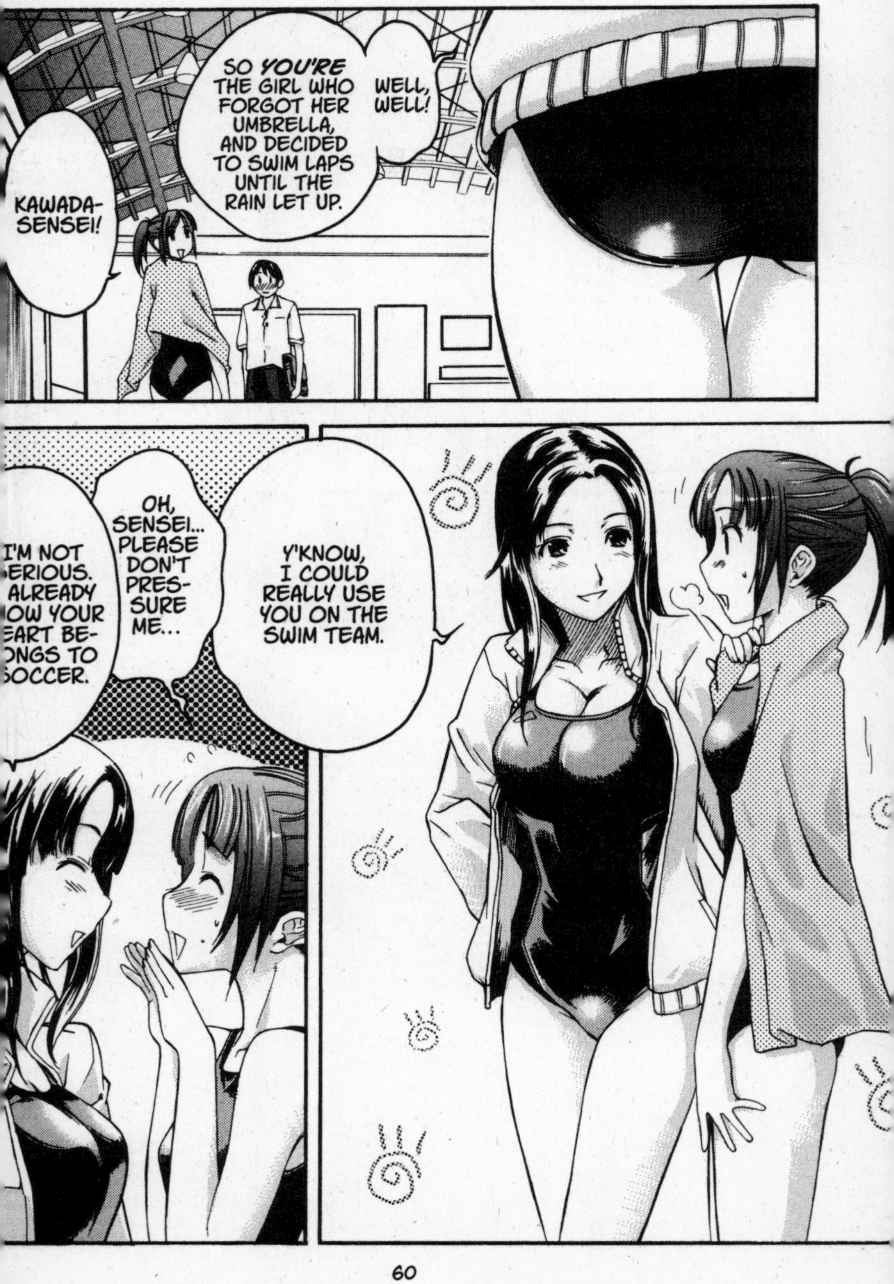
WELL, WELL!
SO *YOU'RE* THE GIRL WHO FORGOT HER UMBRELLA, AND DECIDED TO SWIM LAPS UNTIL THE RAIN LET UP.
KAWADA-SENSEI!
Y'KNOW, I COULD REALLY USE YOU ON THE SWIM TEAM.
OH, SENSEI... PLEASE DON'T PRES-SURE ME...
I'M NOT ERIOUS. ALREADY NOW YOUR EART BE-ONGS TO SOCCER.

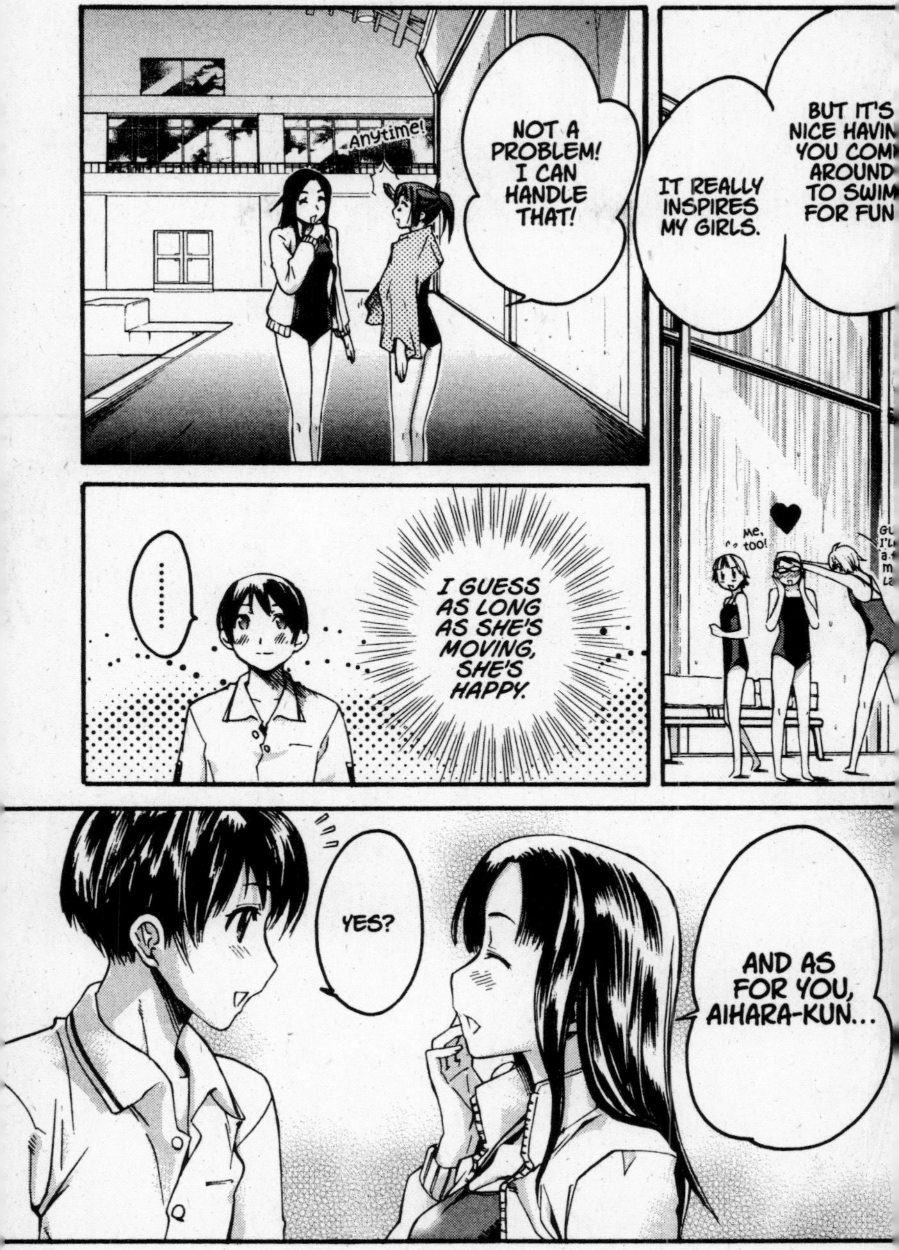
BUT IT'S NICE HAVIN YOU COM AROUND TO SWIM FOR FUN
IT REALLY INSPIRES MY GIRLS.
Me, too!
NOT A PROBLEM! I CAN HANDLE THAT!
Anytime!
I GUESS AS LONG AS SHE'S MOVING, SHE'S HAPPY.
......
AND AS FOR YOU, AIHARA-KUN...
YES?

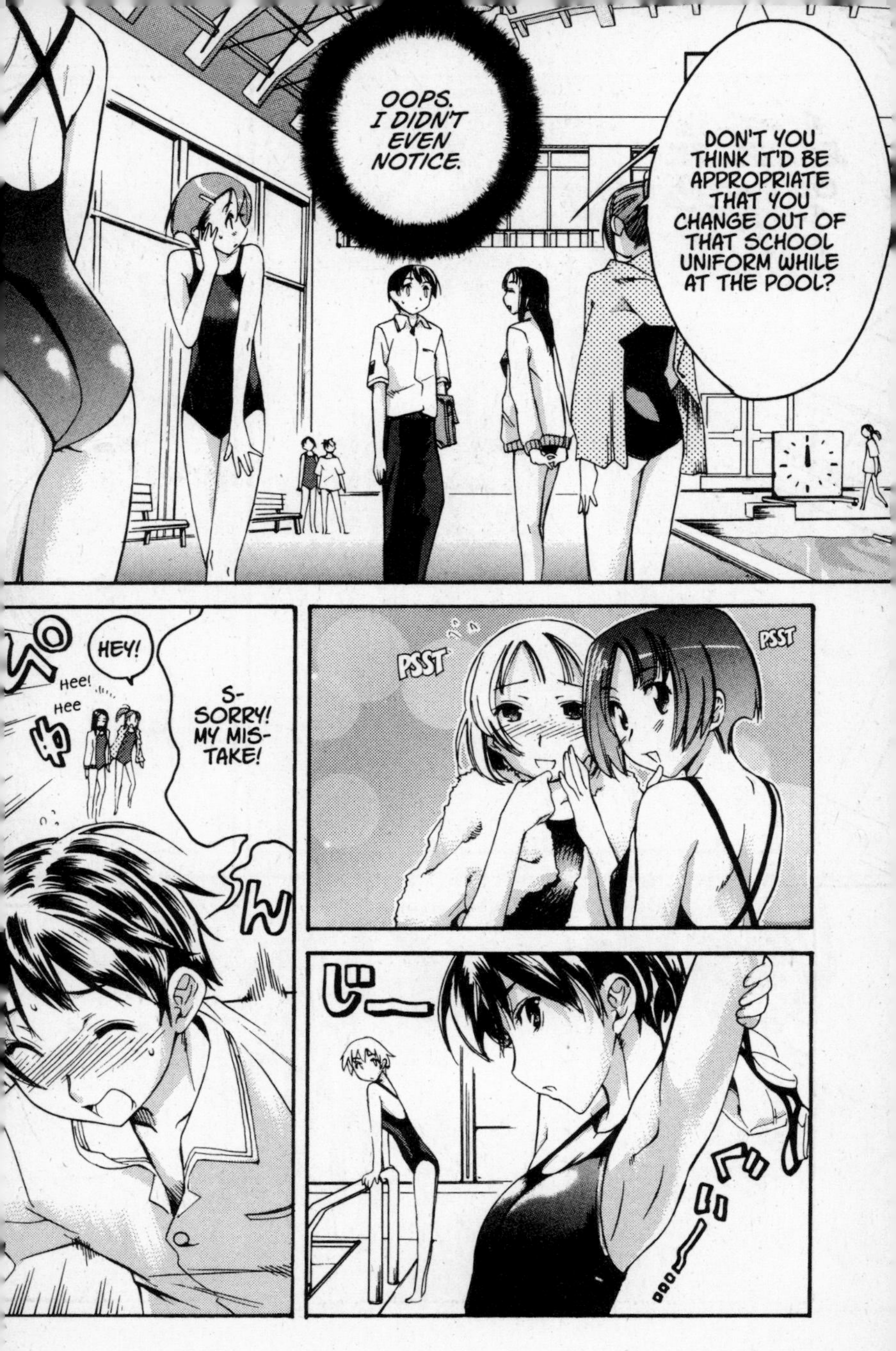
DON'T YOU THINK IT'D BE APPROPRIATE THAT YOU CHANGE OUT OF THAT SCHOOL UNIFORM WHILE AT THE POOL?
OOPS. I DIDN'T EVEN NOTICE.
PSST
PSST
HEY!
Hee! Hee
S-SORRY! MY MISTAKE!

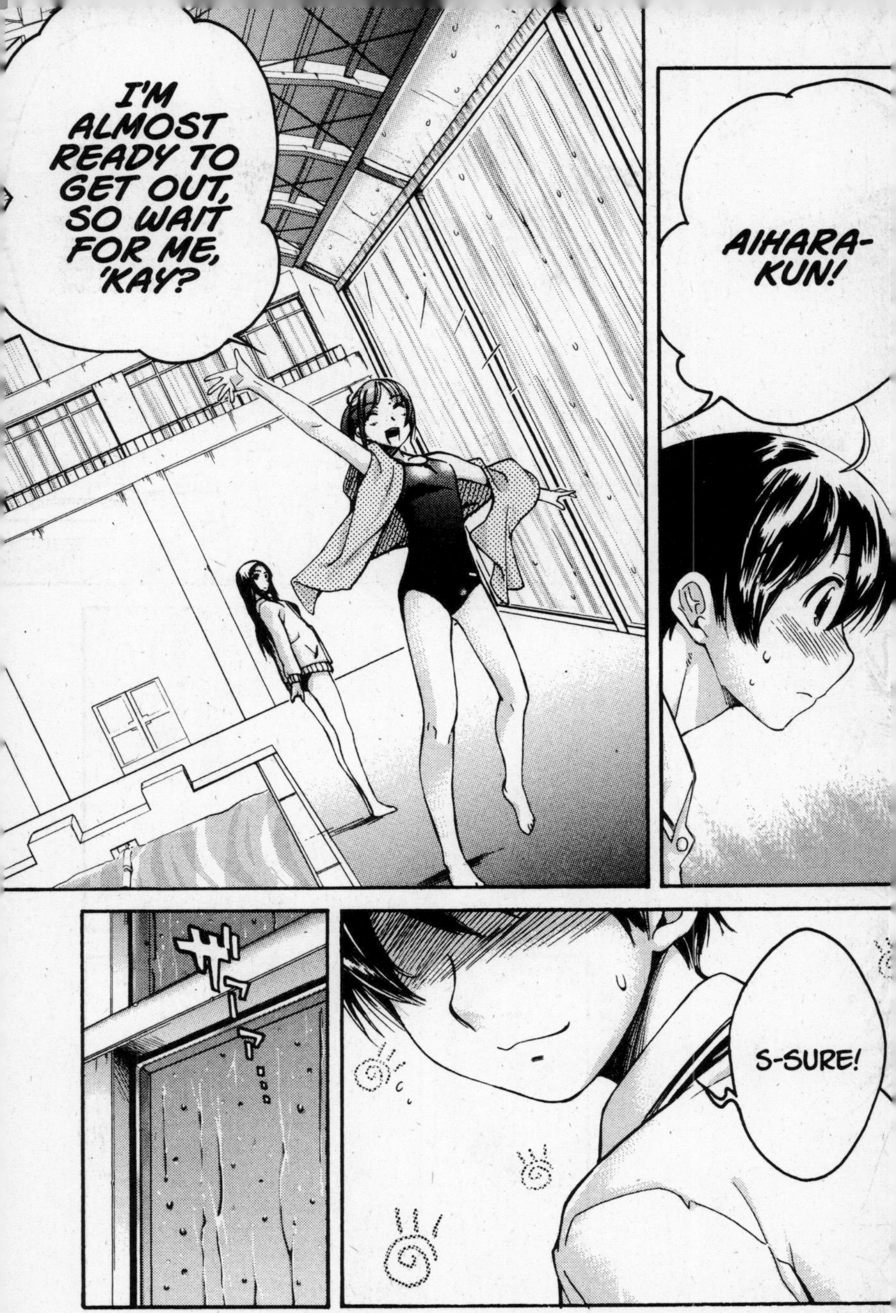
AIHARA-KUN!
I'M ALMOST READY TO GET OUT, SO WAIT FOR ME, 'KAY?
S-SURE!

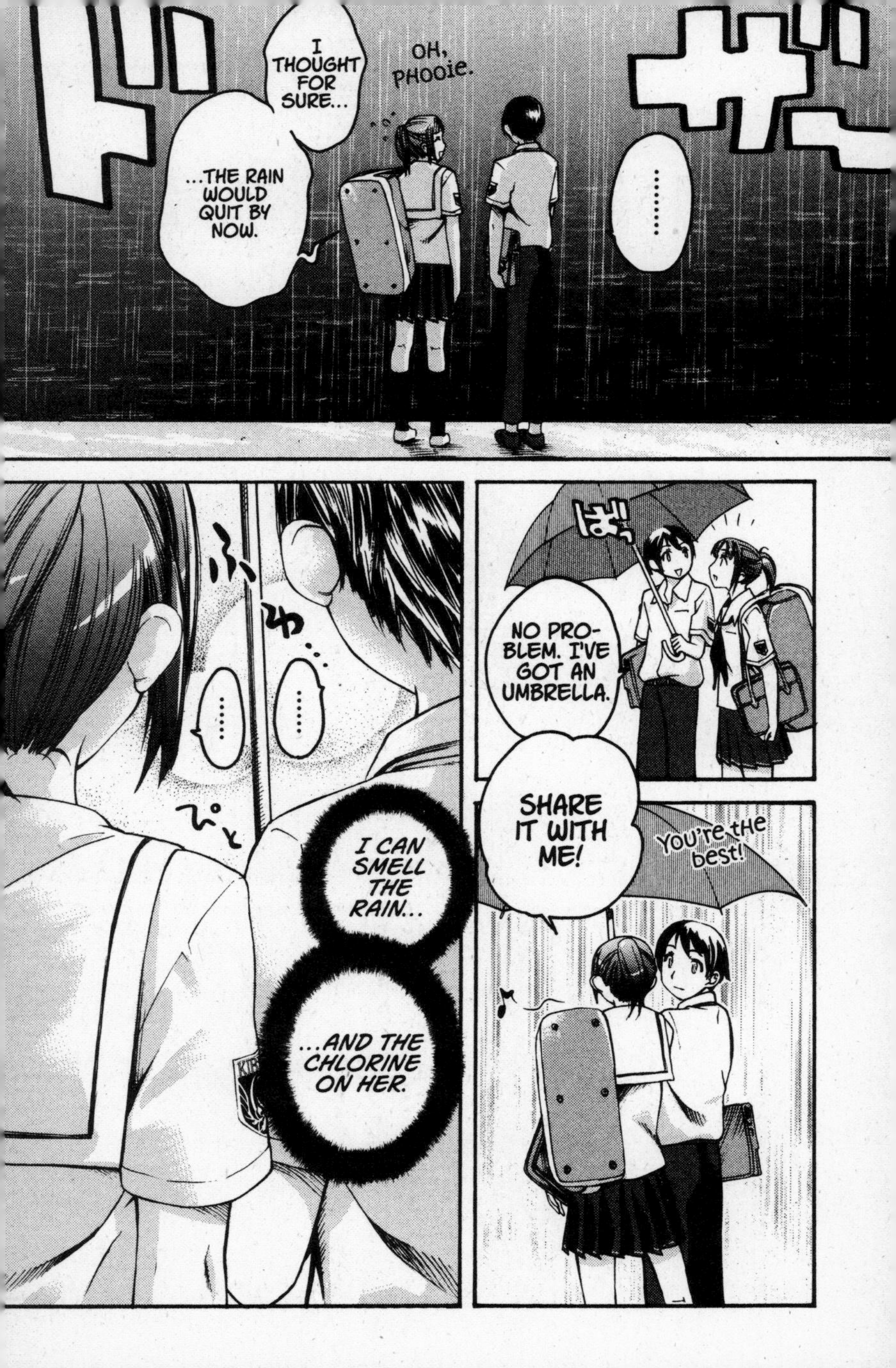

......
OH, PHOOie.
I THOUGHT FOR SURE...
...THE RAIN WOULD QUIT BY NOW.
NO PRO-BLEM. I'VE GOT AN UMBRELLA.
SHARE IT WITH ME!
You're the best!
......
......
I CAN SMELL THE RAIN...
...AND THE CHLORINE ON HER.

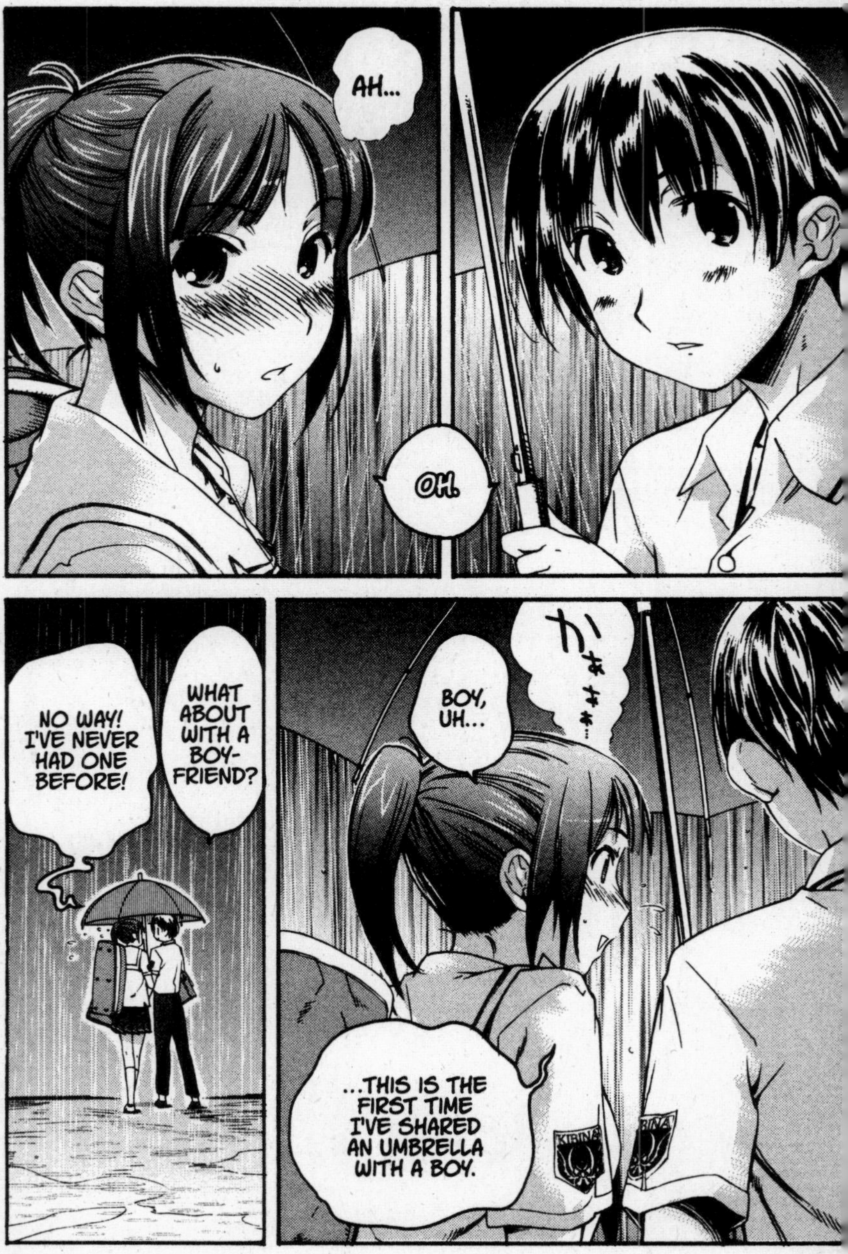
AH...
OH.
かぁぁぁ…
BOY, UH...
...THIS IS THE FIRST TIME I'VE SHARED AN UMBRELLA WITH A BOY.
KIRINA
KIRINA
WHAT ABOUT WITH A BOY-FRIEND?
NO WAY! I'VE NEVER HAD ONE BEFORE!

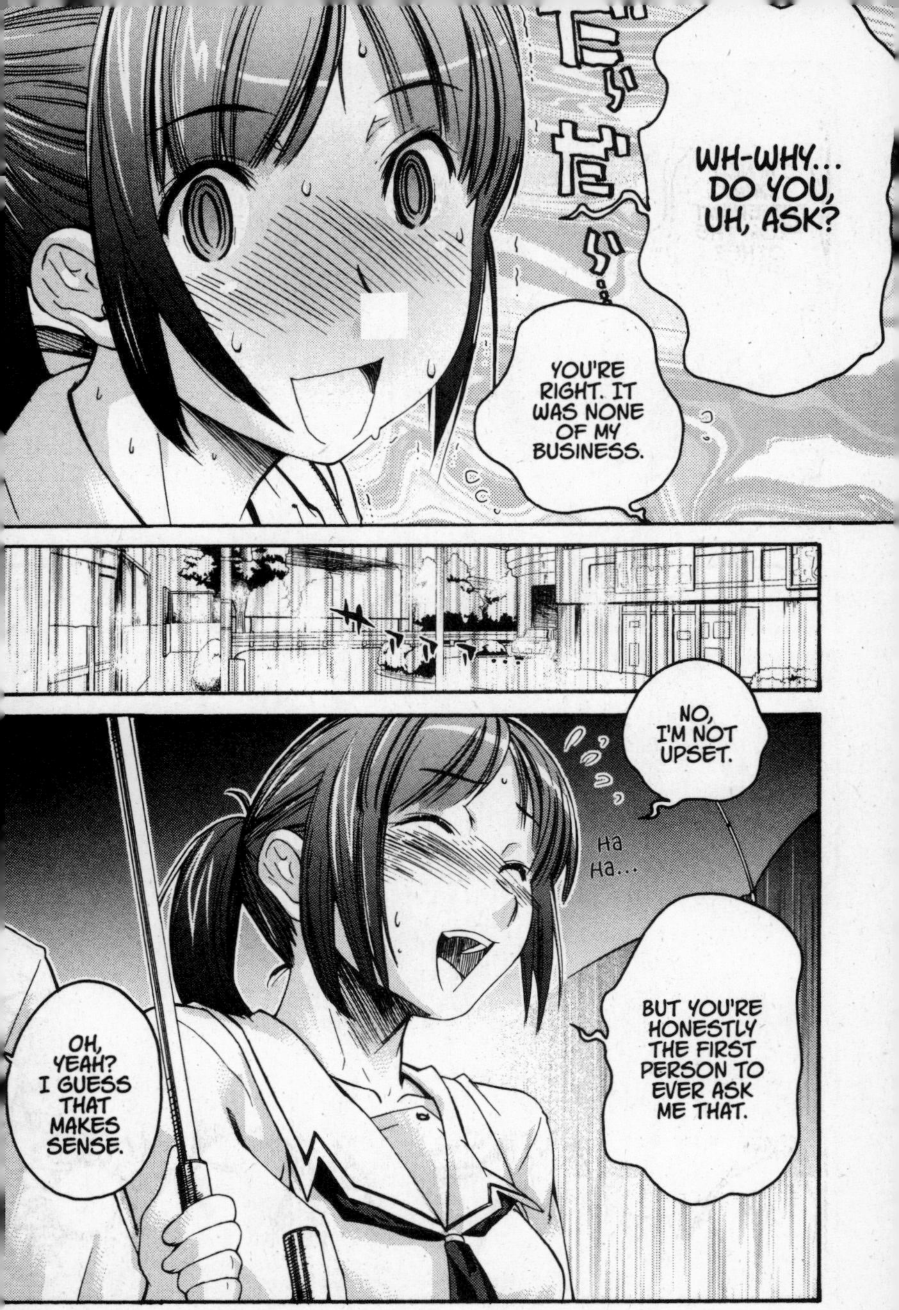
WH-WHY... DO YOU, UH, ASK?
YOU'RE RIGHT. IT WAS NONE OF MY BUSINESS.
NO, I'M NOT UPSET.
Ha Ha...
BUT YOU'RE HONESTLY THE FIRST PERSON TO EVER ASK ME THAT.
OH, YEAH? I GUESS THAT MAKES SENSE.

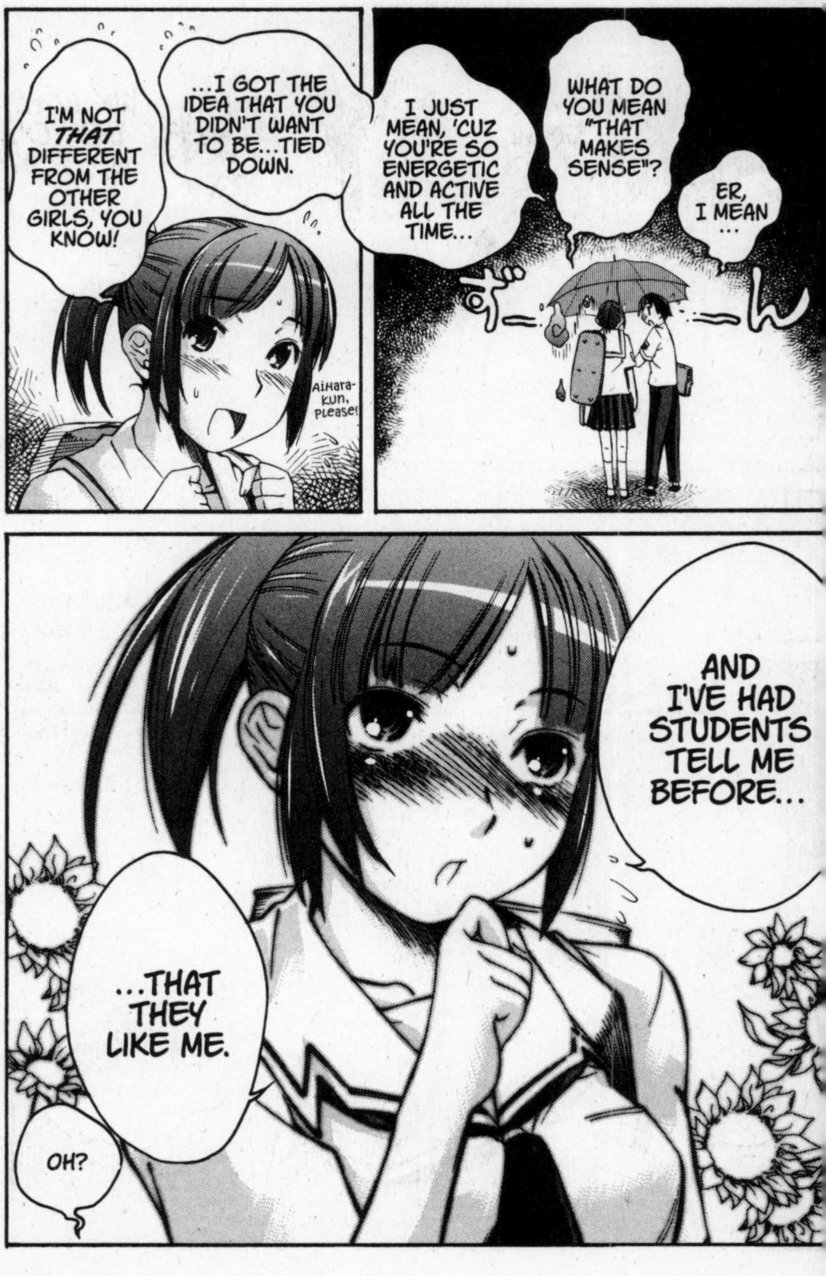
WHAT DO YOU MEAN "THAT MAKES SENSE"?
ER, I MEAN ...
I JUST MEAN, 'CUZ YOU'RE SO ENERGETIC AND ACTIVE ALL THE TIME...
...I GOT THE IDEA THAT YOU DIDN'T WANT TO BE...TIED DOWN.
I'M NOT *THAT* DIFFERENT FROM THE OTHER GIRLS, YOU KNOW!
AiHara-kun, Please!
AND I'VE HAD STUDENTS TELL ME BEFORE...
...THAT THEY LIKE ME.
OH?

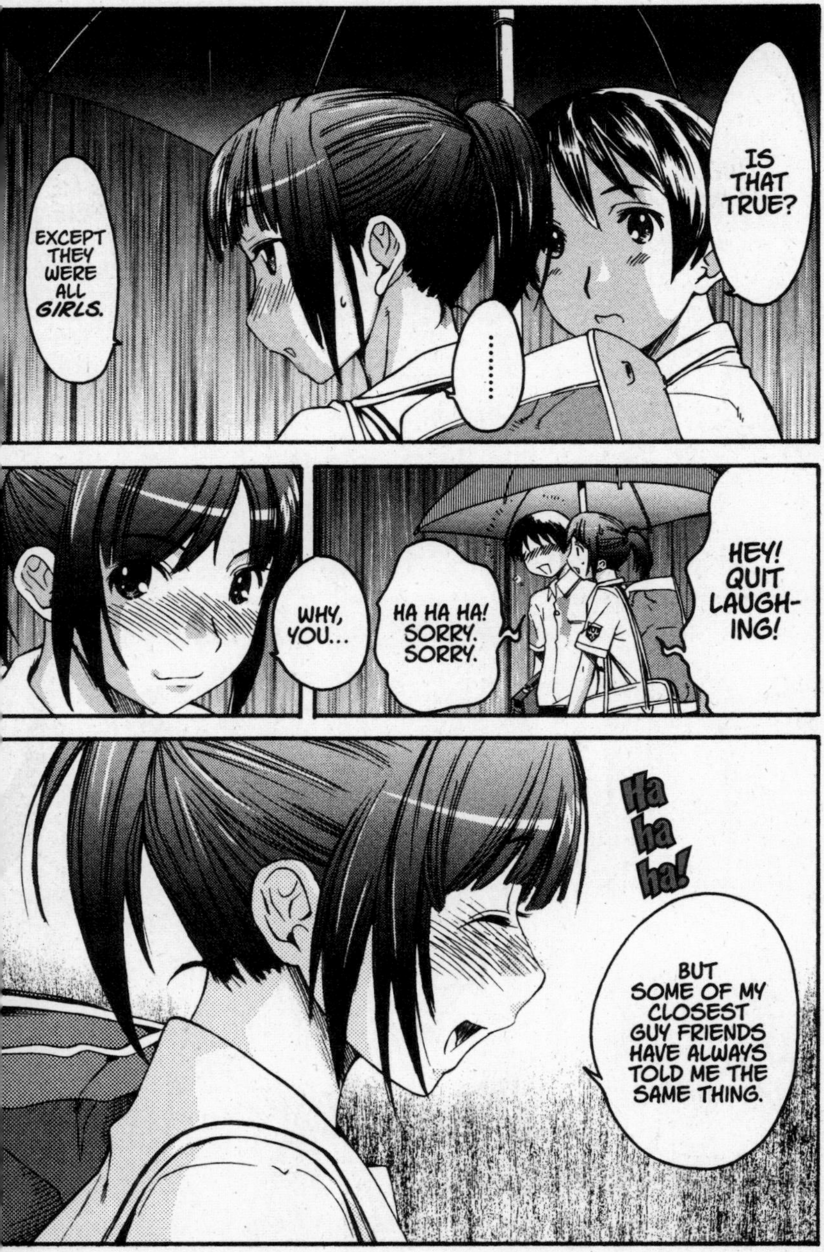
IS THAT TRUE?
EXCEPT THEY WERE ALL GIRLS.
......
HEY! QUIT LAUGH-ING!
HA HA HA! SORRY. SORRY.
WHY, YOU...
Ha ha ha!
BUT SOME OF MY CLOSEST GUY FRIENDS HAVE ALWAYS TOLD ME THE SAME THING.

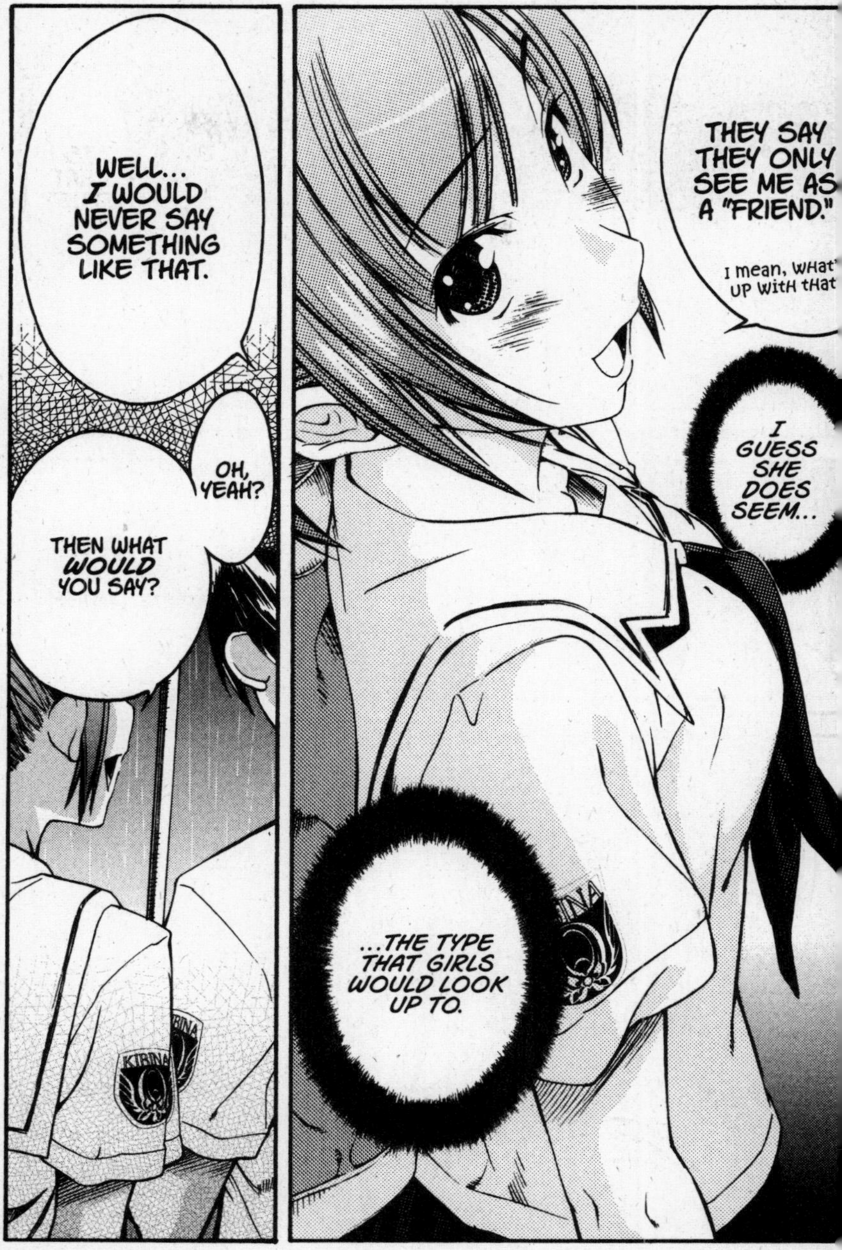
THEY SAY THEY ONLY SEE ME AS A "FRIEND."
I mean, WHAT' UP WITH THAT
I GUESS SHE DOES SEEM...
...THE TYPE THAT GIRLS WOULD LOOK UP TO.
WELL... I WOULD NEVER SAY SOMETHING LIKE THAT.
OH, YEAH?
THEN WHAT WOULD YOU SAY?

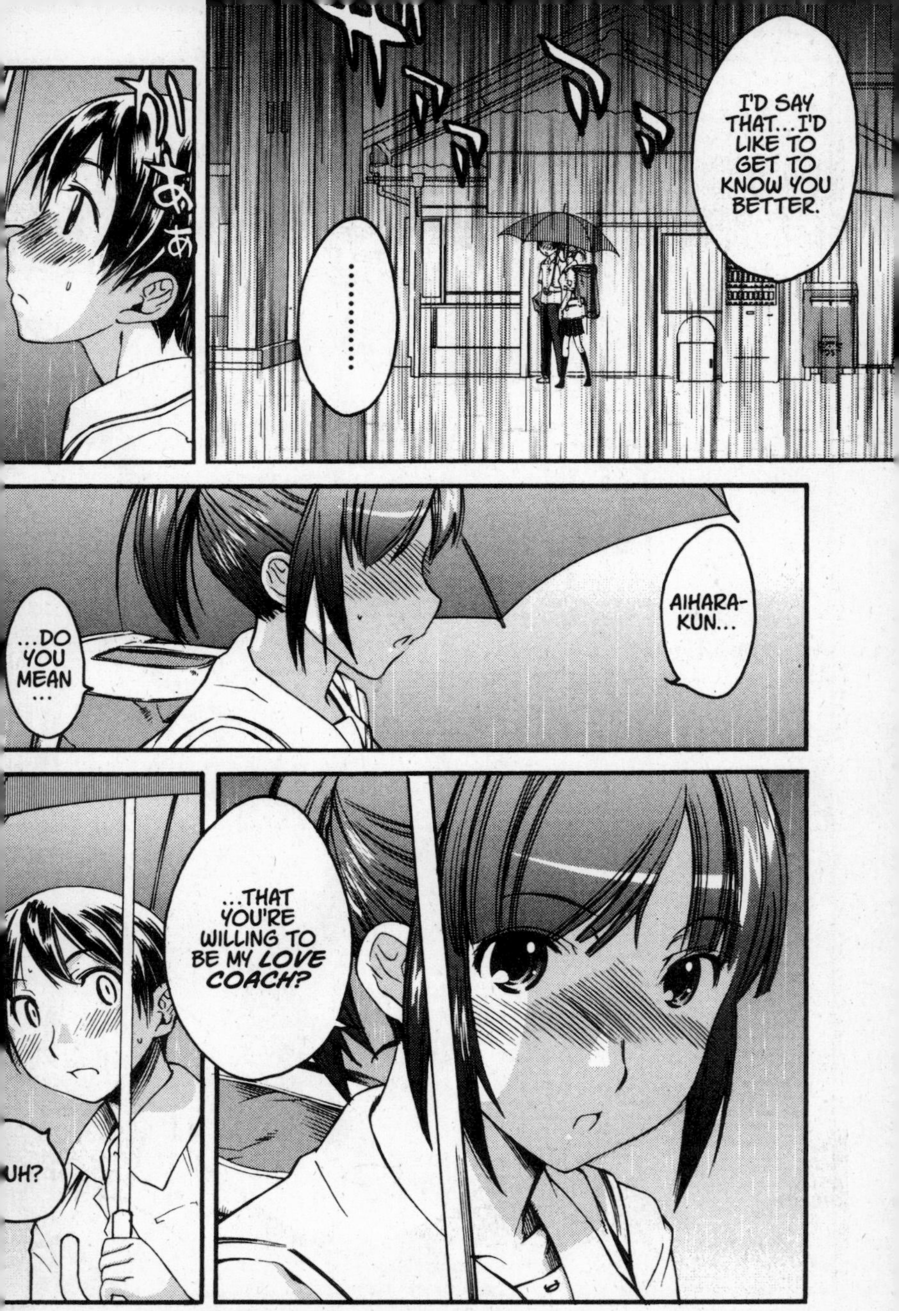
I'D SAY THAT...I'D LIKE TO GET TO KNOW YOU BETTER.
....
AIHARA-KUN...
...DO YOU MEAN...
...THAT YOU'RE WILLING TO BE MY *LOVE COACH?*
UH?

[Asuka 3rd KISS END]

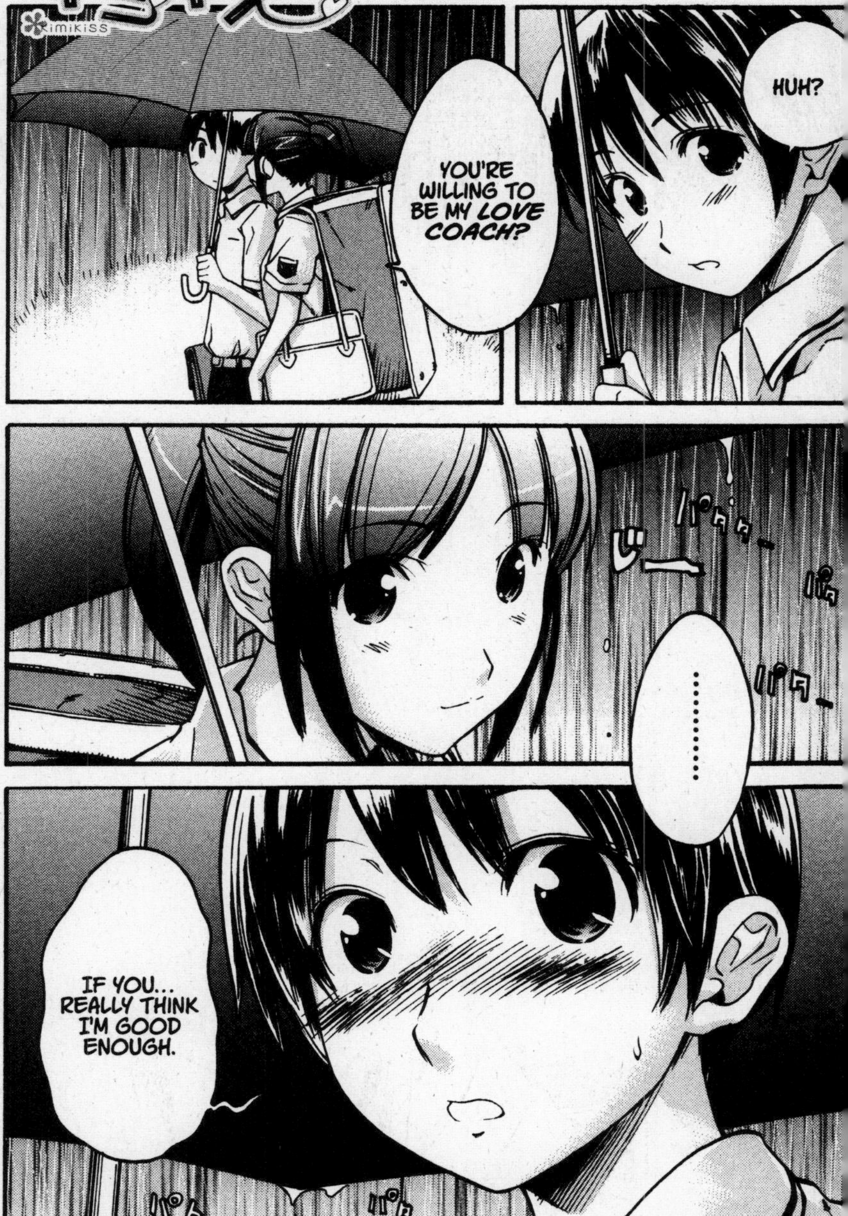
HUH?
YOU'RE WILLING TO BE MY *LOVE COACH?*
……
IF YOU… REALLY THINK I'M GOOD ENOUGH.

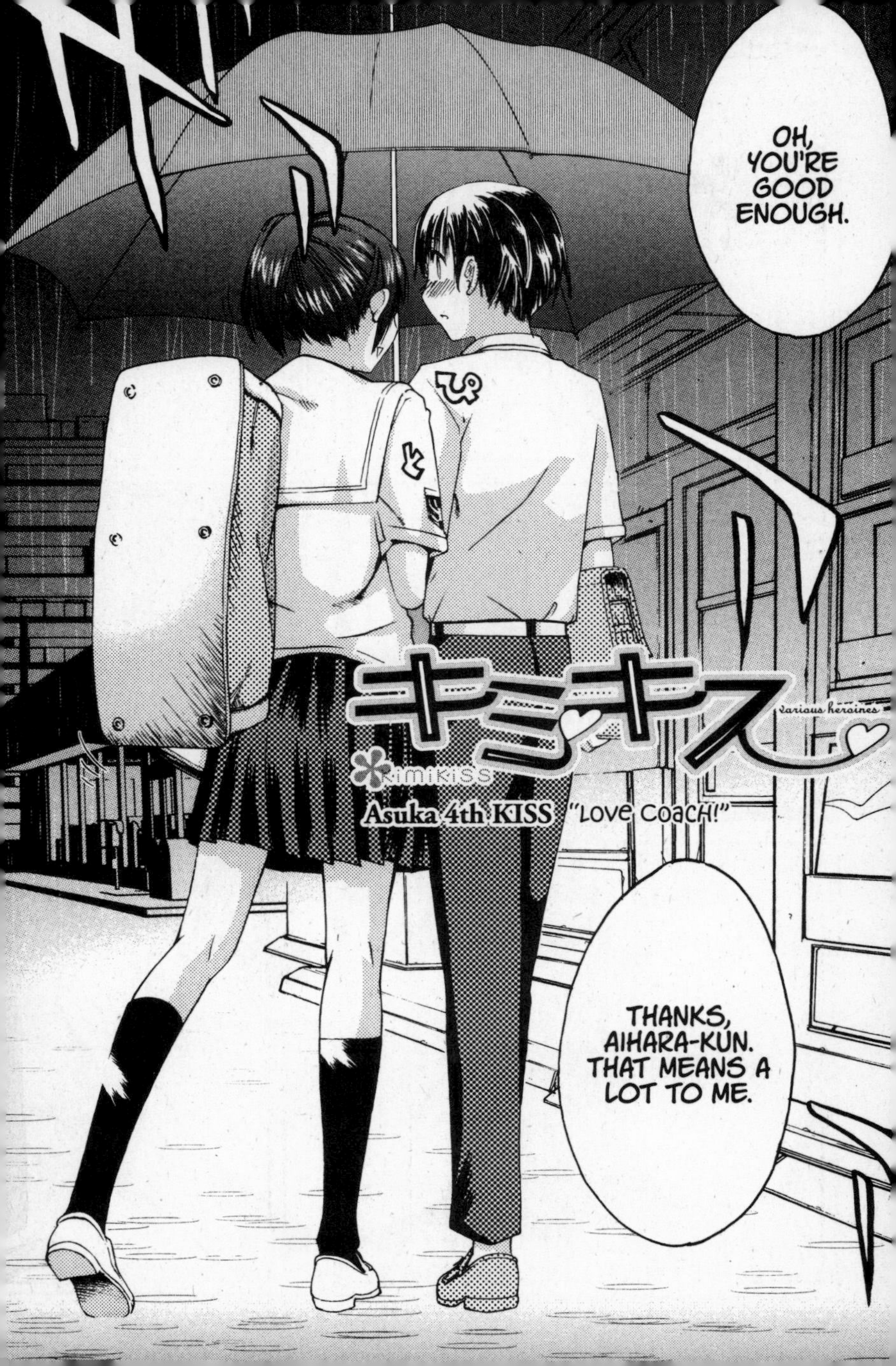
OH, YOU'RE GOOD ENOUGH.
キミキス
various heroines
KIMIKISS
Asuka 4th KISS "Love Coach!"
THANKS, AIHARA-KUN. THAT MEANS A LOT TO ME.

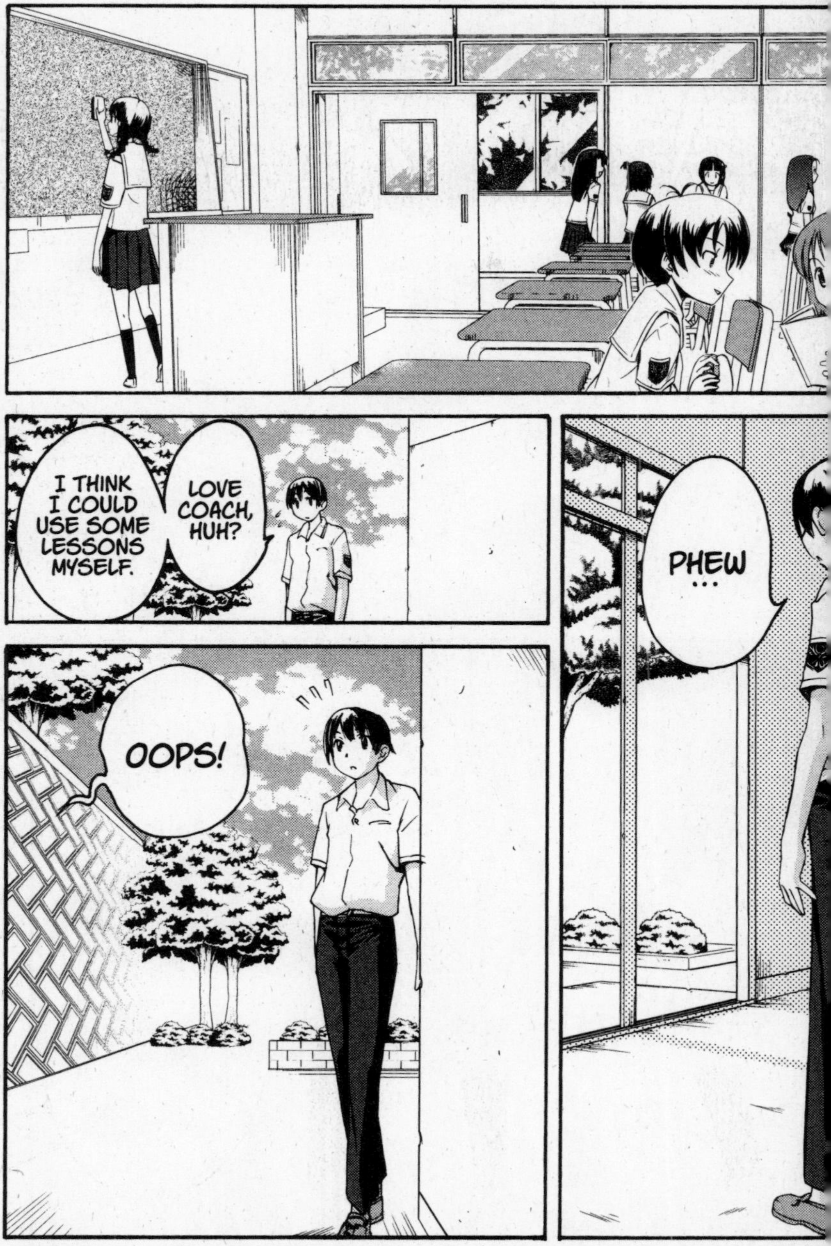
PHEW ...
LOVE COACH, HUH?
I THINK I COULD USE SOME LESSONS MYSELF.
OOPS!

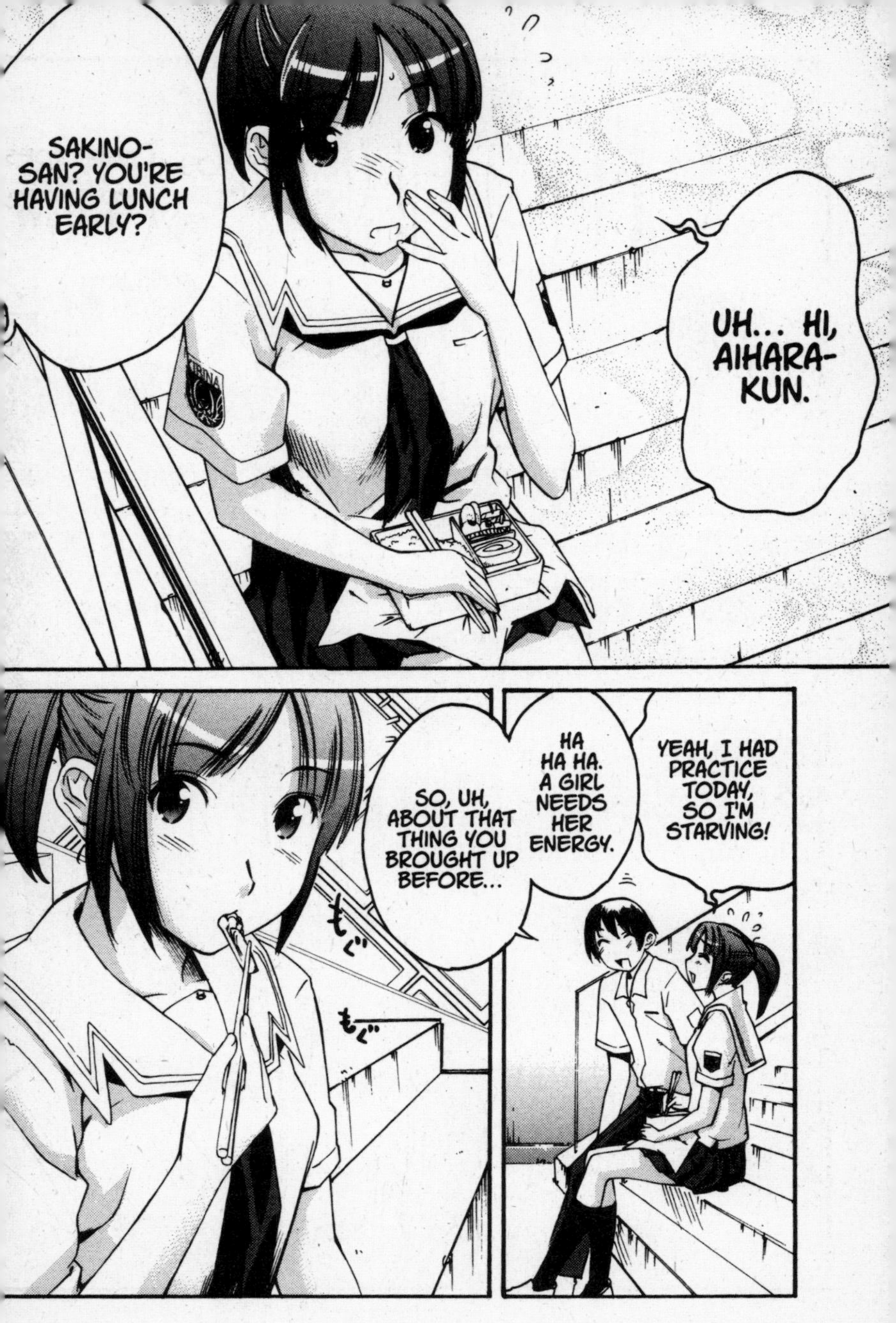
SAKINO-SAN? YOU'RE HAVING LUNCH EARLY?
UH... HI, AIHARA-KUN.
YEAH, I HAD PRACTICE TODAY, SO I'M STARVING!
HA HA HA. A GIRL NEEDS HER ENERGY.
SO, UH, ABOUT THAT THING YOU BROUGHT UP BEFORE...
もぐ
もぐ

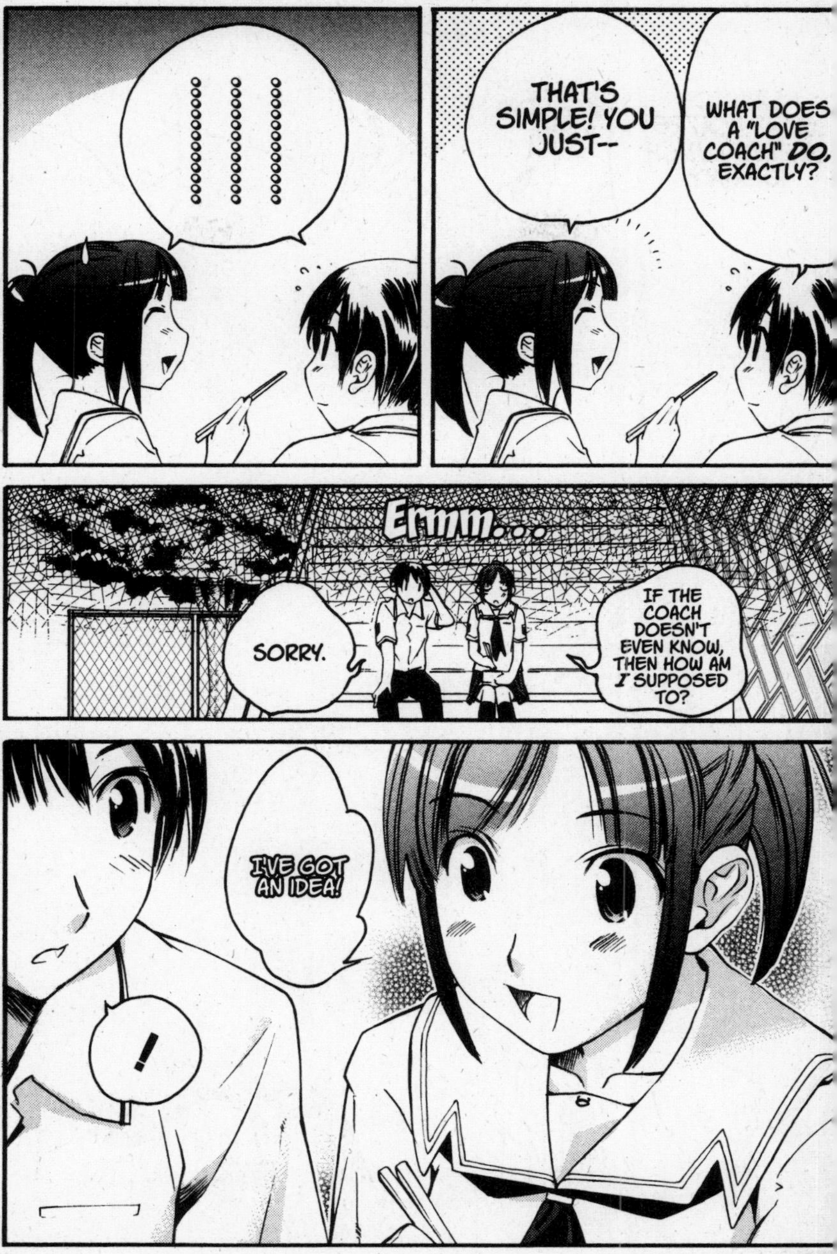
WHAT DOES A "LOVE COACH" DO, EXACTLY?
THAT'S SIMPLE! YOU JUST--
......
Ermmm...
IF THE COACH DOESN'T EVEN KNOW, THEN HOW AM I SUPPOSED TO?
SORRY.
I'VE GOT AN IDEA!
!

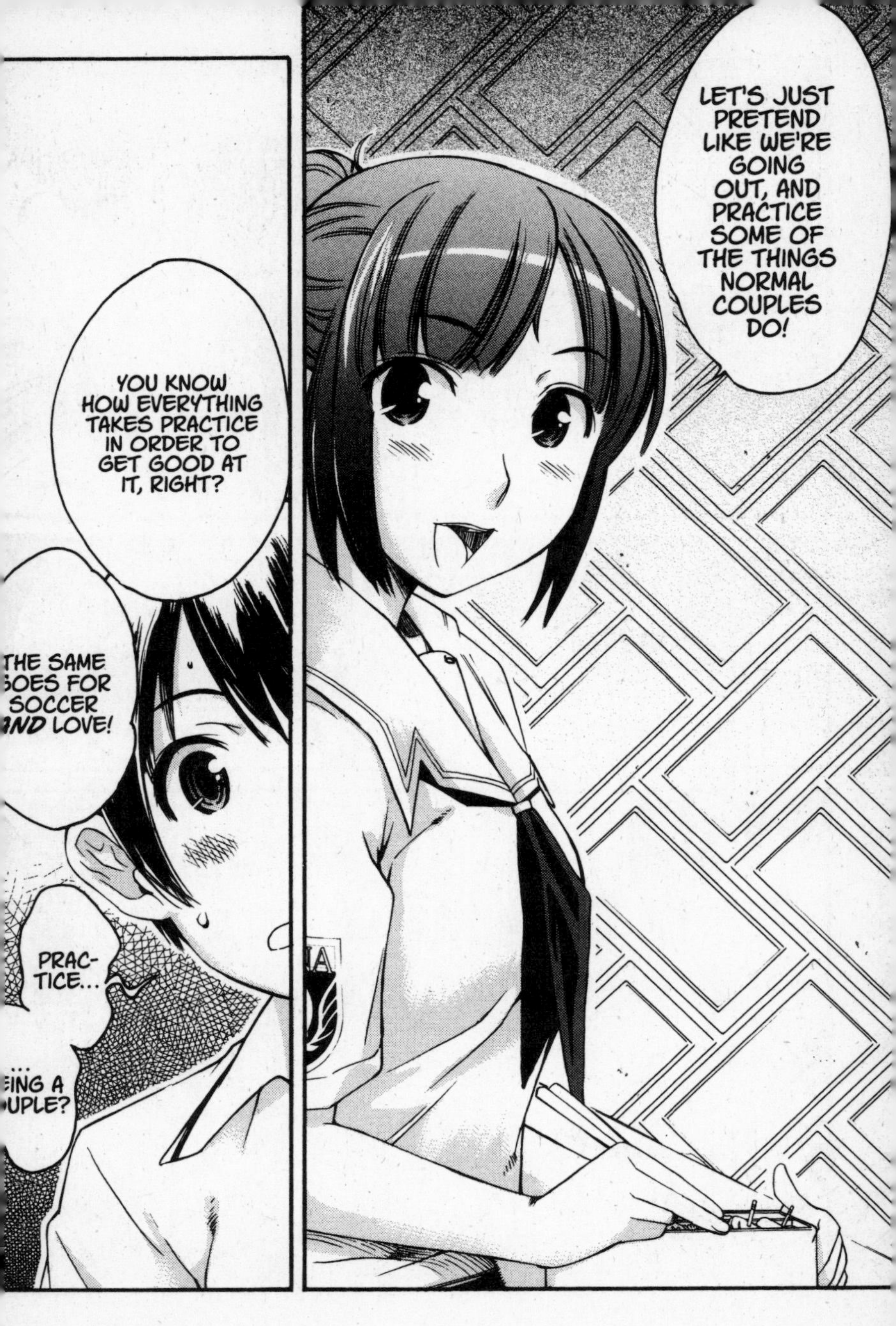
LET'S JUST PRETEND LIKE WE'RE GOING OUT, AND PRACTICE SOME OF THE THINGS NORMAL COUPLES DO!
YOU KNOW HOW EVERYTHING TAKES PRACTICE IN ORDER TO GET GOOD AT IT, RIGHT?
THE SAME OES FOR SOCCER ND LOVE!
PRAC-TICE...
... EING A UPLE?

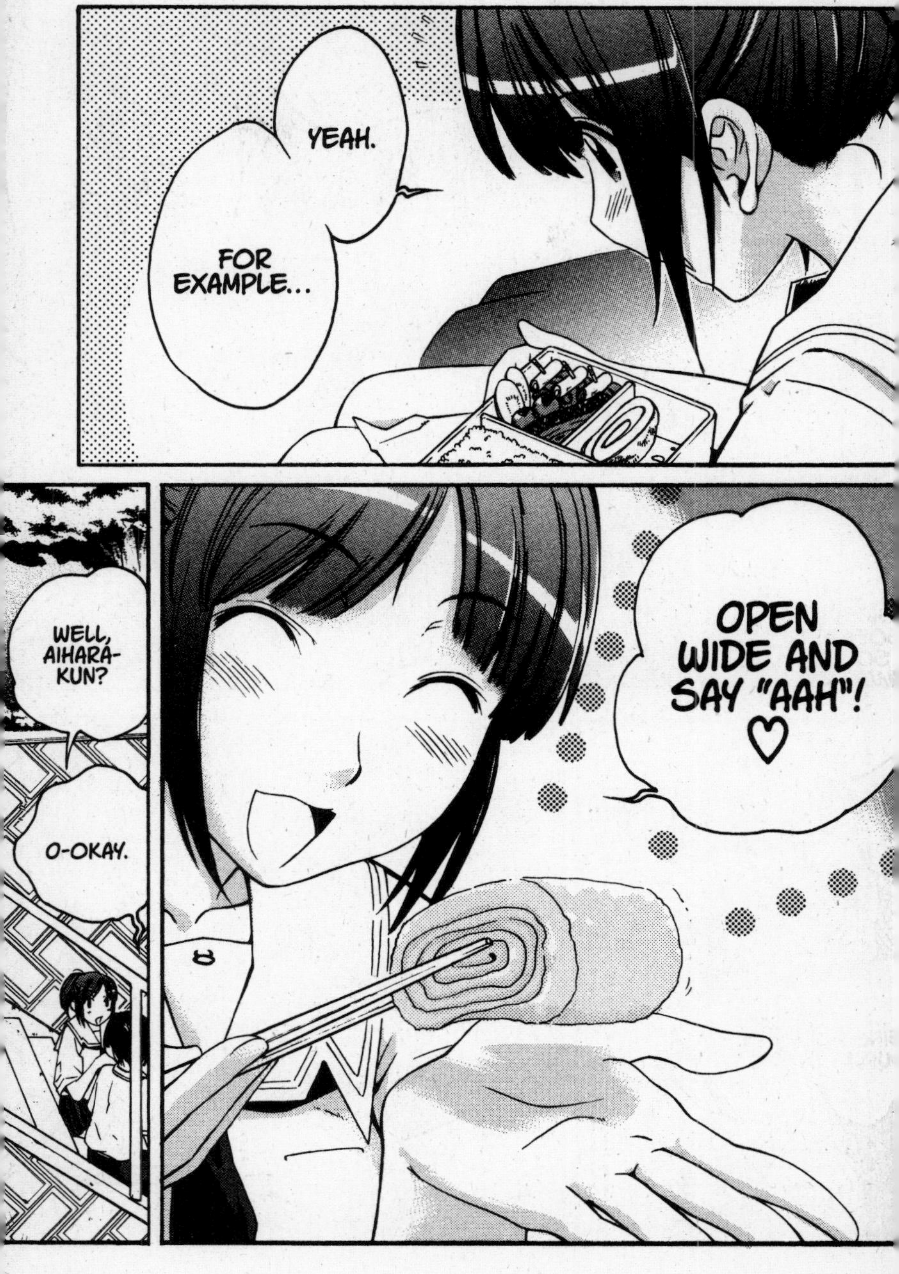
YEAH.
FOR EXAMPLE...
OPEN WIDE AND SAY "AAH"! ♡
WELL, AIHARA-KUN?
O-OKAY.

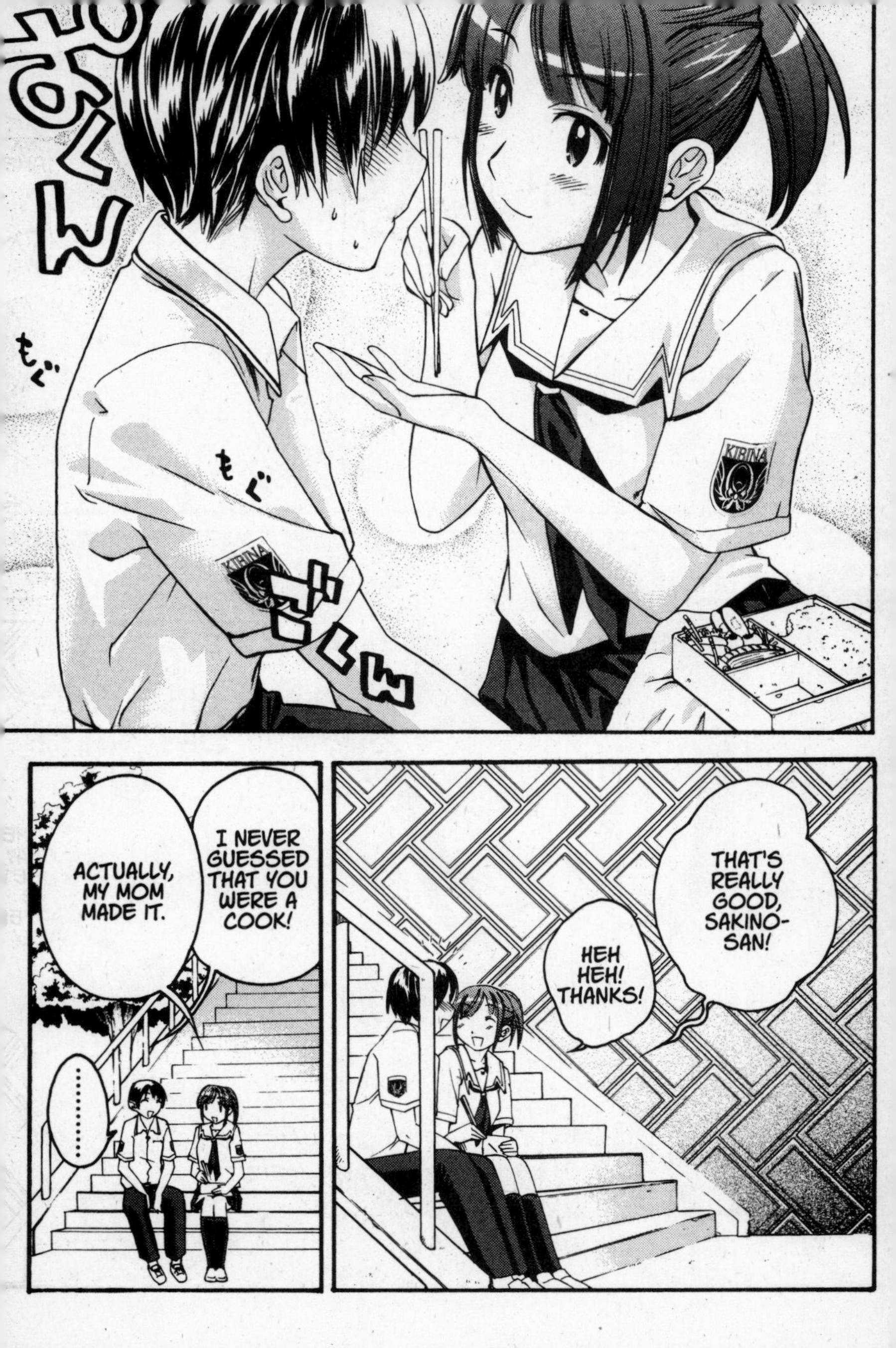
ぱくん
もぐ
もぐ
ごっくん
THAT'S REALLY GOOD, SAKINO-SAN!
HEH HEH! THANKS!
I NEVER GUESSED THAT YOU WERE A COOK!
ACTUALLY, MY MOM MADE IT.
……

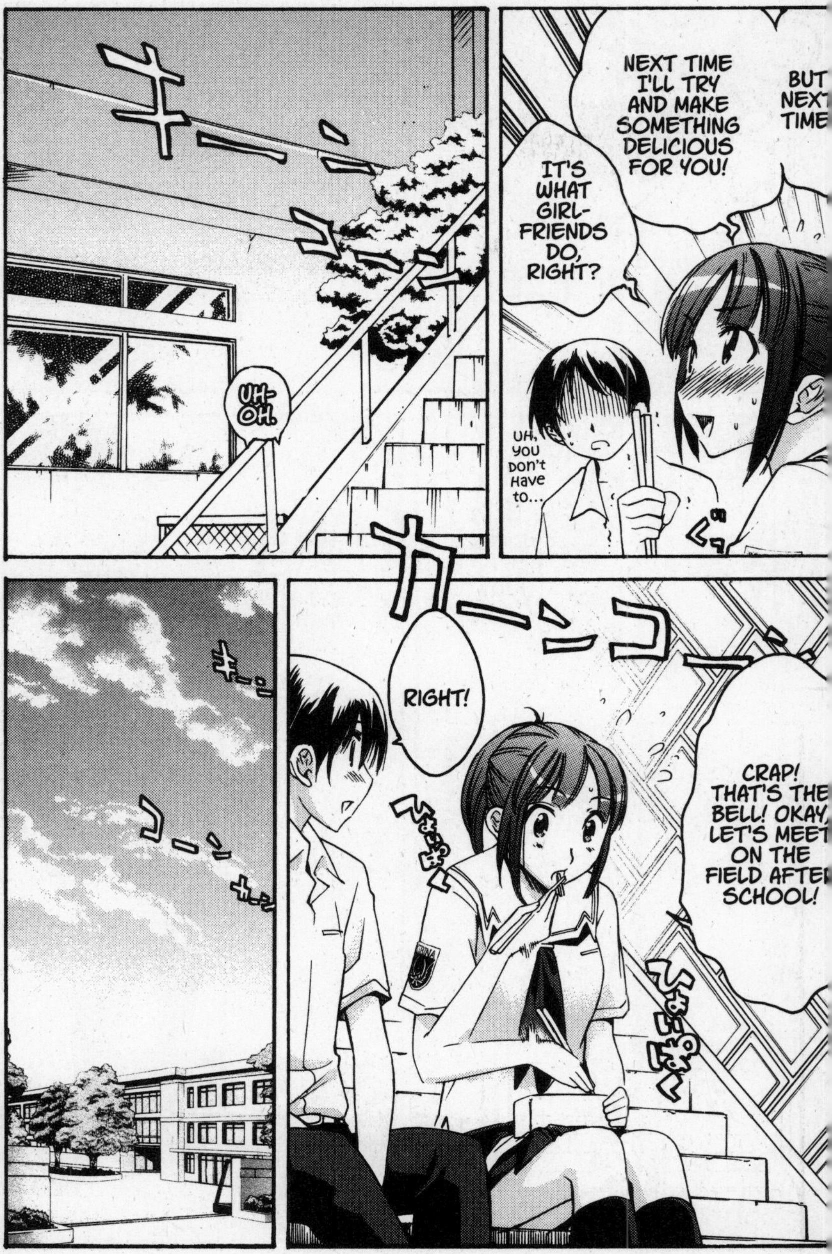
BUT NEXT TIME
NEXT TIME I'LL TRY AND MAKE SOMETHING DELICIOUS FOR YOU!
IT'S WHAT GIRL-FRIENDS DO, RIGHT?
UH, YOU DON'T HAVE TO...
UH-OH.
CRAP! THAT'S THE BELL! OKAY, LET'S MEET ON THE FIELD AFTER SCHOOL!
RIGHT!

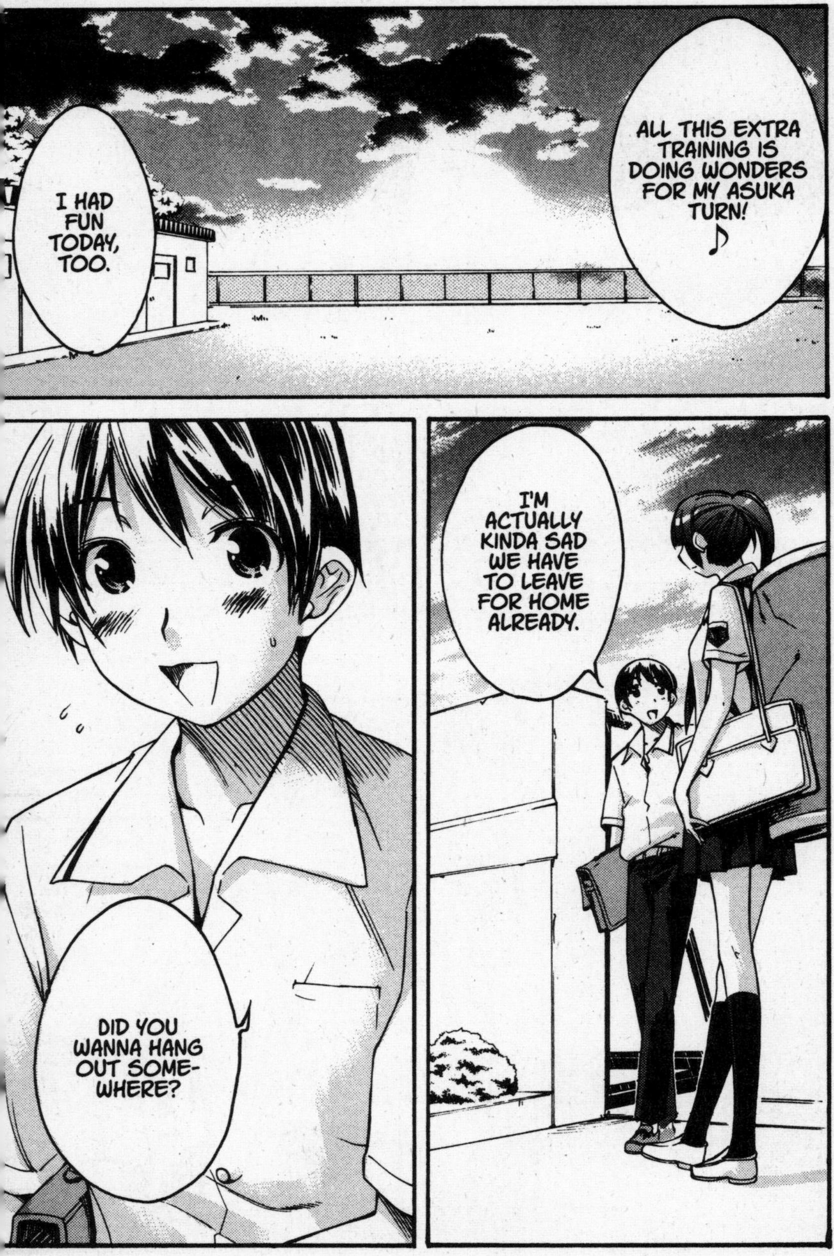
ALL THIS EXTRA TRAINING IS DOING WONDERS FOR MY ASUKA TURN! ♪
I HAD FUN TODAY, TOO.
I'M ACTUALLY KINDA SAD WE HAVE TO LEAVE FOR HOME ALREADY.
DID YOU WANNA HANG OUT SOME-WHERE?

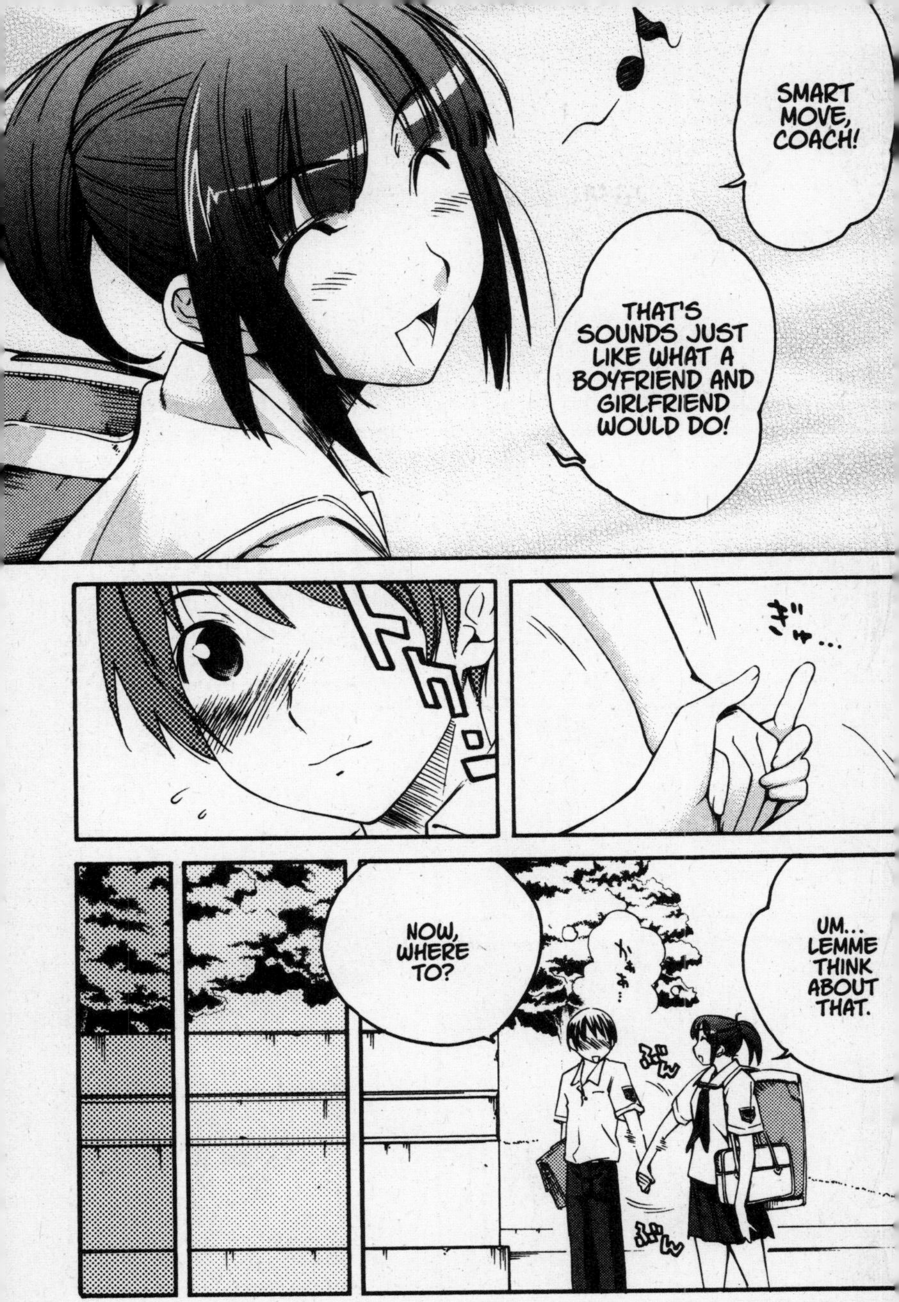
SMART MOVE, COACH!
THAT'S SOUNDS JUST LIKE WHAT A BOYFRIEND AND GIRLFRIEND WOULD DO!
ぎゅ…
UM... LEMME THINK ABOUT THAT.
NOW, WHERE TO?

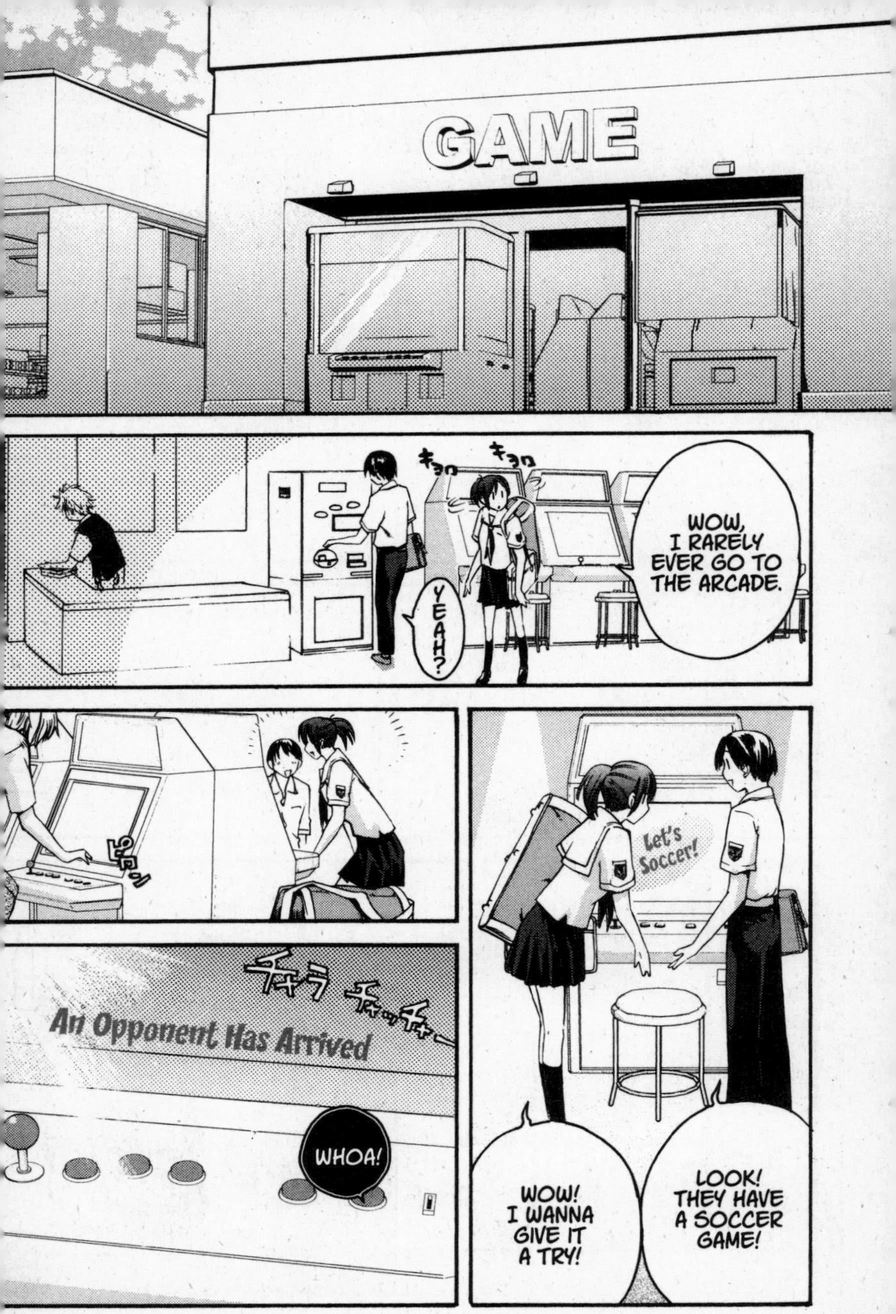
GAME
WOW, I RARELY EVER GO TO THE ARCADE.
YEAH?
キョロ キョロ
Let's Soccer!
LOOK! THEY HAVE A SOCCER GAME!
WOW! I WANNA GIVE IT A TRY!
チャラ チャッチャー
An Opponent Has Arrived
WHOA!

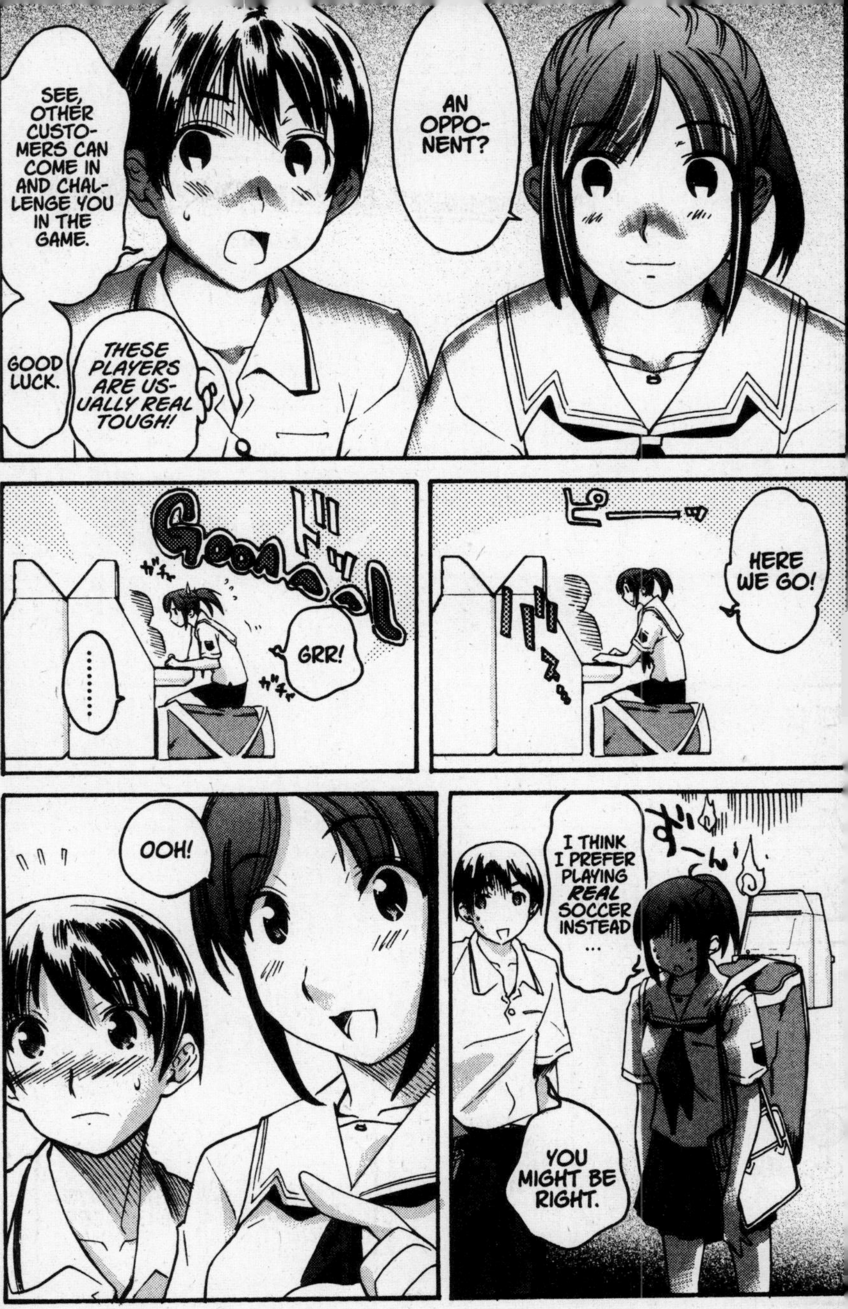
AN OPPONENT?
SEE, OTHER CUSTOMERS CAN COME IN AND CHALLENGE YOU IN THE GAME.
THESE PLAYERS ARE USUALLY REAL TOUGH!
GOOD LUCK.
HERE WE GO!
GRR!
......
I THINK I PREFER PLAYING REAL SOCCER INSTEAD ...
YOU MIGHT BE RIGHT.
OOH!

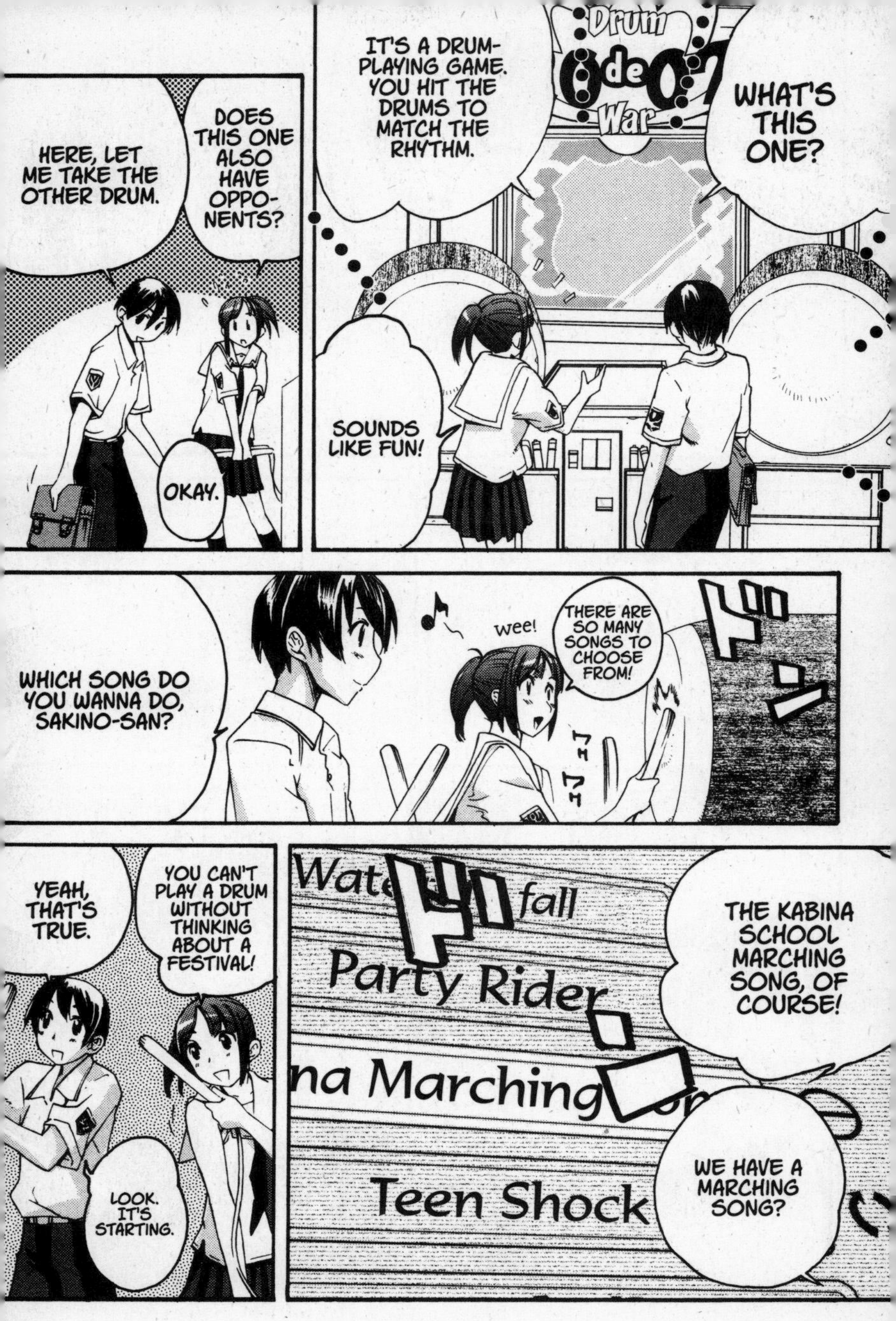
WHAT'S THIS ONE?
Drum
de
War
IT'S A DRUM-PLAYING GAME. YOU HIT THE DRUMS TO MATCH THE RHYTHM.
SOUNDS LIKE FUN!
DOES THIS ONE ALSO HAVE OPPO-NENTS?
HERE, LET ME TAKE THE OTHER DRUM.
OKAY.
ドン
THERE ARE SO MANY SONGS TO CHOOSE FROM!
wee!
WHICH SONG DO YOU WANNA DO, SAKINO-SAN?
THE KABINA SCHOOL MARCHING SONG, OF COURSE!
Wate fall
Party Rider
na Marching
Teen Shock
WE HAVE A MARCHING SONG?
YOU CAN'T PLAY A DRUM WITHOUT THINKING ABOUT A FESTIVAL!
YEAH, THAT'S TRUE.
LOOK. IT'S STARTING.

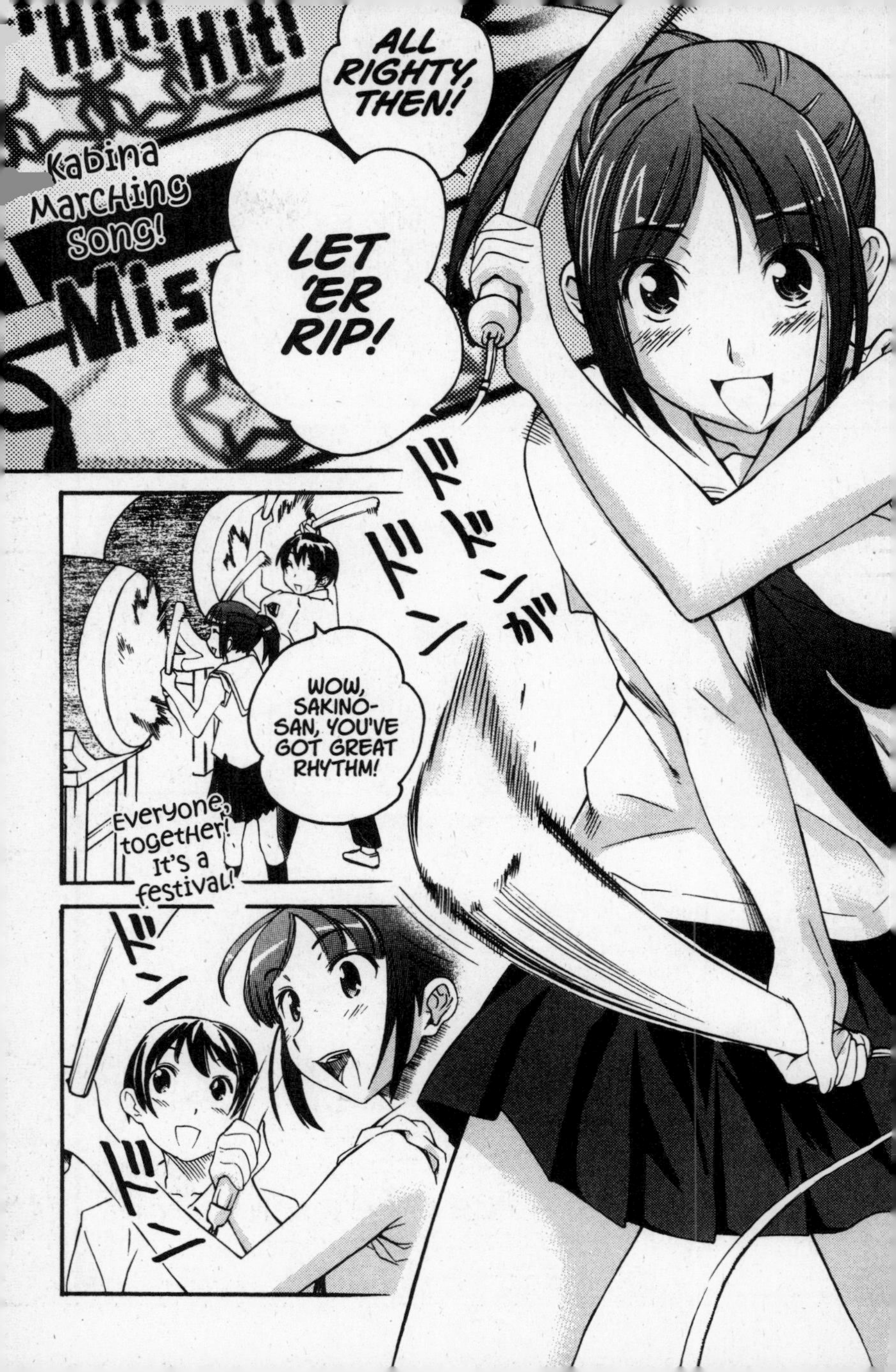ALL RIGHTY, THEN!
LET 'ER RIP!
Hit! Hit!
Kabina Marching song!
Mis
ドーンが
ドーン
WOW, SAKINO-SAN, YOU'VE GOT GREAT RHYTHM!
Everyone, together! It's a festival!
ドン
ドーン

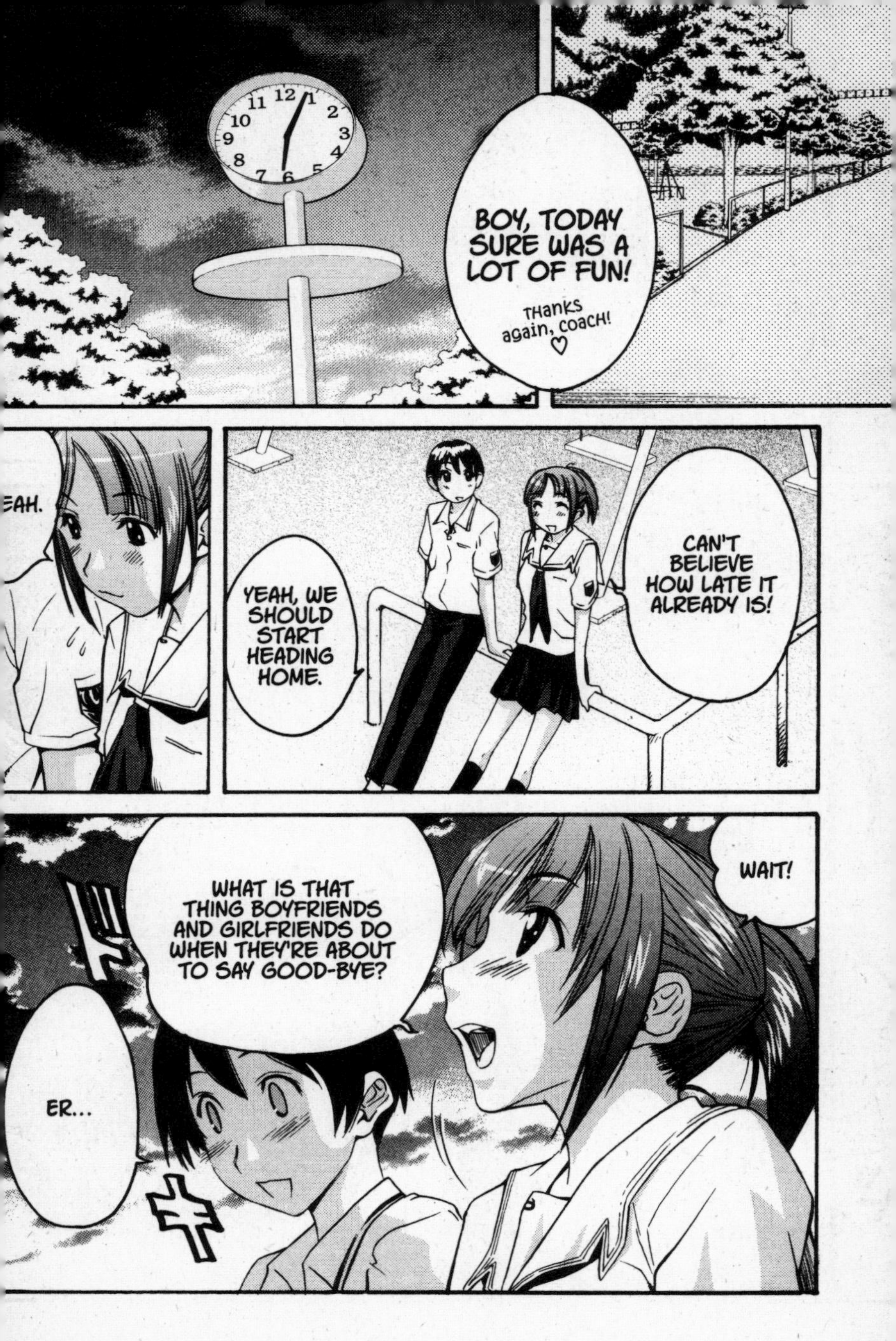
BOY, TODAY SURE WAS A LOT OF FUN!
Thanks again, coach! ♡
CAN'T BELIEVE HOW LATE IT ALREADY IS!
YEAH, WE SHOULD START HEADING HOME.
EAH.
WAIT!
WHAT IS THAT THING BOYFRIENDS AND GIRLFRIENDS DO WHEN THEY'RE ABOUT TO SAY GOOD-BYE?
ER...

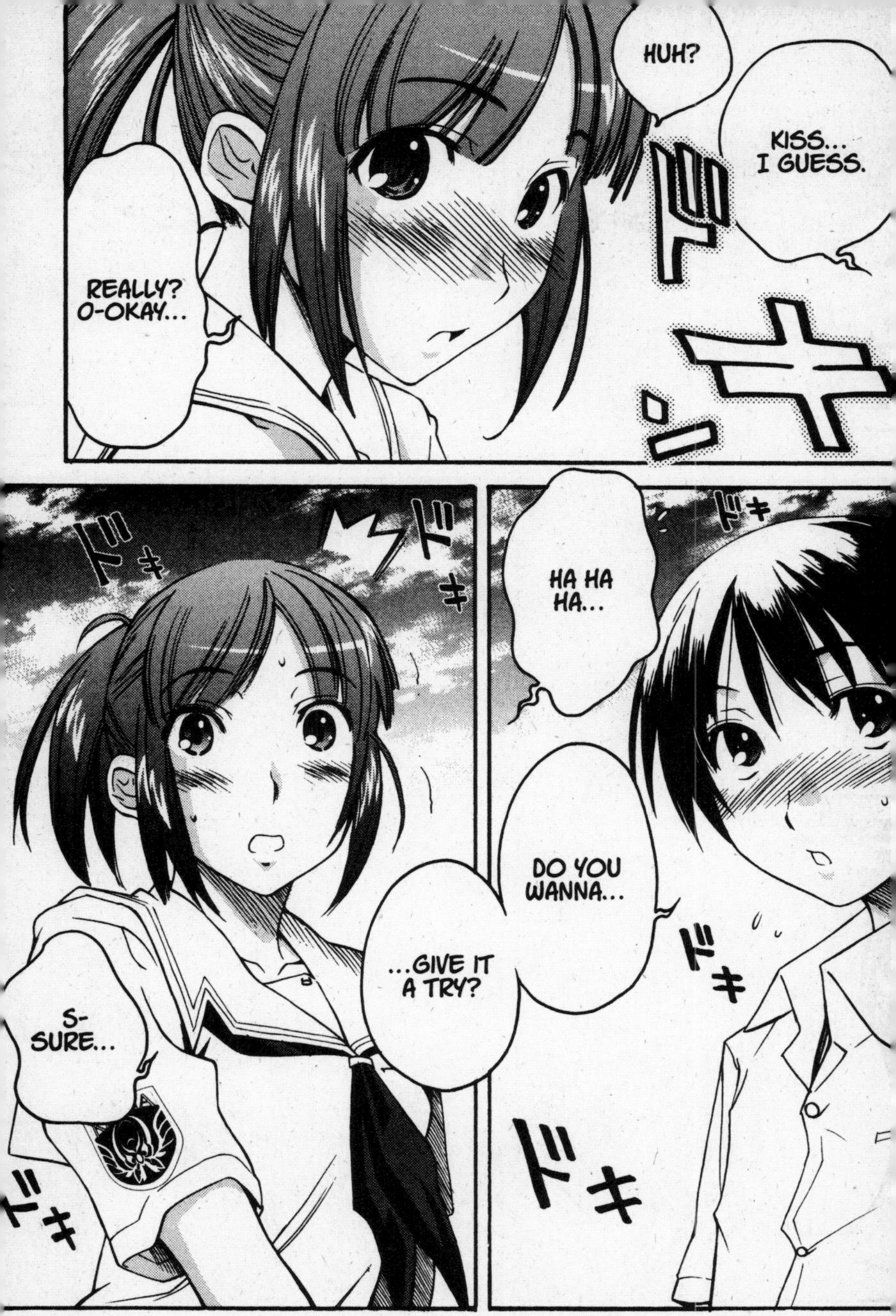
HUH?
KISS... I GUESS.
ドキン
REALLY? O-OKAY...
ドキ
HA HA HA...
DO YOU WANNA...
ドキ
ドキ
ドキ
ドキ
...GIVE IT A TRY?
S-SURE...
ドキ

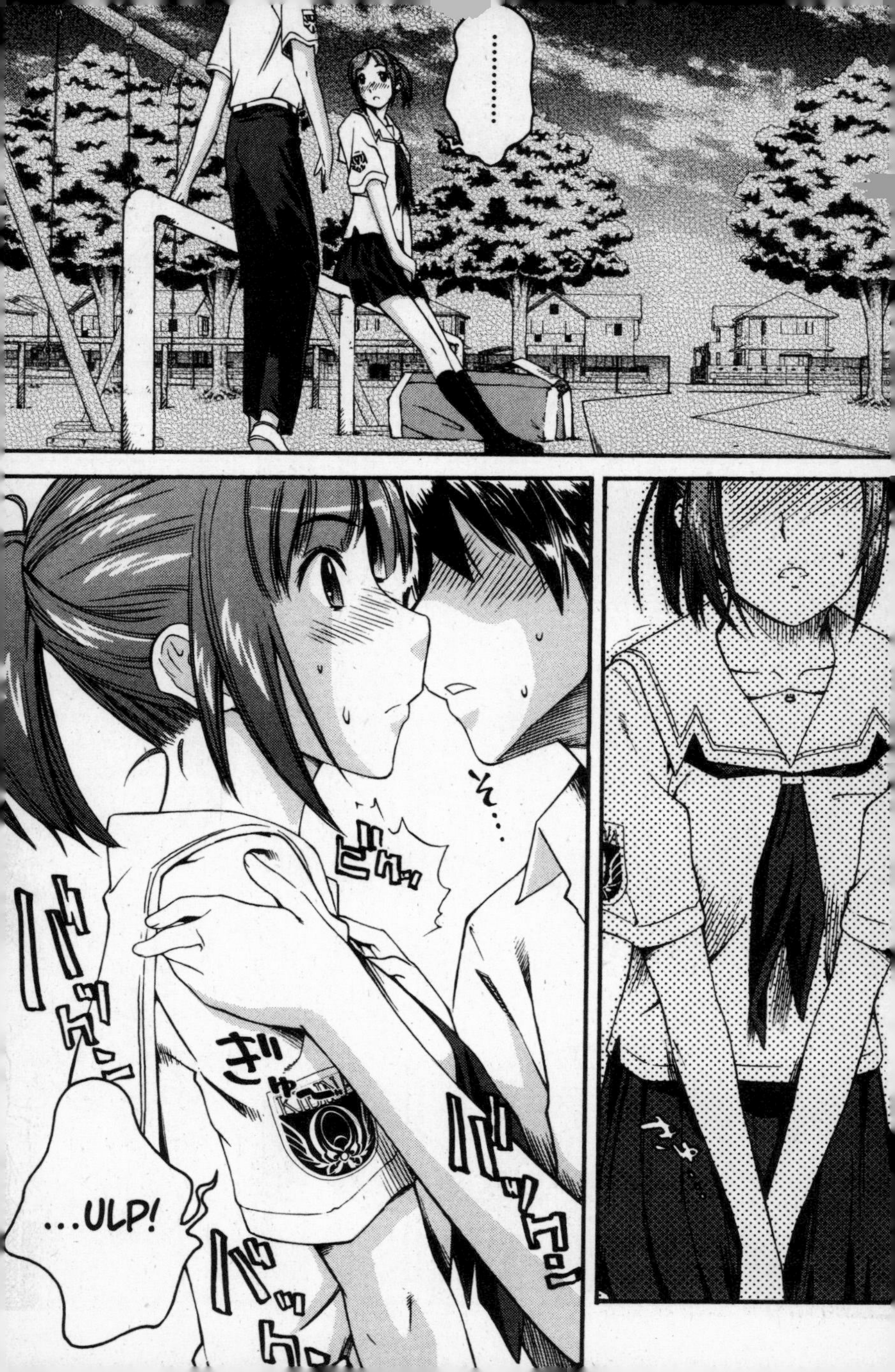
……
...ULP!

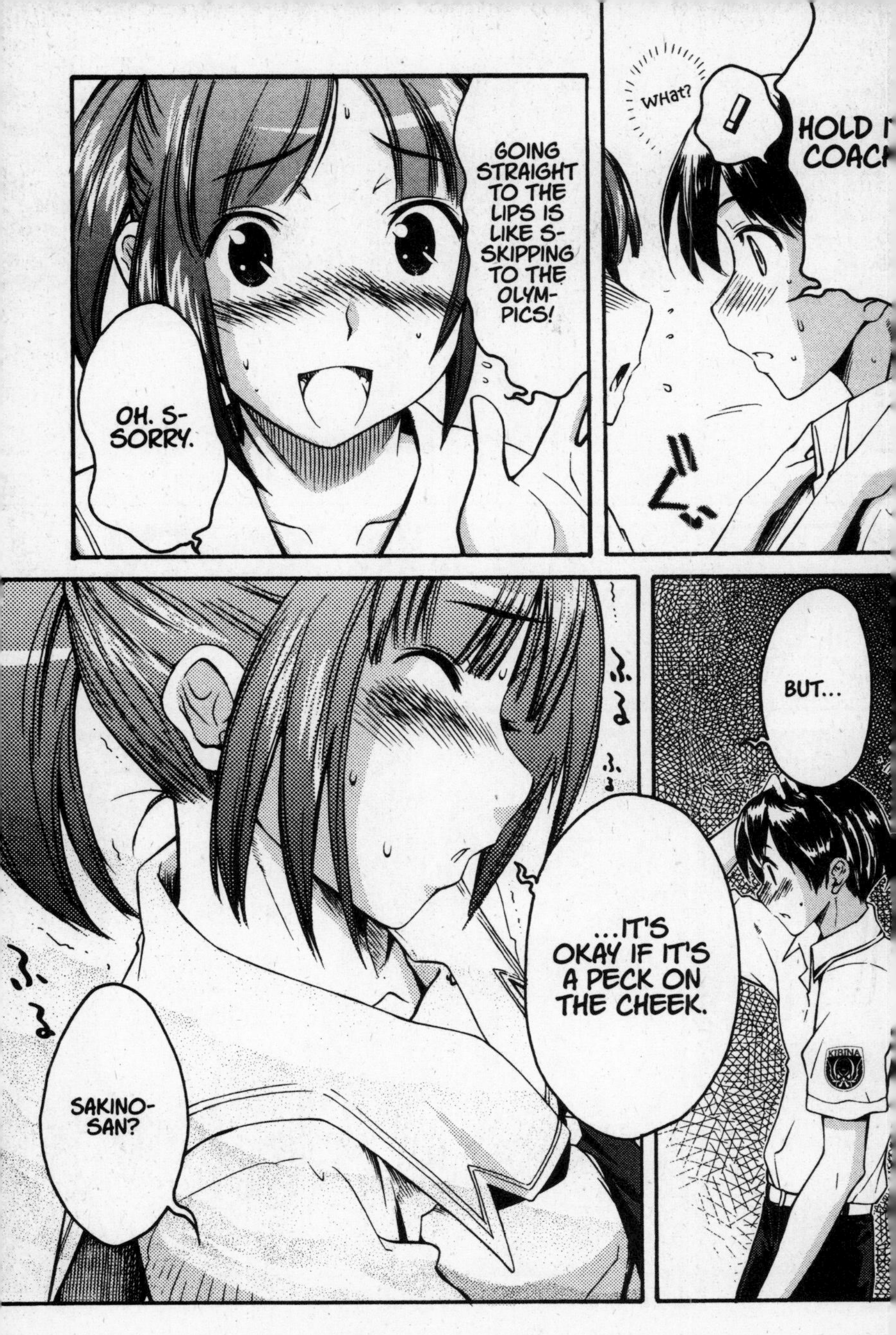
WHAT?
!
HOLD I
COACH
GOING STRAIGHT TO THE LIPS IS LIKE S-SKIPPING TO THE OLYMPICS!
OH. S-SORRY.
BUT...
ふるふる
...IT'S OKAY IF IT'S A PECK ON THE CHEEK.
ふる
SAKINO-SAN?

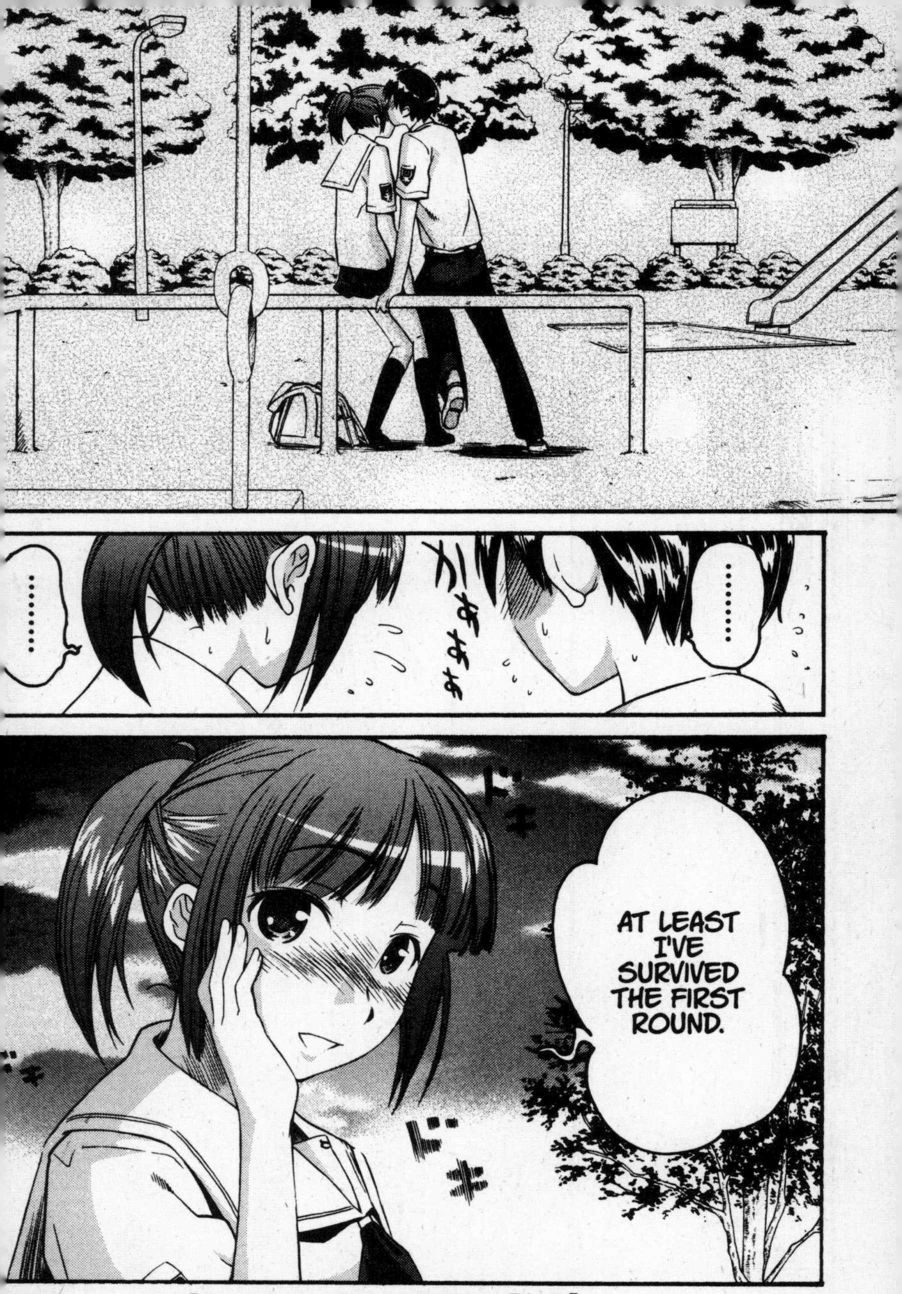
……
かあああ
……
ドキ
AT LEAST I'VE SURVIVED THE FIRST ROUND.
ドキ
ドキ

[Asuka 4th KISS END]

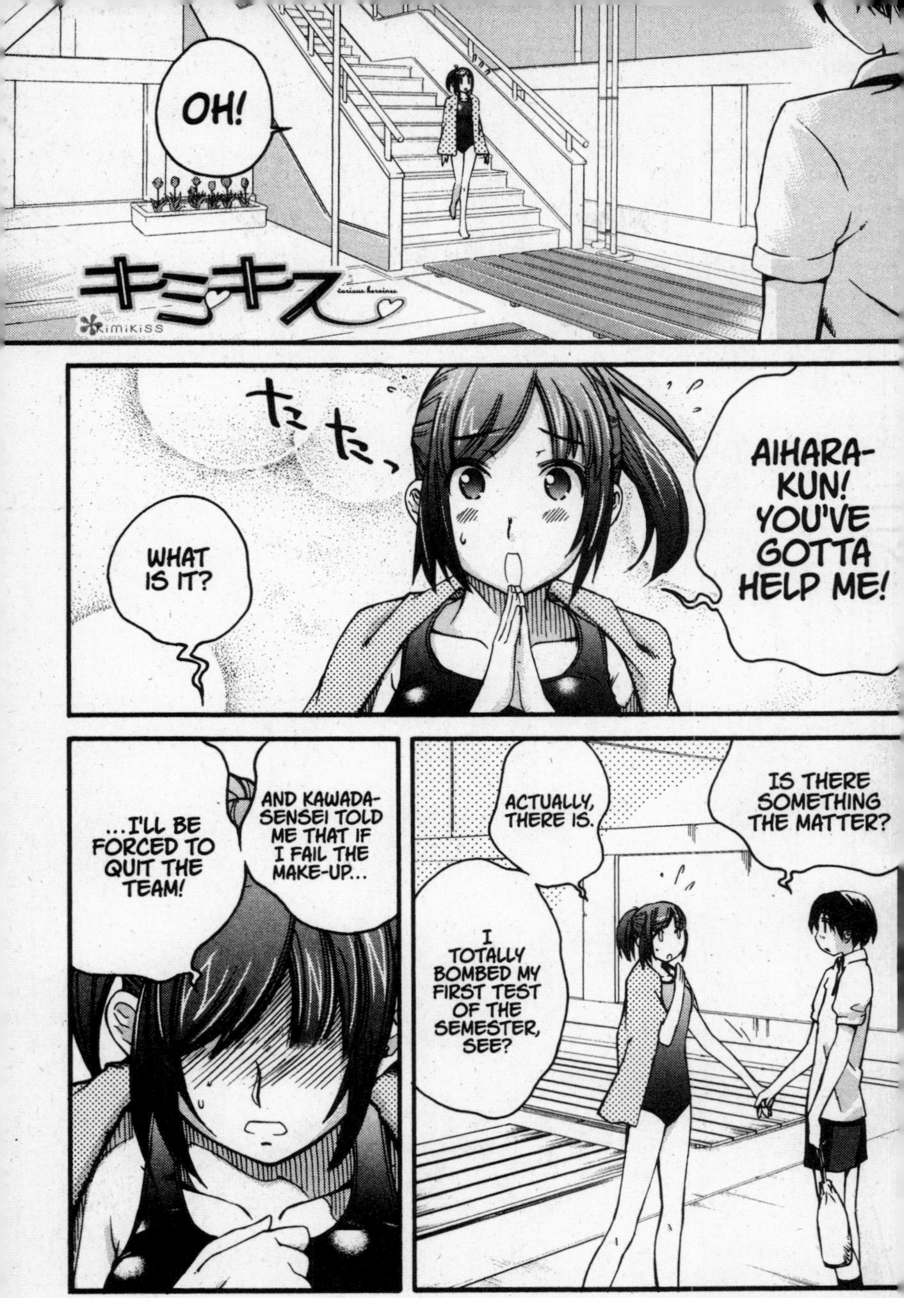
OH!
キミキス
various heroines
KimiKiss
AIHARA-KUN! YOU'VE GOTTA HELP ME!
たたっ
WHAT IS IT?
IS THERE SOMETHING THE MATTER?
ACTUALLY, THERE IS.
I TOTALLY BOMBED MY FIRST TEST OF THE SEMESTER, SEE?
AND KAWADA-SENSEI TOLD ME THAT IF I FAIL THE MAKE-UP...
...I'LL BE FORCED TO QUIT THE TEAM!

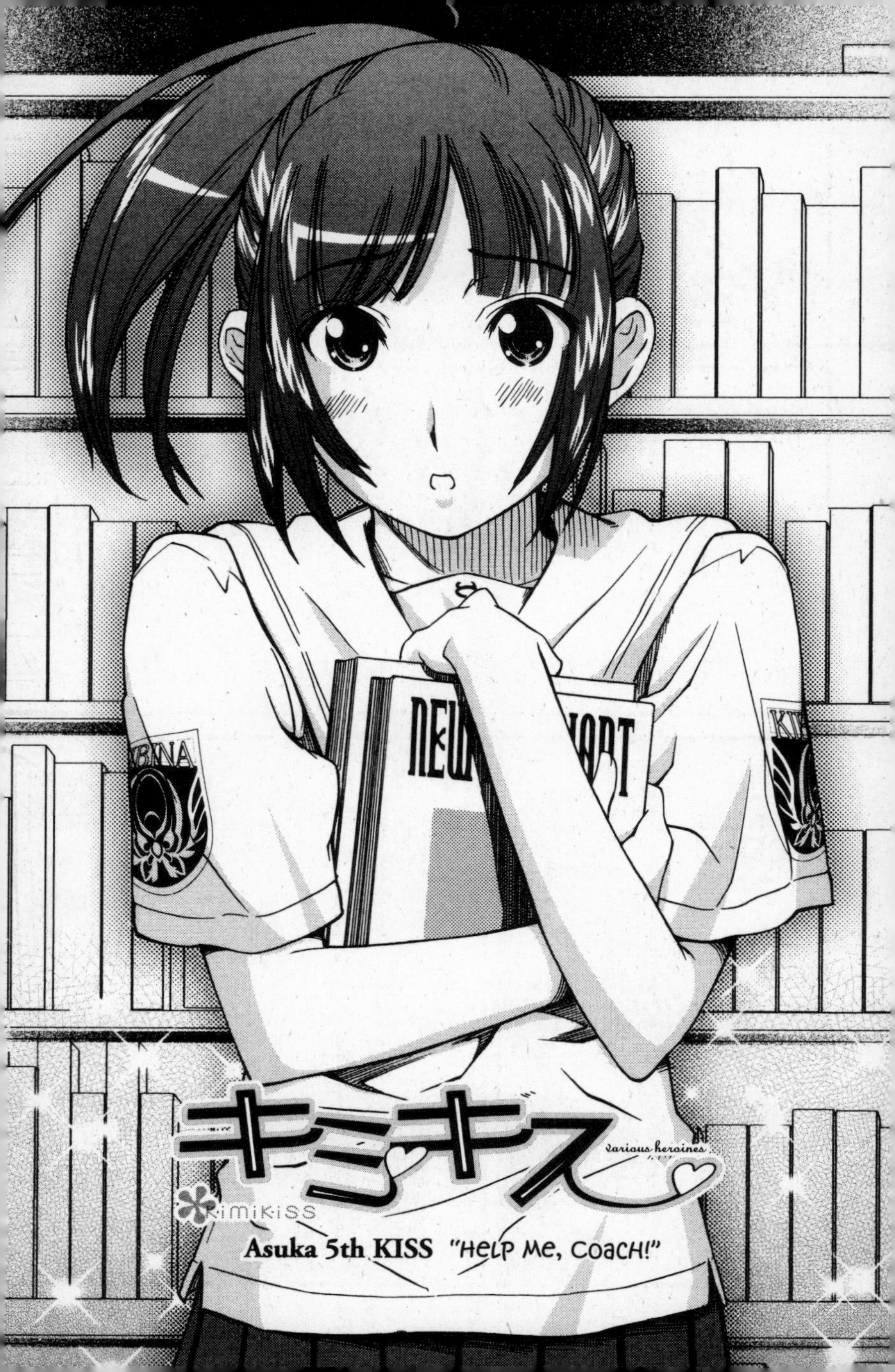
キミキス
various heroines
KimiKiss
Asuka 5th KISS "HELP ME, COACH!"

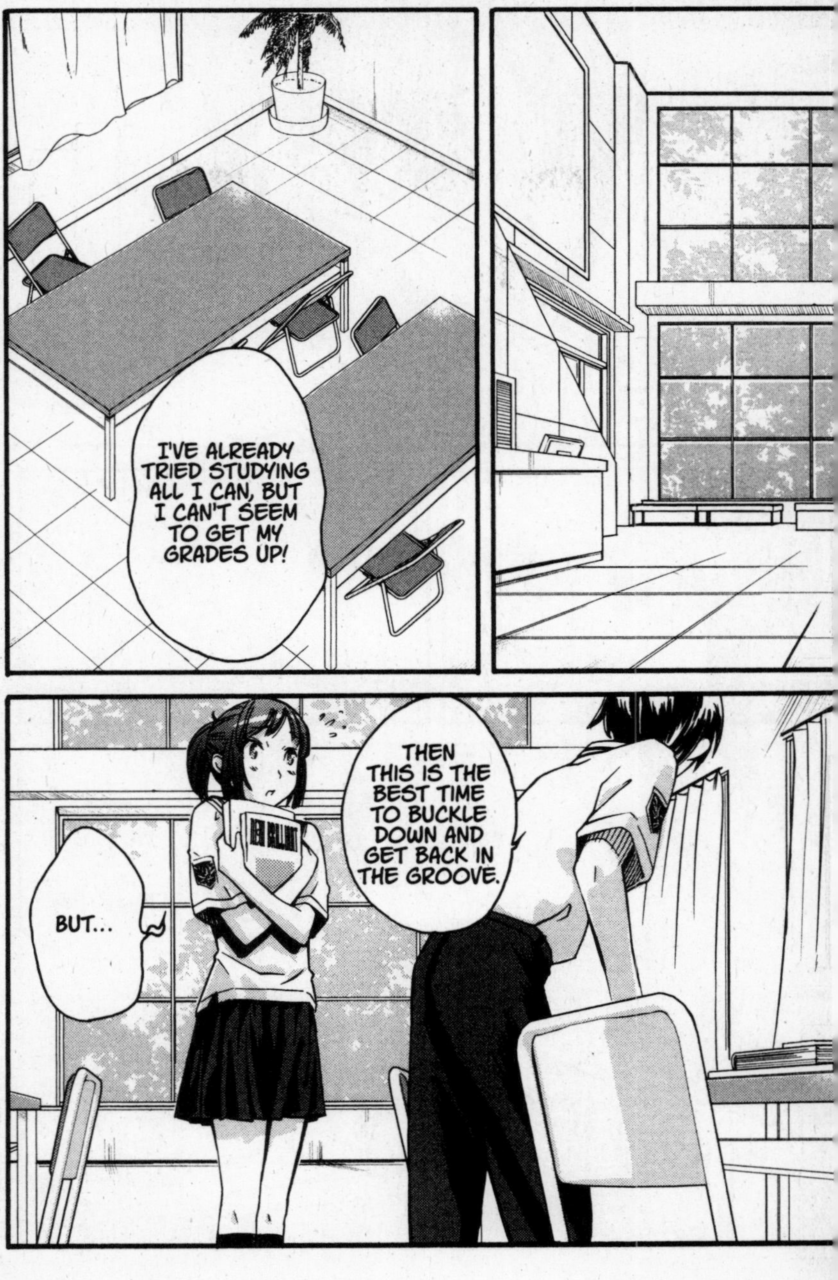
I'VE ALREADY TRIED STUDYING ALL I CAN, BUT I CAN'T SEEM TO GET MY GRADES UP!
THEN THIS IS THE BEST TIME TO BUCKLE DOWN AND GET BACK IN THE GROOVE.
BUT...

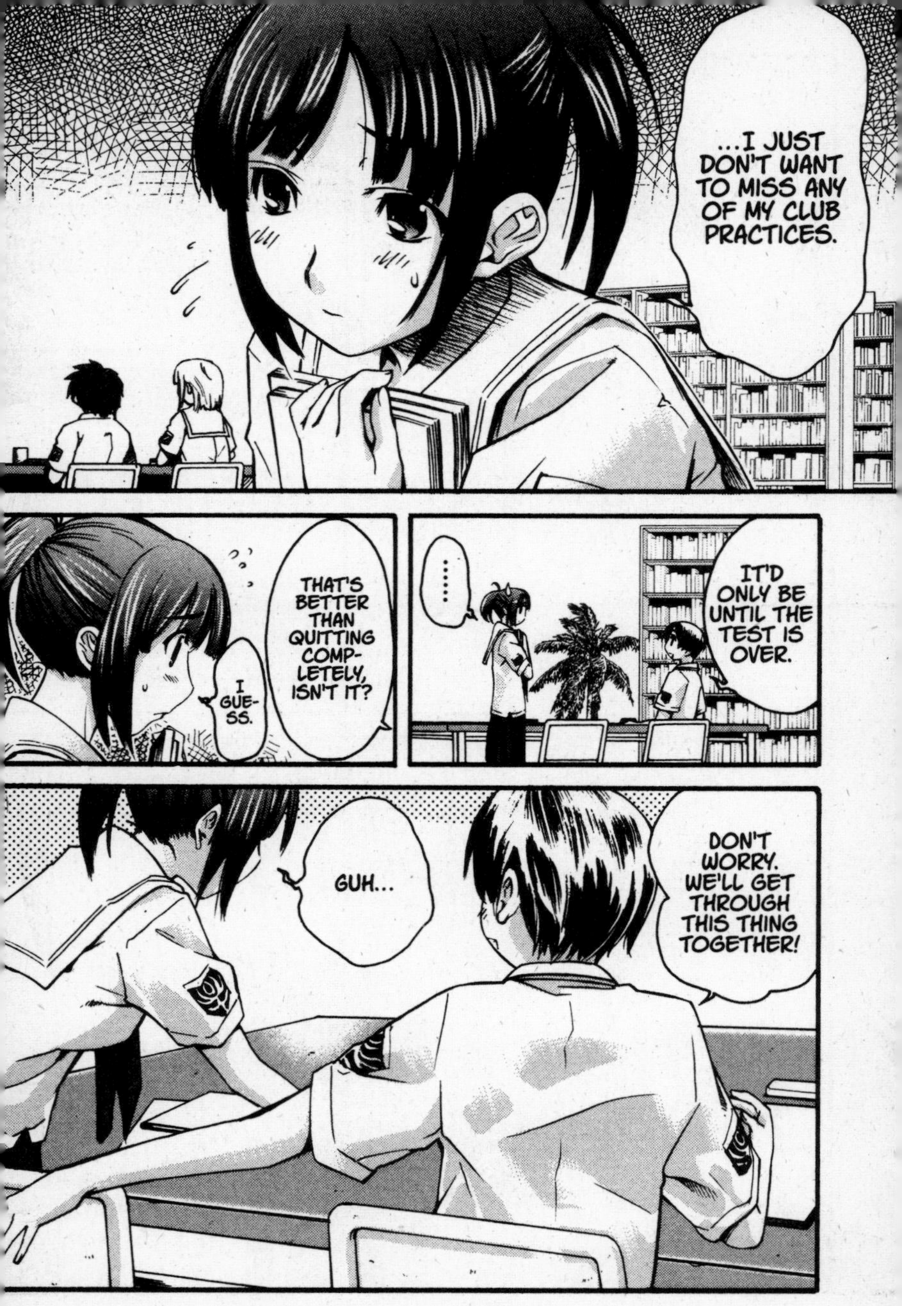
...I JUST DON'T WANT TO MISS ANY OF MY CLUB PRACTICES.
IT'D ONLY BE UNTIL THE TEST IS OVER.
......
THAT'S BETTER THAN QUITTING COMP-LETELY, ISN'T IT?
I GUE-SS.
DON'T WORRY. WE'LL GET THROUGH THIS THING TOGETHER!
GUH...

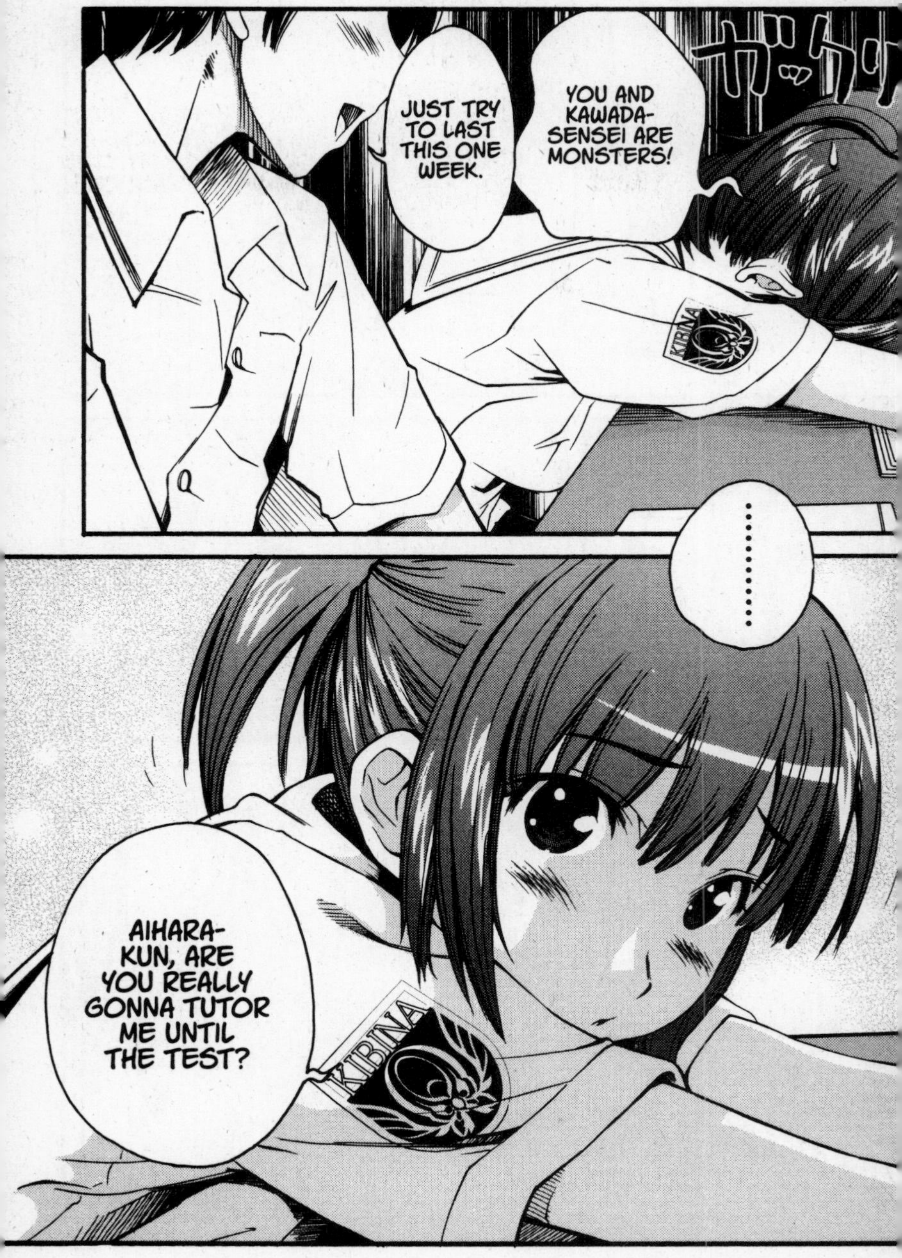
ガックリ
YOU AND KAWADA-SENSEI ARE MONSTERS!
JUST TRY TO LAST THIS ONE WEEK.
KIBINA
…………
AIHARA-KUN, ARE YOU REALLY GONNA TUTOR ME UNTIL THE TEST?
KIBINA

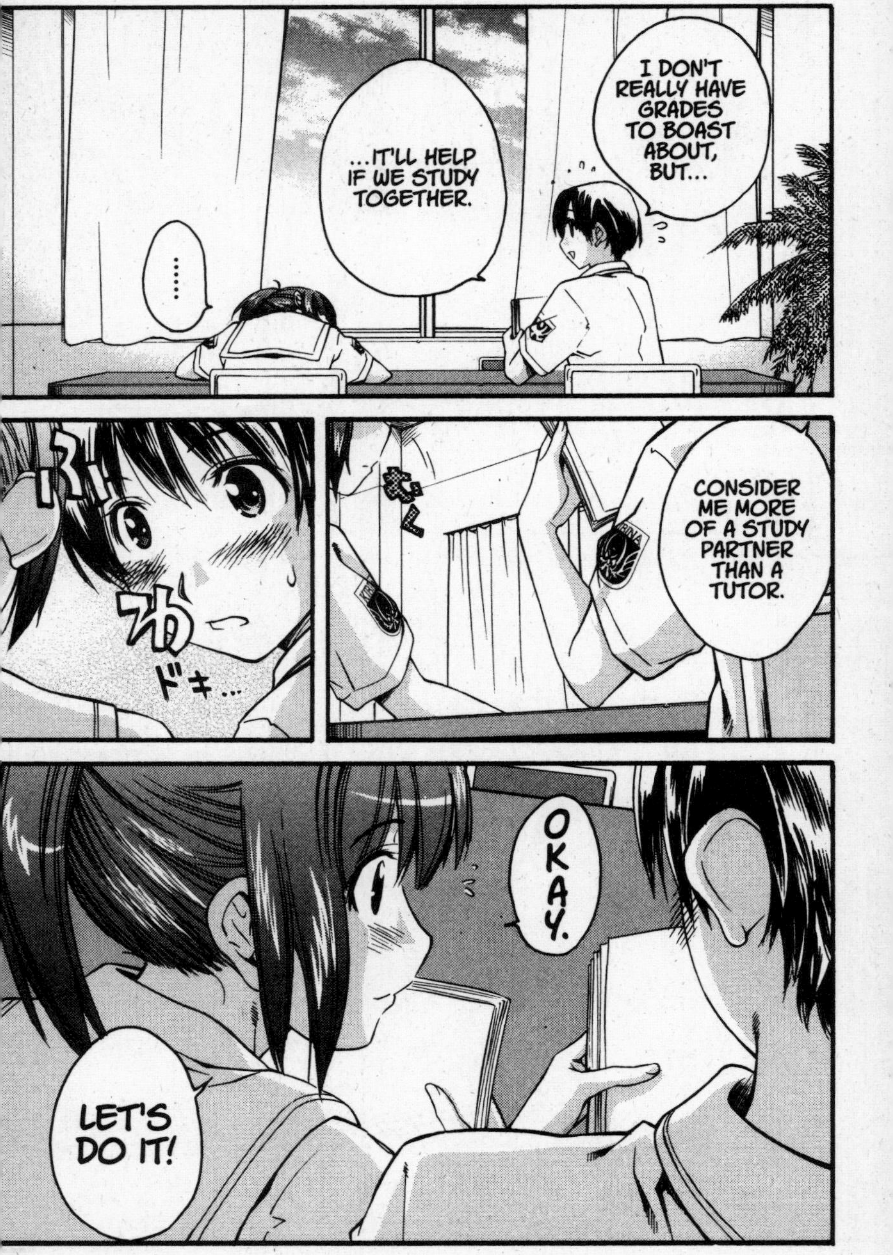
I DON'T REALLY HAVE GRADES TO BOAST ABOUT, BUT...
...IT'LL HELP IF WE STUDY TOGETHER.
......
CONSIDER ME MORE OF A STUDY PARTNER THAN A TUTOR.
ドキ...
OKAY.
LET'S DO IT!

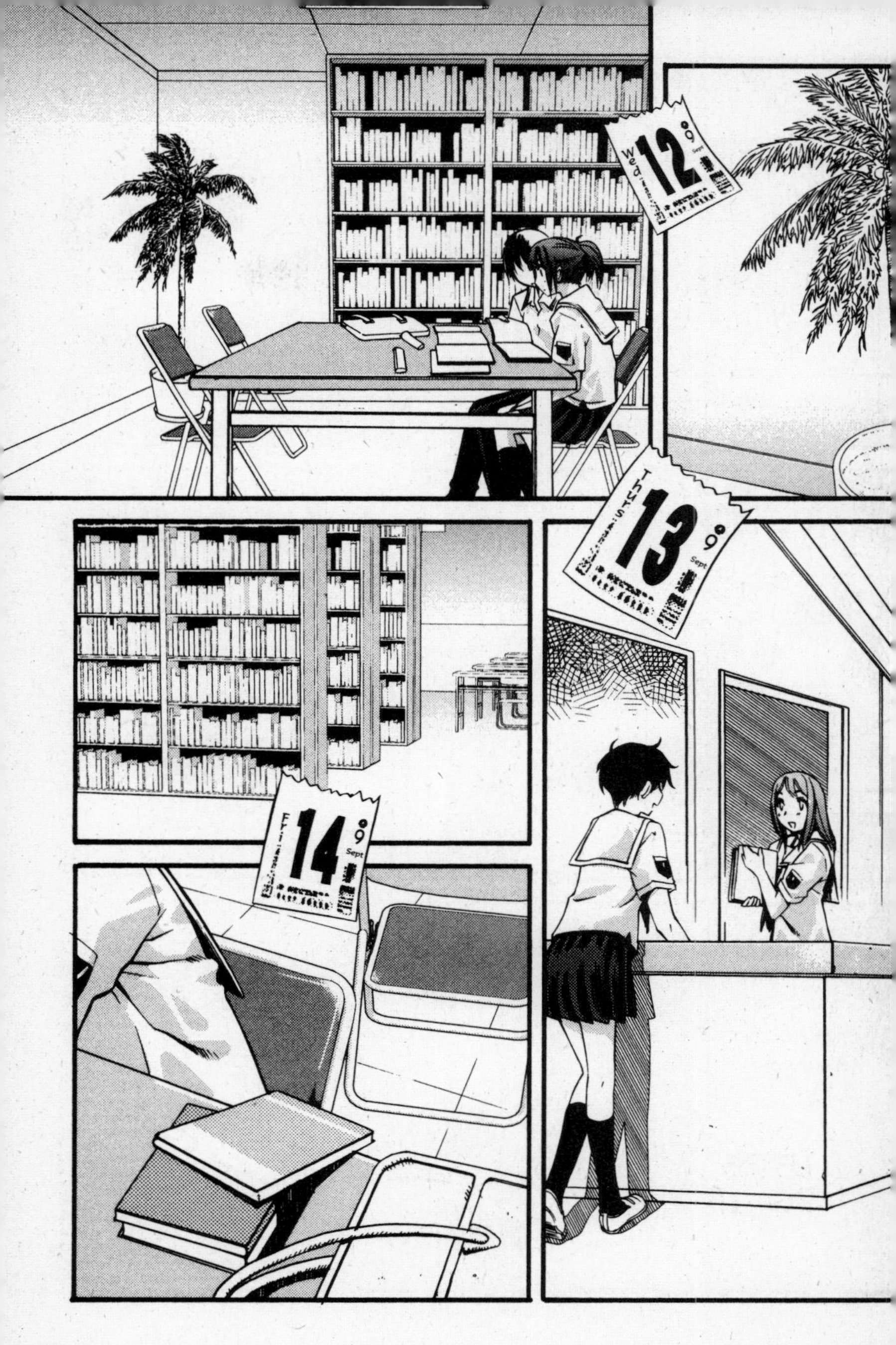
Wed 12 9 Sept
Thurs 13 9 Sept
Fri 14 9 Sept

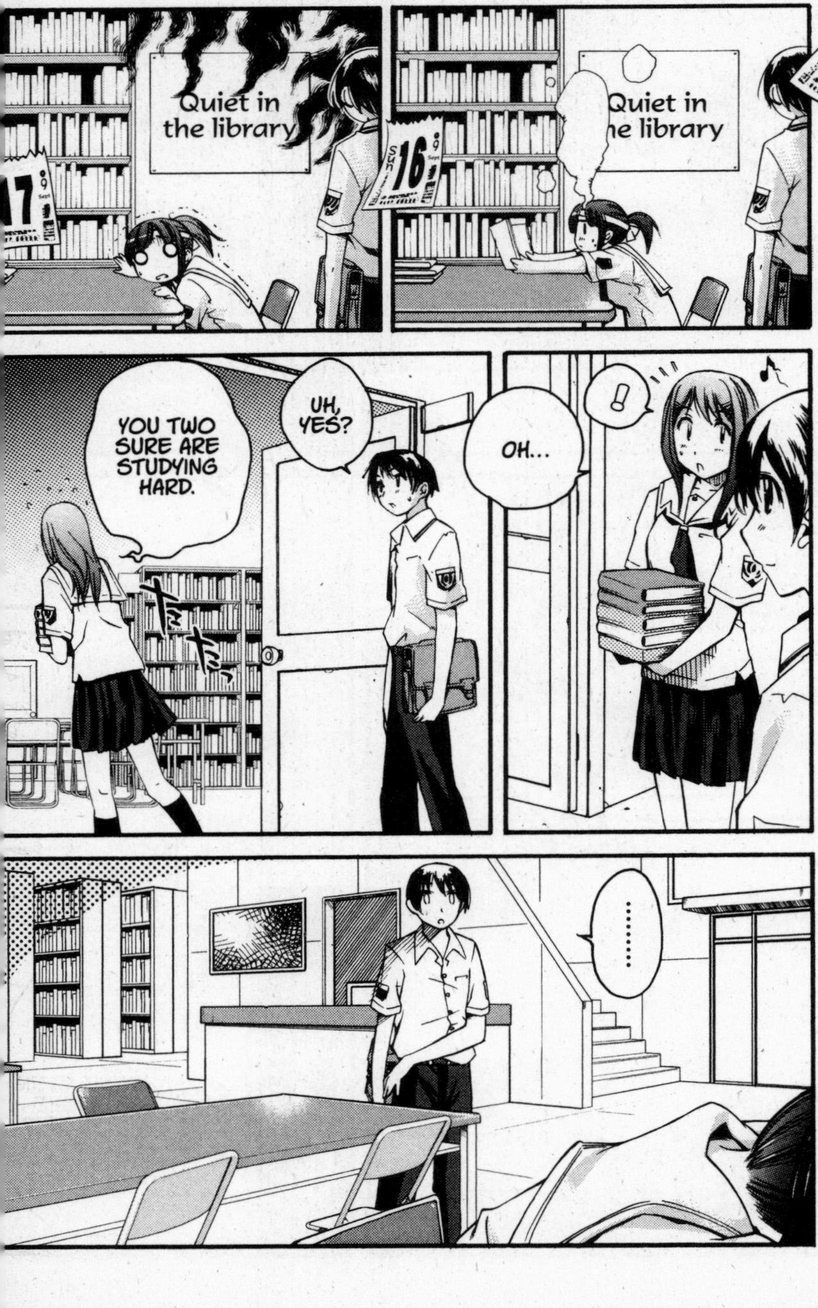
15
Quiet in
he library
16
Quiet in
the library
17
!
OH...
UH, YES?
YOU TWO SURE ARE STUDYING HARD.
......

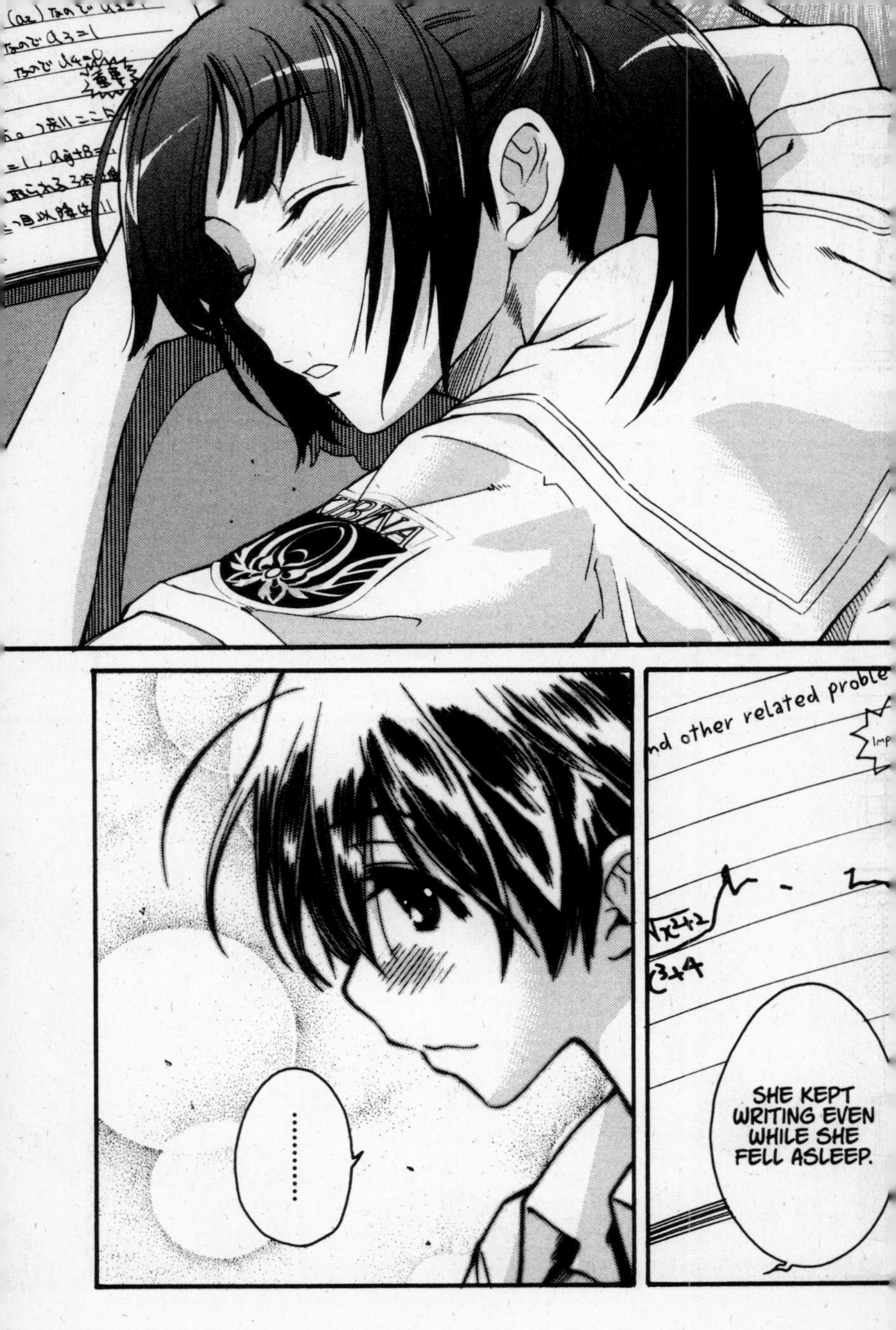
SHE KEPT WRITING EVEN WHILE SHE FELL ASLEEP.
......

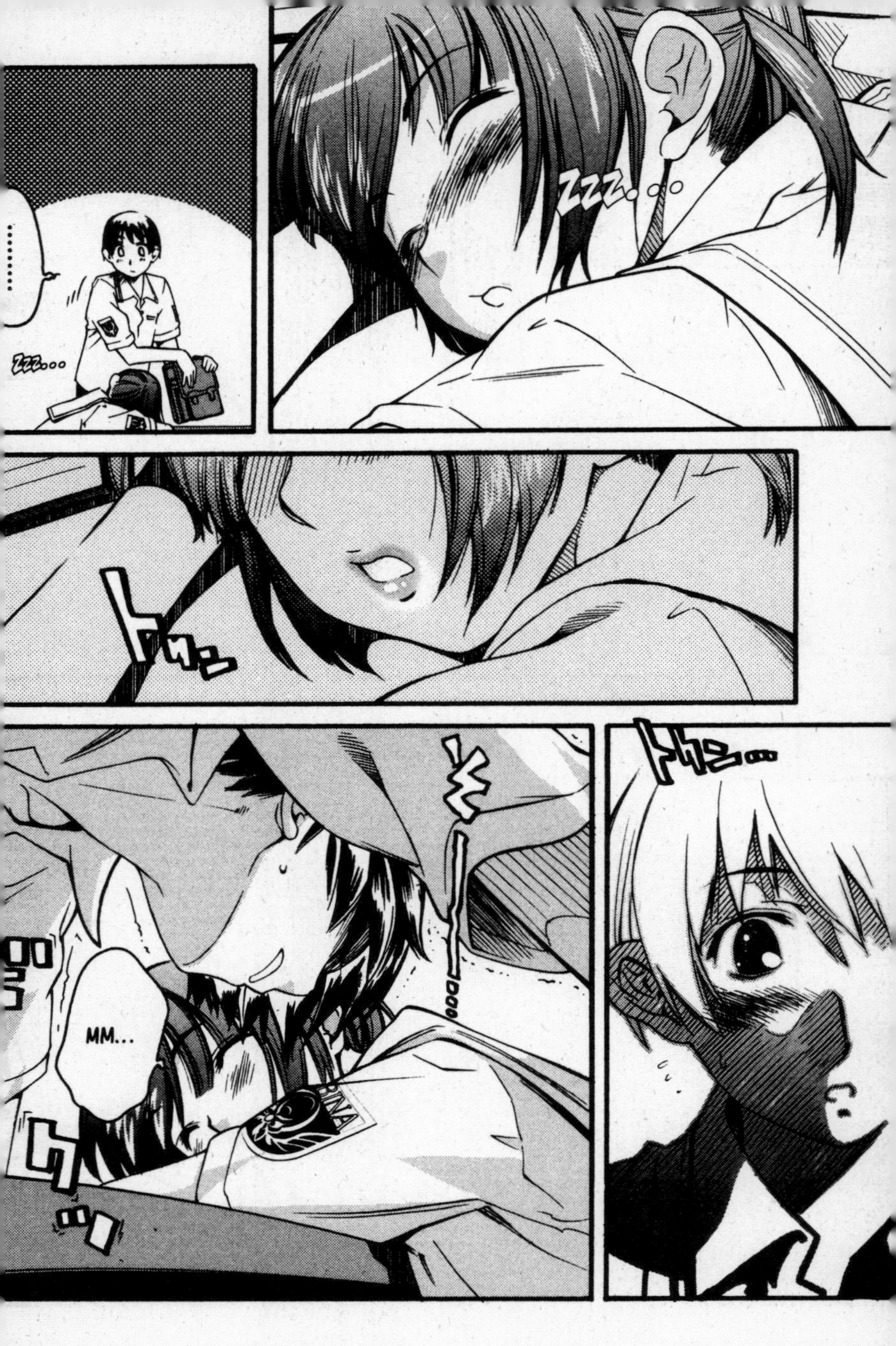
ZZZ...
......
ZZZ...
トクン
トクン…
MM...

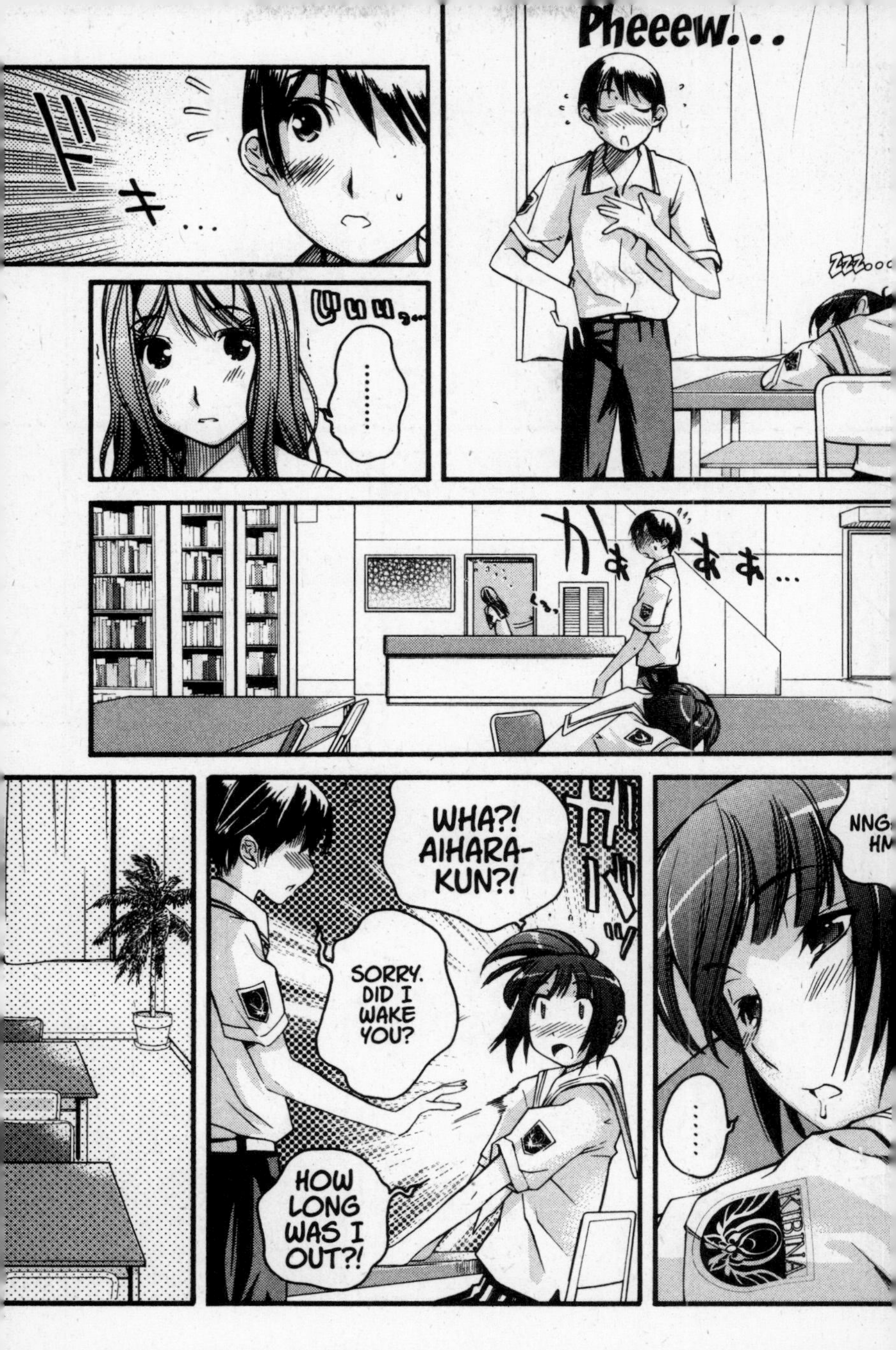
Pheeew...
zzz...
ドキ...
......
NNG
HM
......
WHA?! AIHARA-KUN?!
SORRY. DID I WAKE YOU?
HOW LONG WAS I OUT?!

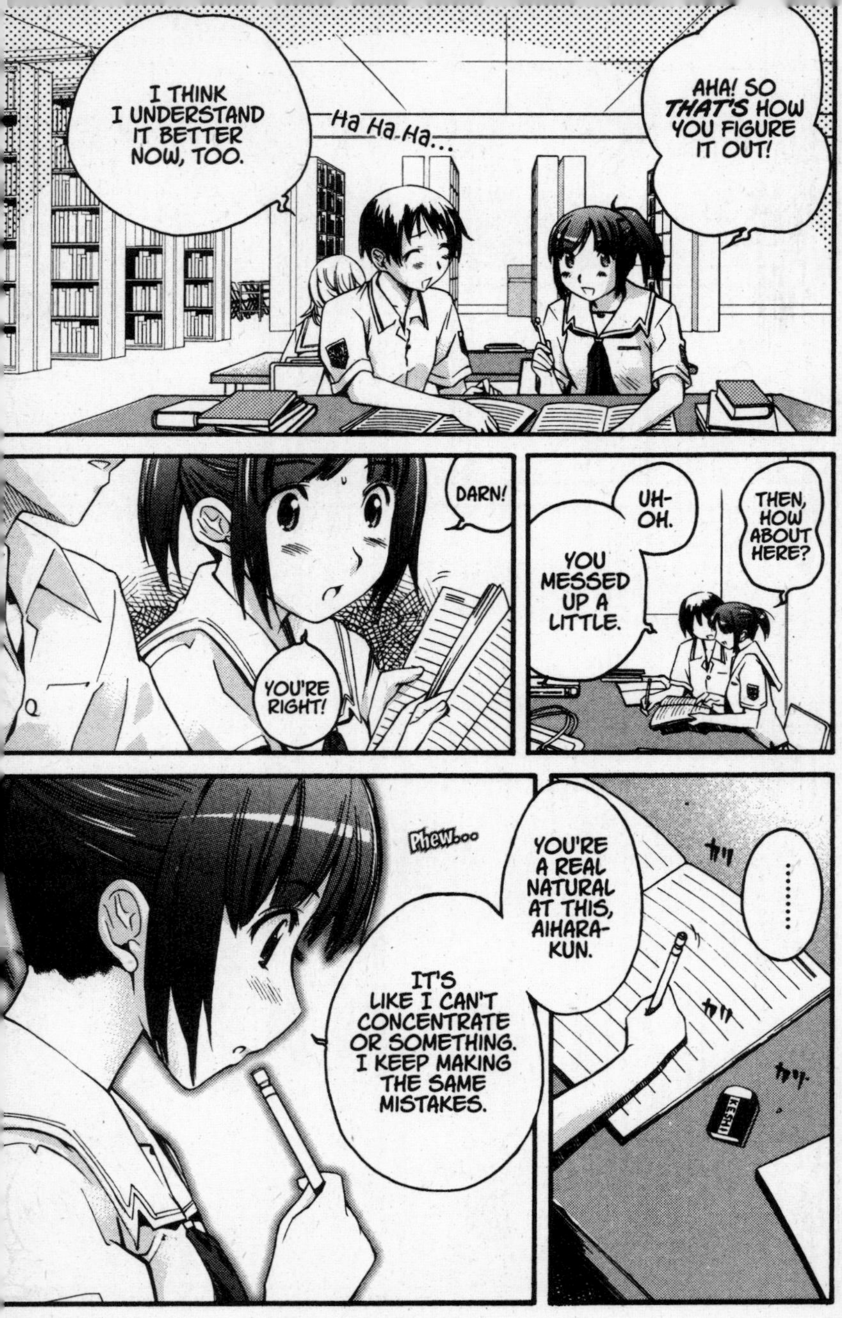
AHA! SO THAT'S HOW YOU FIGURE IT OUT!
Ha Ha Ha...
I THINK I UNDERSTAND IT BETTER NOW, TOO.
THEN, HOW ABOUT HERE?
UH-OH.
YOU MESSED UP A LITTLE.
DARN!
YOU'RE RIGHT!
......
YOU'RE A REAL NATURAL AT THIS, AIHARA-KUN.
KESHI
Phewboo
IT'S LIKE I CAN'T CONCENTRATE OR SOMETHING. I KEEP MAKING THE SAME MISTAKES.

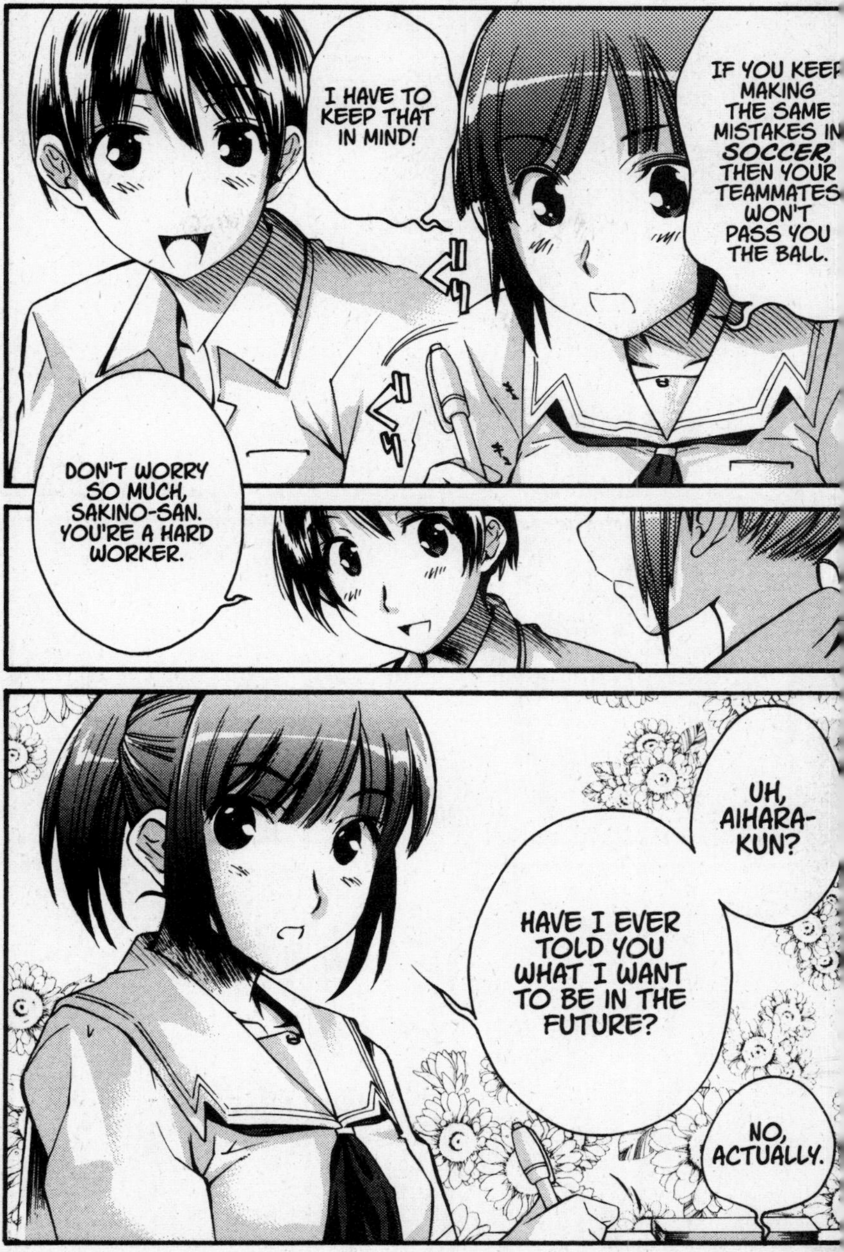

IF YOU KEEP MAKING THE SAME MISTAKES IN *SOCCER,* THEN YOUR TEAMMATES WON'T PASS YOU THE BALL.
I HAVE TO KEEP THAT IN MIND!
DON'T WORRY SO MUCH, SAKINO-SAN. YOU'RE A HARD WORKER.
UH, AIHARA-KUN?
HAVE I EVER TOLD YOU WHAT I WANT TO BE IN THE FUTURE?
NO, ACTUALLY.

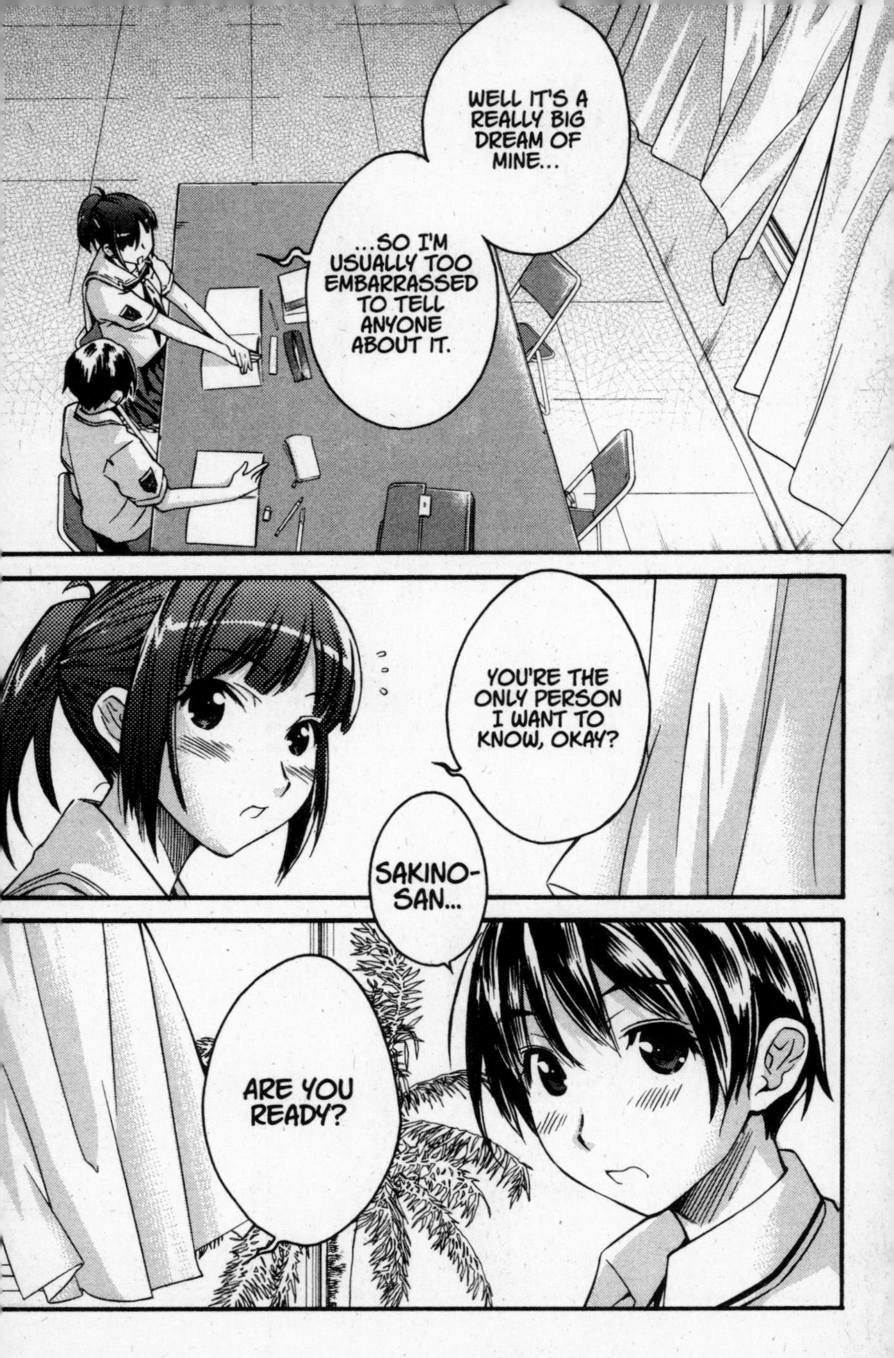
WELL IT'S A REALLY BIG DREAM OF MINE...
...SO I'M USUALLY TOO EMBARRASSED TO TELL ANYONE ABOUT IT.
YOU'RE THE ONLY PERSON I WANT TO KNOW, OKAY?
SAKINO-SAN...
ARE YOU READY?

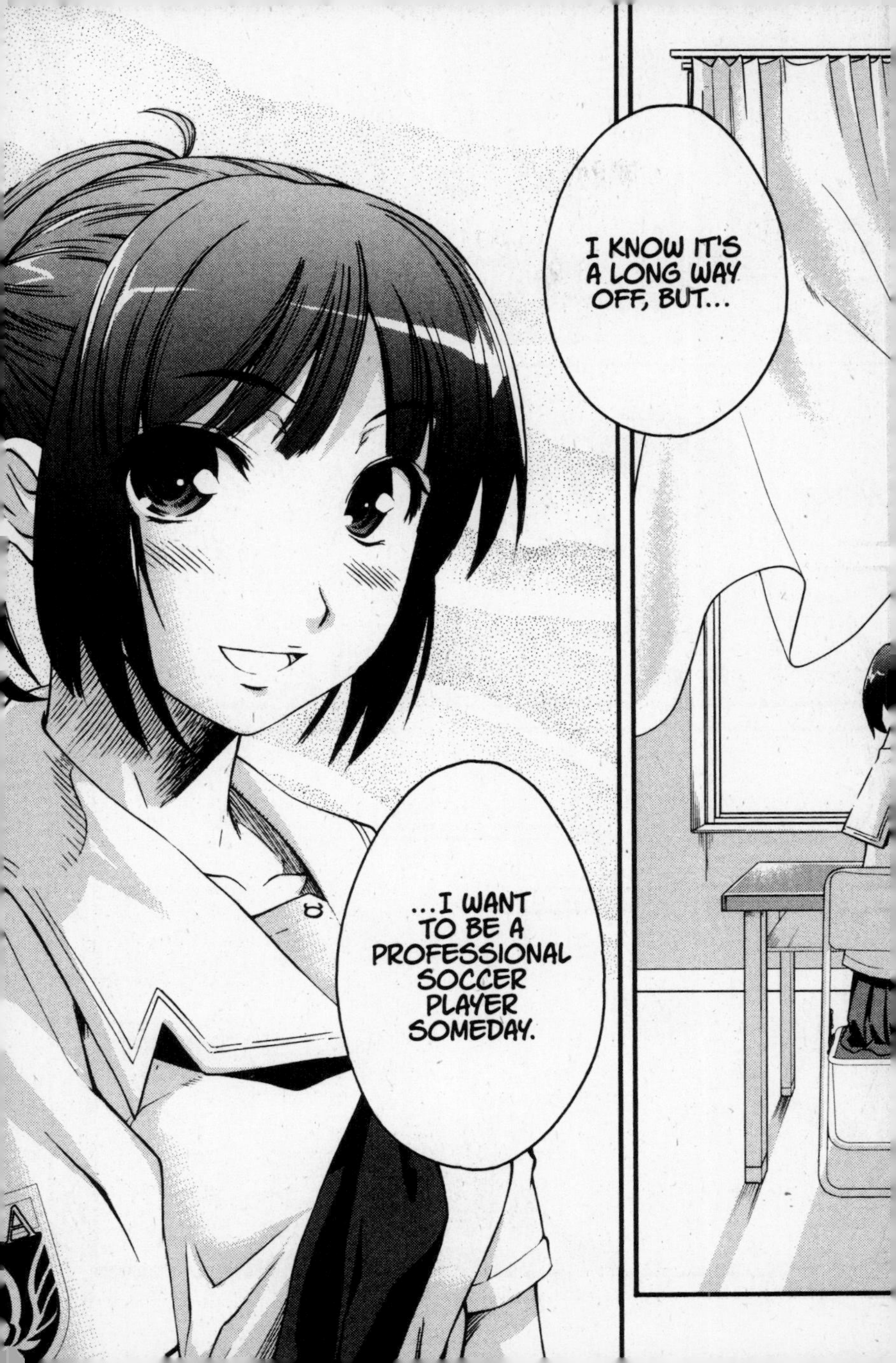
I KNOW IT'S A LONG WAY OFF, BUT...
...I WANT TO BE A PROFESSIONAL SOCCER PLAYER SOMEDAY.

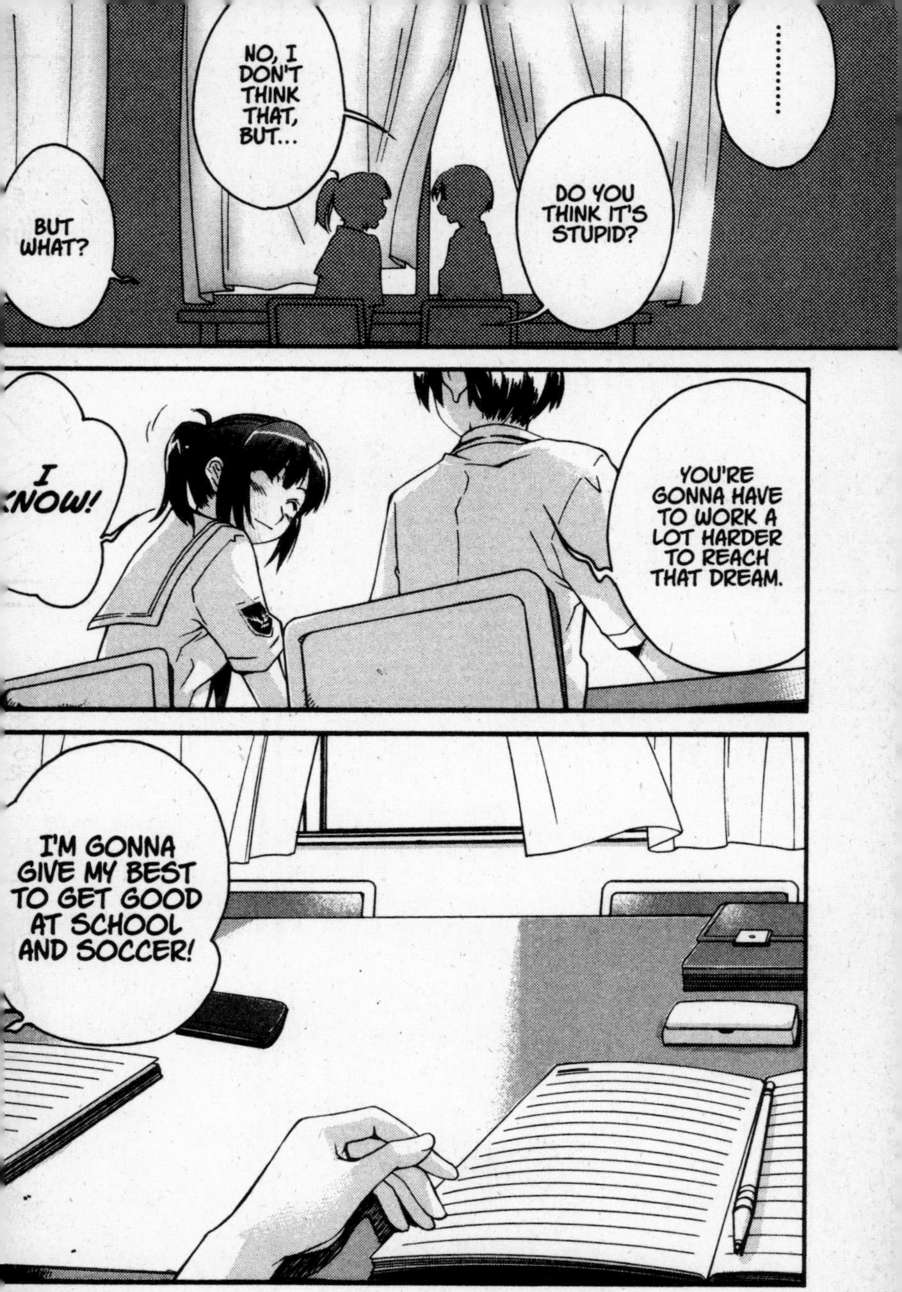
....
DO YOU THINK IT'S STUPID?
NO, I DON'T THINK THAT, BUT...
BUT WHAT?
YOU'RE GONNA HAVE TO WORK A LOT HARDER TO REACH THAT DREAM.
I KNOW!
I'M GONNA GIVE MY BEST TO GET GOOD AT SCHOOL AND SOCCER!

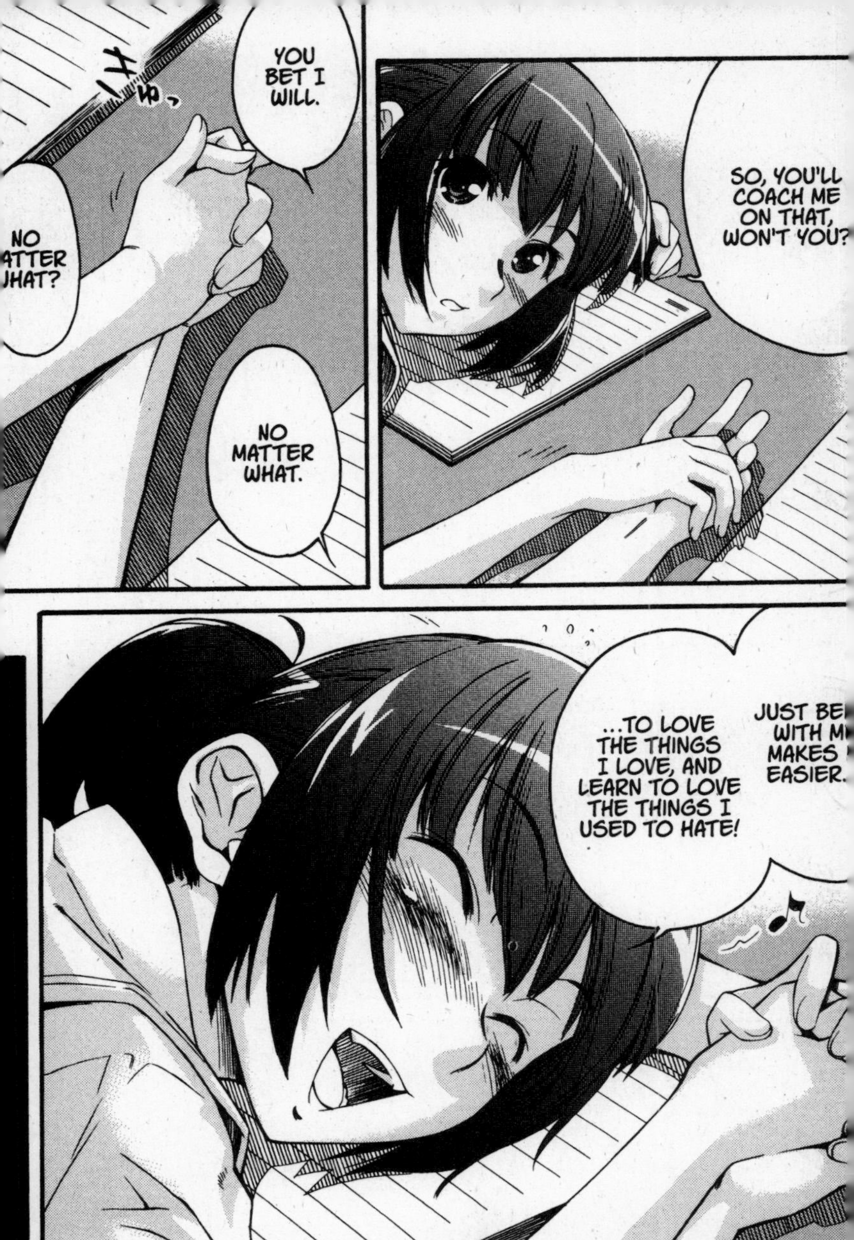
SO, YOU'LL COACH ME ON THAT, WON'T YOU?
YOU BET I WILL.
NO ATTER HAT?
NO MATTER WHAT.
JUST BE WITH M MAKES EASIER.
...TO LOVE THE THINGS I LOVE, AND LEARN TO LOVE THE THINGS I USED TO HATE!

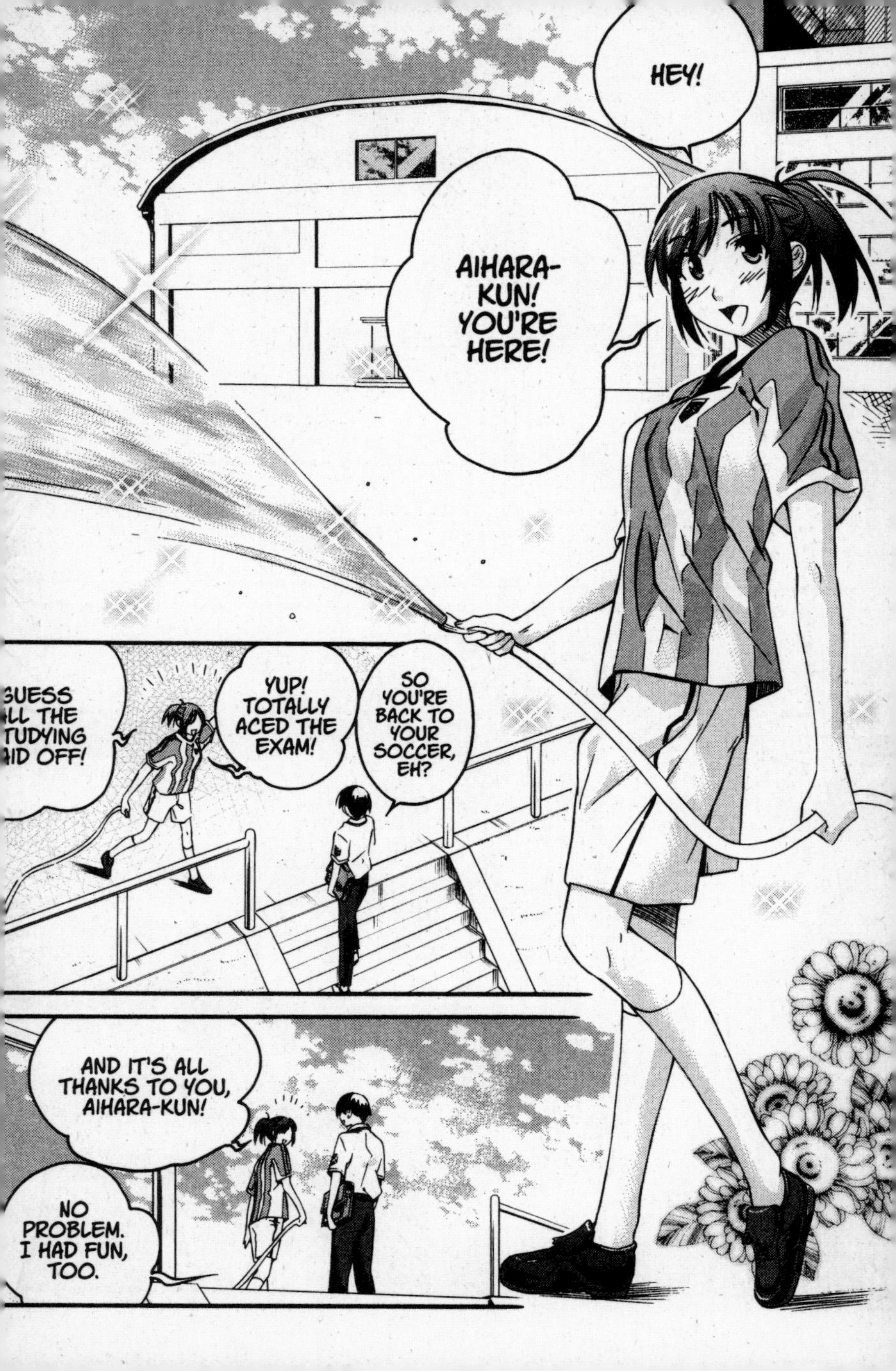
HEY!
AIHARA-KUN! YOU'RE HERE!
SO YOU'RE BACK TO YOUR SOCCER, EH?
YUP! TOTALLY ACED THE EXAM!
GUESS LL THE TUDYING AID OFF!
AND IT'S ALL THANKS TO YOU, AIHARA-KUN!
NO PROBLEM. I HAD FUN, TOO.

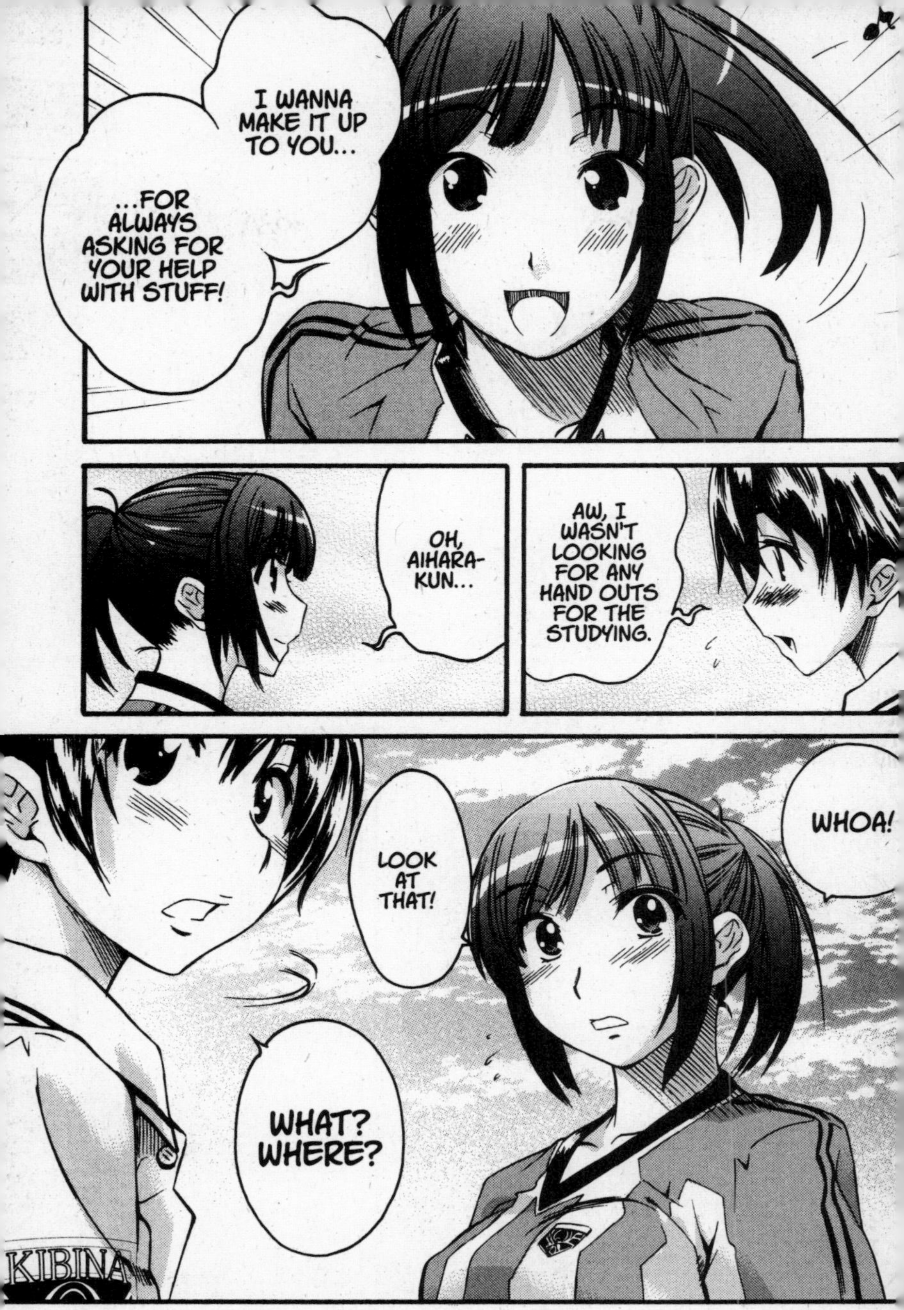
I WANNA MAKE IT UP TO YOU...
...FOR ALWAYS ASKING FOR YOUR HELP WITH STUFF!
AW, I WASN'T LOOKING FOR ANY HAND OUTS FOR THE STUDYING.
OH, AIHARA-KUN...
WHOA!
LOOK AT THAT!
WHAT? WHERE?
KIBINA

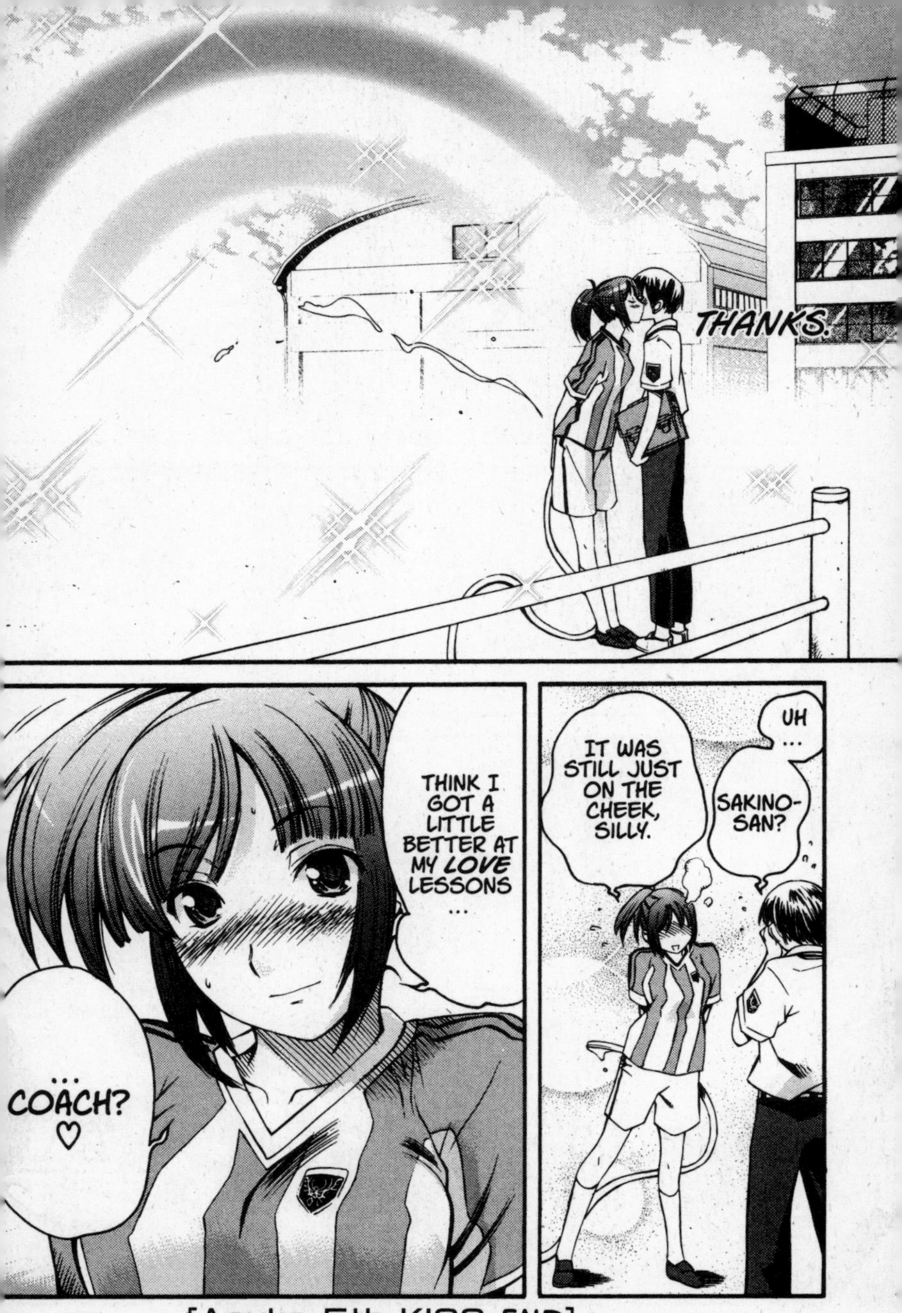
THANKS.
UH ... SAKINO-SAN?
IT WAS STILL JUST ON THE CHEEK, SILLY.
THINK I GOT A LITTLE BETTER AT MY *LOVE* LESSONS ...
... COACH? ♡

[Asuka 5th KISS END]

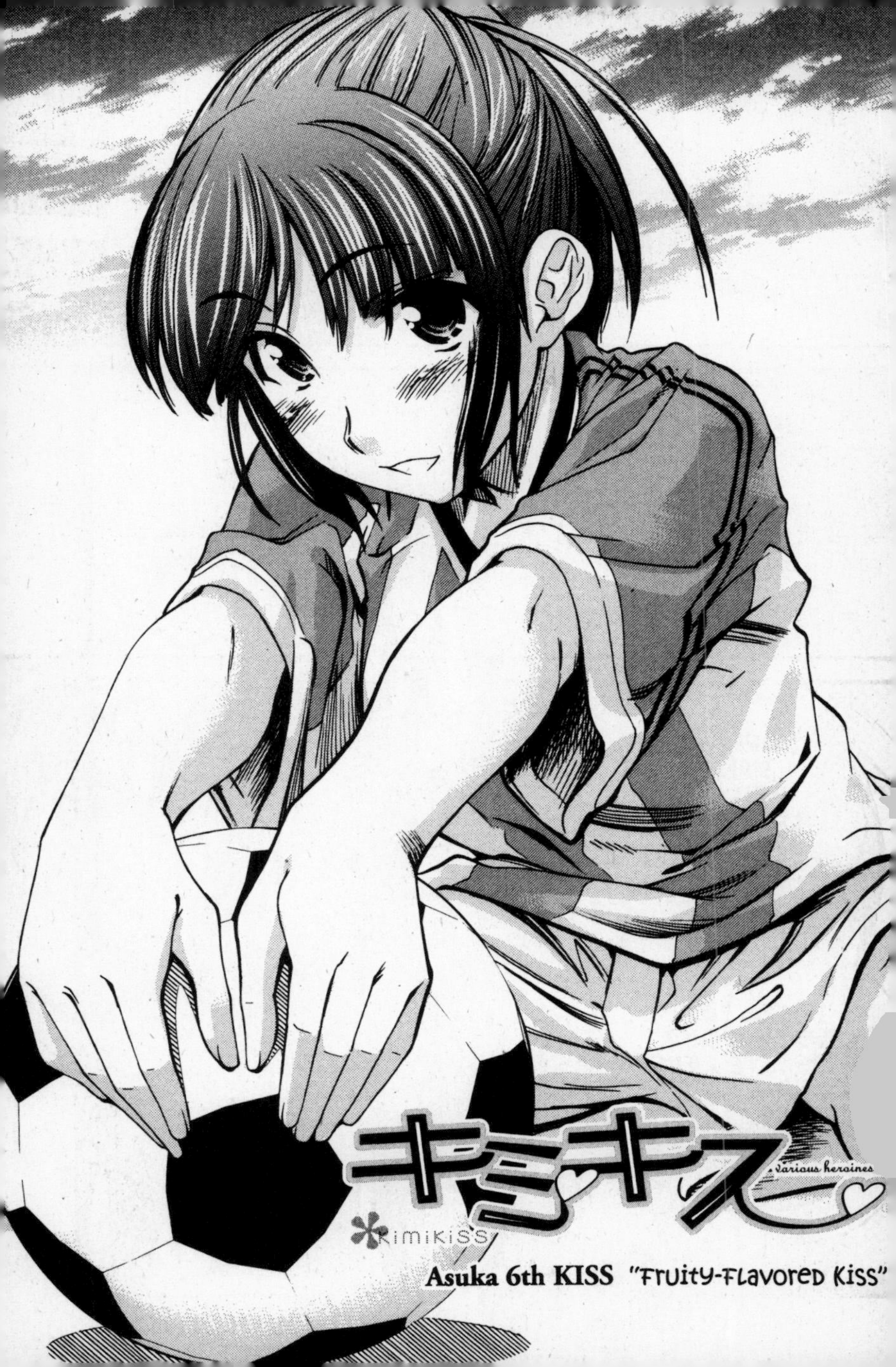
キミキス
various heroines
kimikiss
Asuka 6th KISS "Fruity-Flavored Kiss"

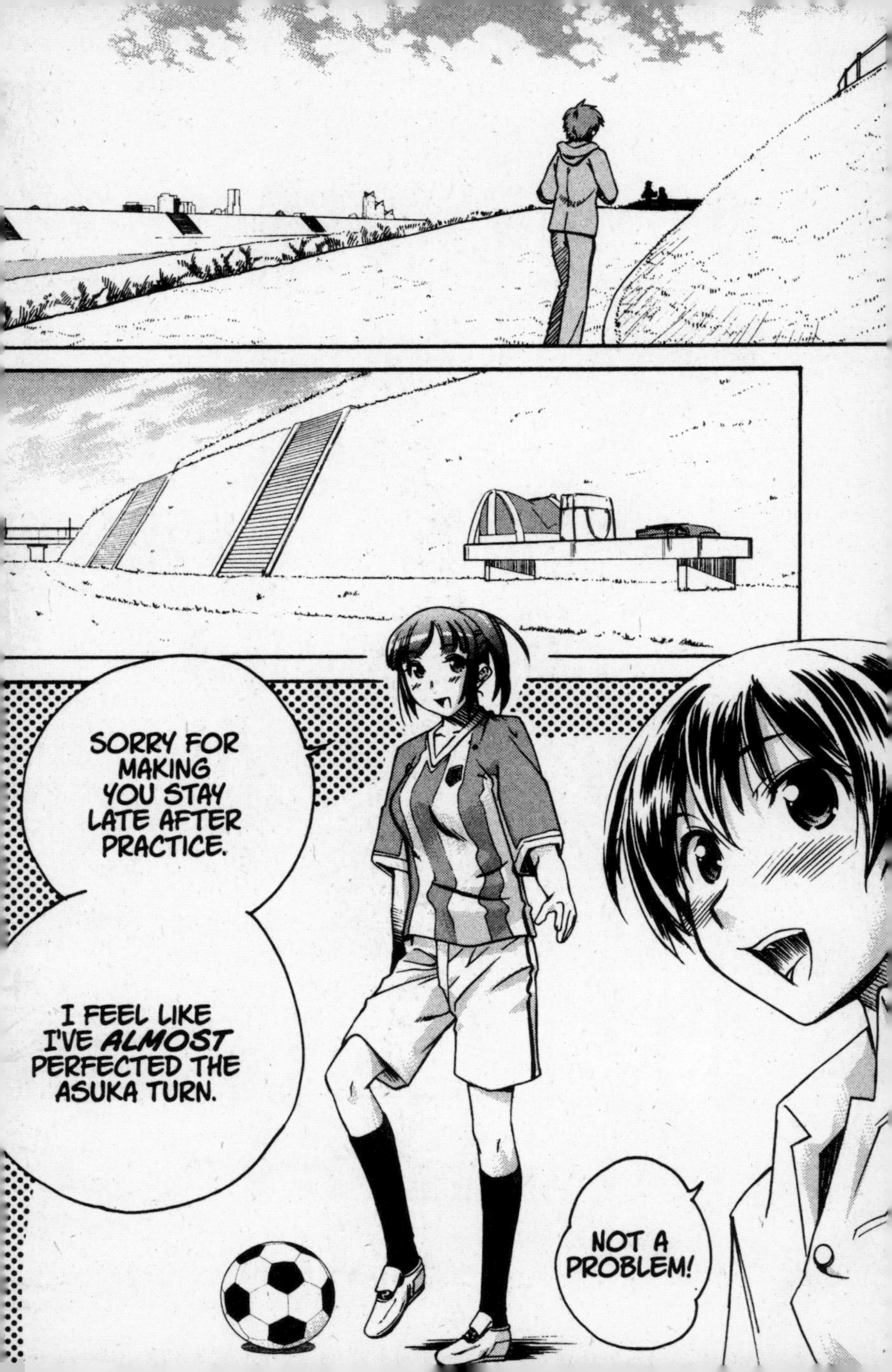
SORRY FOR MAKING YOU STAY LATE AFTER PRACTICE.
I FEEL LIKE I'VE *ALMOST* PERFECTED THE ASUKA TURN.
NOT A PROBLEM!

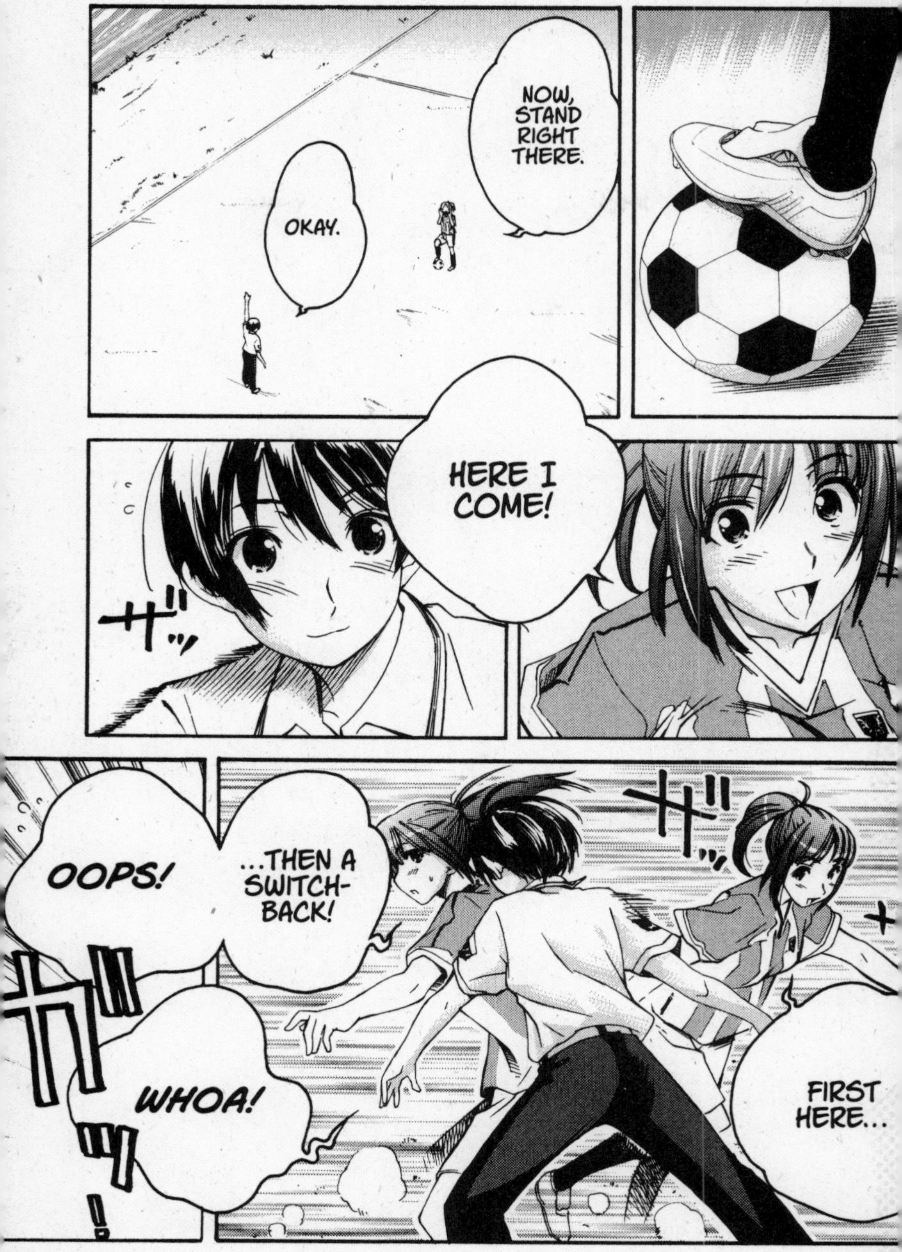
NOW, STAND RIGHT THERE.
OKAY.
HERE I COME!
ザッ
ザッ
FIRST HERE...
...THEN A SWITCH-BACK!
WHOA!
ガッ
OOPS!

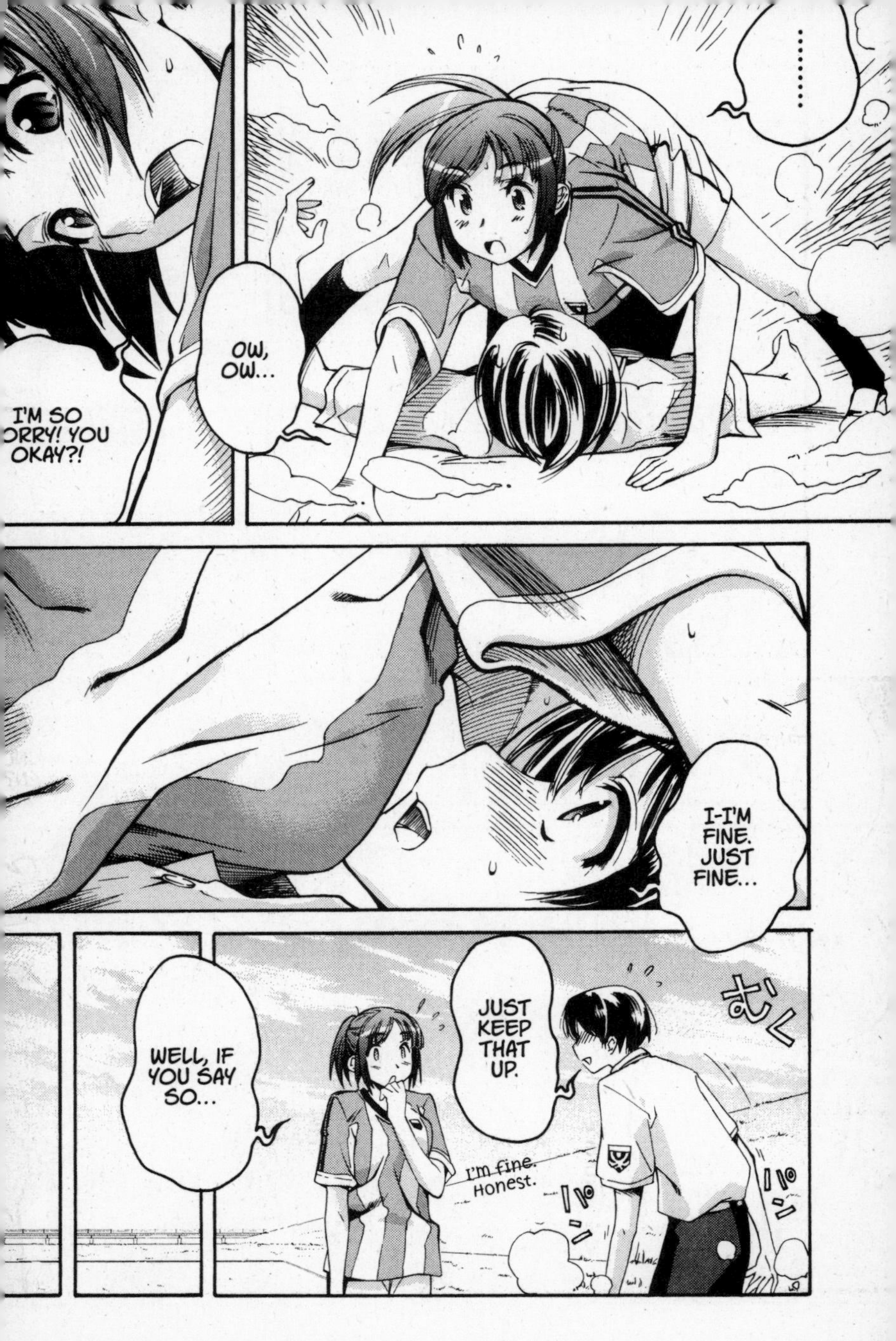
......
OW, OW...
I'M SO ORRY! YOU OKAY?!
I-I'M FINE. JUST FINE...
むく
JUST KEEP THAT UP.
パン
WELL, IF YOU SAY SO...
I'm fine. Honest.
パン

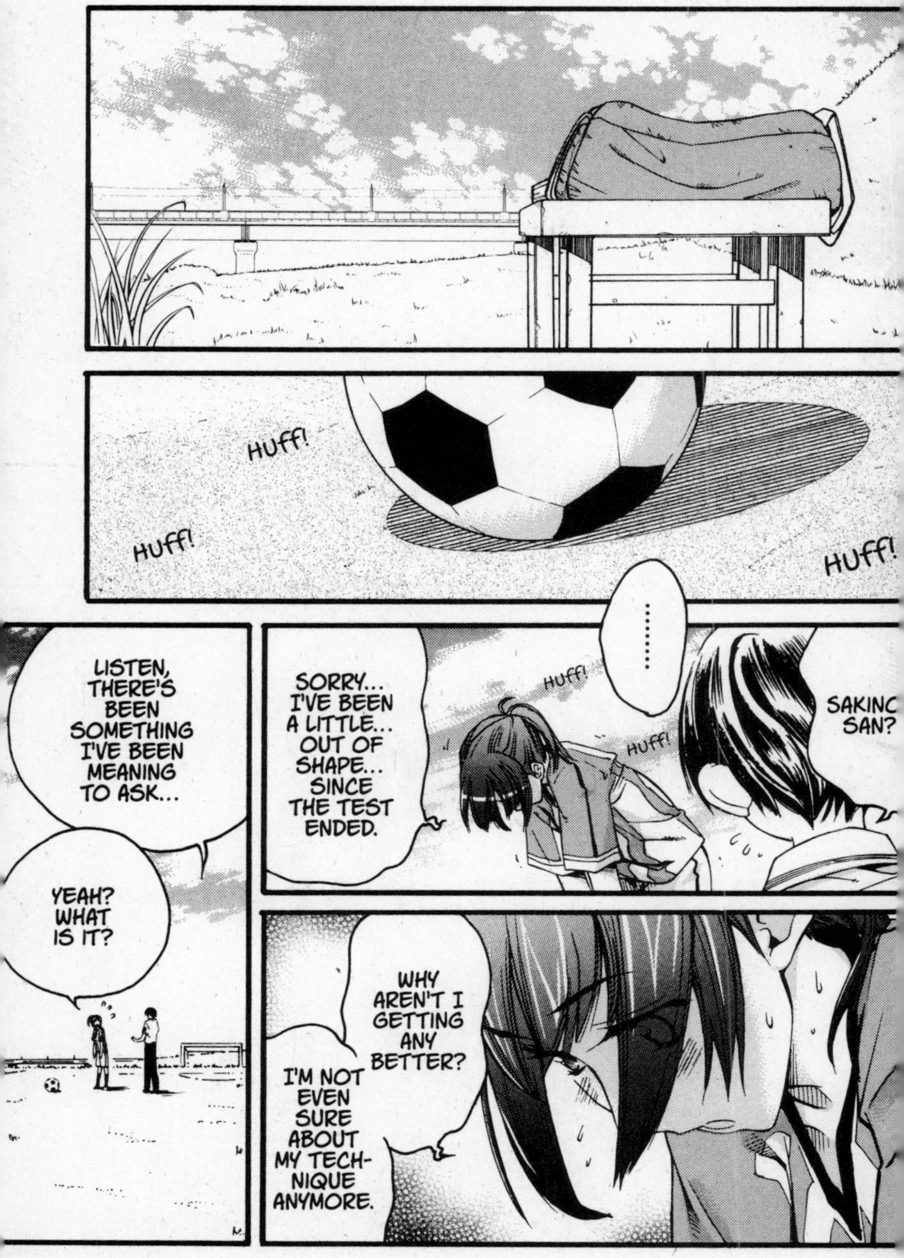

HUFF!
HUFF!
HUFF!
SAKINC SAN?
......
HUFF!
HUFF!
SORRY... I'VE BEEN A LITTLE... OUT OF SHAPE... SINCE THE TEST ENDED.
WHY AREN'T I GETTING ANY BETTER?
I'M NOT EVEN SURE ABOUT MY TECH-NIQUE ANYMORE.
LISTEN, THERE'S BEEN SOMETHING I'VE BEEN MEANING TO ASK...
YEAH? WHAT IS IT?

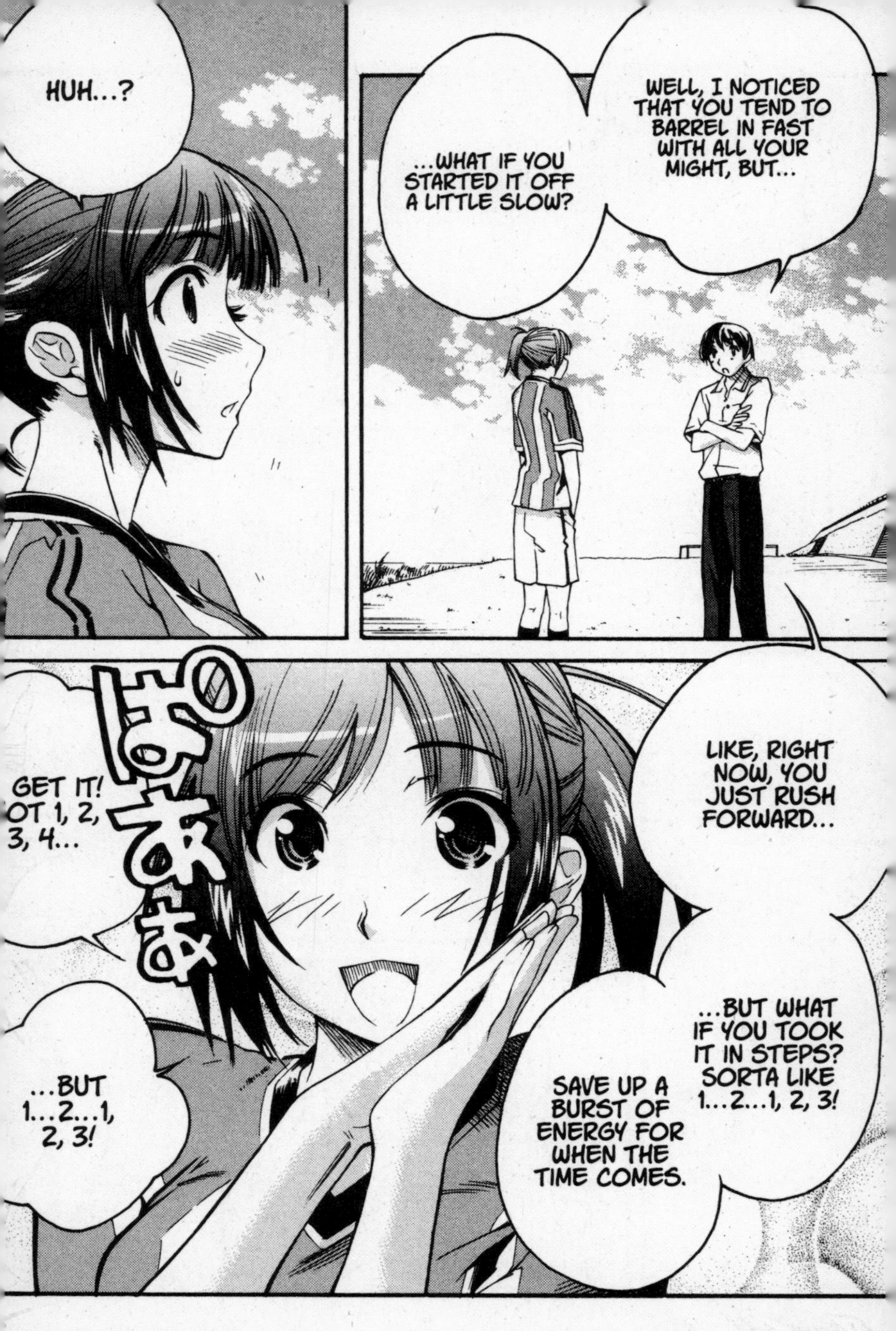
WELL, I NOTICED THAT YOU TEND TO BARREL IN FAST WITH ALL YOUR MIGHT, BUT...
...WHAT IF YOU STARTED IT OFF A LITTLE SLOW?
HUH...?
LIKE, RIGHT NOW, YOU JUST RUSH FORWARD...
...BUT WHAT IF YOU TOOK IT IN STEPS? SORTA LIKE 1...2...1, 2, 3!
SAVE UP A BURST OF ENERGY FOR WHEN THE TIME COMES.
ぱああ
GET IT! OT 1, 2, 3, 4...
...BUT 1...2...1, 2, 3!

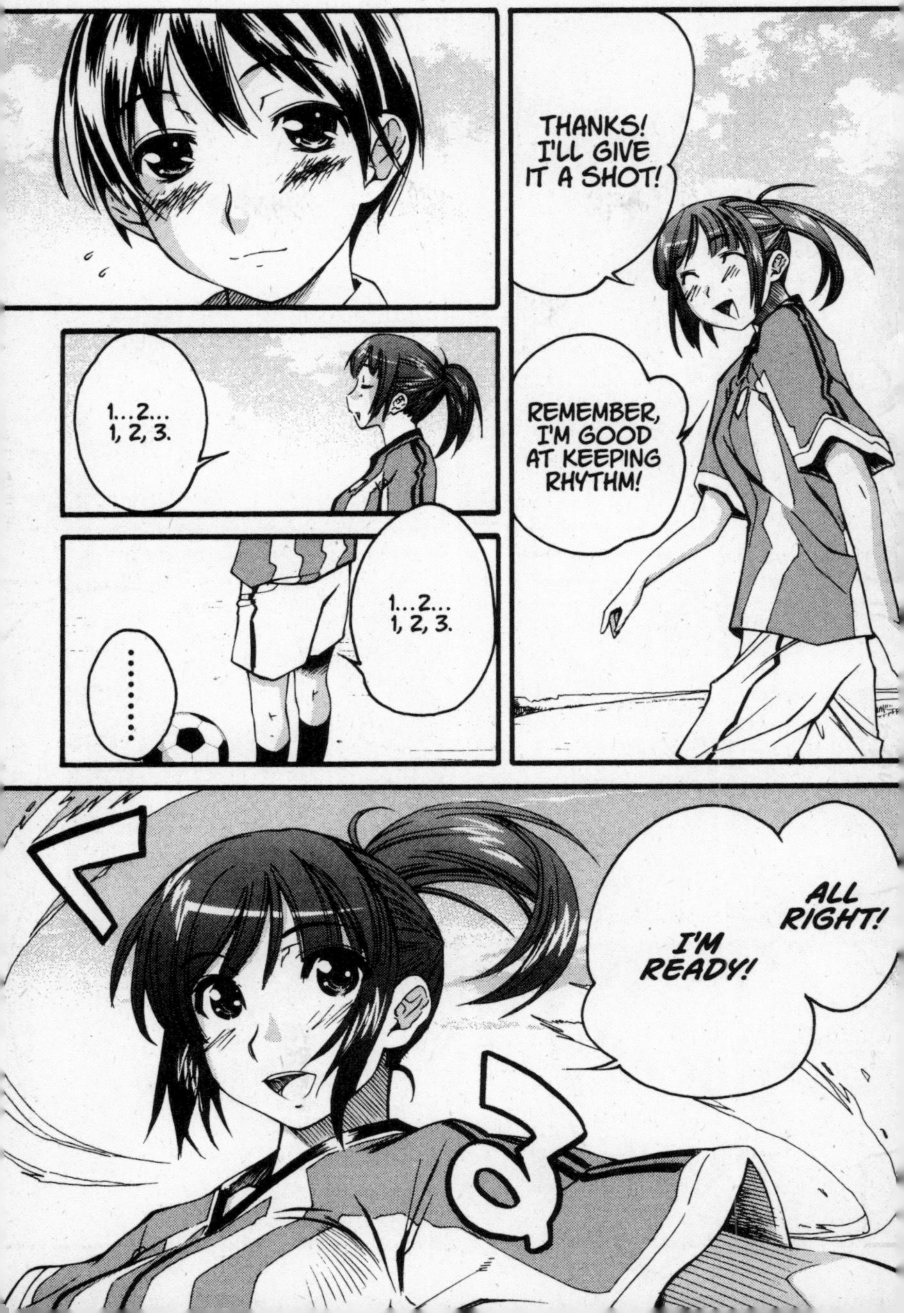
THANKS! I'LL GIVE IT A SHOT!
REMEMBER, I'M GOOD AT KEEPING RHYTHM!
1...2... 1, 2, 3.
1...2... 1, 2, 3.
....
ALL RIGHT! I'M READY!

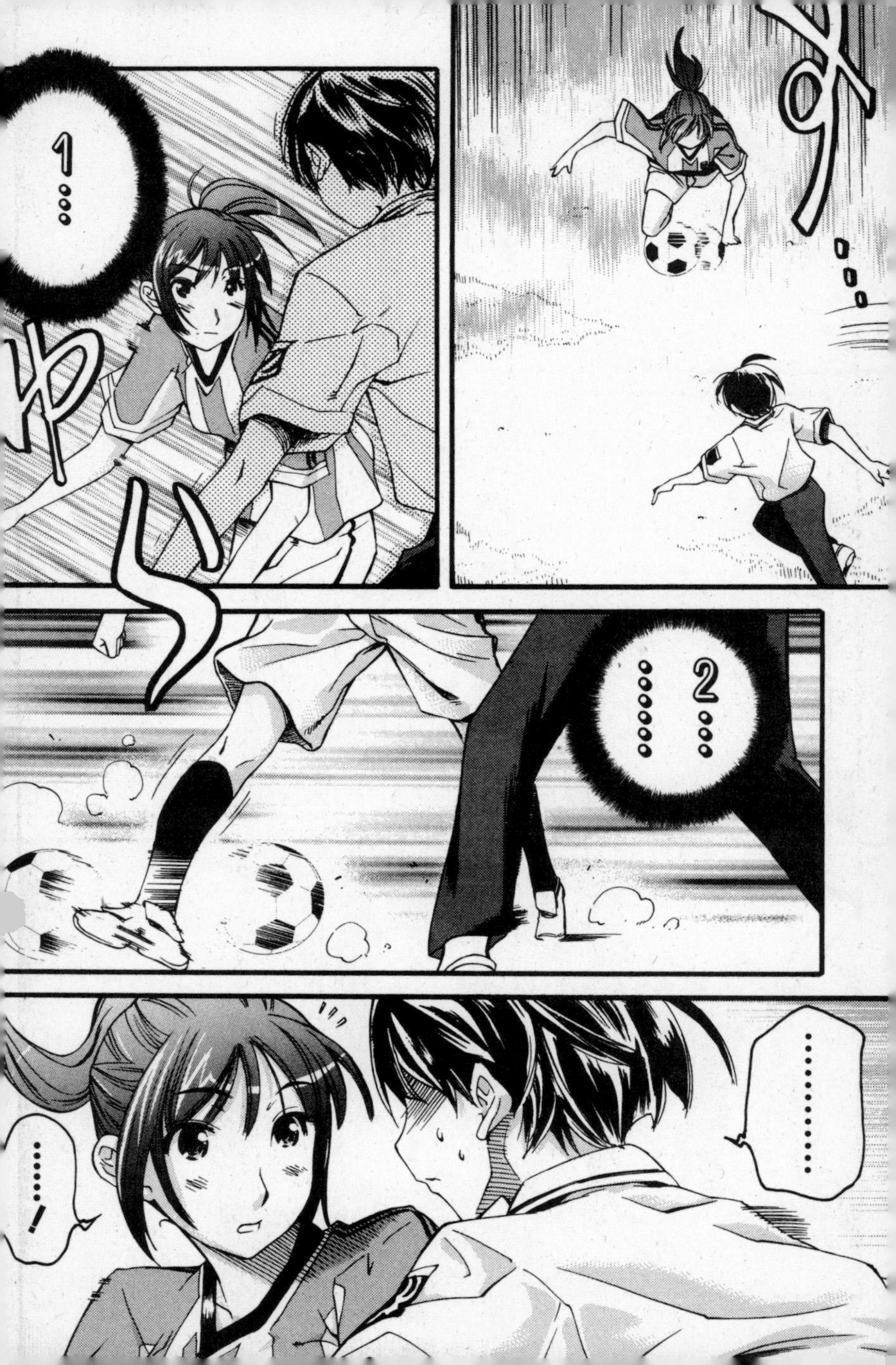
す…
1…
ゆ
2……
……
……!

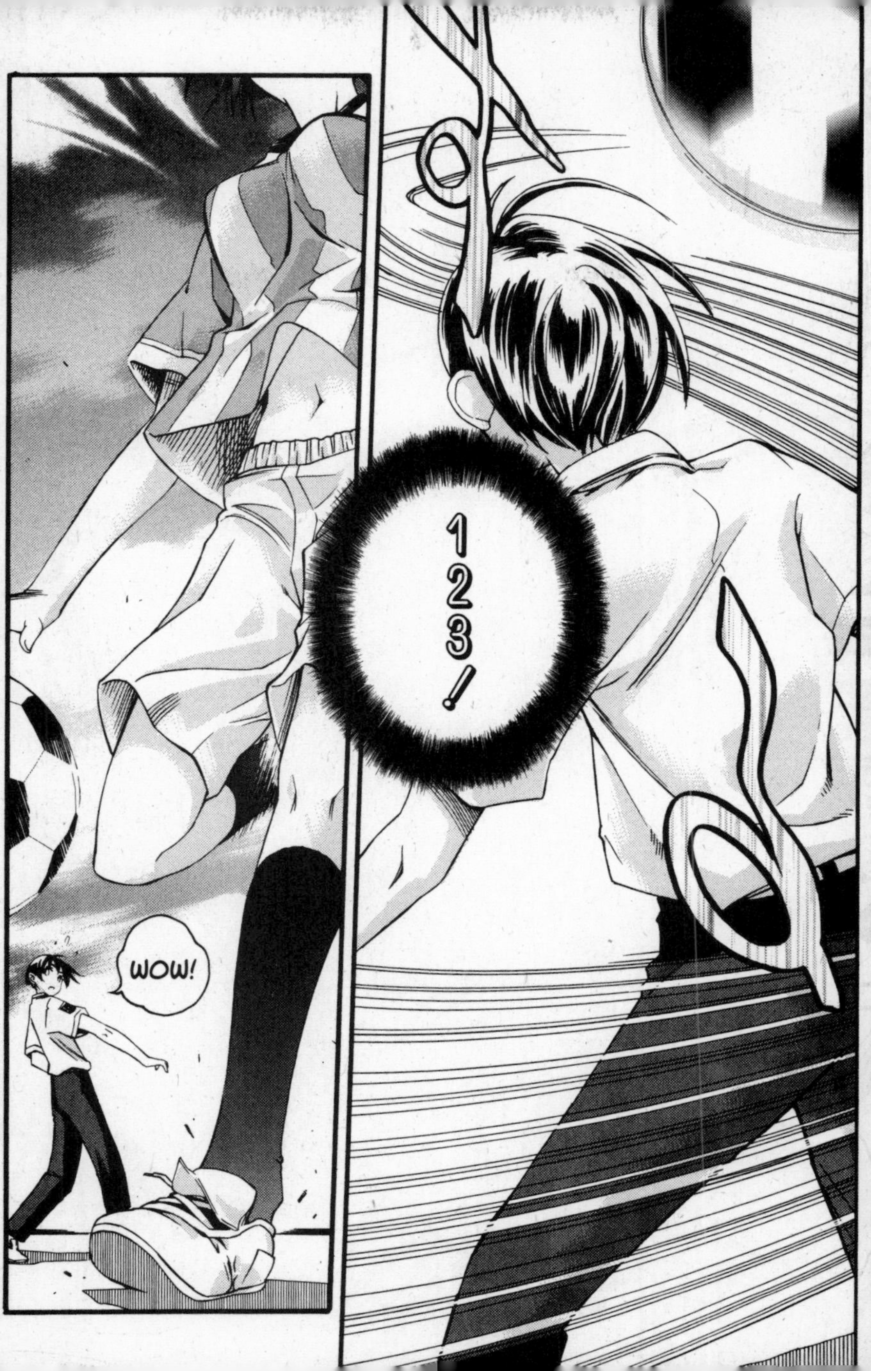
123!
WOW!

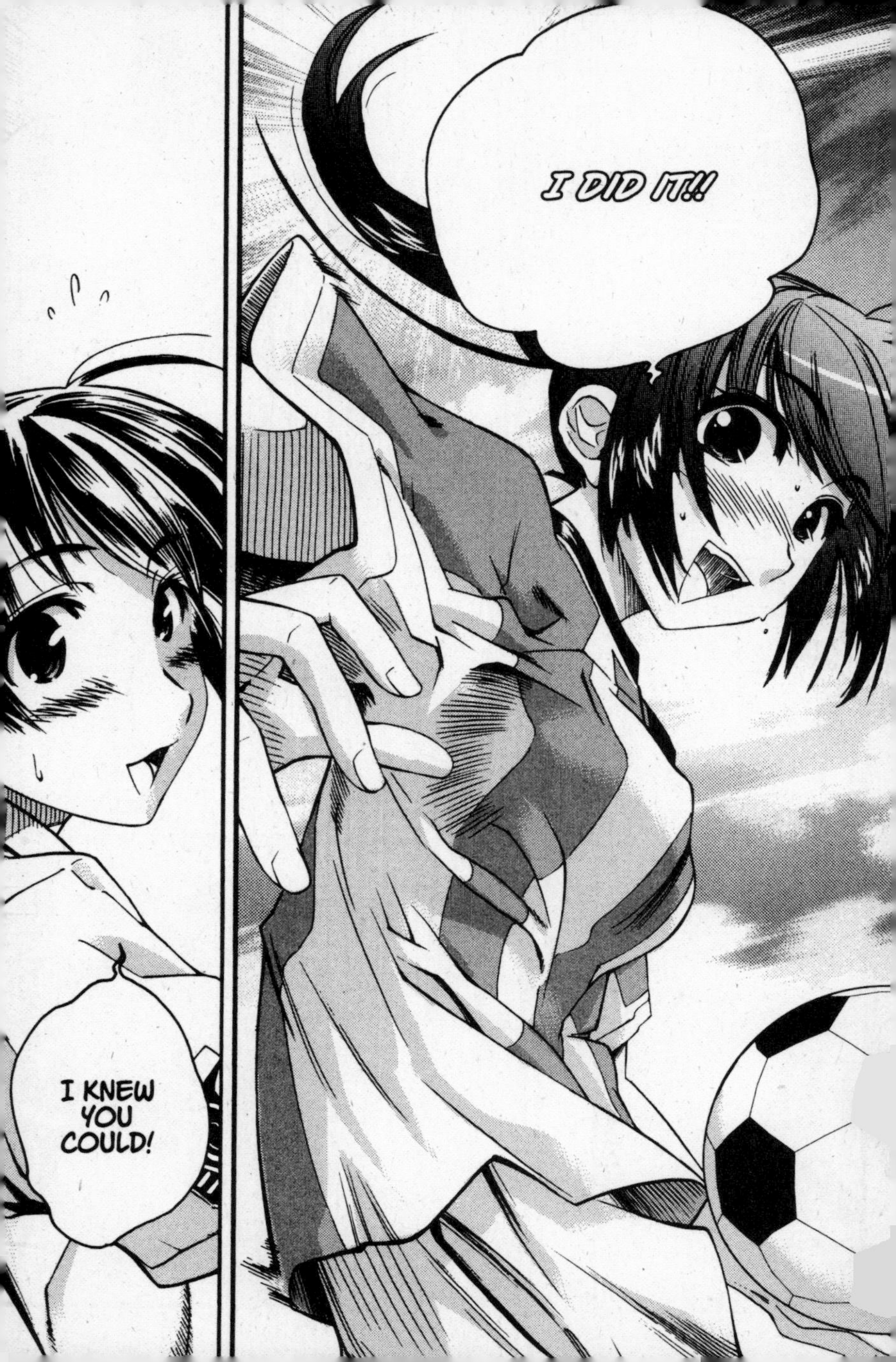
I DID IT!!
I KNEW YOU COULD!

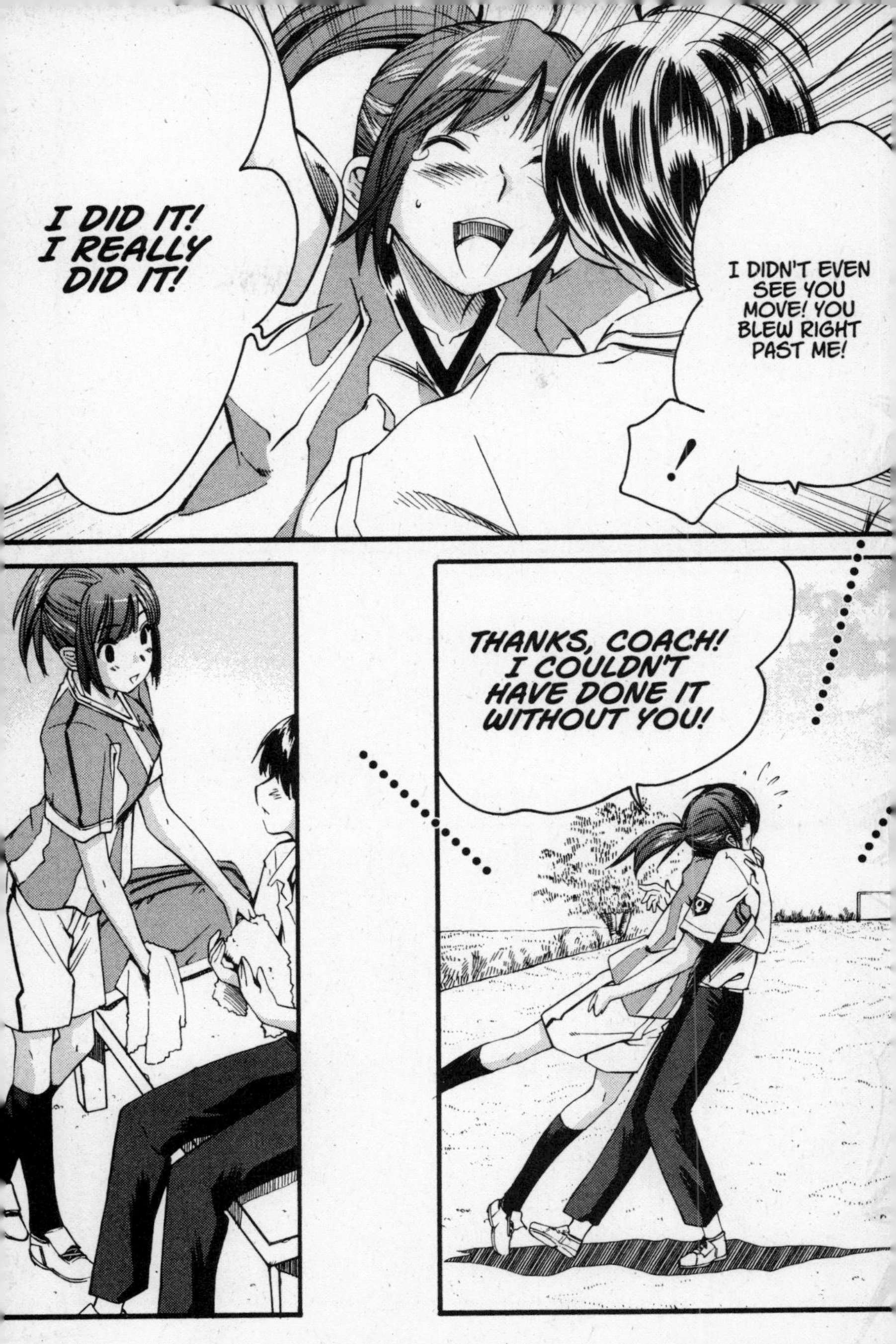
I DIDN'T EVEN SEE YOU MOVE! YOU BLEW RIGHT PAST ME!
!
I DID IT! I REALLY DID IT!
THANKS, COACH! I COULDN'T HAVE DONE IT WITHOUT YOU!

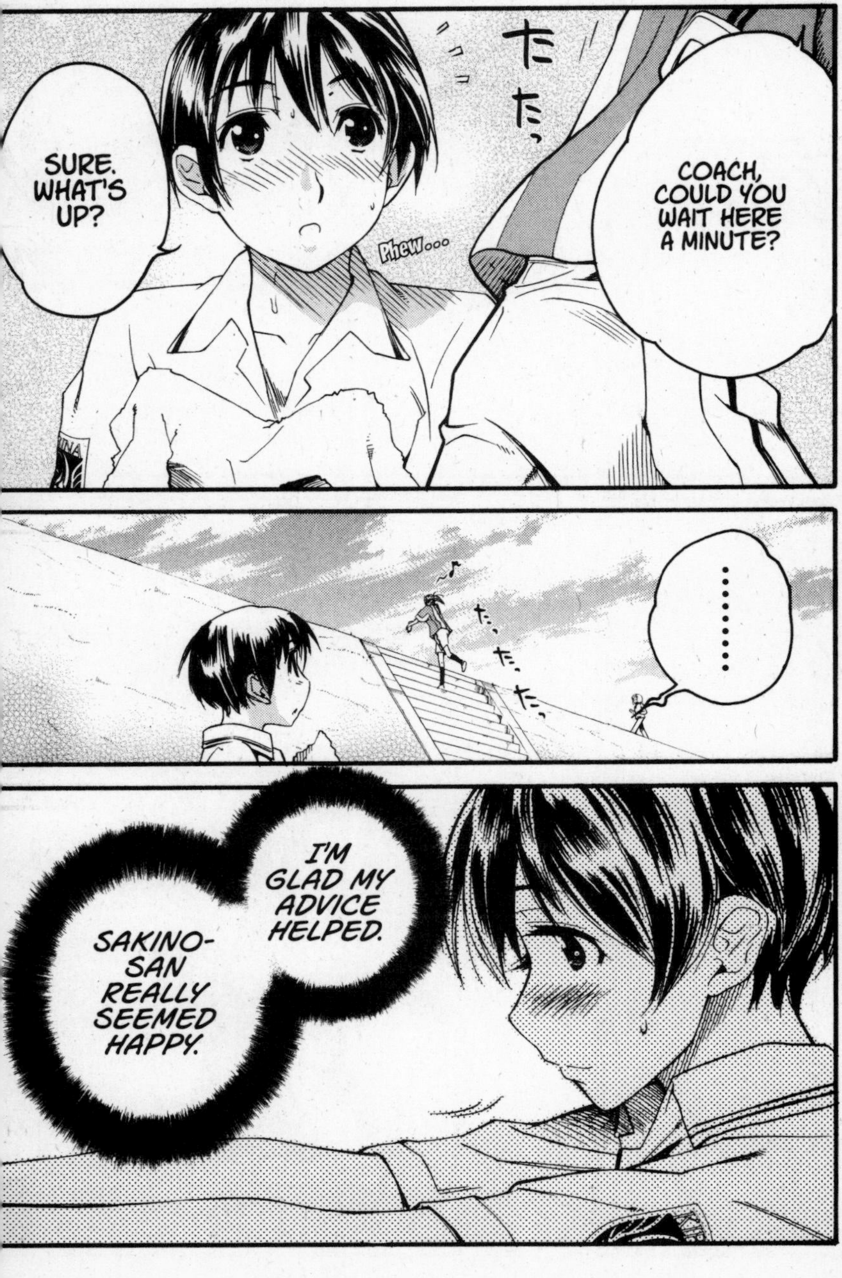
COACH, COULD YOU WAIT HERE A MINUTE?
たた、
SURE. WHAT'S UP?
Phew...
......
た、た、た、
I'M GLAD MY ADVICE HELPED.
SAKINO-SAN REALLY SEEMED HAPPY.

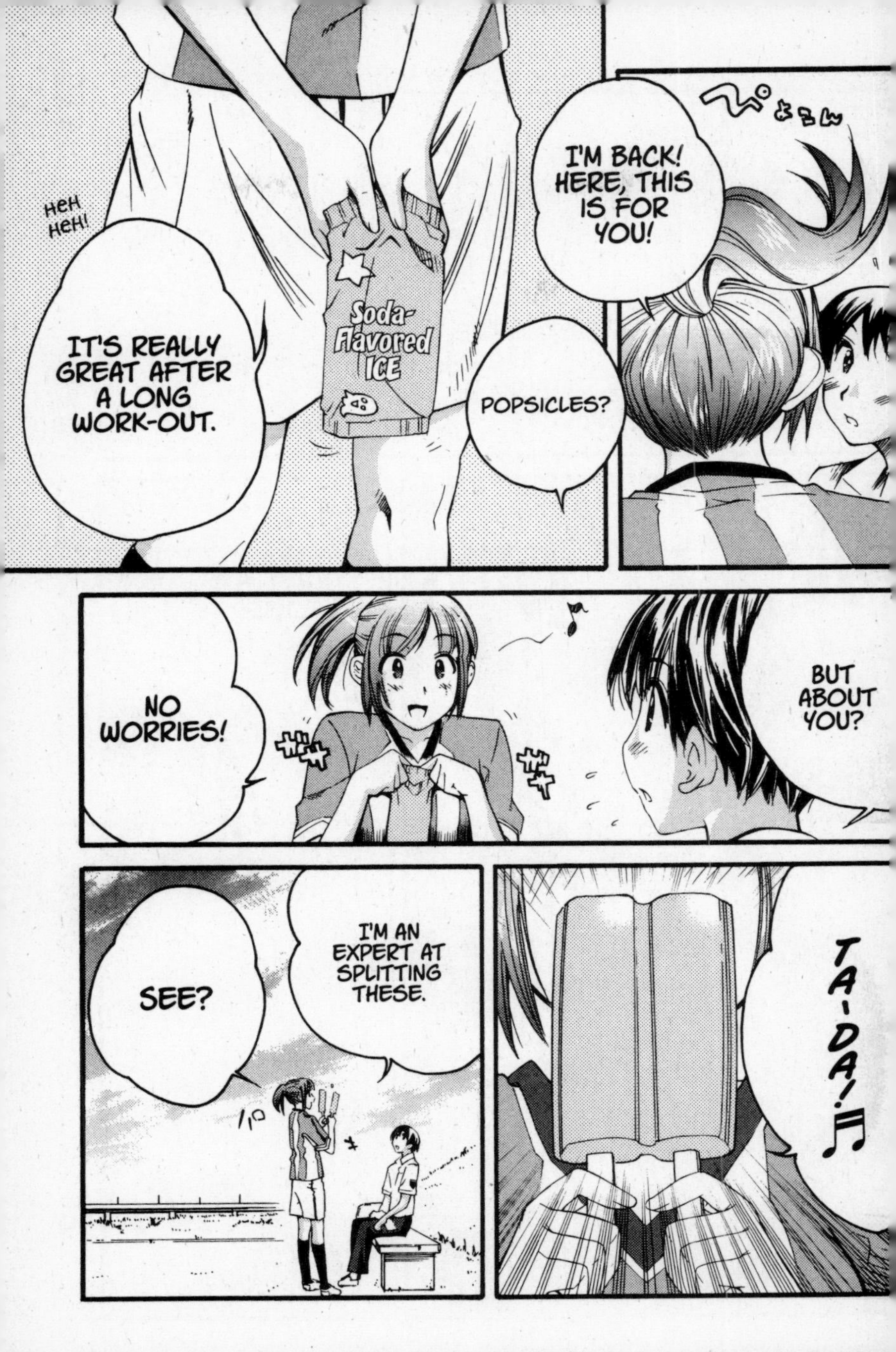
I'M BACK! HERE, THIS IS FOR YOU!
POPSICLES?
Soda-Flavored ICE
HEH HEH!
IT'S REALLY GREAT AFTER A LONG WORK-OUT.
BUT ABOUT YOU?
NO WORRIES!
TA-DA!
I'M AN EXPERT AT SPLITTING THESE.
SEE?

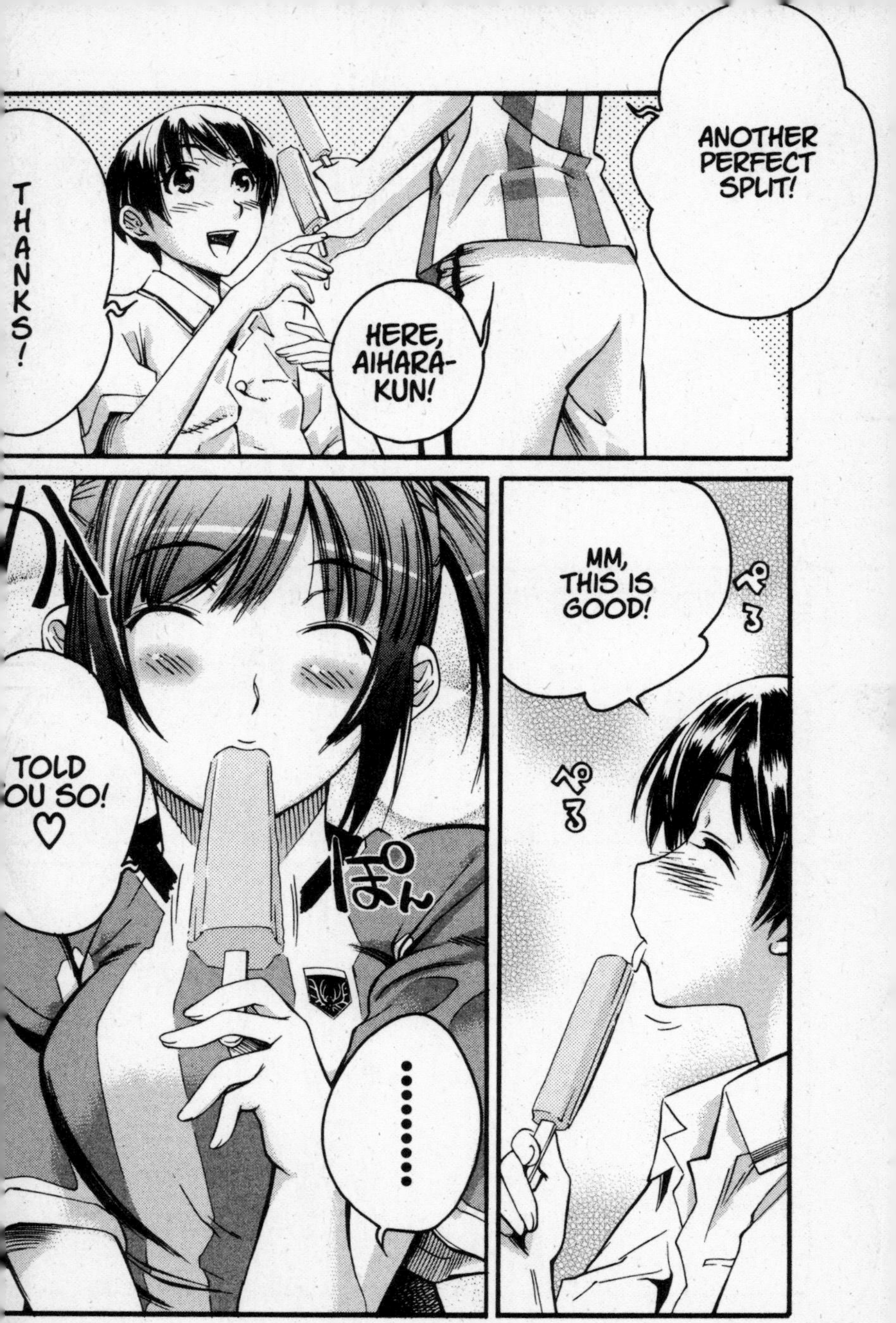
ANOTHER PERFECT SPLIT!
HERE, AIHARA-KUN!
THANKS!
MM, THIS IS GOOD!
ぺろ
ぺろ
ぽん
TOLD
OU SO! ♡
....

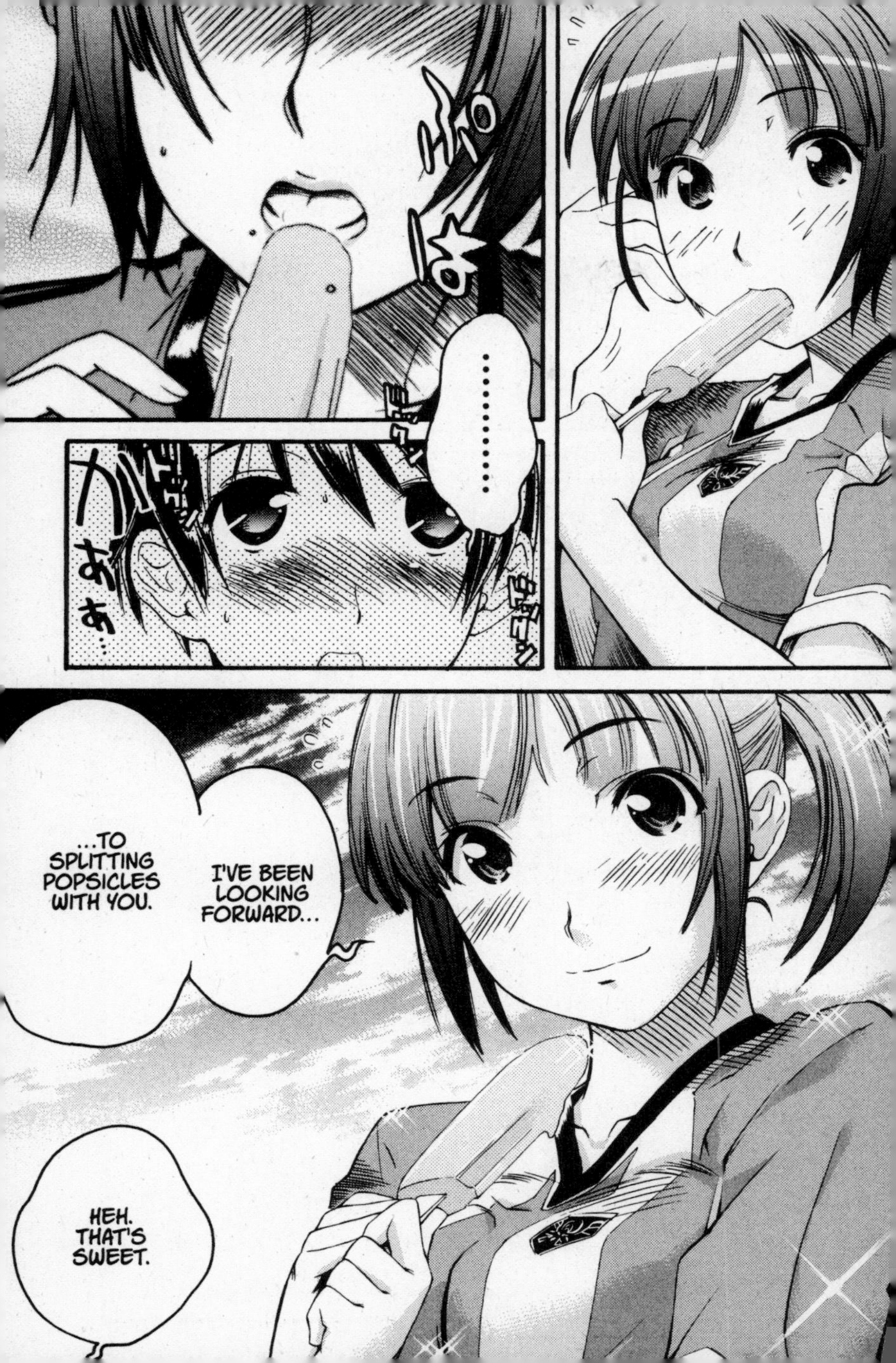
……
かぁぁ…
I'VE BEEN LOOKING FORWARD...
...TO SPLITTING POPSICLES WITH YOU.
HEH. THAT'S SWEET.

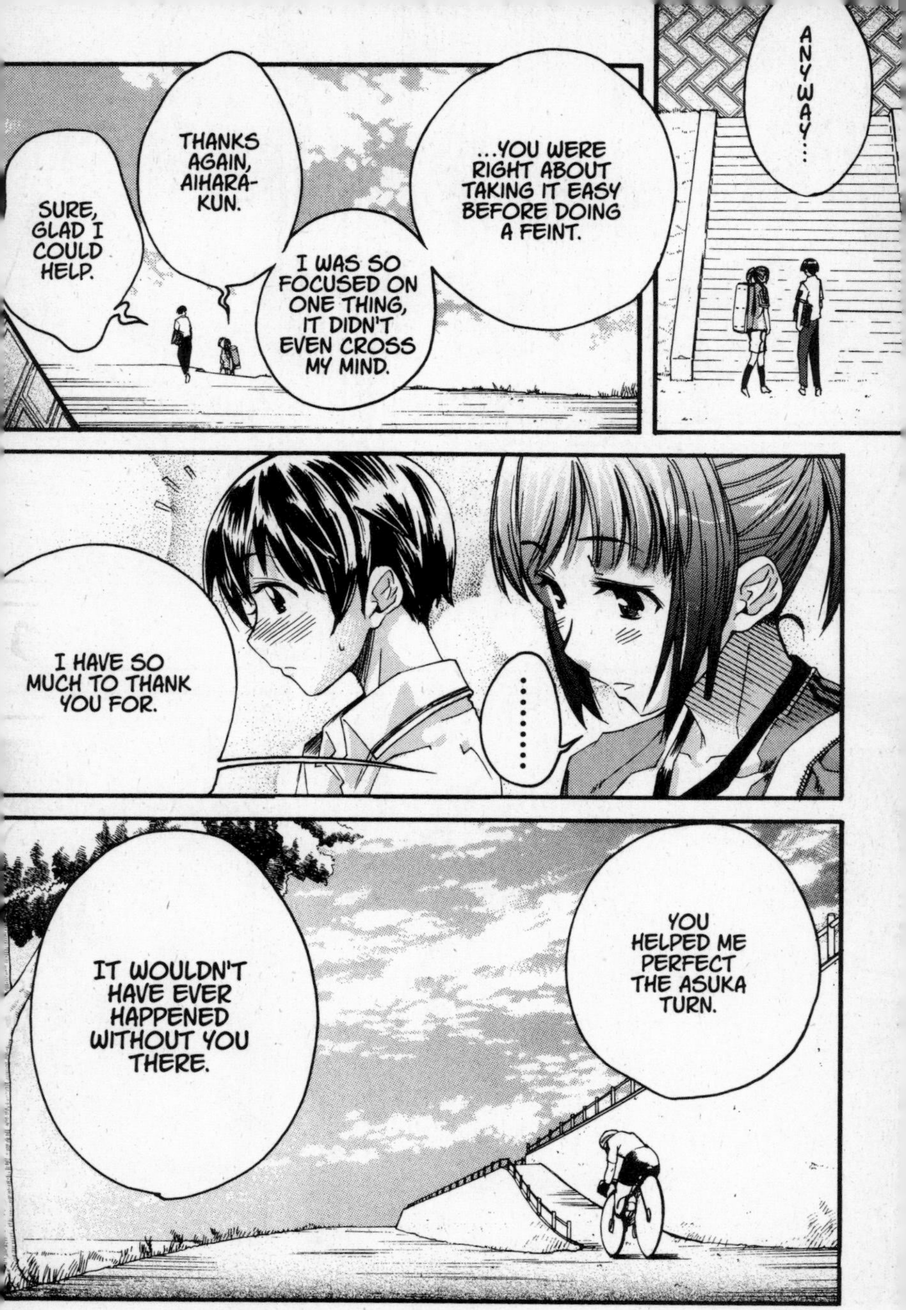
ANYWAY...
...YOU WERE RIGHT ABOUT TAKING IT EASY BEFORE DOING A FEINT.
I WAS SO FOCUSED ON ONE THING, IT DIDN'T EVEN CROSS MY MIND.
THANKS AGAIN, AIHARA-KUN.
SURE, GLAD I COULD HELP.
......
I HAVE SO MUCH TO THANK YOU FOR.
YOU HELPED ME PERFECT THE ASUKA TURN.
IT WOULDN'T HAVE EVER HAPPENED WITHOUT YOU THERE.

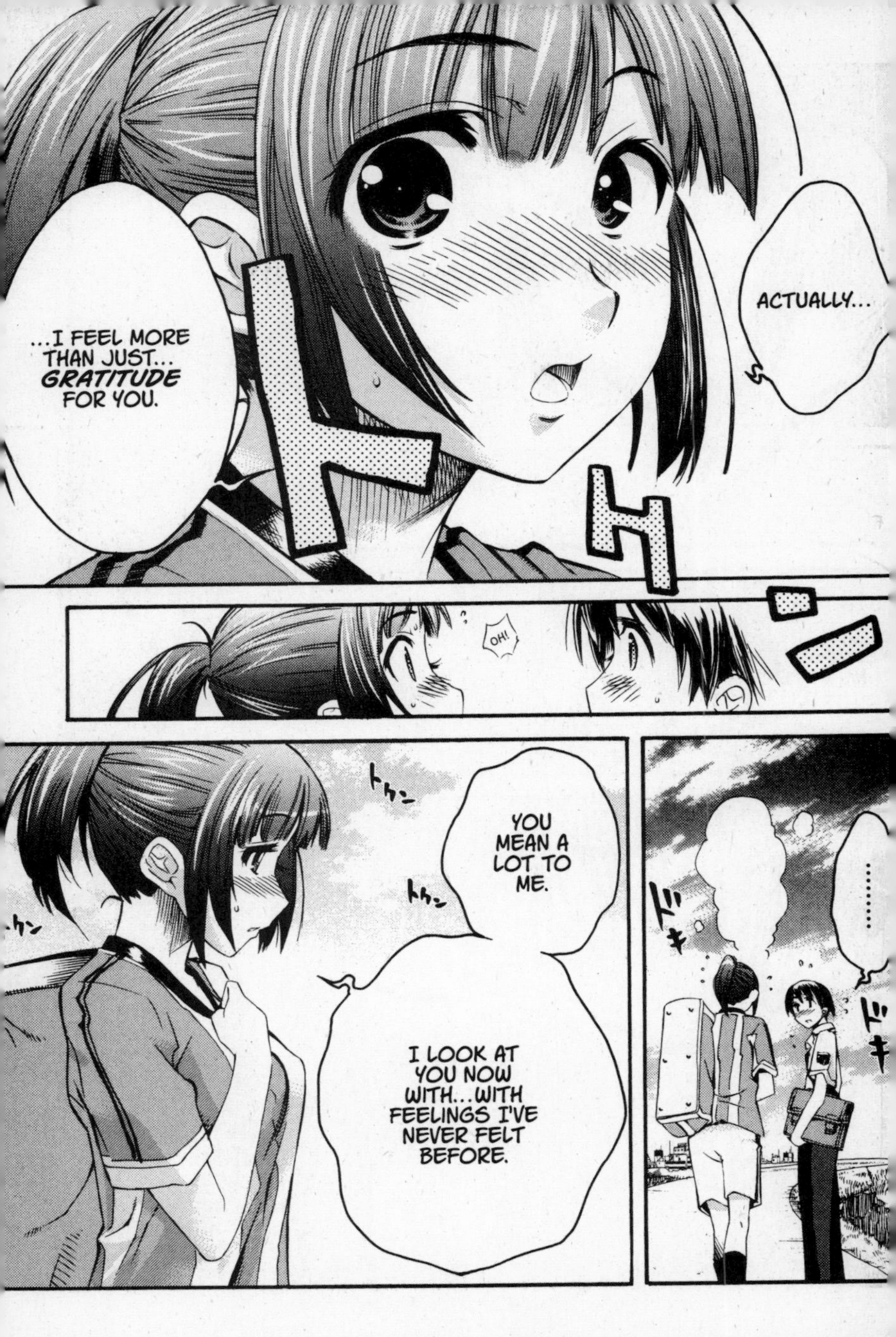
ACTUALLY...
...I FEEL MORE THAN JUST... *GRATITUDE* FOR YOU.
OH!
......
ドキ
ドキ
YOU MEAN A LOT TO ME.
I LOOK AT YOU NOW WITH...WITH FEELINGS I'VE NEVER FELT BEFORE.

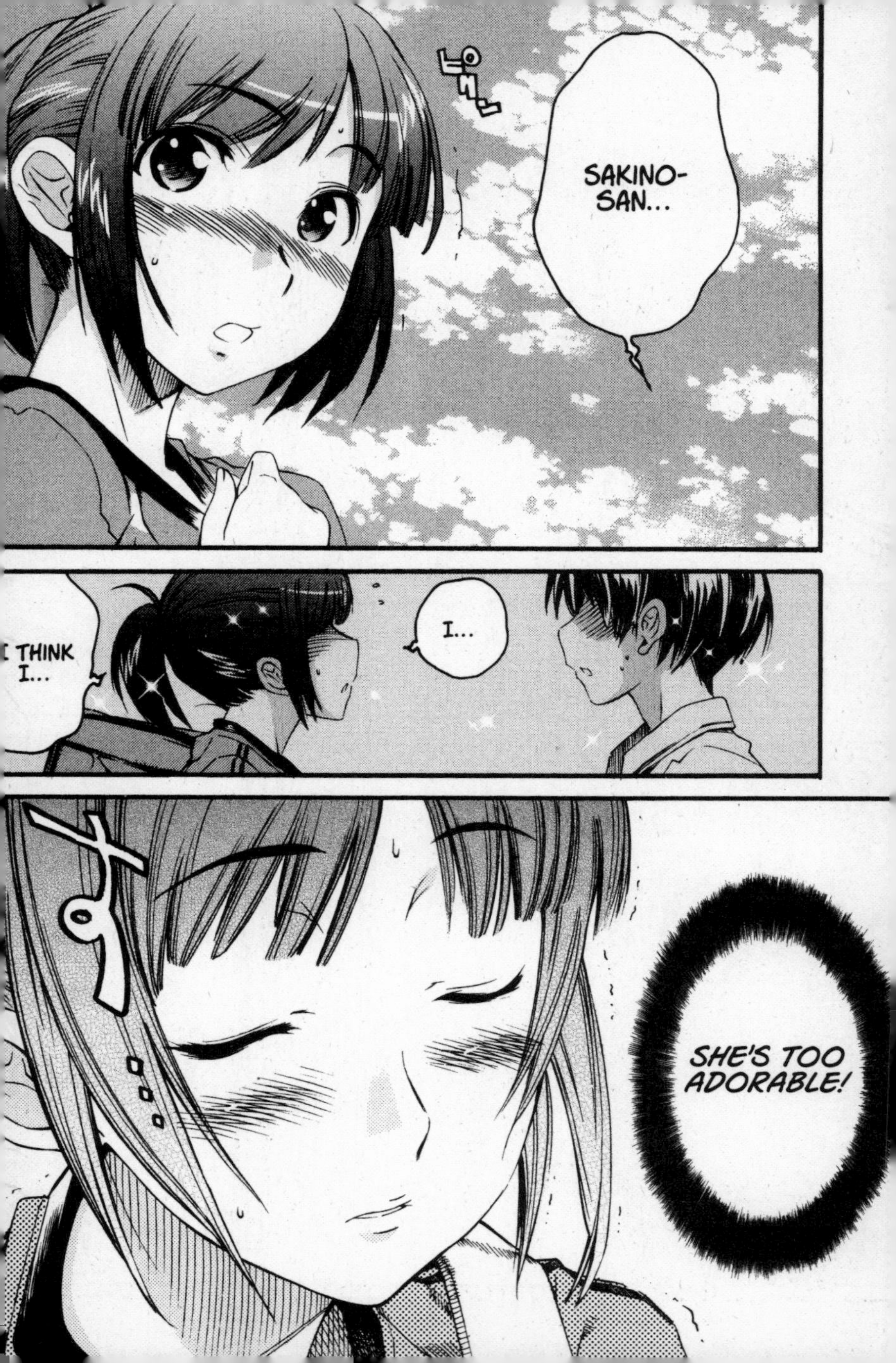
SAKINO-SAN...
I...
I THINK I...
SHE'S TOO ADORABLE!

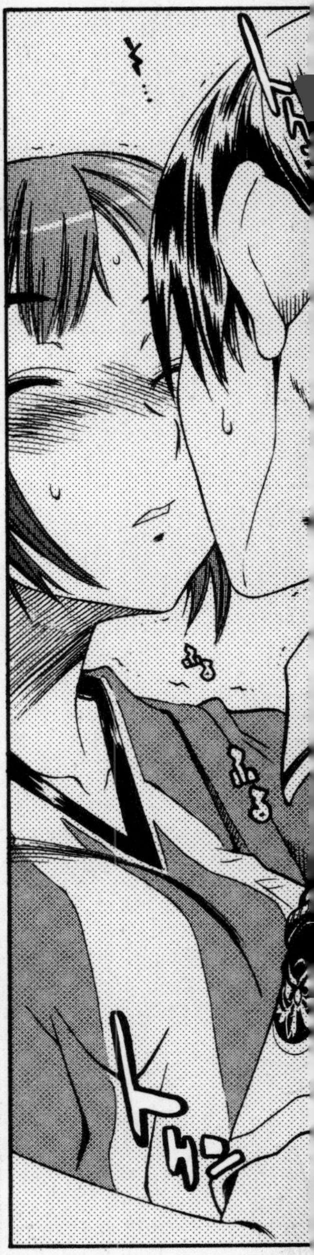
ン…
ドクン
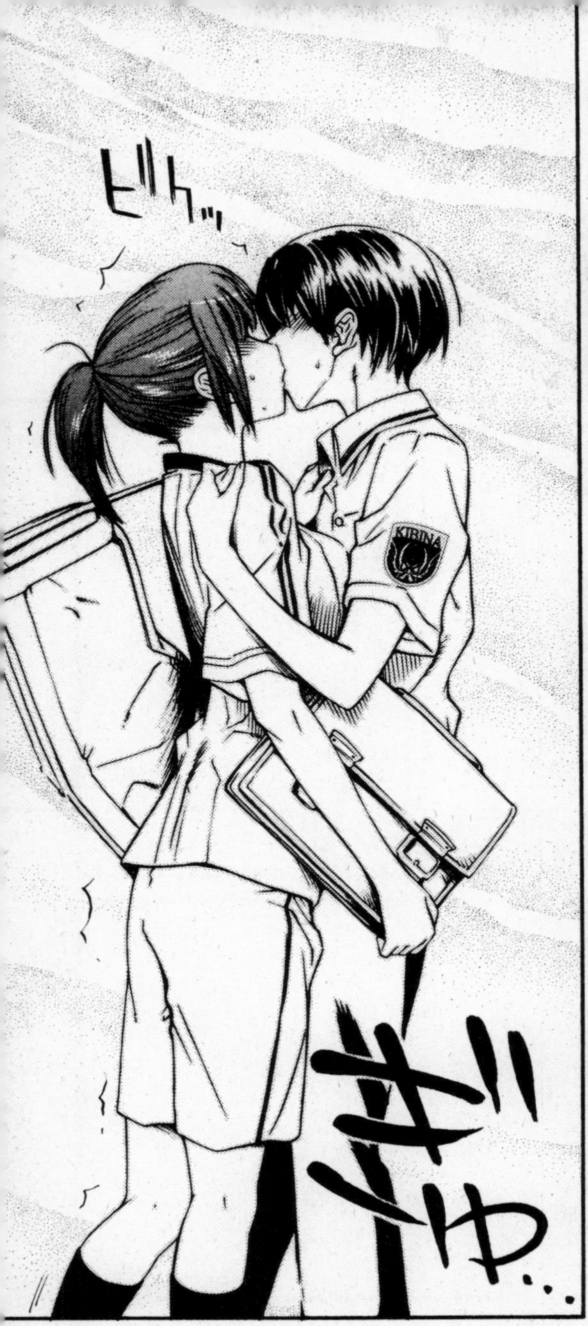
ビクッ
ギュ…

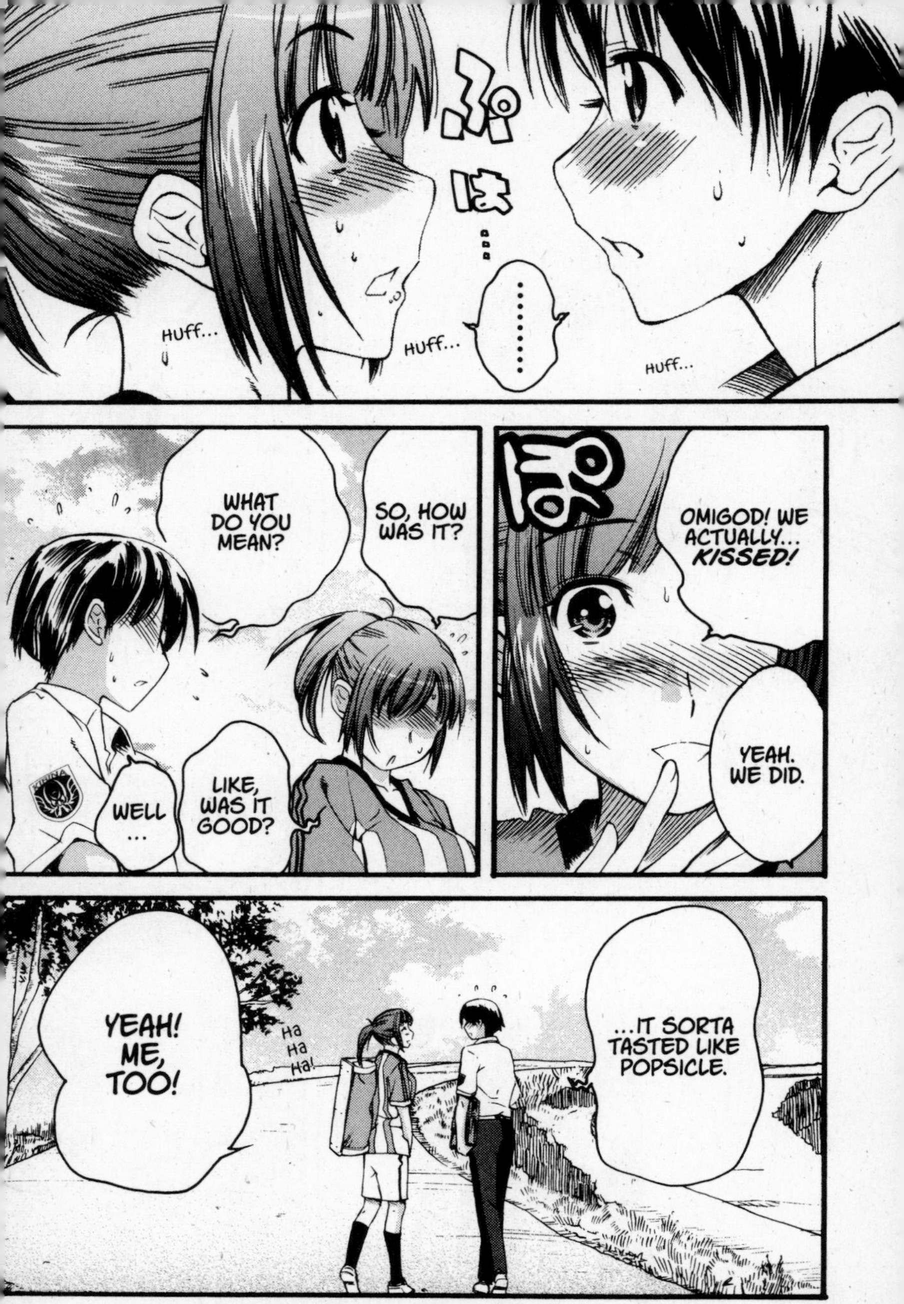
ぷは
...
HUFF...
....
HUFF...
HUFF...
ぽ
OMIGOD! WE ACTUALLY... KISSED!
YEAH. WE DID.
SO, HOW WAS IT?
WHAT DO YOU MEAN?
LIKE, WAS IT GOOD?
WELL ...
...IT SORTA TASTED LIKE POPSICLE.
Ha Ha Ha!
YEAH! ME, TOO!

[Asuka 6th KISS END]

キスキス *kimikiss

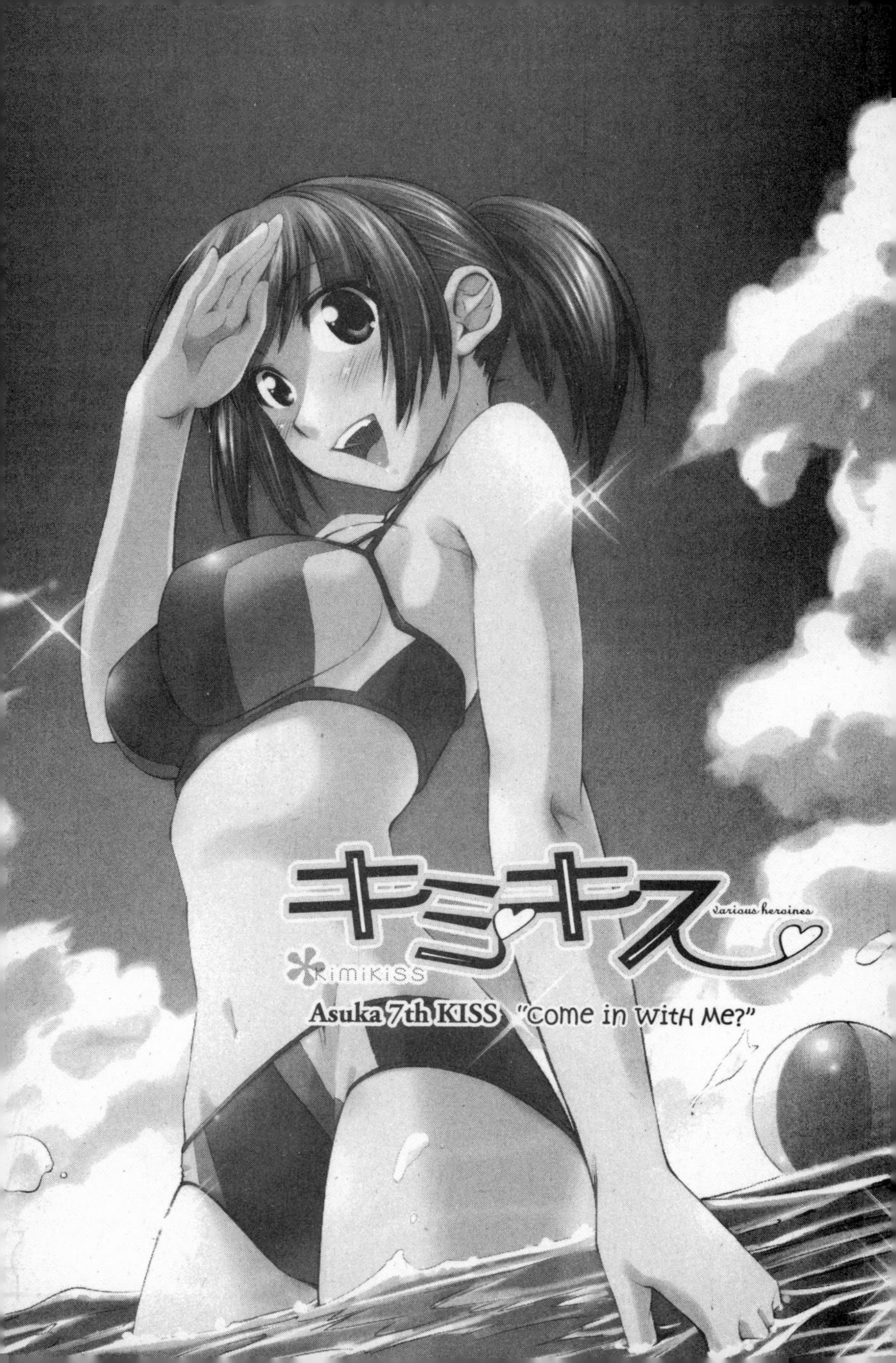
キミキス
various heroines
KimiKiSS
Asuka 7th KISS "Come in With Me?"

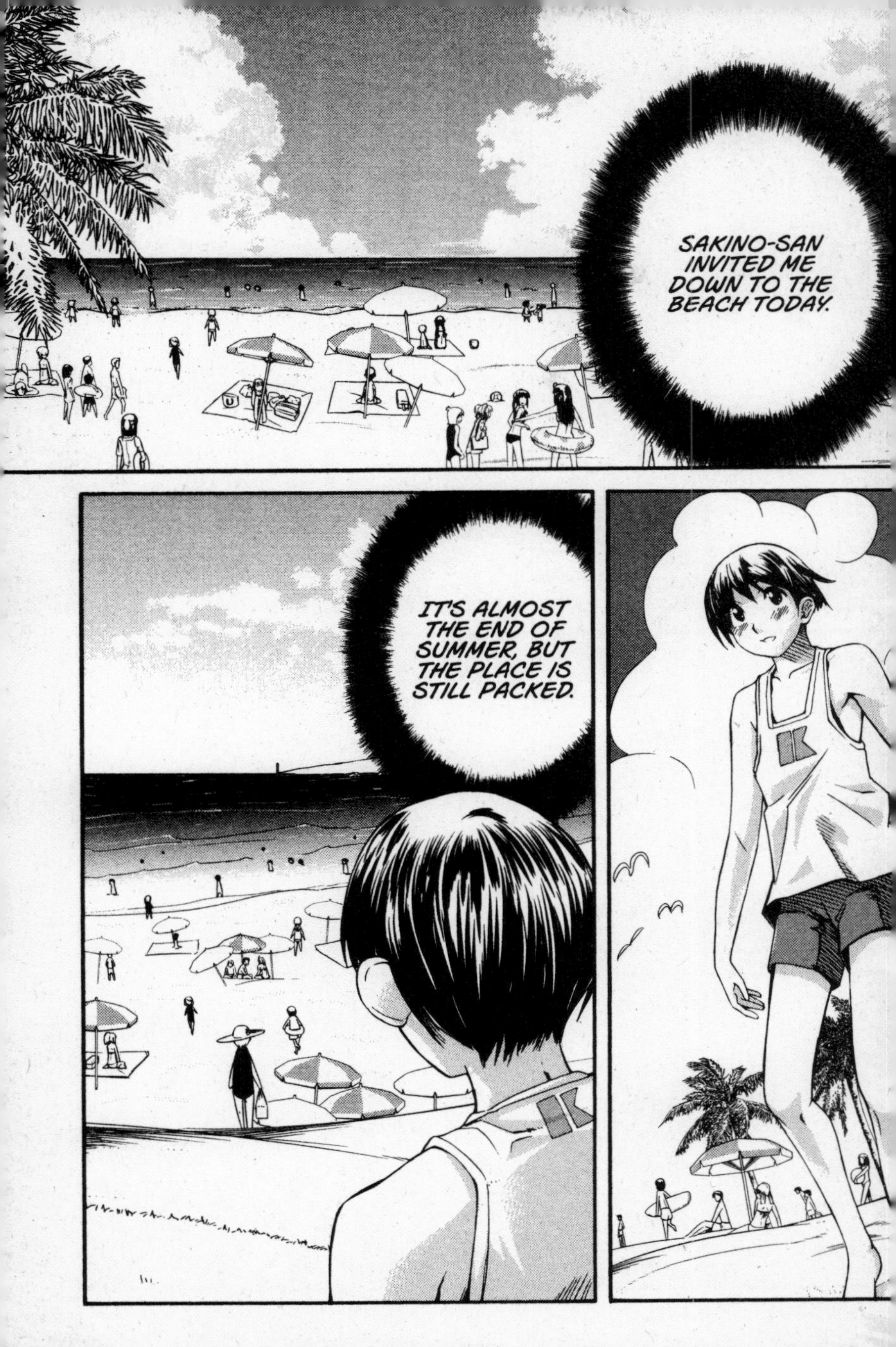
SAKINO-SAN INVITED ME DOWN TO THE BEACH TODAY.
IT'S ALMOST THE END OF SUMMER, BUT THE PLACE IS STILL PACKED.

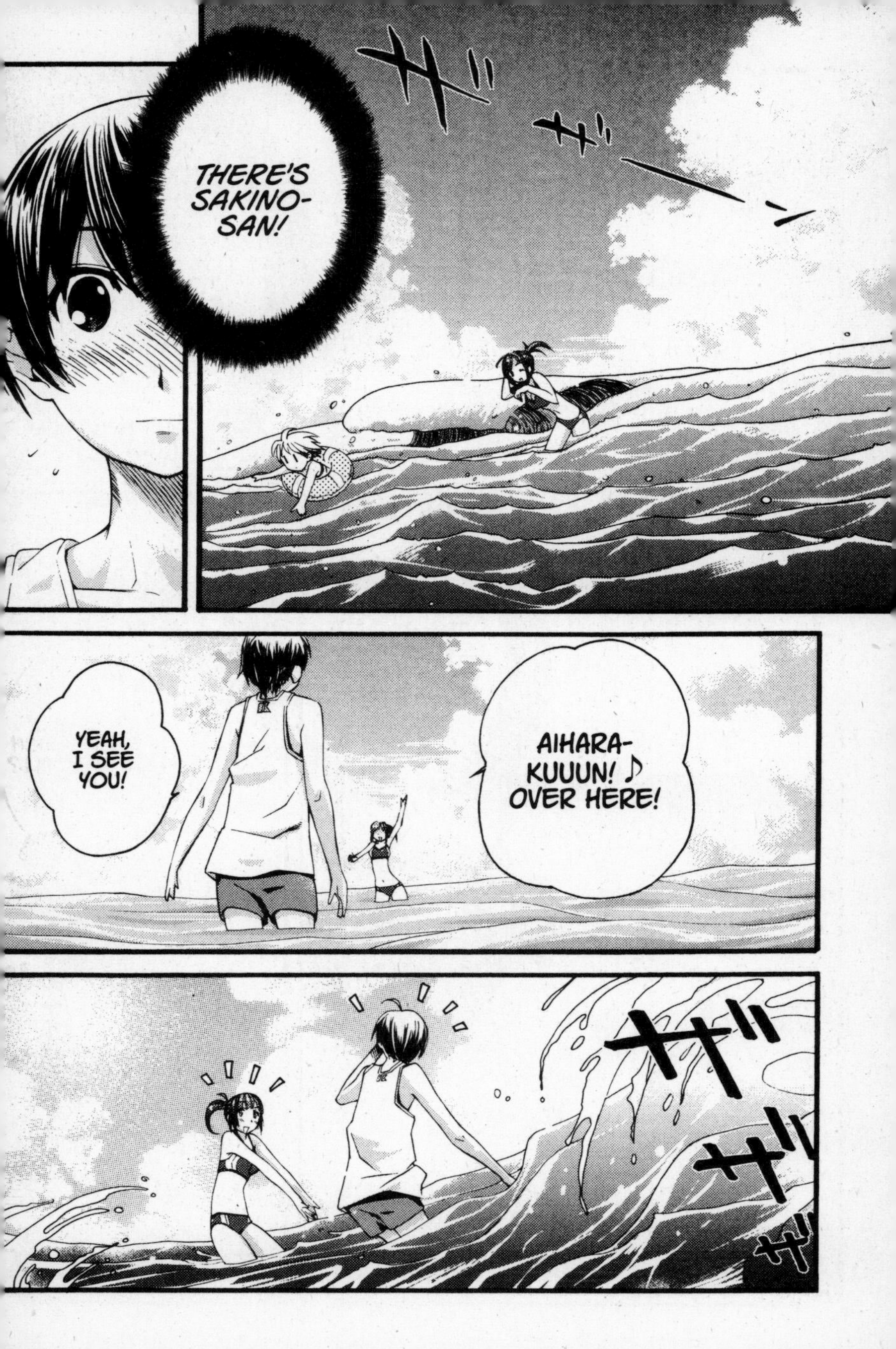
THERE'S SAKINO-SAN!
AIHARA-KUUUN! ♪ OVER HERE!
YEAH, I SEE YOU!

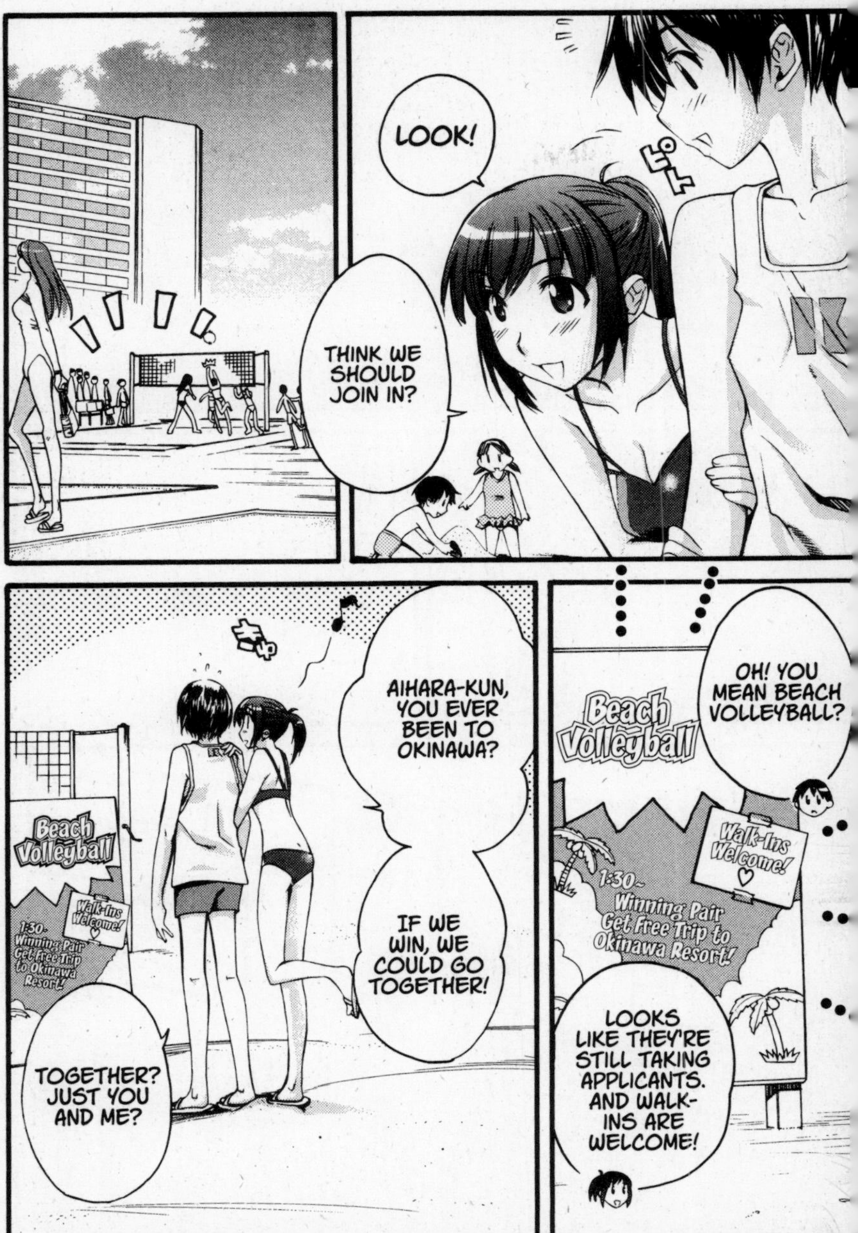
LOOK!
THINK WE SHOULD JOIN IN?
OH! YOU MEAN BEACH VOLLEYBALL?
Beach Volleyball
Walk-Ins Welcome!
1:30~ Winning Pair Get Free Trip to Okinawa Resort!
LOOKS LIKE THEY'RE STILL TAKING APPLICANTS. AND WALK-INS ARE WELCOME!
AIHARA-KUN, YOU EVER BEEN TO OKINAWA?
IF WE WIN, WE COULD GO TOGETHER!
Beach Volleyball
Walk-Ins Welcome!
1:30~ Winning Pair Get Free Trip to Okinawa Resort!
TOGETHER? JUST YOU AND ME?

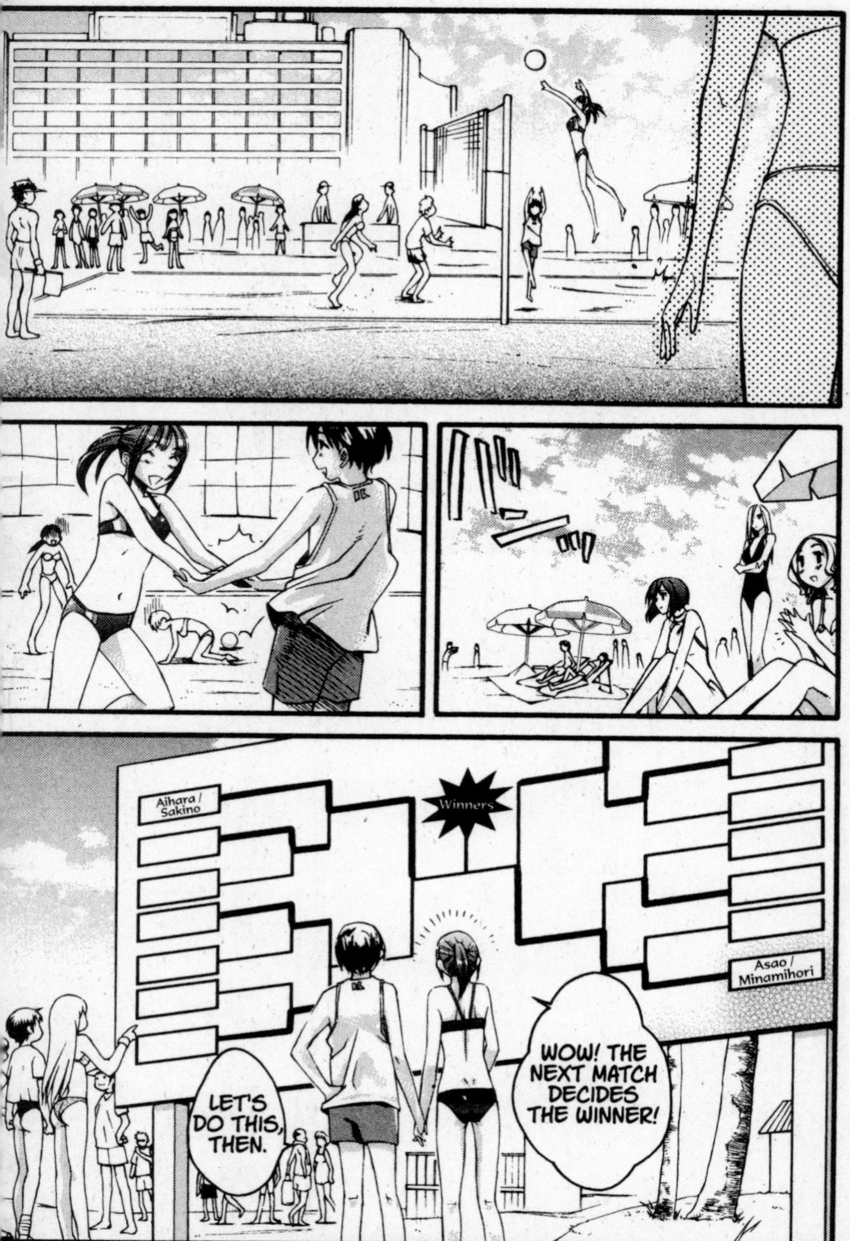
Winners
Aihara / Sakino
Asao / Minamihori
WOW! THE NEXT MATCH DECIDES THE WINNER!
LET'S DO THIS, THEN.

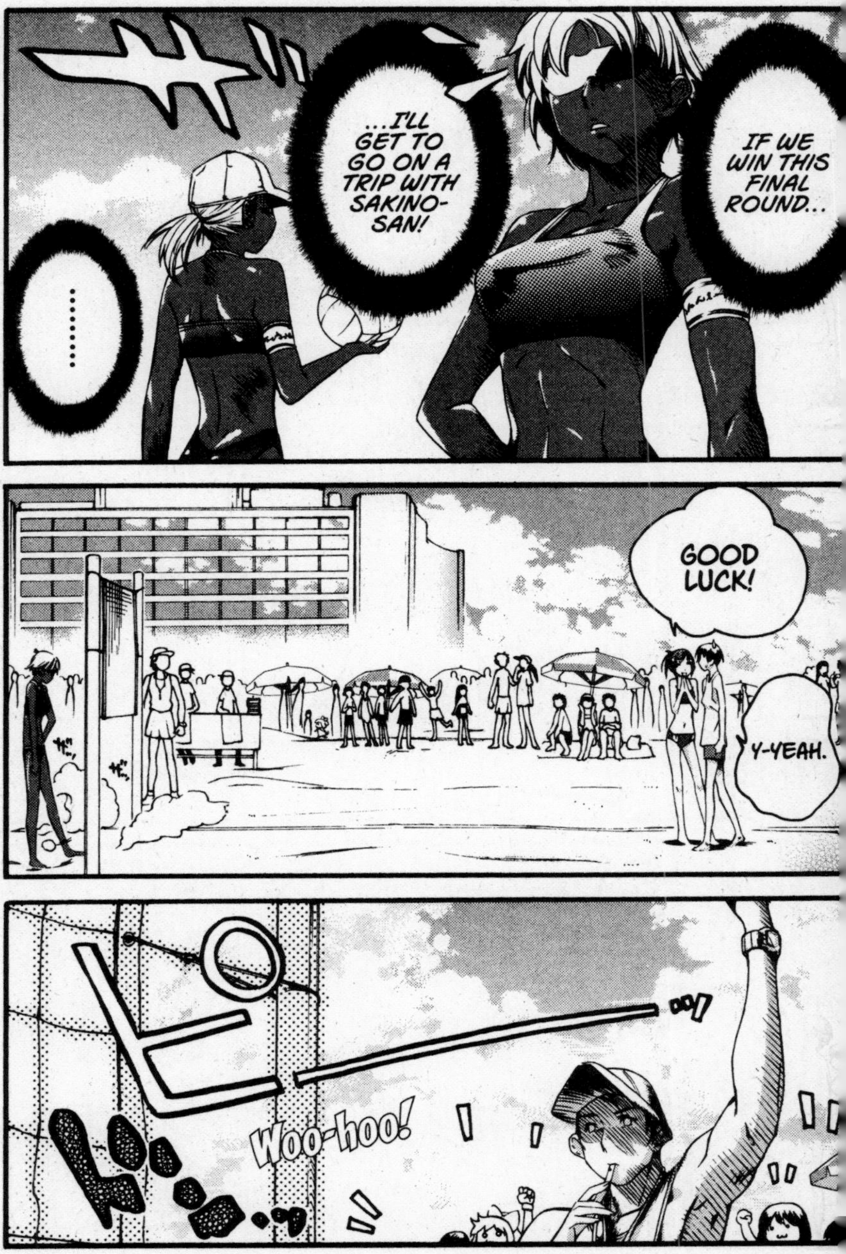
IF WE WIN THIS FINAL ROUND...
...I'LL GET TO GO ON A TRIP WITH SAKINO-SAN!
......
GOOD LUCK!
Y-YEAH.
Woo-hoo!

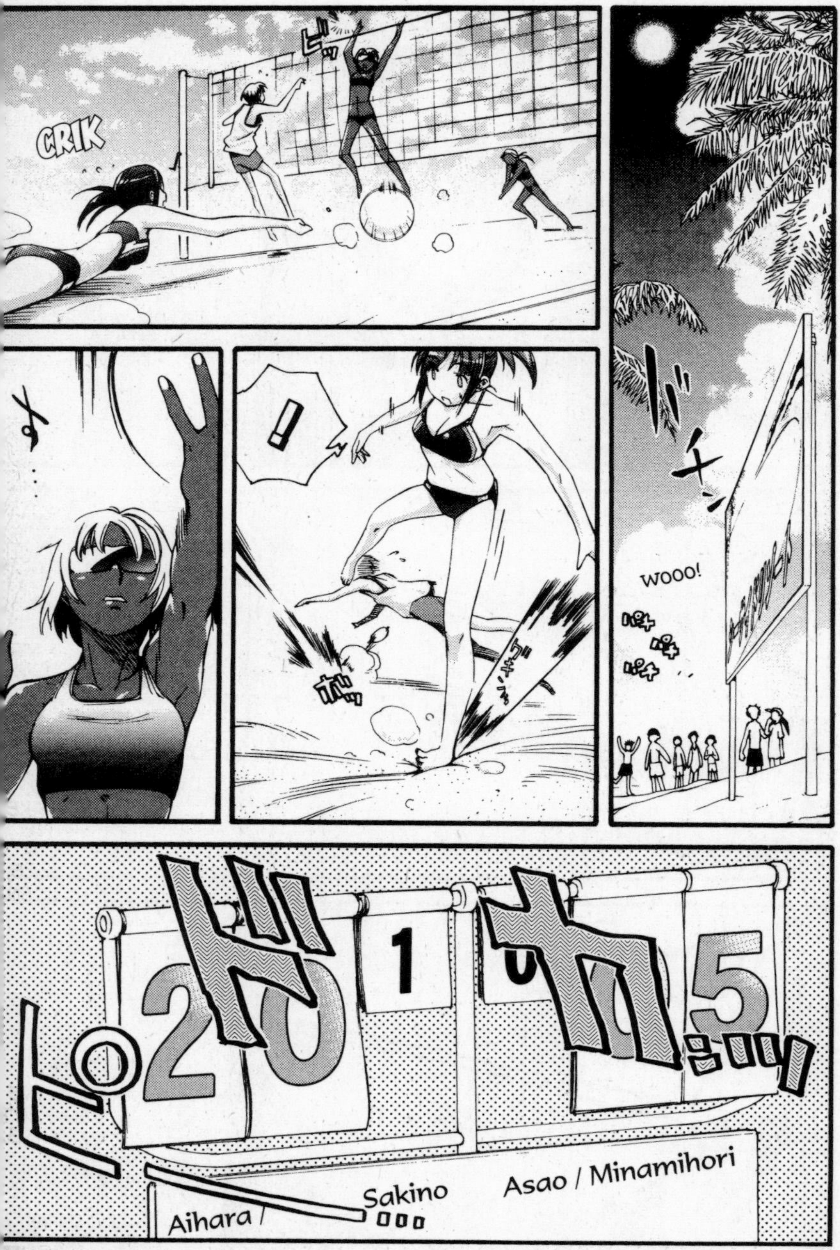

WOOO!
パチ
パチ
パチ
CRIK
!
20
1
5
Aihara / Sakino
Asao / Minamihori

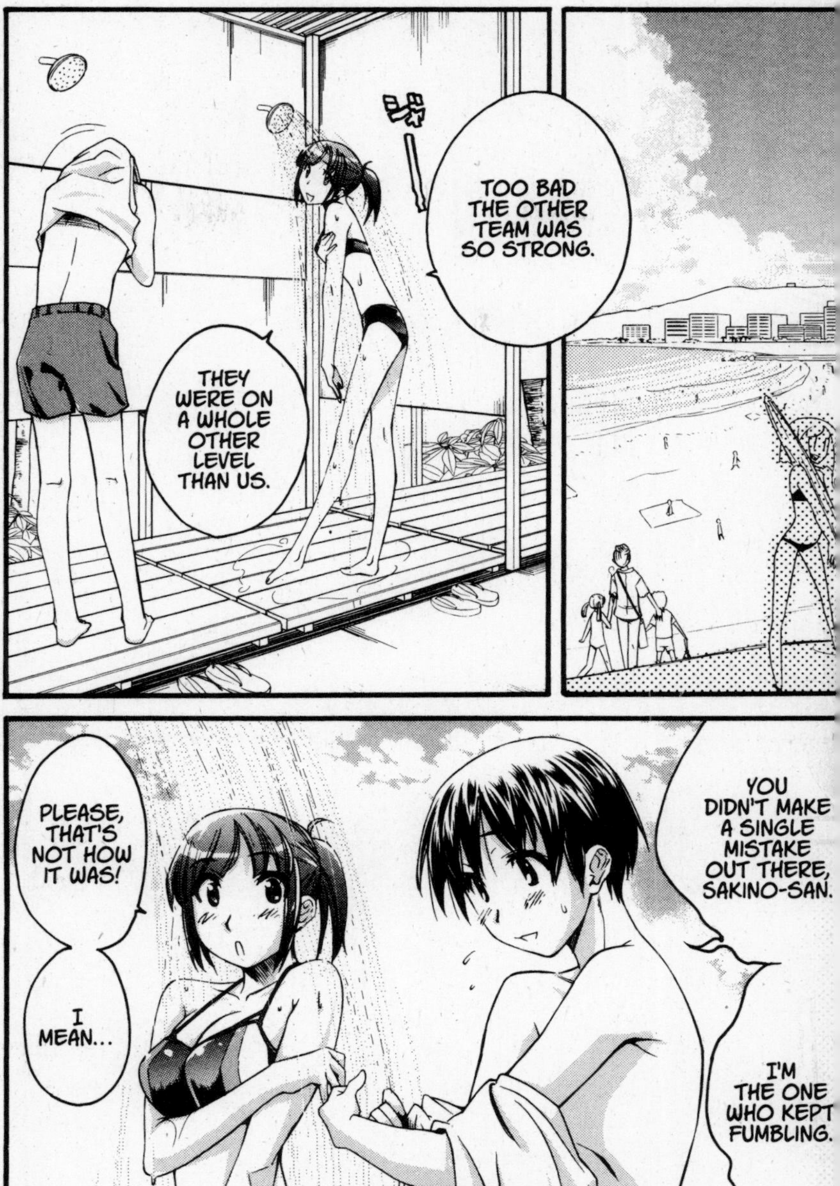
TOO BAD THE OTHER TEAM WAS SO STRONG.
THEY WERE ON A WHOLE OTHER LEVEL THAN US.
YOU DIDN'T MAKE A SINGLE MISTAKE OUT THERE, SAKINO-SAN.
I'M THE ONE WHO KEPT FUMBLING.
PLEASE, THAT'S NOT HOW IT WAS!
I MEAN...

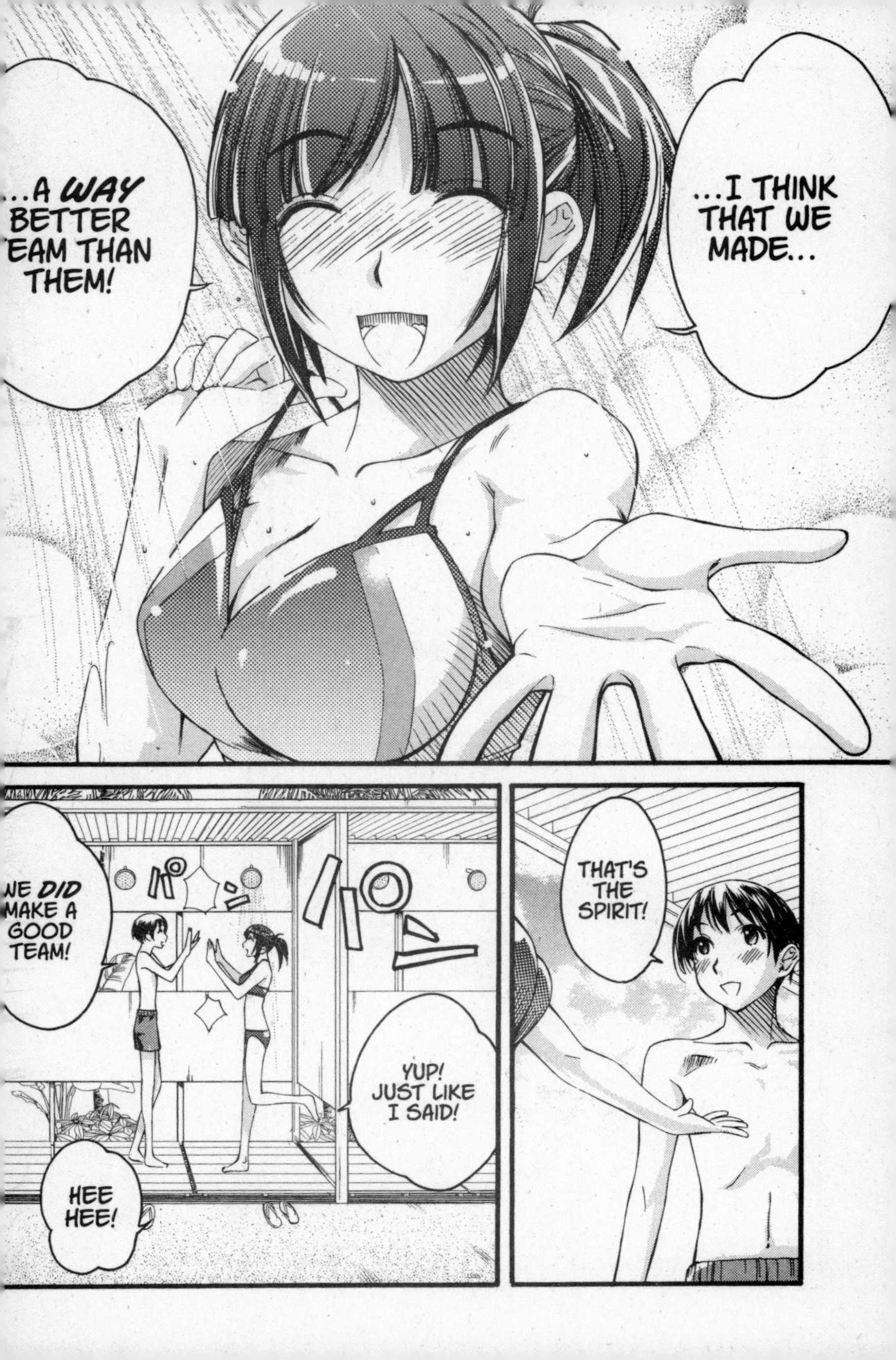
...I THINK THAT WE MADE...
...A *WAY* BETTER EAM THAN THEM!
THAT'S THE SPIRIT!
WE *DID* MAKE A GOOD TEAM!
YUP! JUST LIKE I SAID!
HEE HEE!

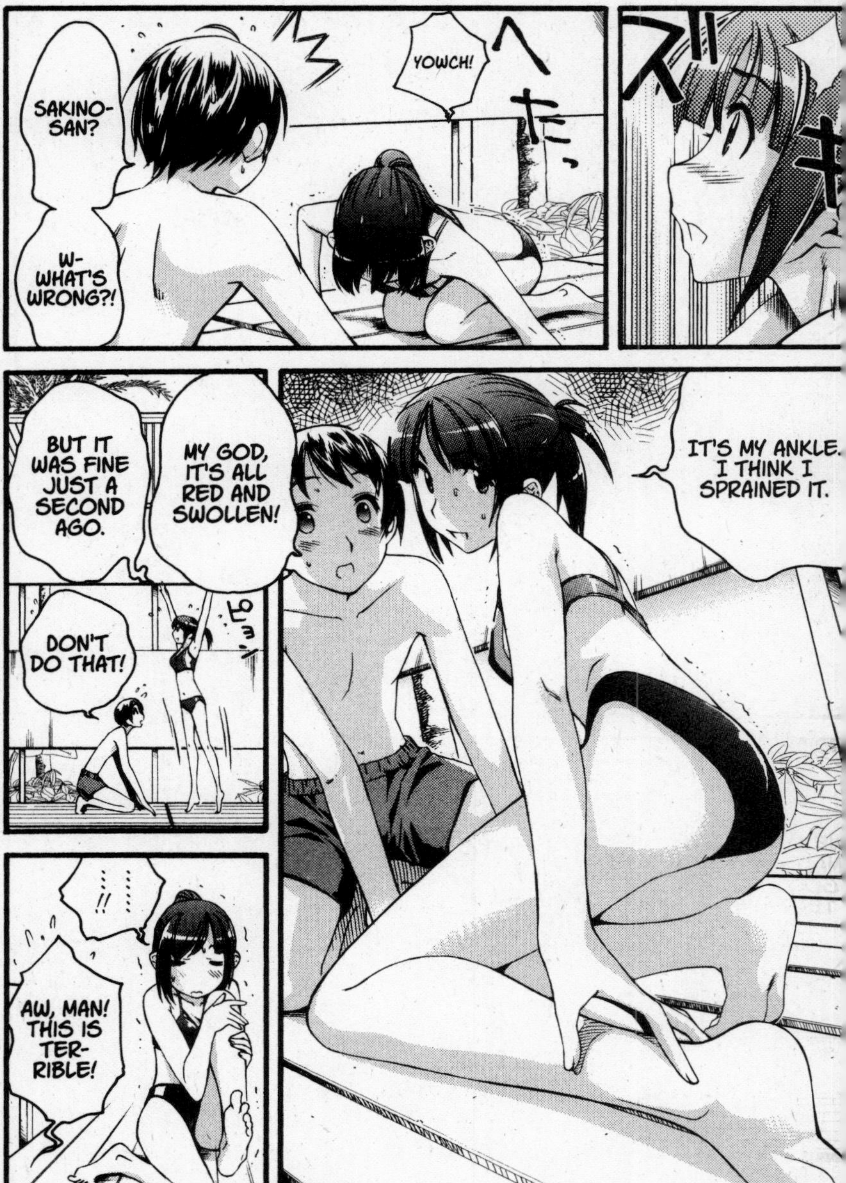
YOWCH!
SAKINO-SAN?
W-WHAT'S WRONG?!
IT'S MY ANKLE. I THINK I SPRAINED IT.
MY GOD, IT'S ALL RED AND SWOLLEN!
BUT IT WAS FINE JUST A SECOND AGO.
DON'T DO THAT!
......!!
AW, MAN! THIS IS TER-RIBLE!

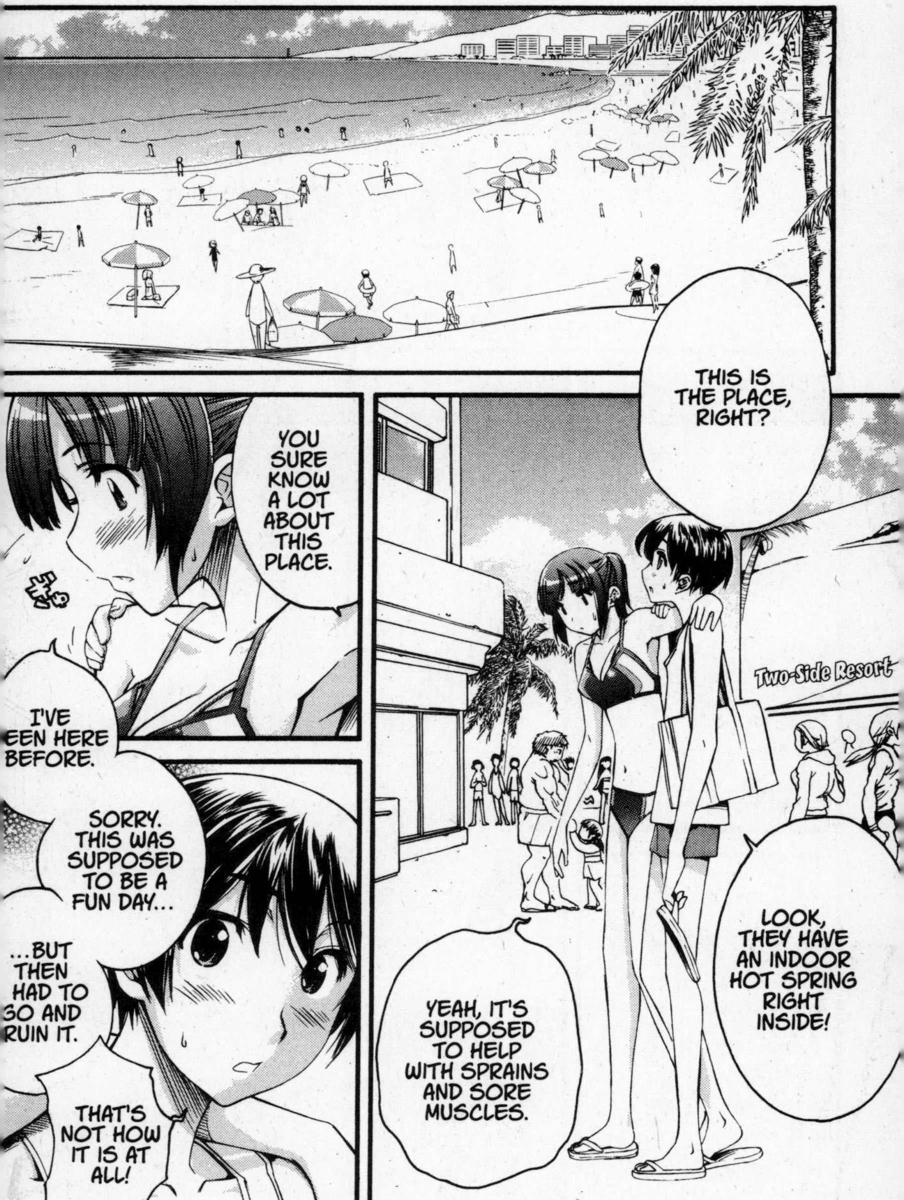
THIS IS THE PLACE, RIGHT?
Two-Side Resort
LOOK, THEY HAVE AN INDOOR HOT SPRING RIGHT INSIDE!
YEAH, IT'S SUPPOSED TO HELP WITH SPRAINS AND SORE MUSCLES.
YOU SURE KNOW A LOT ABOUT THIS PLACE.
I'VE EEN HERE BEFORE.
SORRY. THIS WAS SUPPOSED TO BE A FUN DAY...
...BUT THEN HAD TO GO AND RUIN IT.
THAT'S NOT HOW IT IS AT ALL!

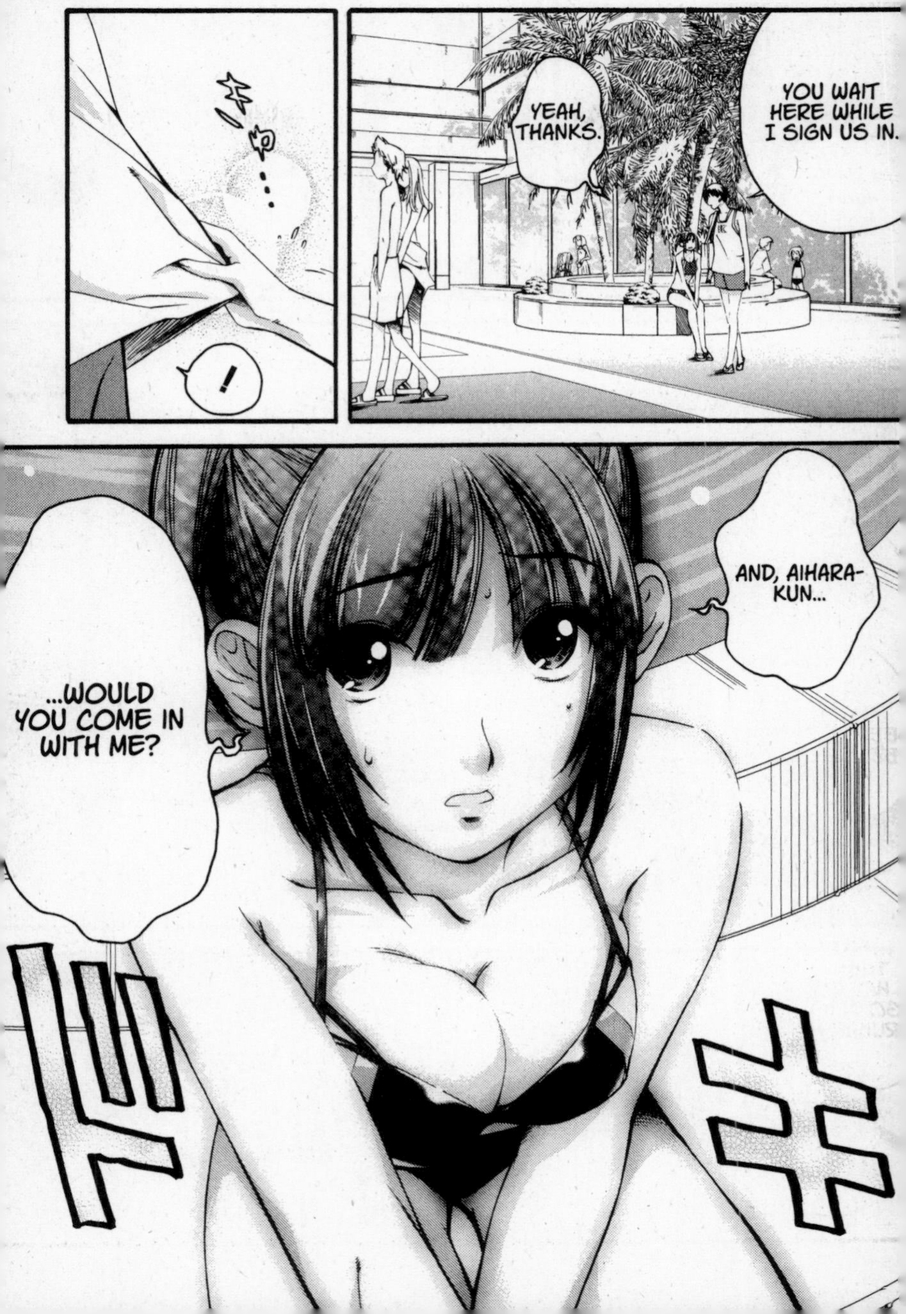
YOU WAIT HERE WHILE I SIGN US IN.
YEAH, THANKS.
!
AND, AIHARA-KUN...
...WOULD YOU COME IN WITH ME?

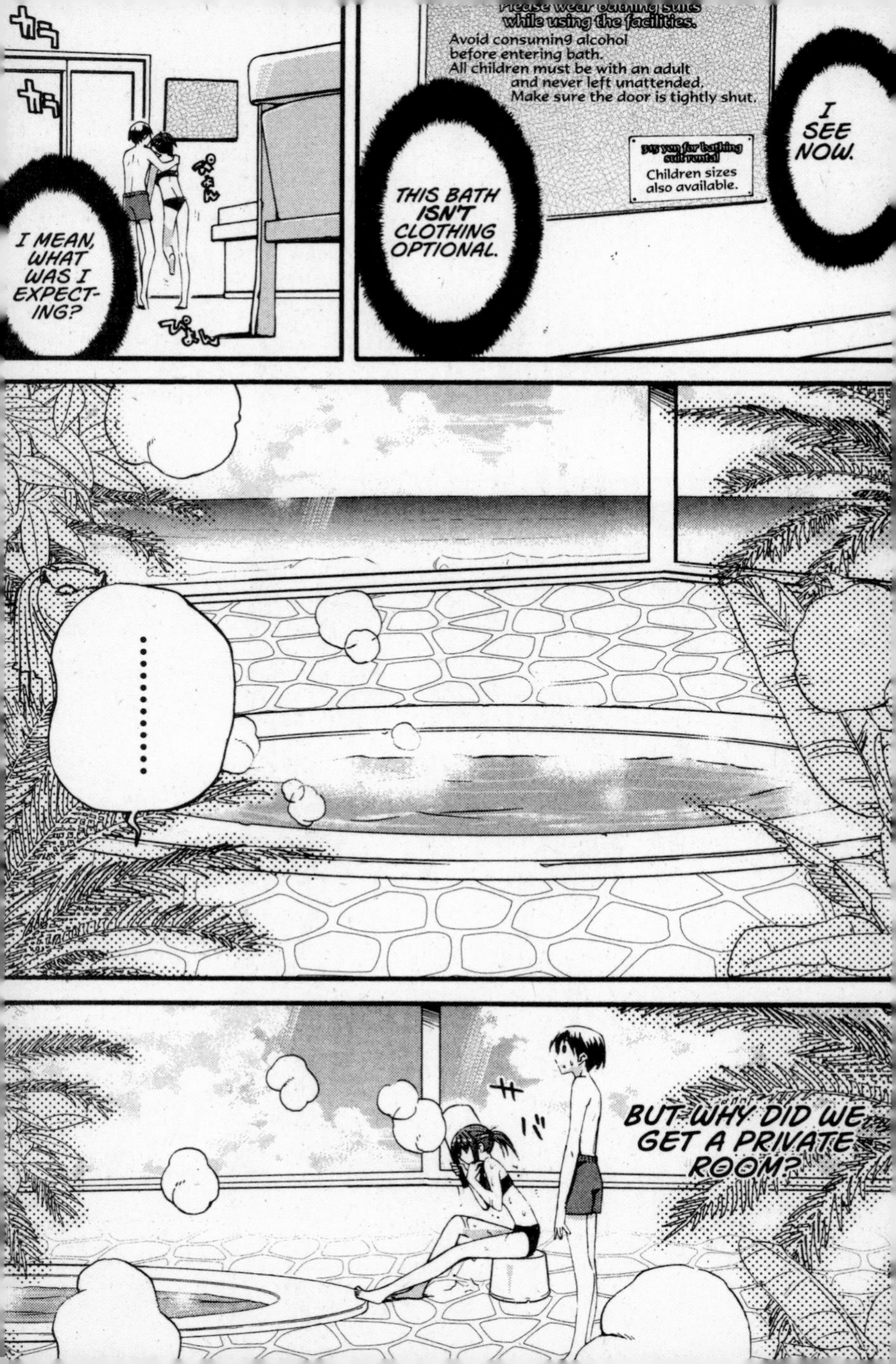
Please wear bathing suits while using the facilities.
Avoid consuming alcohol before entering bath.
All children must be with an adult and never left unattended.
Make sure the door is tightly shut.
Children sizes also available.
I SEE NOW.
THIS BATH ISN'T CLOTHING OPTIONAL.
I MEAN, WHAT WAS I EXPECTING?
......
BUT WHY DID WE GET A PRIVATE ROOM?

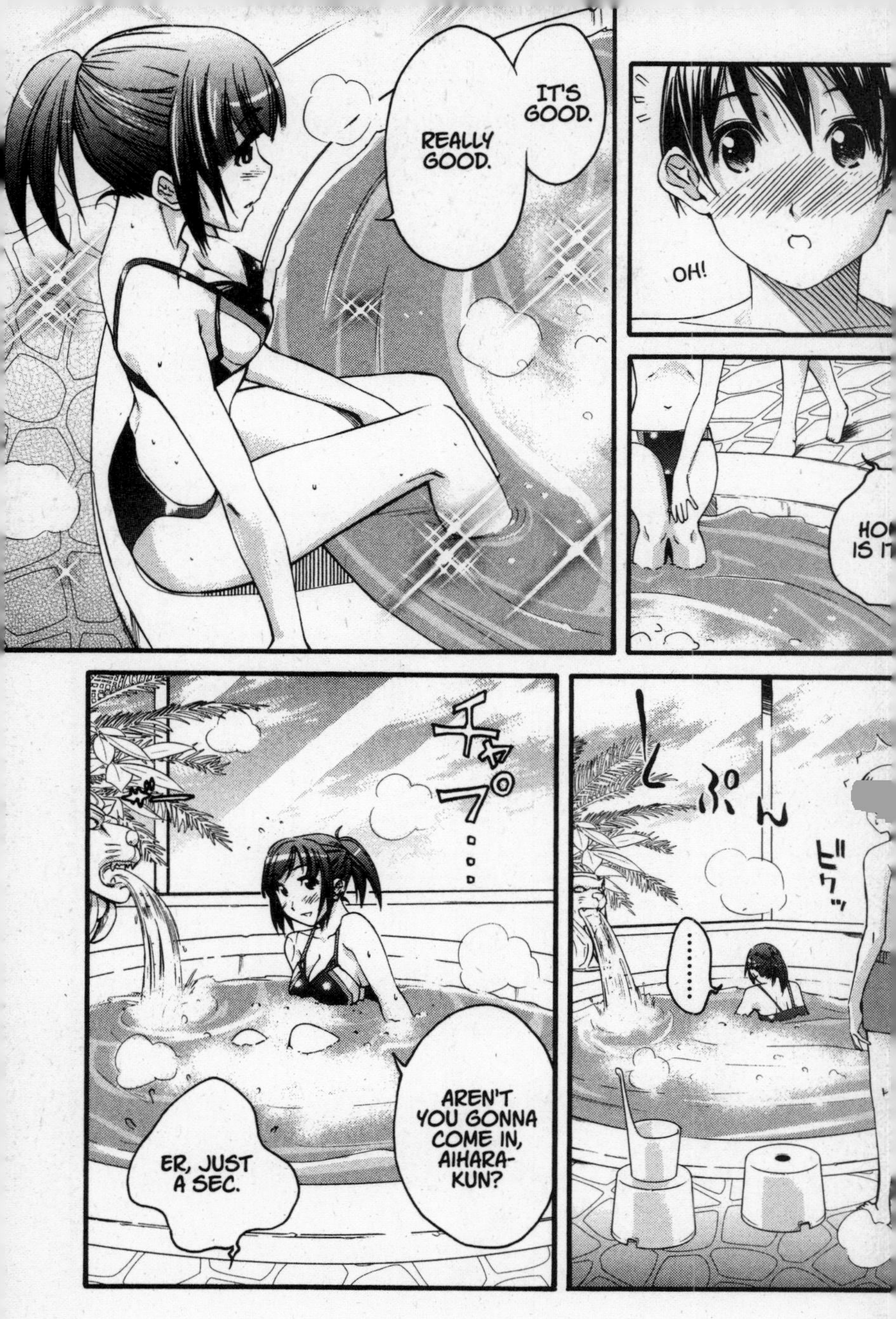
OH!
HO
IS IT
IT'S GOOD.
REALLY GOOD.
しぷん
ビクッ
......
チャプ...
AREN'T YOU GONNA COME IN, AIHARA-KUN?
ER, JUST A SEC.

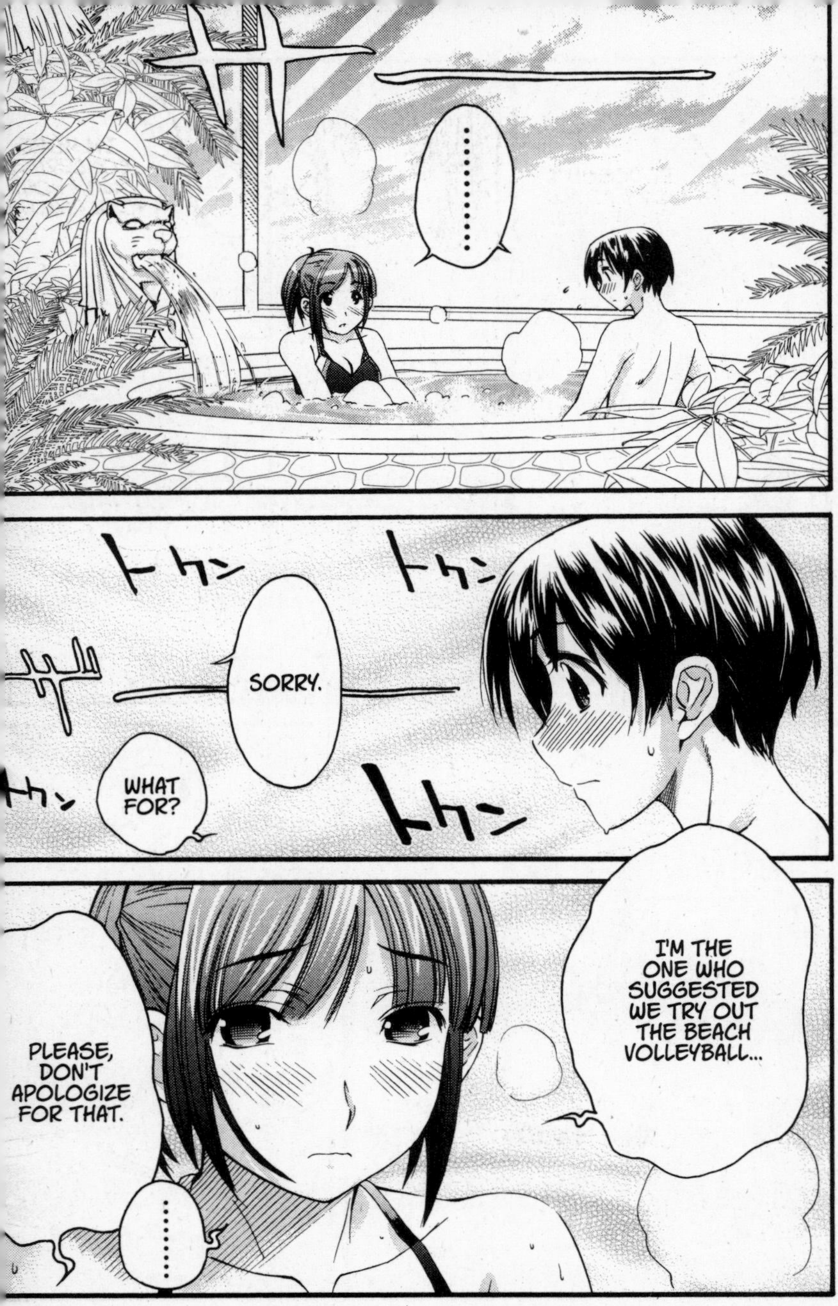
……
トクン
トクン
SORRY.
WHAT FOR?
トクン
トクン
I'M THE ONE WHO SUGGESTED WE TRY OUT THE BEACH VOLLEYBALL...
PLEASE, DON'T APOLOGIZE FOR THAT.
……

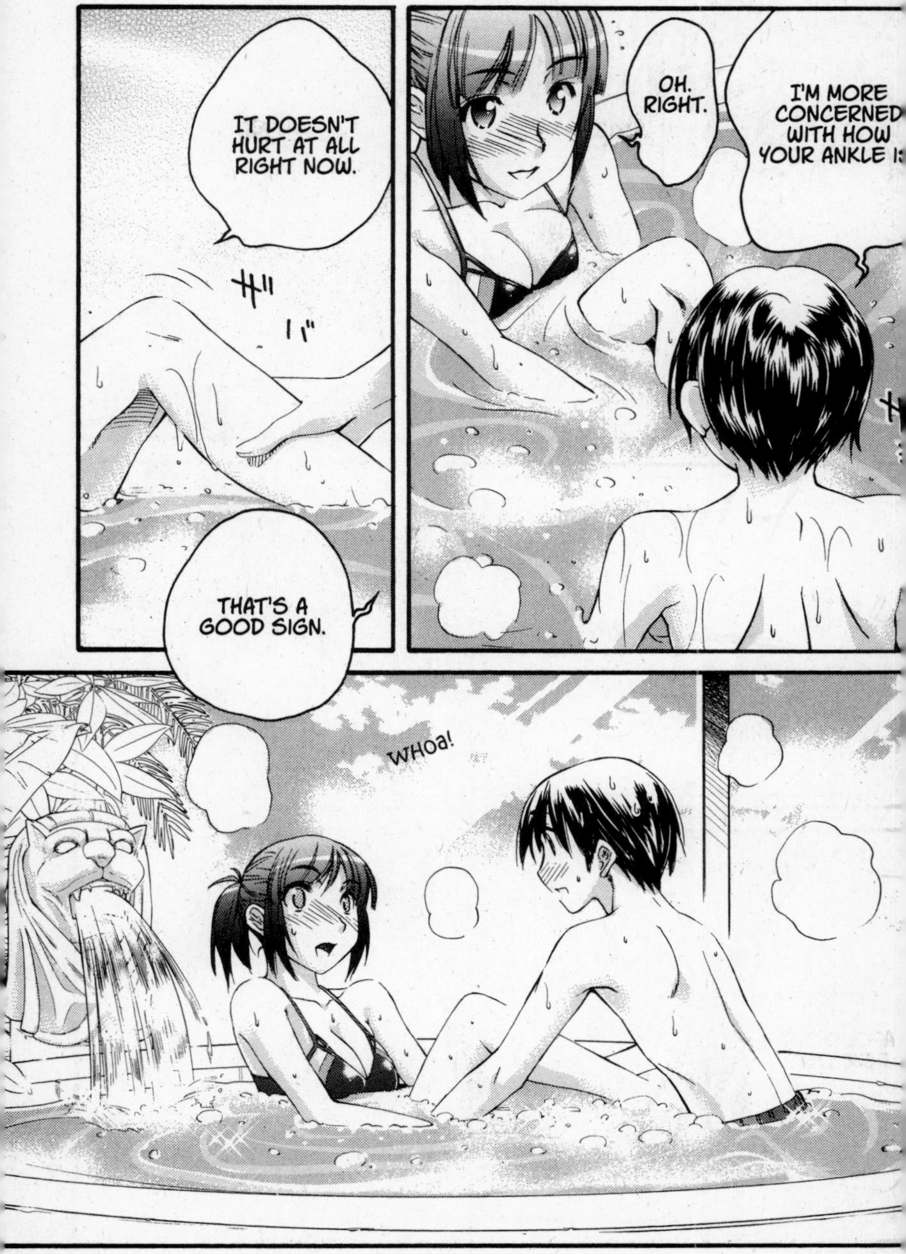
I'M MORE CONCERNED WITH HOW YOUR ANKLE I
OH. RIGHT.
IT DOESN'T HURT AT ALL RIGHT NOW.
THAT'S A GOOD SIGN.
WHOa!

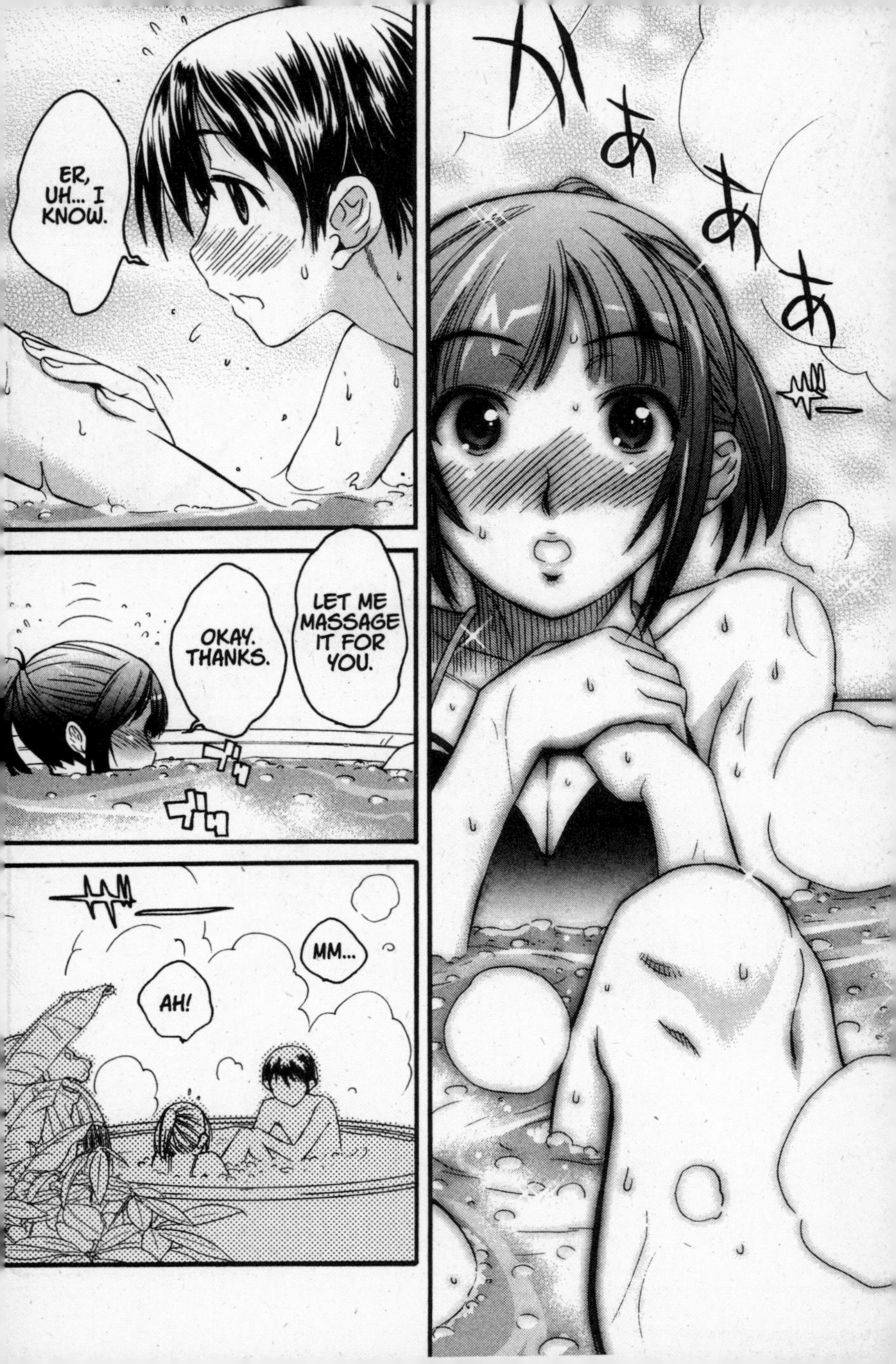
かあああ
ER, UH... I KNOW.
LET ME MASSAGE IT FOR YOU.
OKAY. THANKS.
MM...
AH!

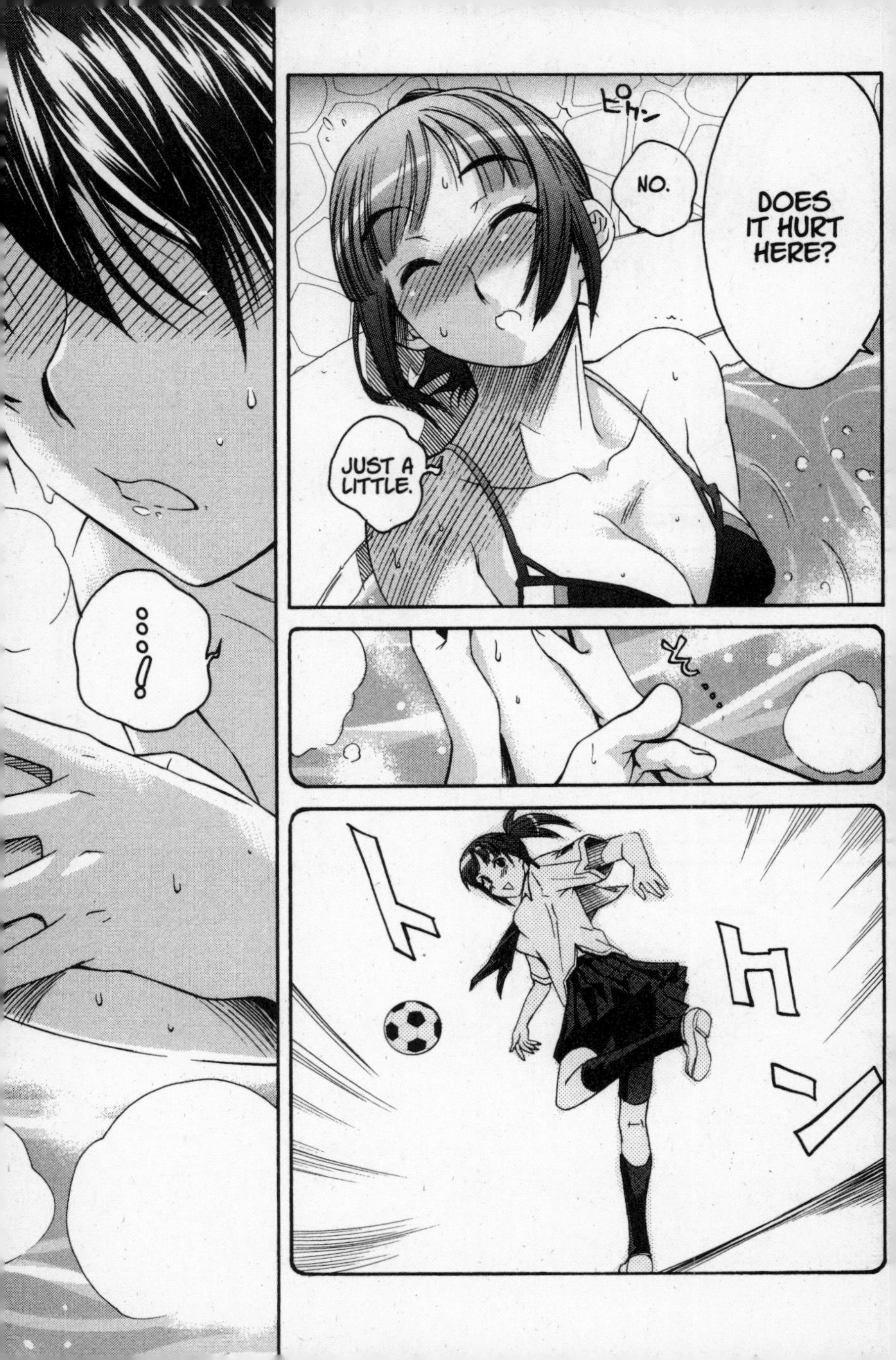
DOES IT HURT HERE?
NO.
JUST A LITTLE.
ooo!

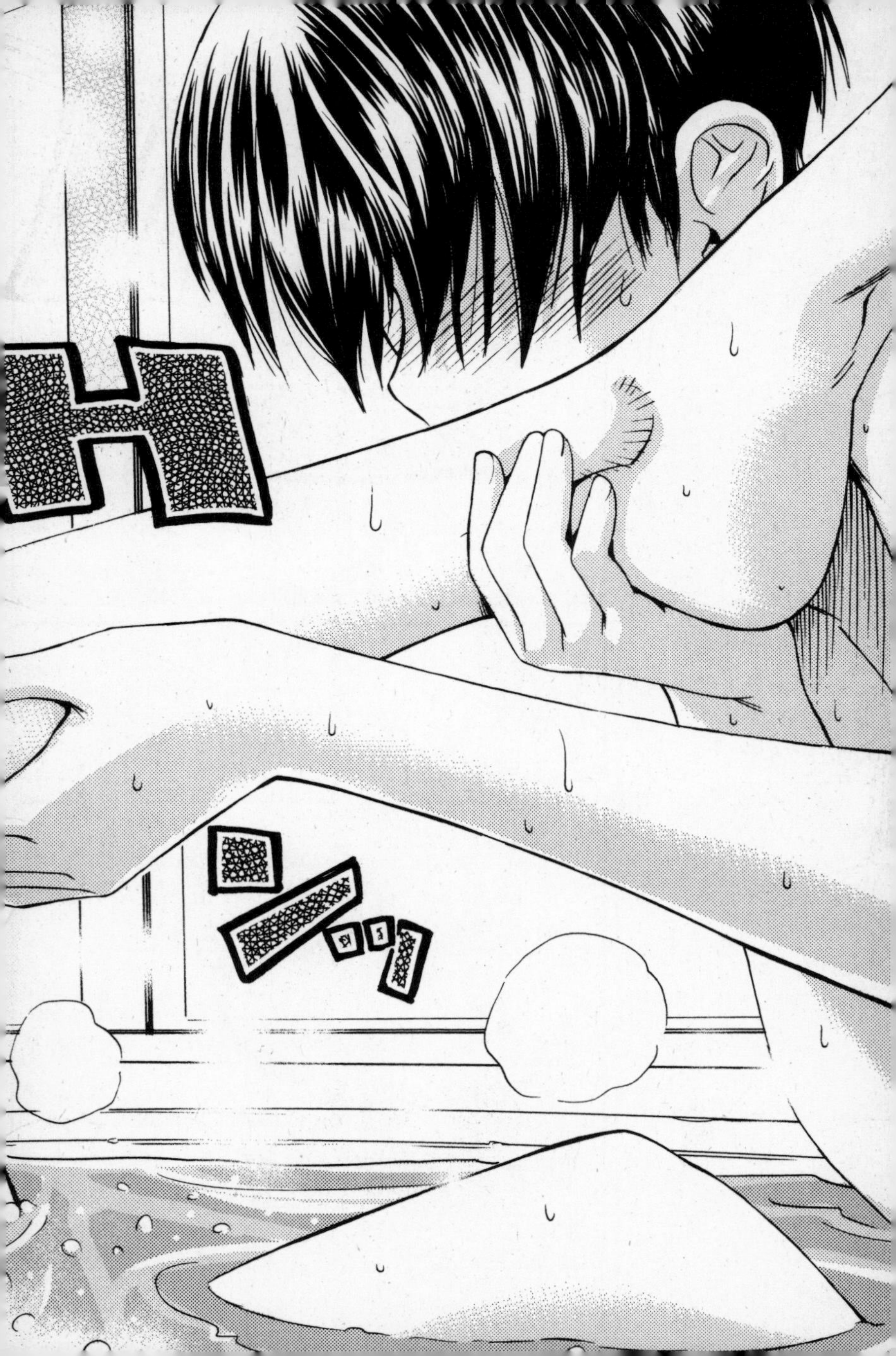
H

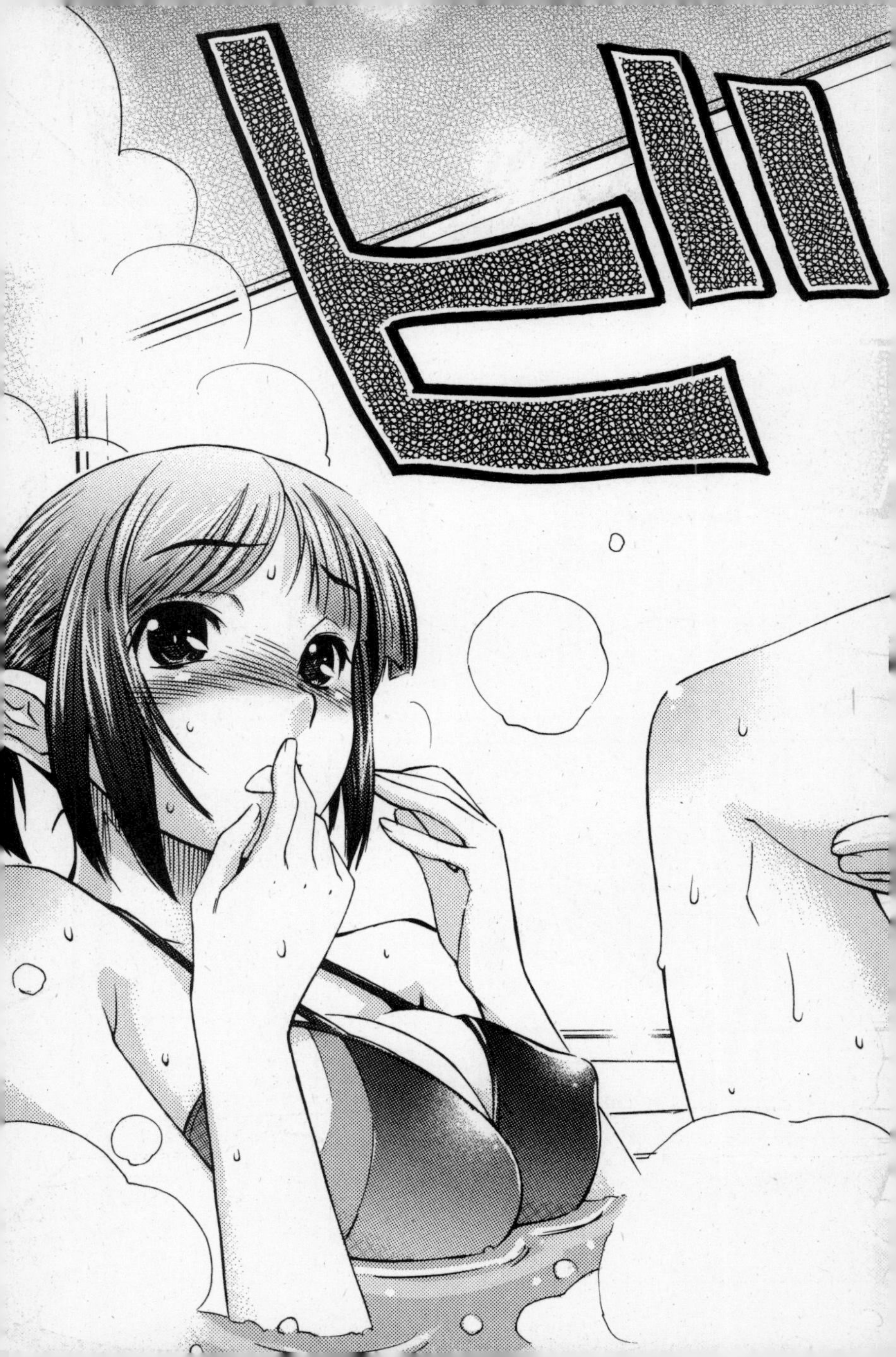
ヒッ

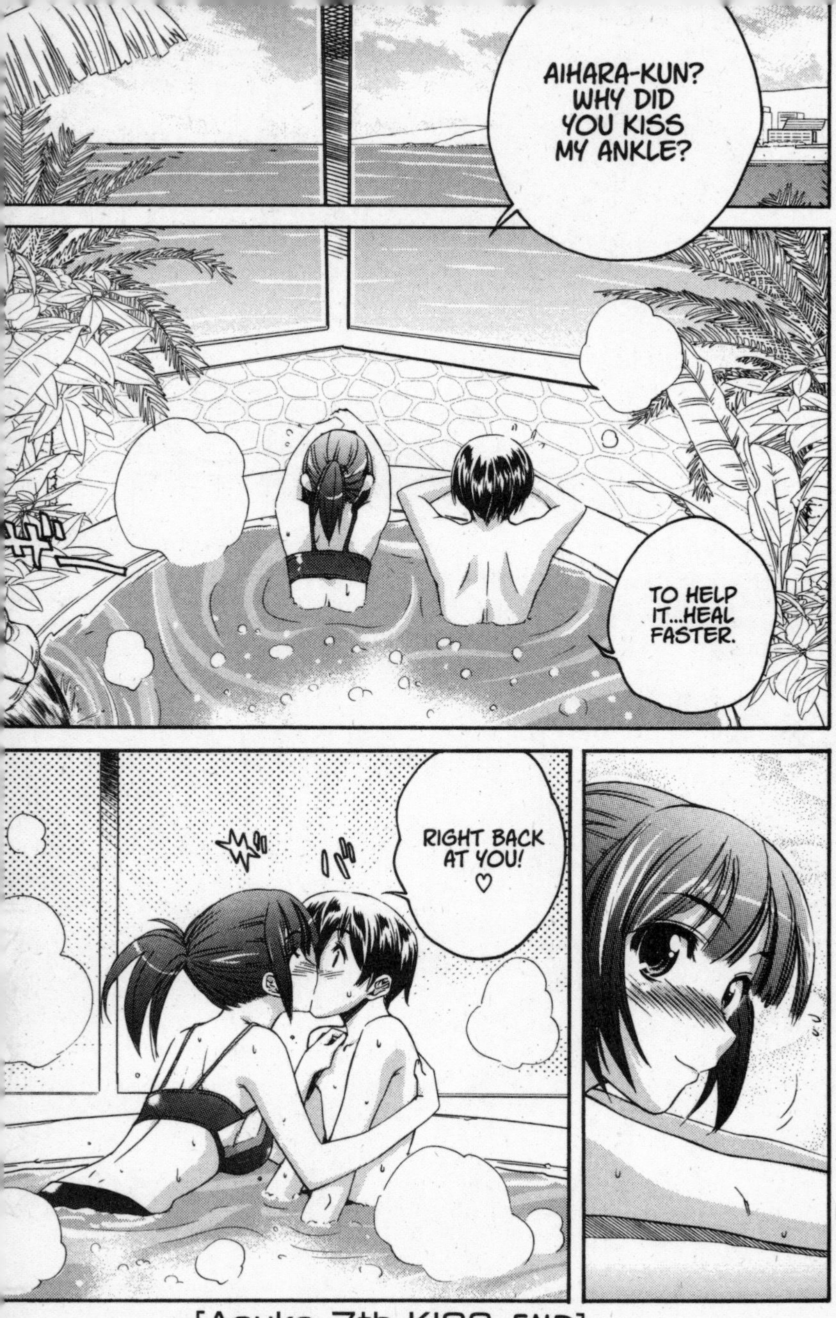
AIHARA-KUN? WHY DID YOU KISS MY ANKLE?
TO HELP IT...HEAL FASTER.
RIGHT BACK AT YOU! ♡

[Asuka 7th KISS END]

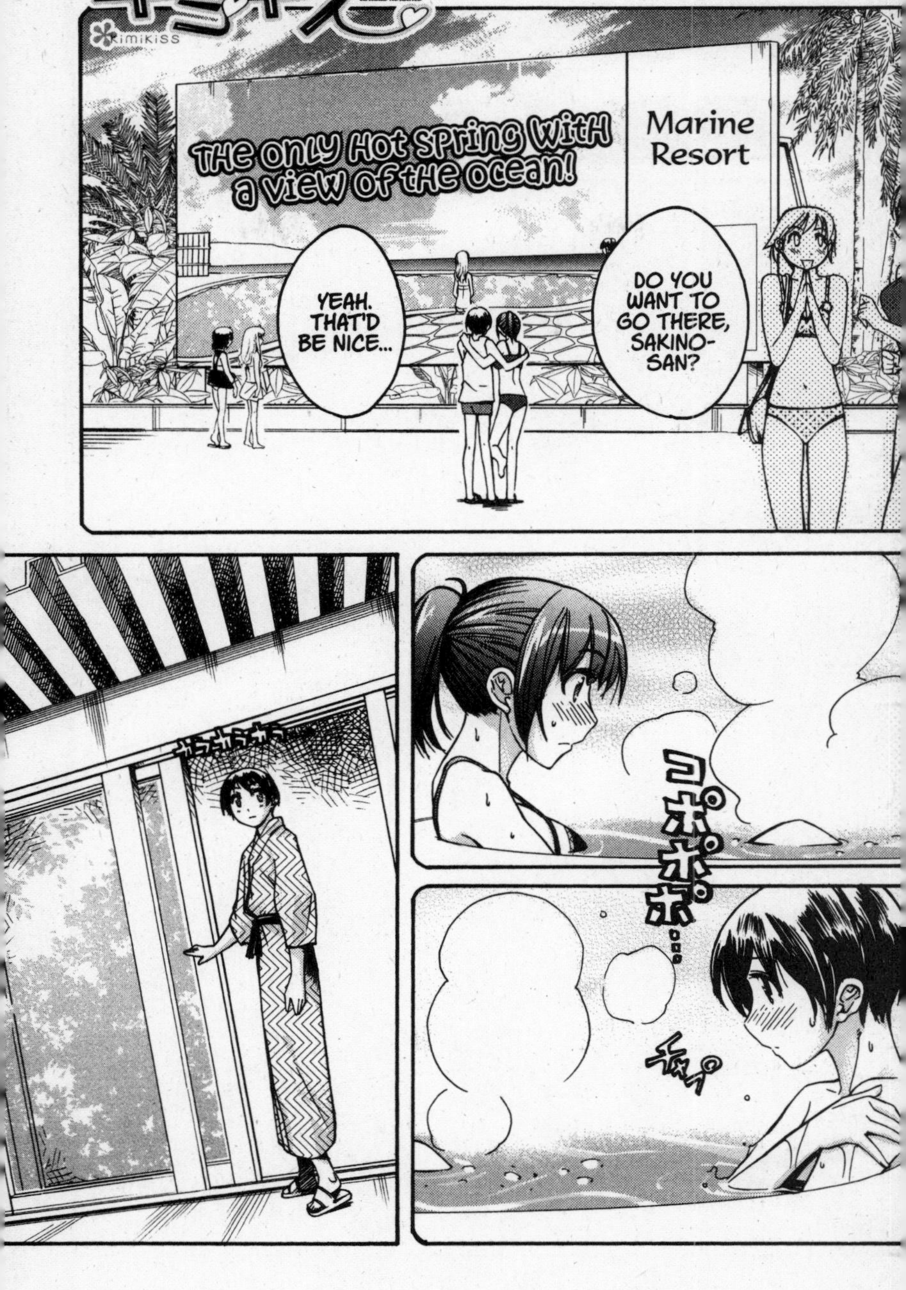
Marine
Resort
THE ONLY HOT SPRING WITH
A VIEW OF THE OCEAN!
DO YOU WANT TO GO THERE, SAKINO-SAN?
YEAH. THAT'D BE NICE...
コポポポ…

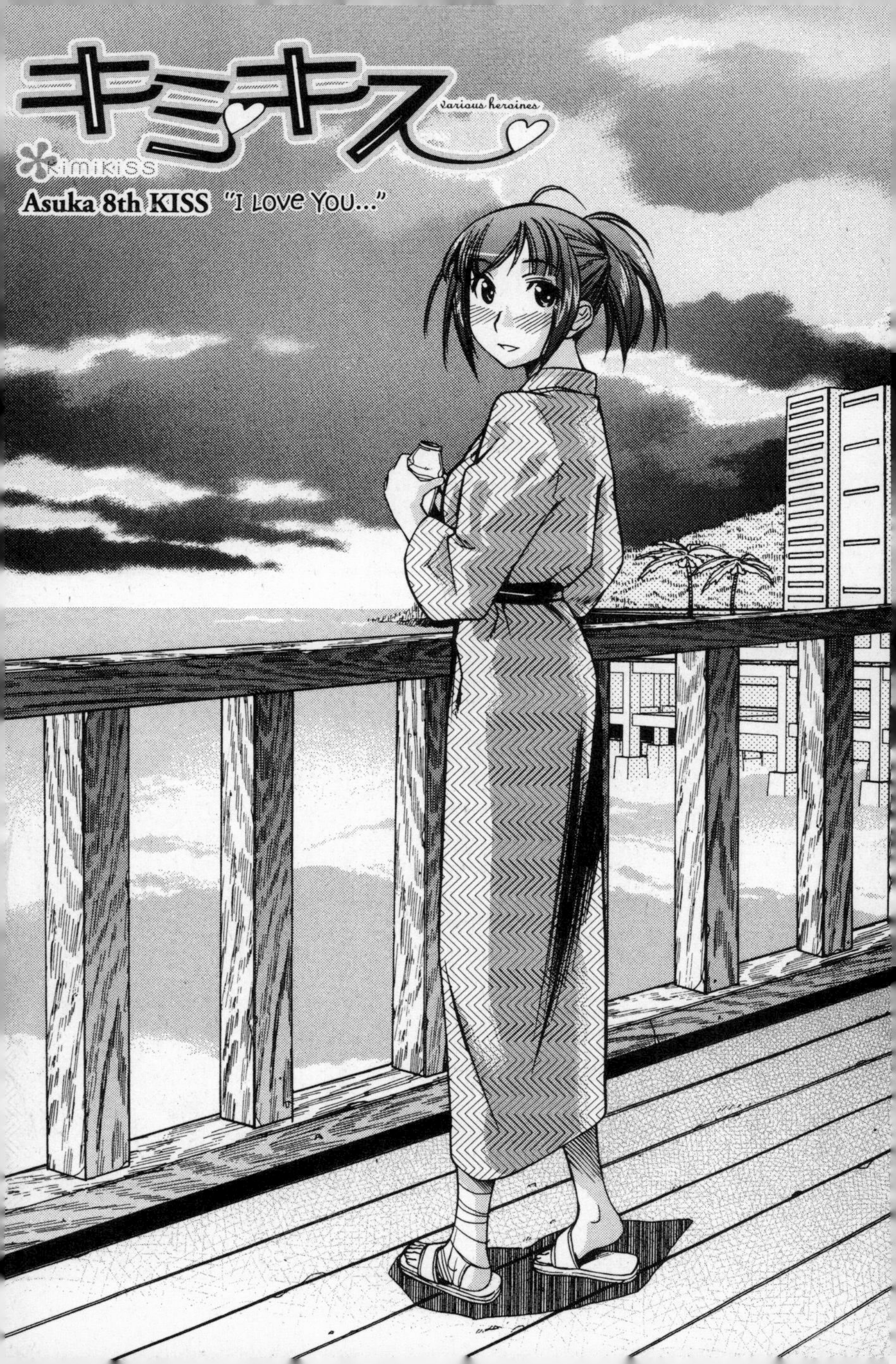

キミキス
various heroines
KimiKiss
Asuka 8th KISS "I Love You..."

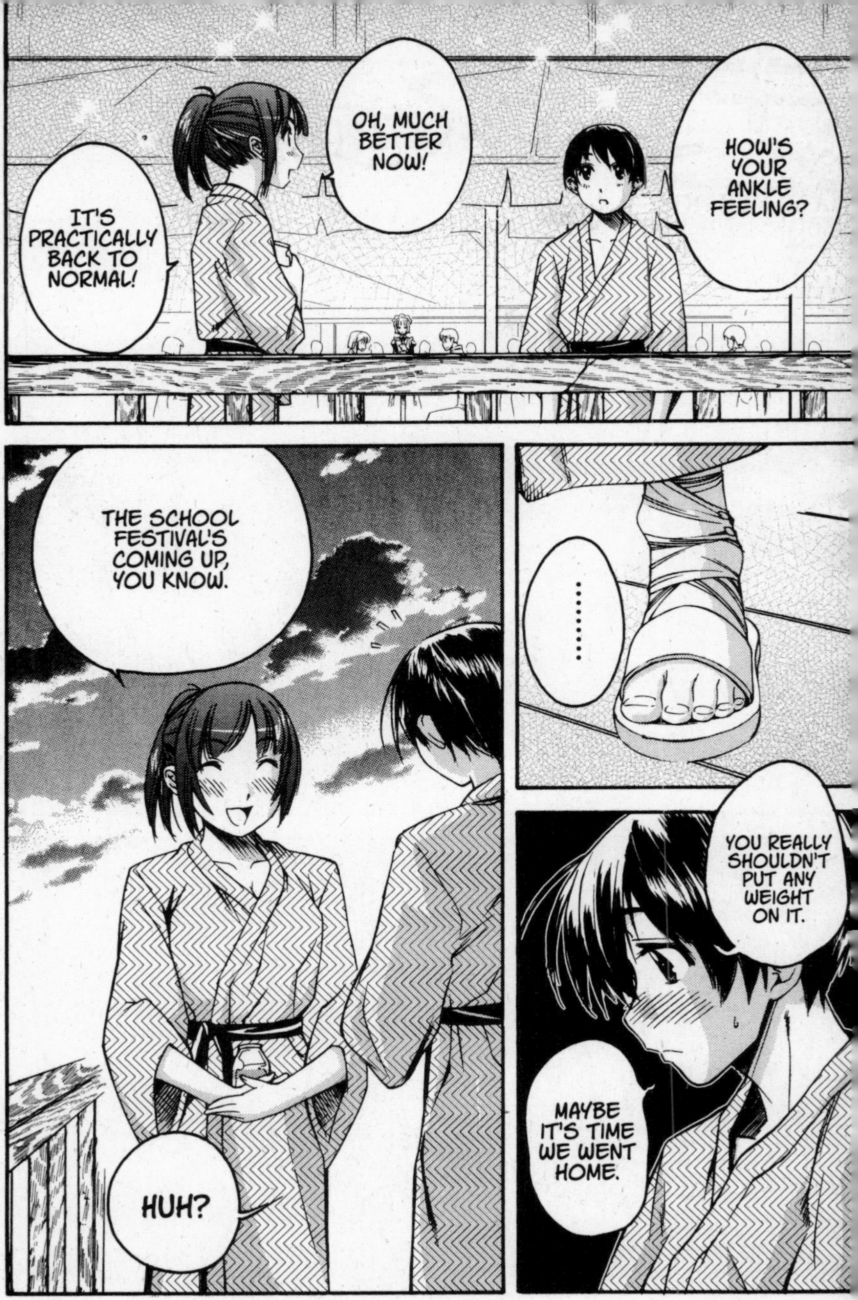
HOW'S YOUR ANKLE FEELING?
OH, MUCH BETTER NOW!
IT'S PRACTICALLY BACK TO NORMAL!
......
YOU REALLY SHOULDN'T PUT ANY WEIGHT ON IT.
MAYBE IT'S TIME WE WENT HOME.
THE SCHOOL FESTIVAL'S COMING UP, YOU KNOW.
HUH?

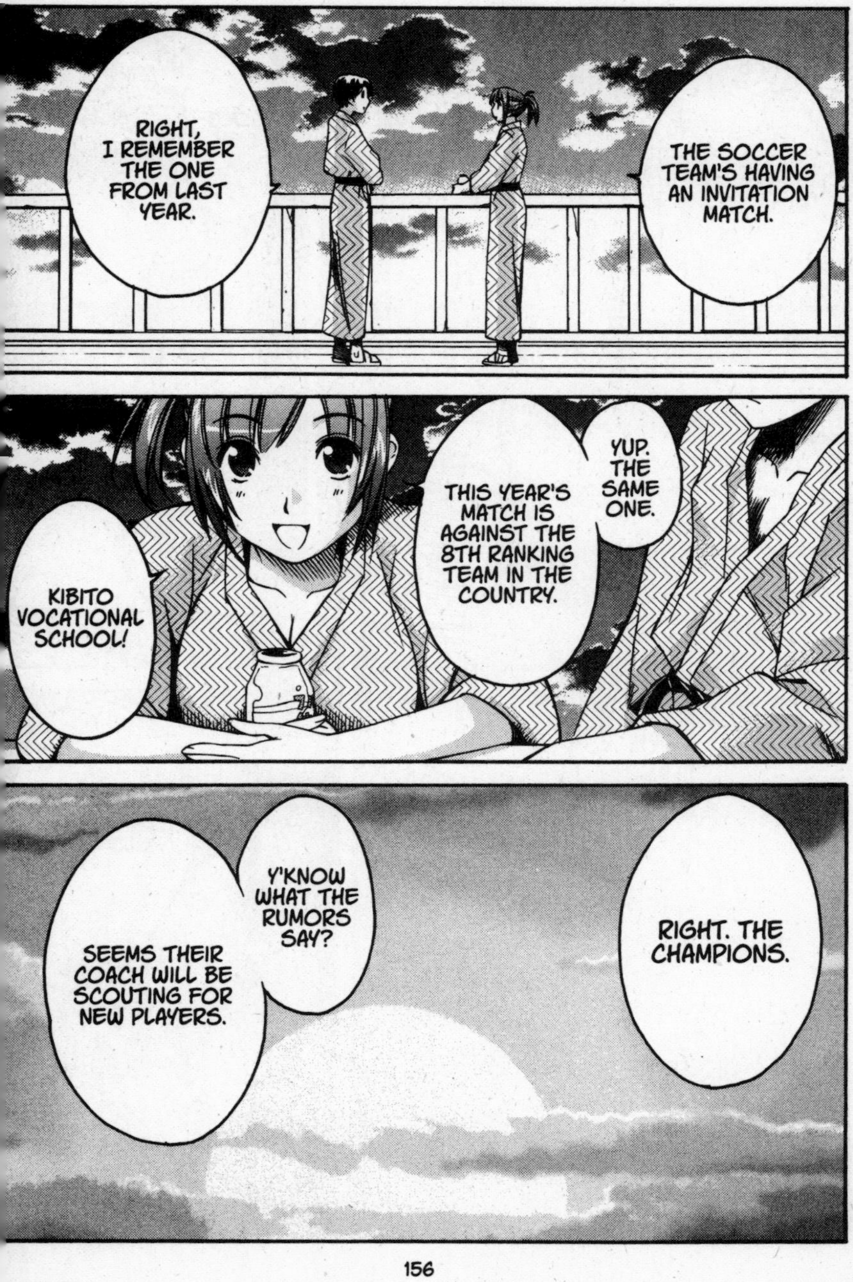
THE SOCCER TEAM'S HAVING AN INVITATION MATCH.
RIGHT, I REMEMBER THE ONE FROM LAST YEAR.
YUP. THE SAME ONE.
THIS YEAR'S MATCH IS AGAINST THE 8TH RANKING TEAM IN THE COUNTRY.
KIBITO VOCATIONAL SCHOOL!
RIGHT. THE CHAMPIONS.
Y'KNOW WHAT THE RUMORS SAY?
SEEMS THEIR COACH WILL BE SCOUTING FOR NEW PLAYERS.

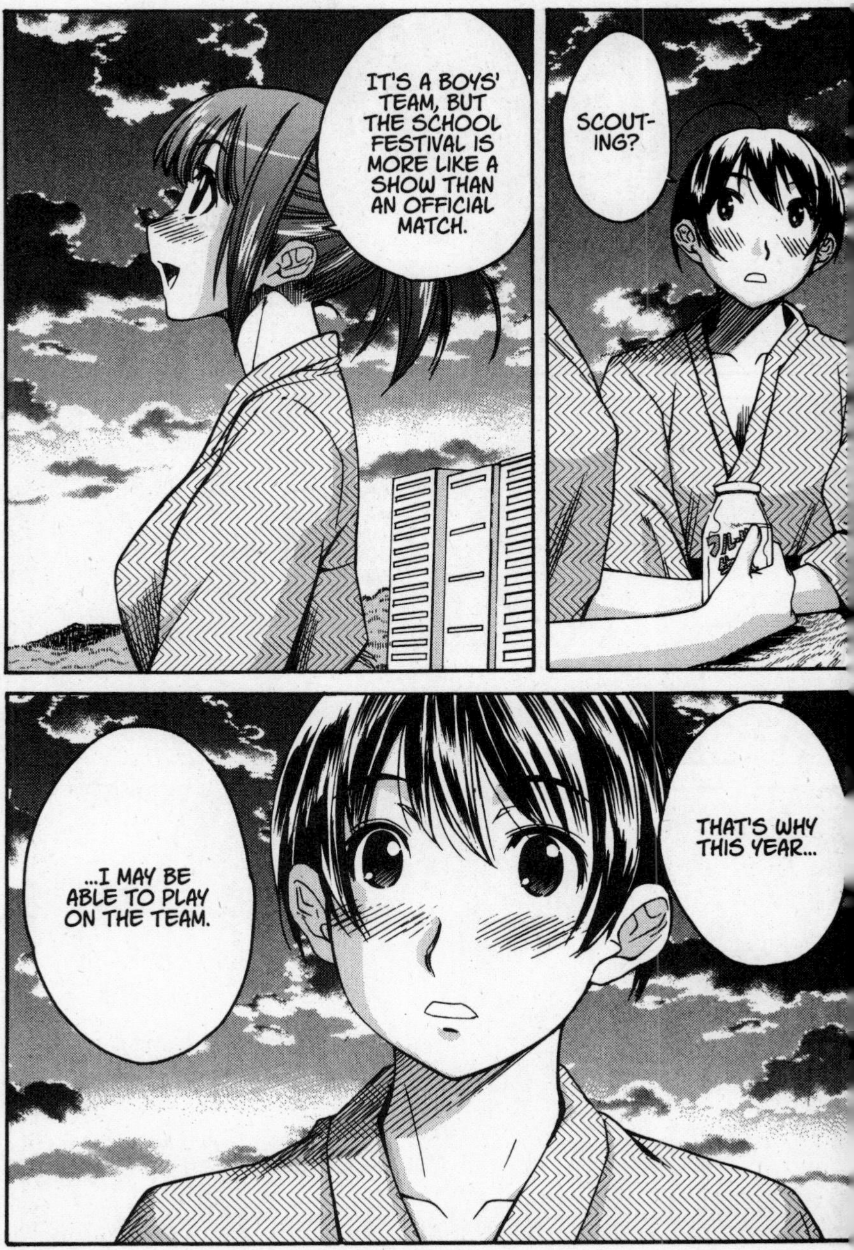
SCOUT-ING?
IT'S A BOYS' TEAM, BUT THE SCHOOL FESTIVAL IS MORE LIKE A SHOW THAN AN OFFICIAL MATCH.
THAT'S WHY THIS YEAR...
...I MAY BE ABLE TO PLAY ON THE TEAM.

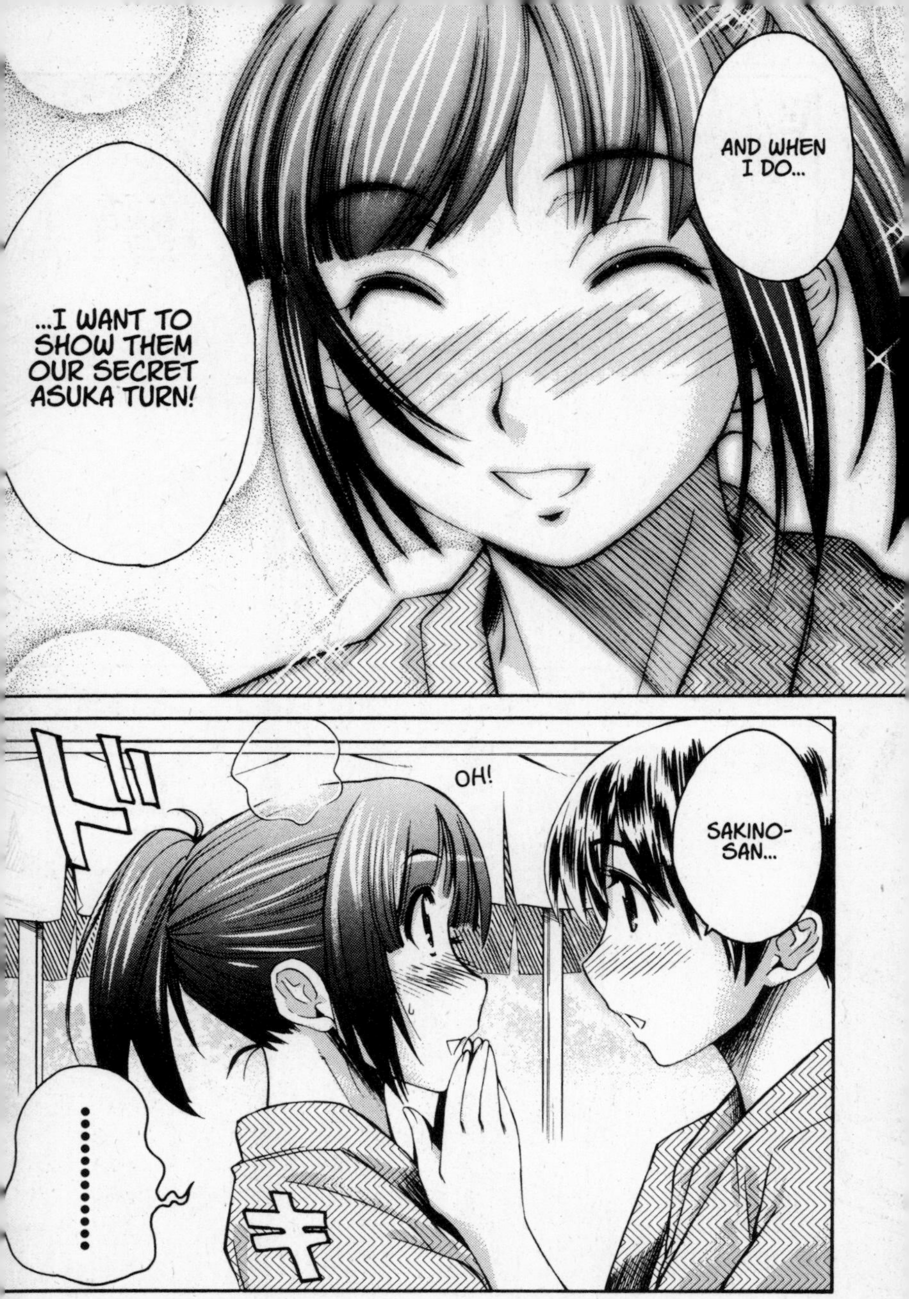
AND WHEN I DO...
...I WANT TO SHOW THEM OUR SECRET ASUKA TURN!
SAKINO-SAN...
OH!
ドッ
....
キ

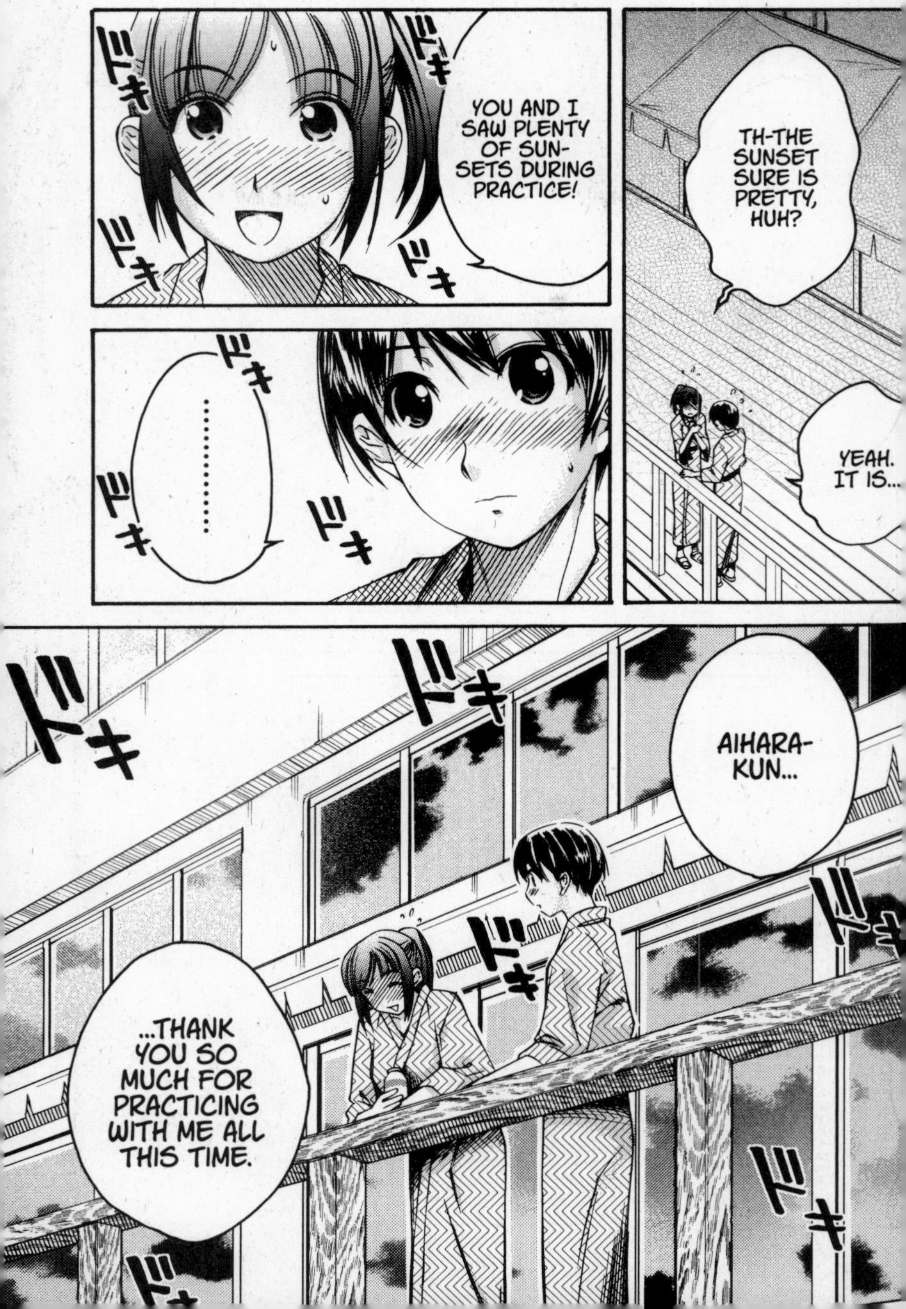
TH-THE SUNSET SURE IS PRETTY, HUH?
YEAH. IT IS...
ドキ
ドキ
YOU AND I SAW PLENTY OF SUN-SETS DURING PRACTICE!
ドキ
ドキ
ドキ
......
ドキ
ドキ
ドキ
ドキ
AIHARA-KUN...
ドキ
ドキ
...THANK YOU SO MUCH FOR PRACTICING WITH ME ALL THIS TIME.
ドキ

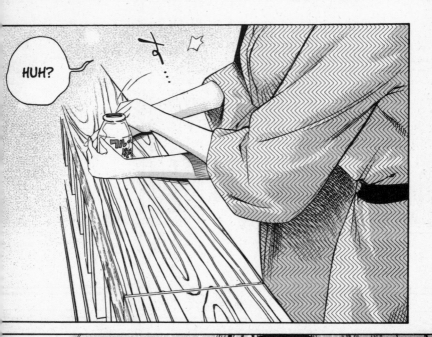

HUH?

WHAT--?

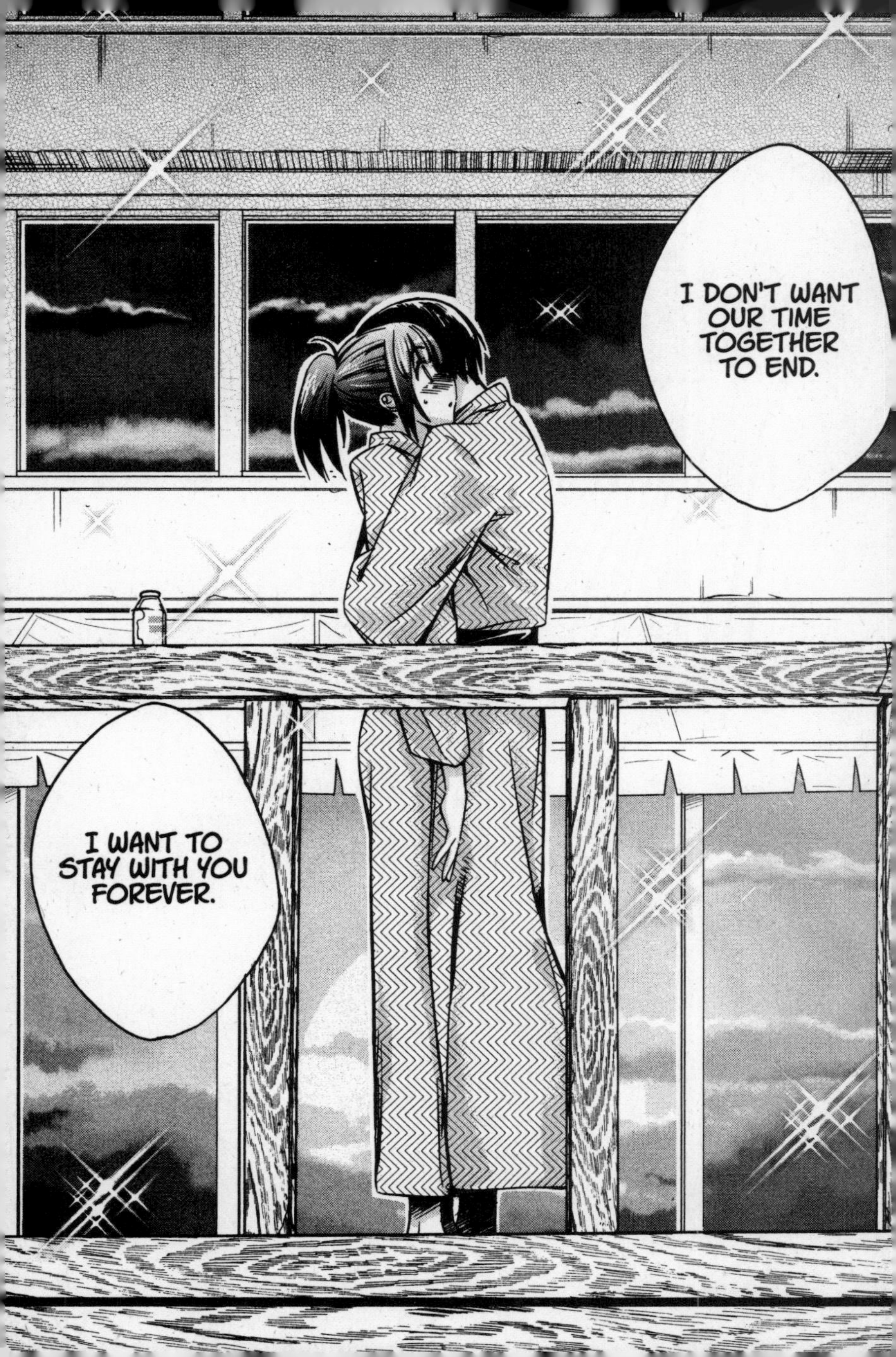
I DON'T WANT OUR TIME TOGETHER TO END.
I WANT TO STAY WITH YOU FOREVER.

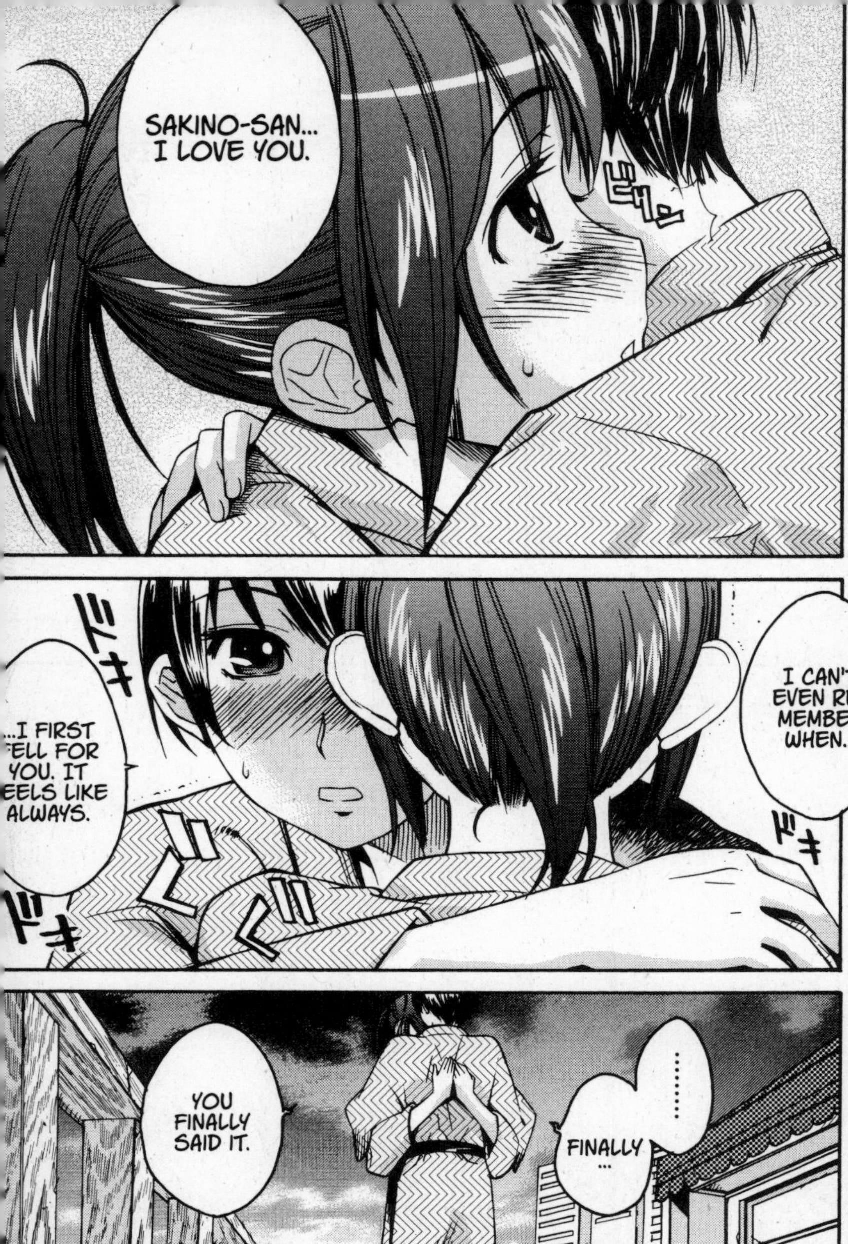
SAKINO-SAN... I LOVE YOU.
I CAN'T EVEN RE-MEMBER WHEN...
ドキ
...I FIRST ELL FOR YOU. IT EELS LIKE ALWAYS.
ドキ
......
FINALLY ...
YOU FINALLY SAID IT.

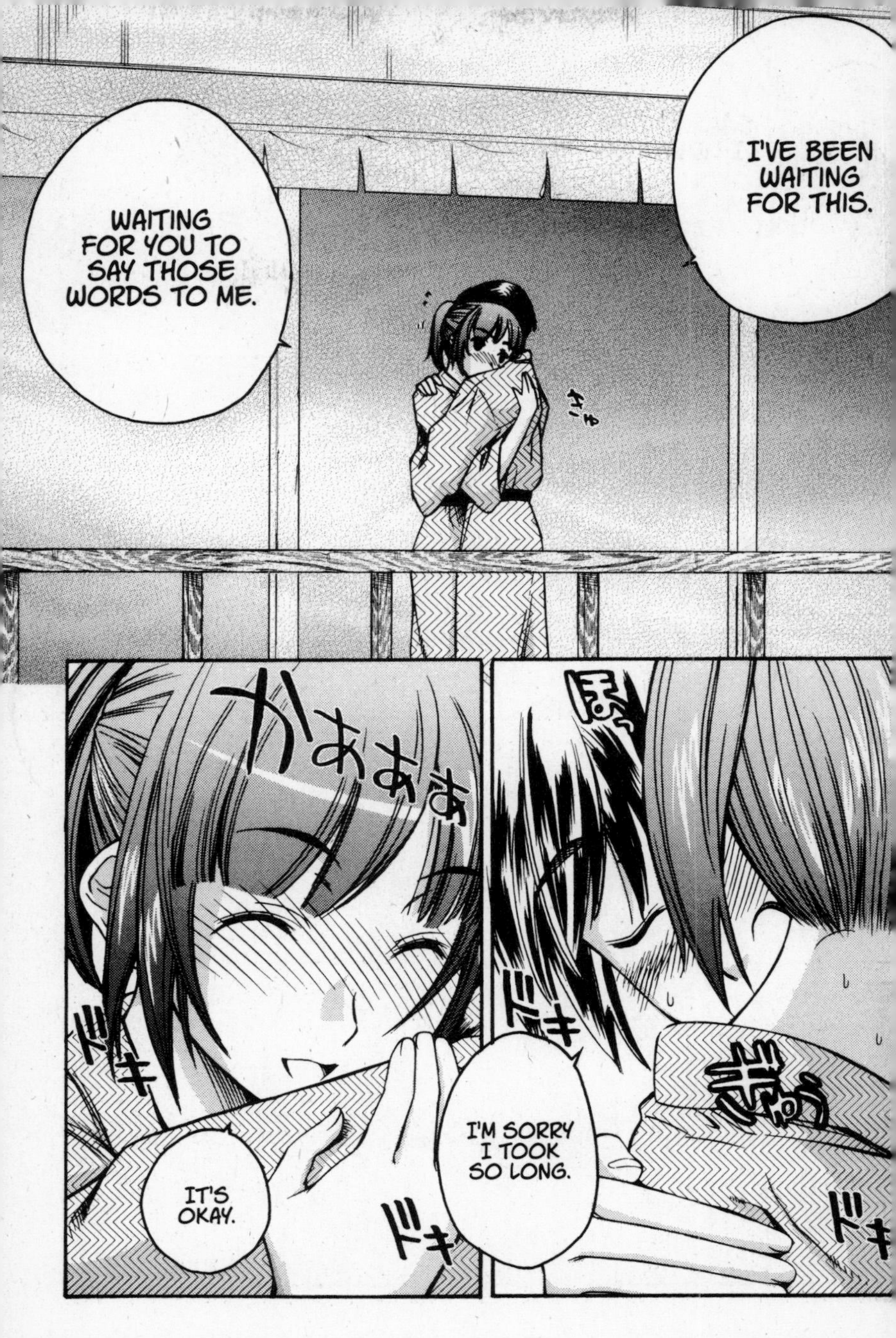
I'VE BEEN WAITING FOR THIS.
WAITING FOR YOU TO SAY THOSE WORDS TO ME.
ほっ
ドキ
ぎゅう
ドキ
I'M SORRY I TOOK SO LONG.
かあああ
ドキ
IT'S OKAY.
ドキ

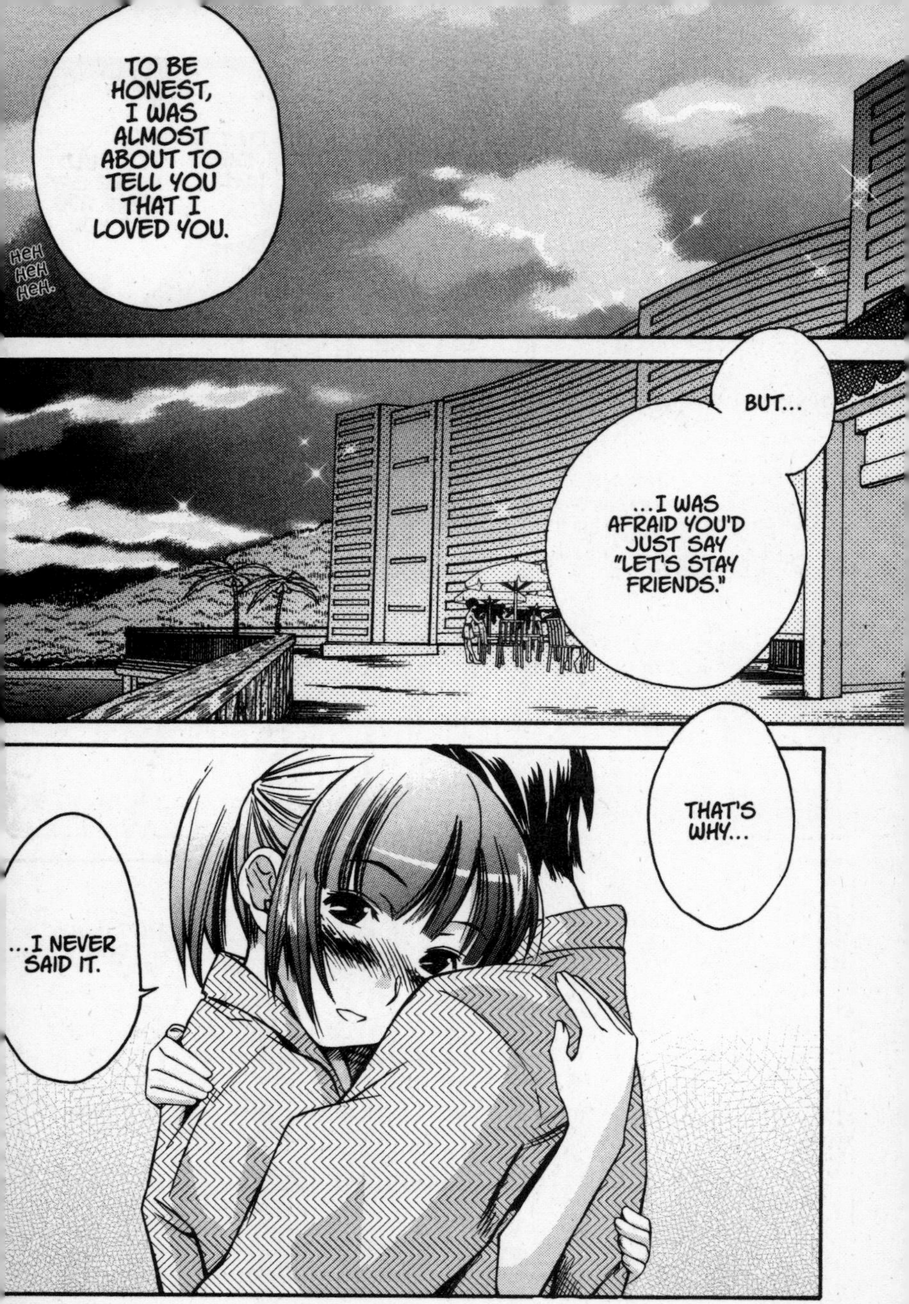
TO BE HONEST, I WAS ALMOST ABOUT TO TELL YOU THAT I LOVED YOU.
HEH HEH HEH.
BUT...
...I WAS AFRAID YOU'D JUST SAY "LET'S STAY FRIENDS."
THAT'S WHY...
...I NEVER SAID IT.

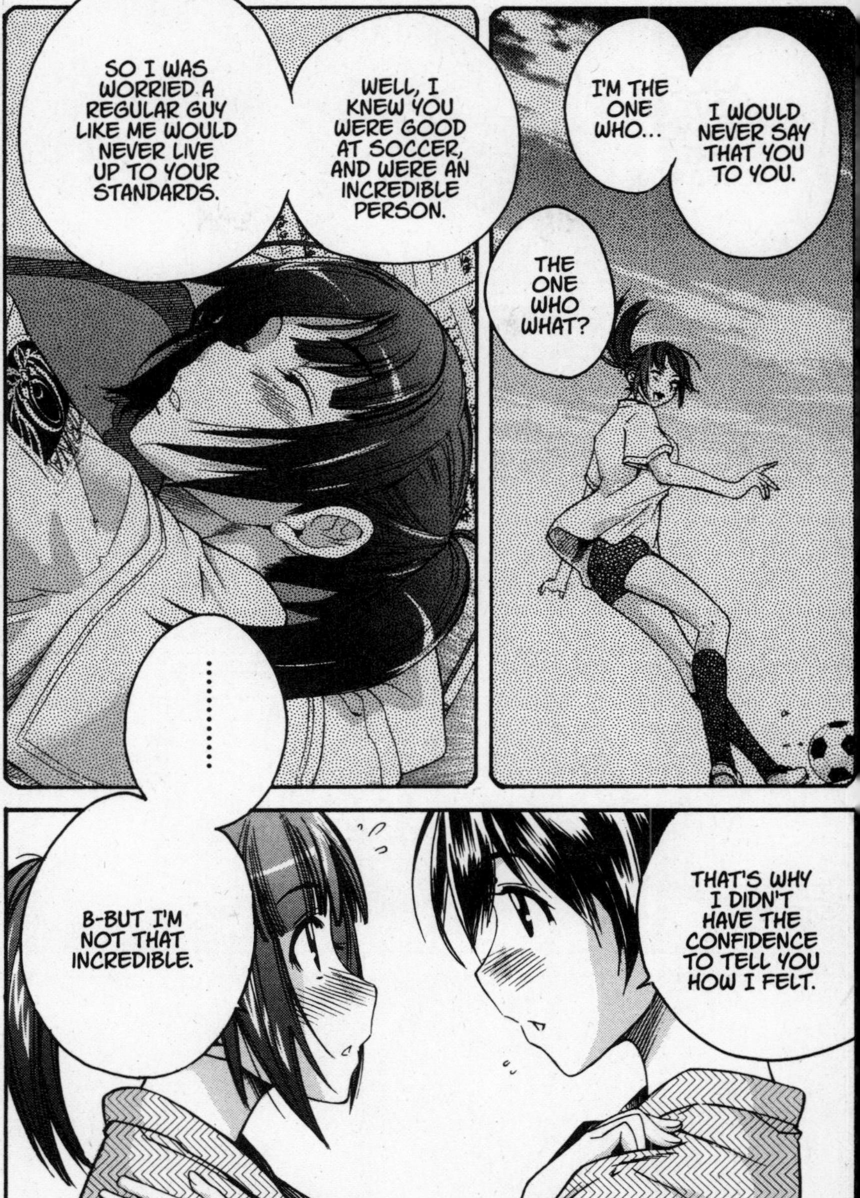
I WOULD NEVER SAY THAT YOU TO YOU.
I'M THE ONE WHO...
THE ONE WHO WHAT?
WELL, I KNEW YOU WERE GOOD AT SOCCER, AND WERE AN INCREDIBLE PERSON.
SO I WAS WORRIED A REGULAR GUY LIKE ME WOULD NEVER LIVE UP TO YOUR STANDARDS.
......
THAT'S WHY I DIDN'T HAVE THE CONFIDENCE TO TELL YOU HOW I FELT.
B-BUT I'M NOT THAT INCREDIBLE.

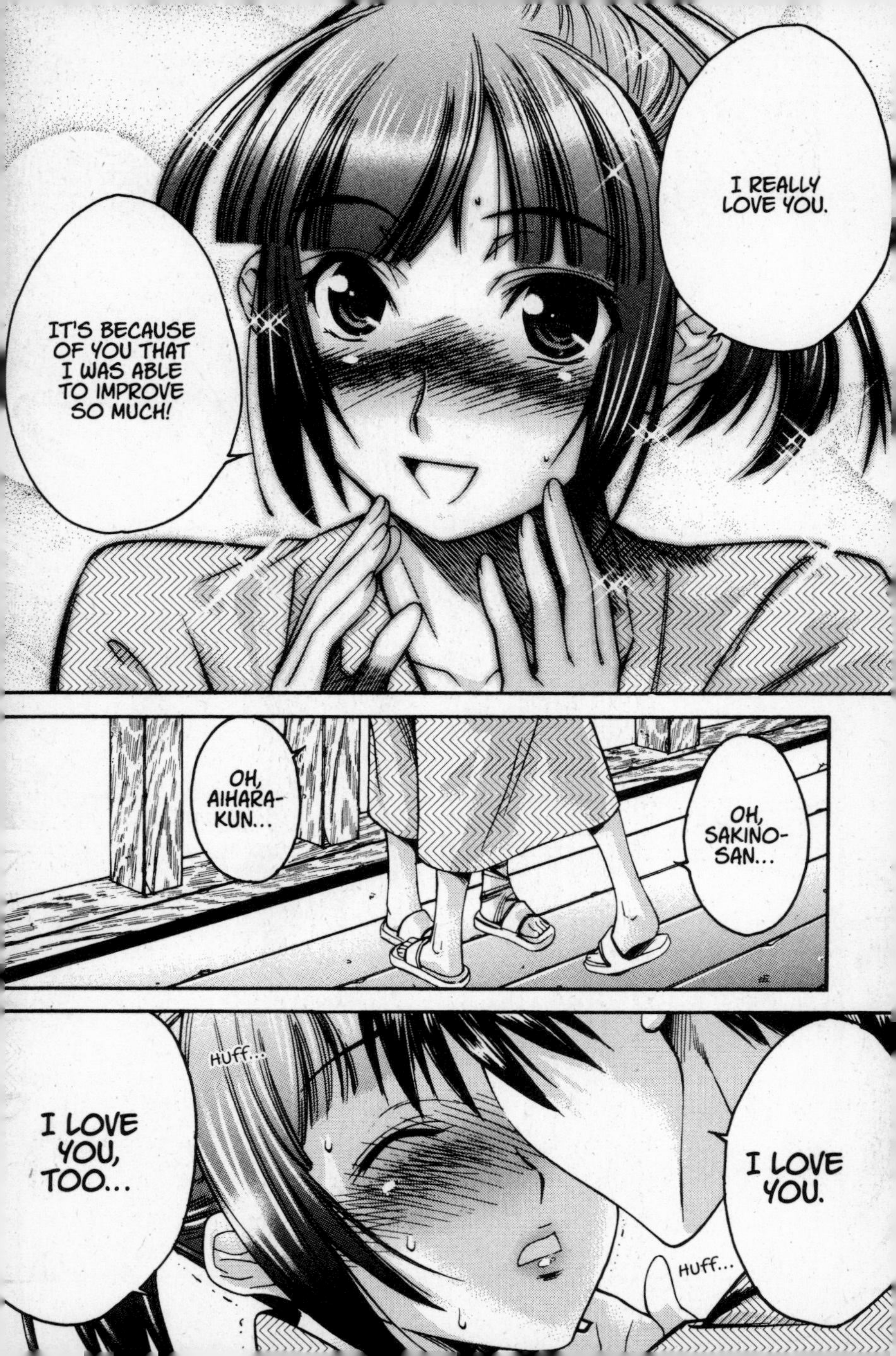
I REALLY LOVE YOU.
IT'S BECAUSE OF YOU THAT I WAS ABLE TO IMPROVE SO MUCH!
OH, SAKINO-SAN...
OH, AIHARA-KUN...
I LOVE YOU.
HUFF...
I LOVE YOU, TOO...
HUFF...

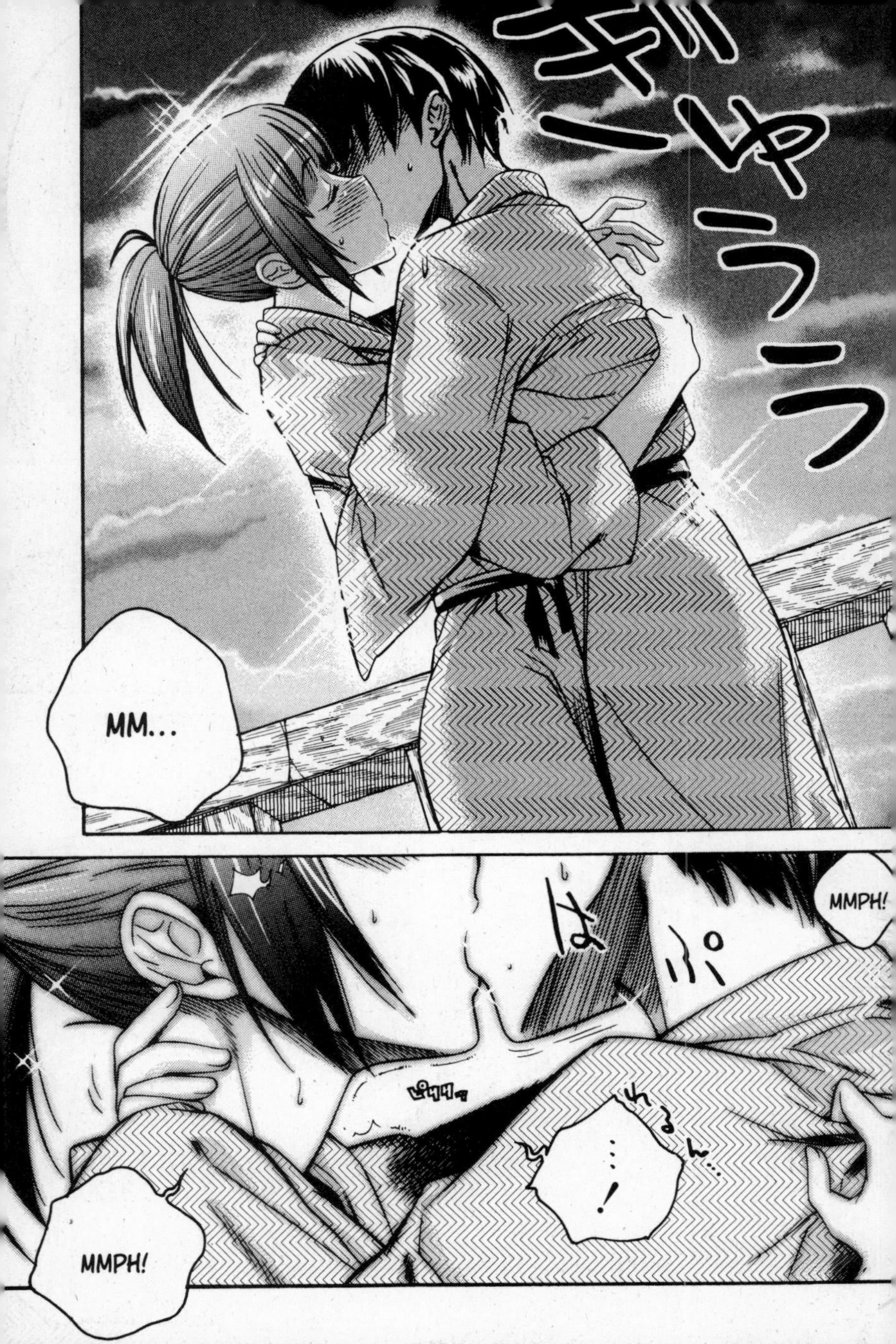
ぎゅううう
MM...
MMPH!
ぷ
は
れるん…
…!
MMPH!

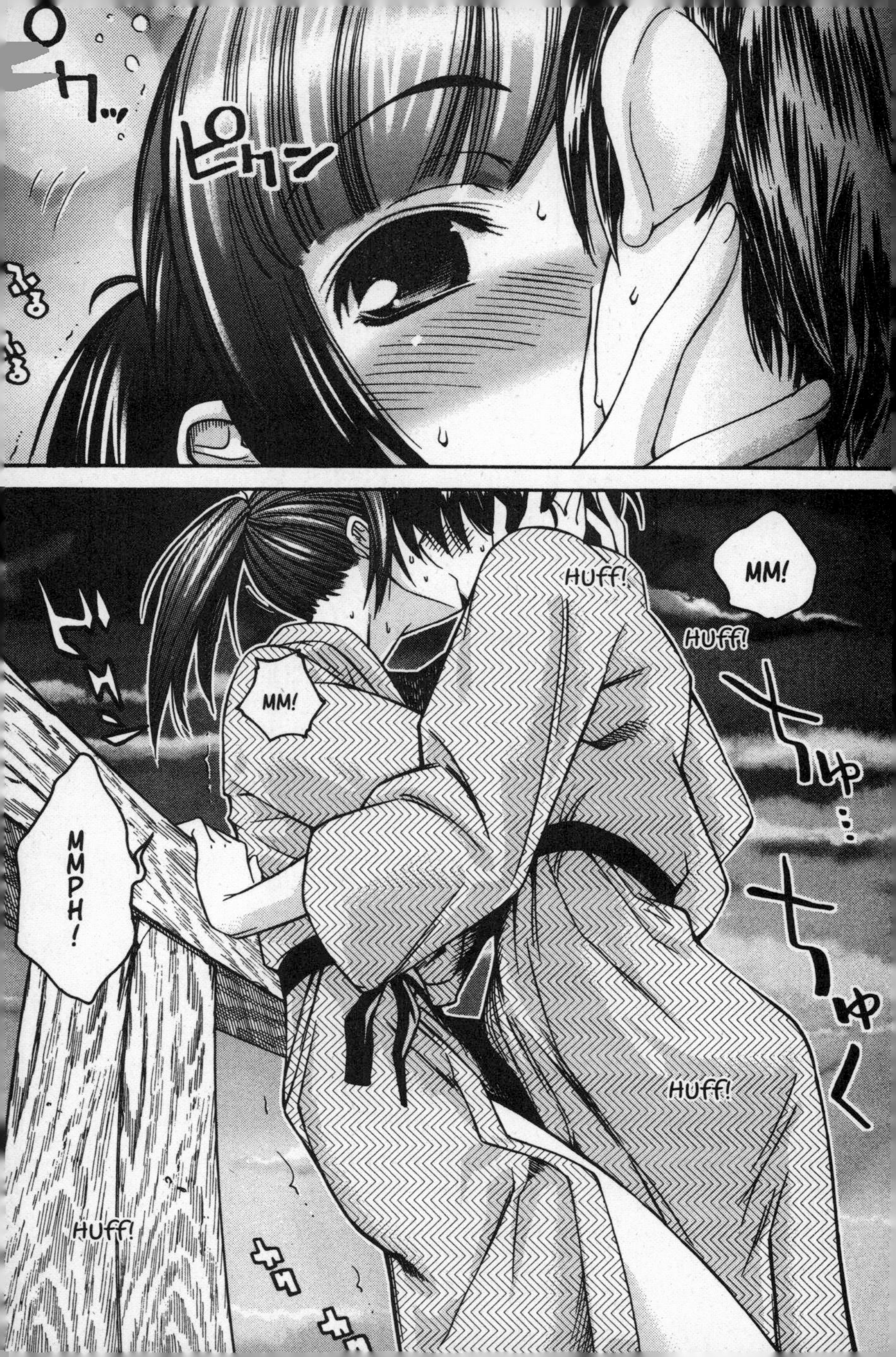
MM!
HUFF!
HUFF!
MM!
MMPH!
HUFF!
HUFF!

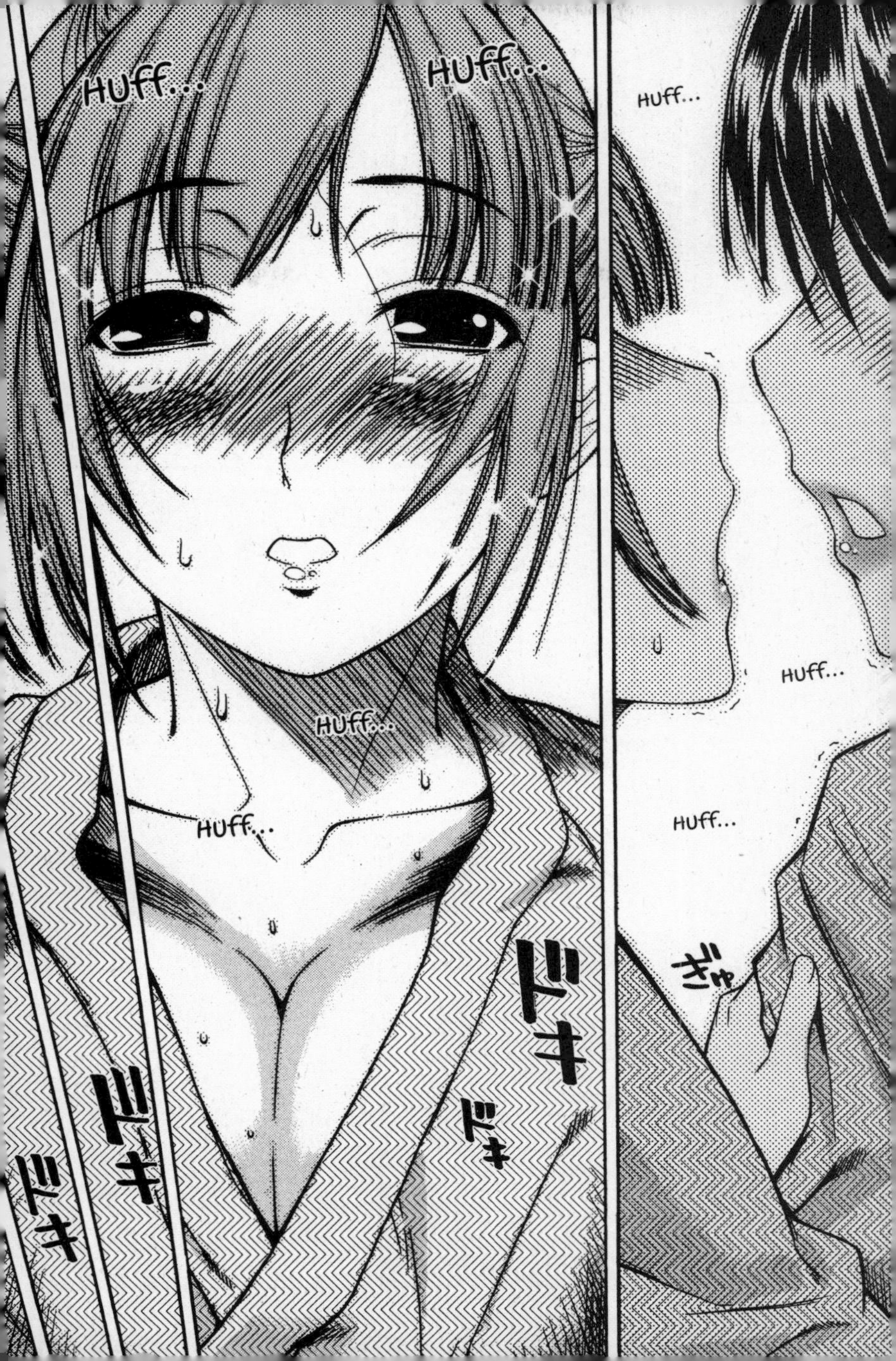
HUFF...
HUFF...
HUFF...
ぎゅ
HUFF...
HUFF...
HUFF...
HUFF...
ドキ
ドキ
ドキ
ドキ

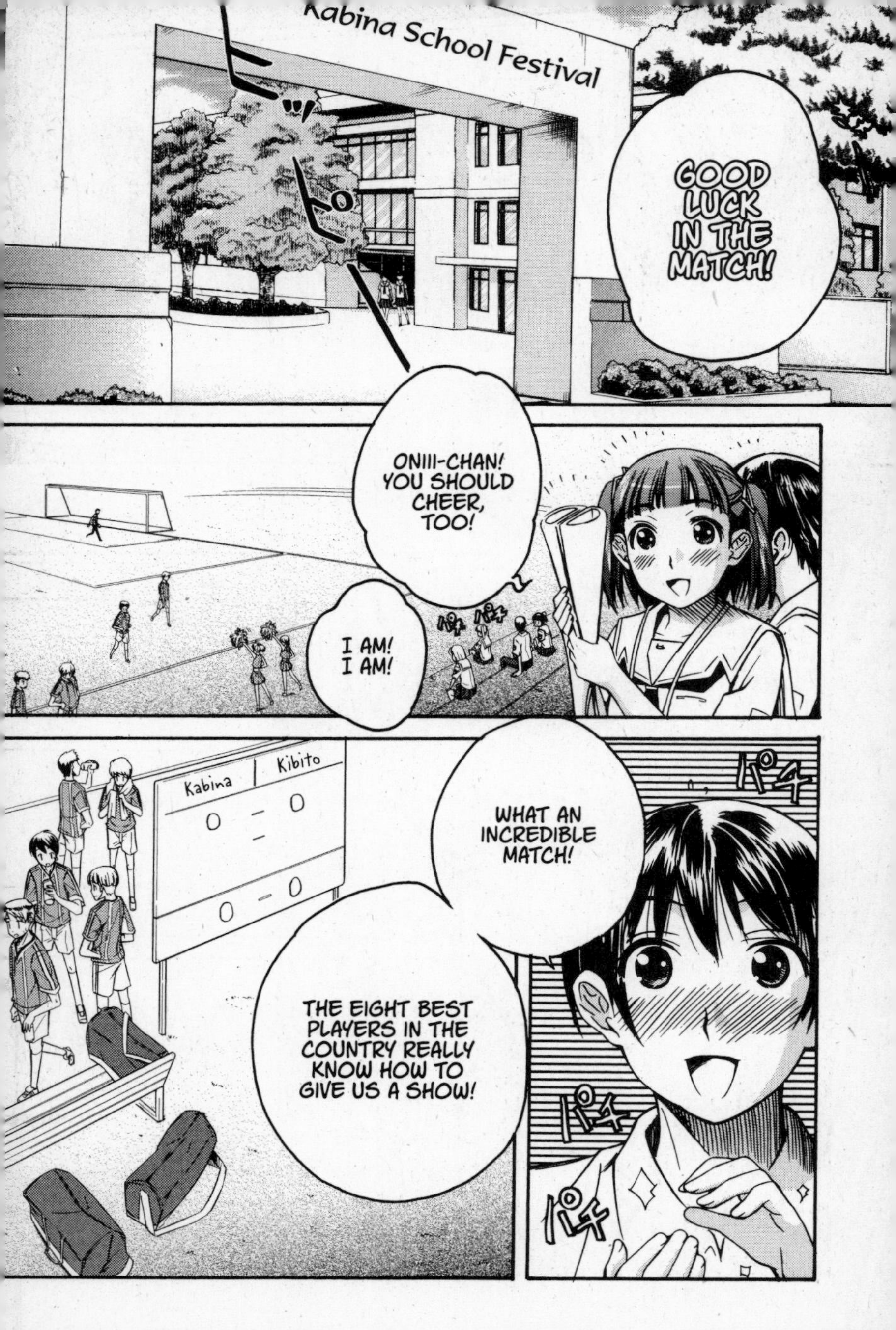
Kabina School Festival
GOOD LUCK IN THE MATCH!
ONIII-CHAN! YOU SHOULD CHEER, TOO!
I AM! I AM!
WHAT AN INCREDIBLE MATCH!
THE EIGHT BEST PLAYERS IN THE COUNTRY REALLY KNOW HOW TO GIVE US A SHOW!
Kabina
Kibito
0 - 0
0 - 0

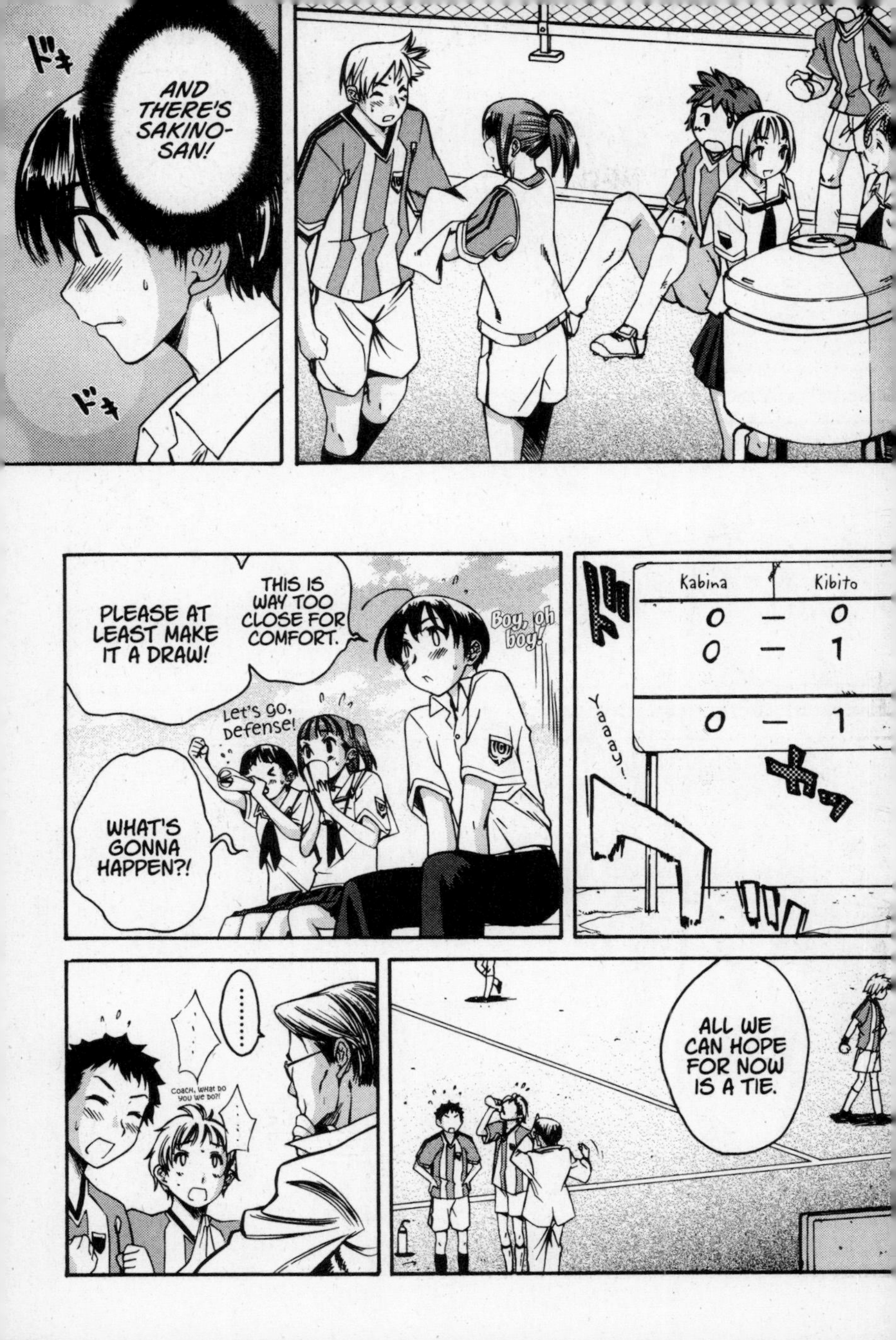
AND THERE'S SAKINO-SAN!
ドキ
ドキ
Kabina
Kibito
0 — 0
0 — 1
0 — 1
Yaaay!
THIS IS WAY TOO CLOSE FOR COMFORT.
Boy, oh boy!
PLEASE AT LEAST MAKE IT A DRAW!
Let's go, Defense!
WHAT'S GONNA HAPPEN?!
ALL WE CAN HOPE FOR NOW IS A TIE.
......
Coach, what do you we do?!
...

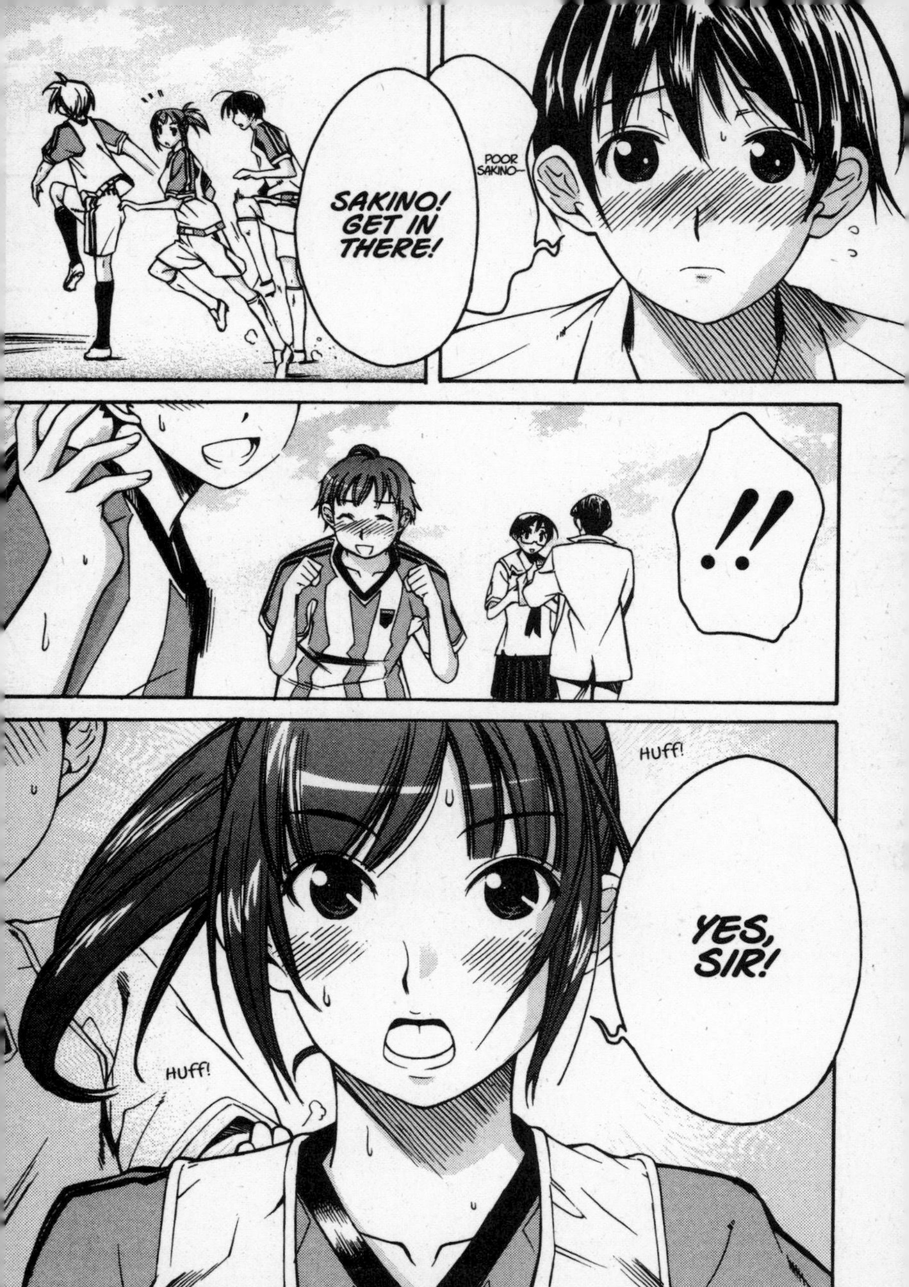
SAKINO! GET IN THERE!
POOR SAKINO~
!!
HUFF!
YES, SIR!
HUFF!

[Asuka 8th KISS END]

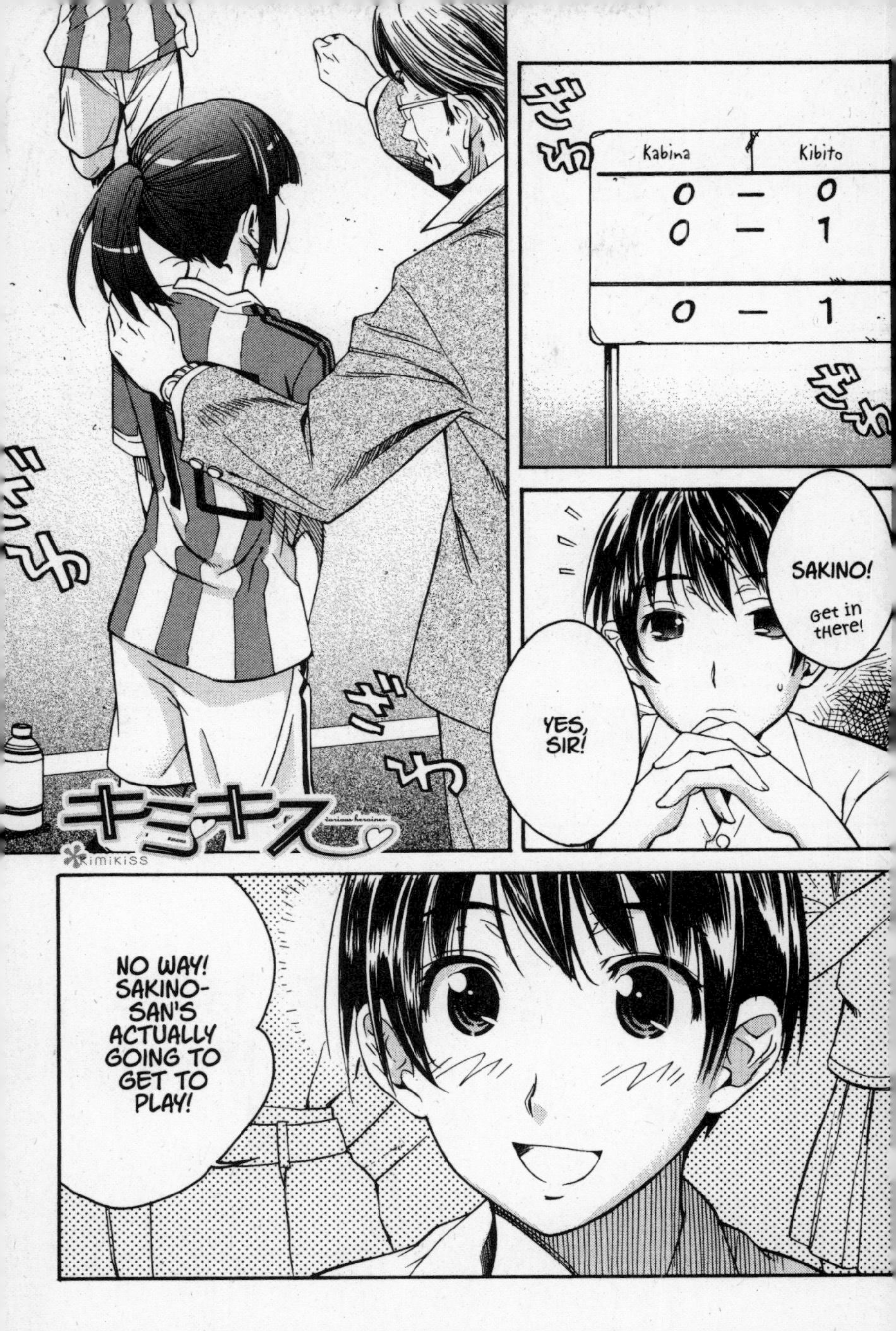
ざわ
Kabina
Kibito
0 — 0
0 — 1
0 — 1
ざわ
SAKINO!
Get in tHere!
YES, SIR!
ざわ
キミキス
various heroines
KimiKiss
NO WAY! SAKINO-SAN'S ACTUALLY GOING TO GET TO PLAY!

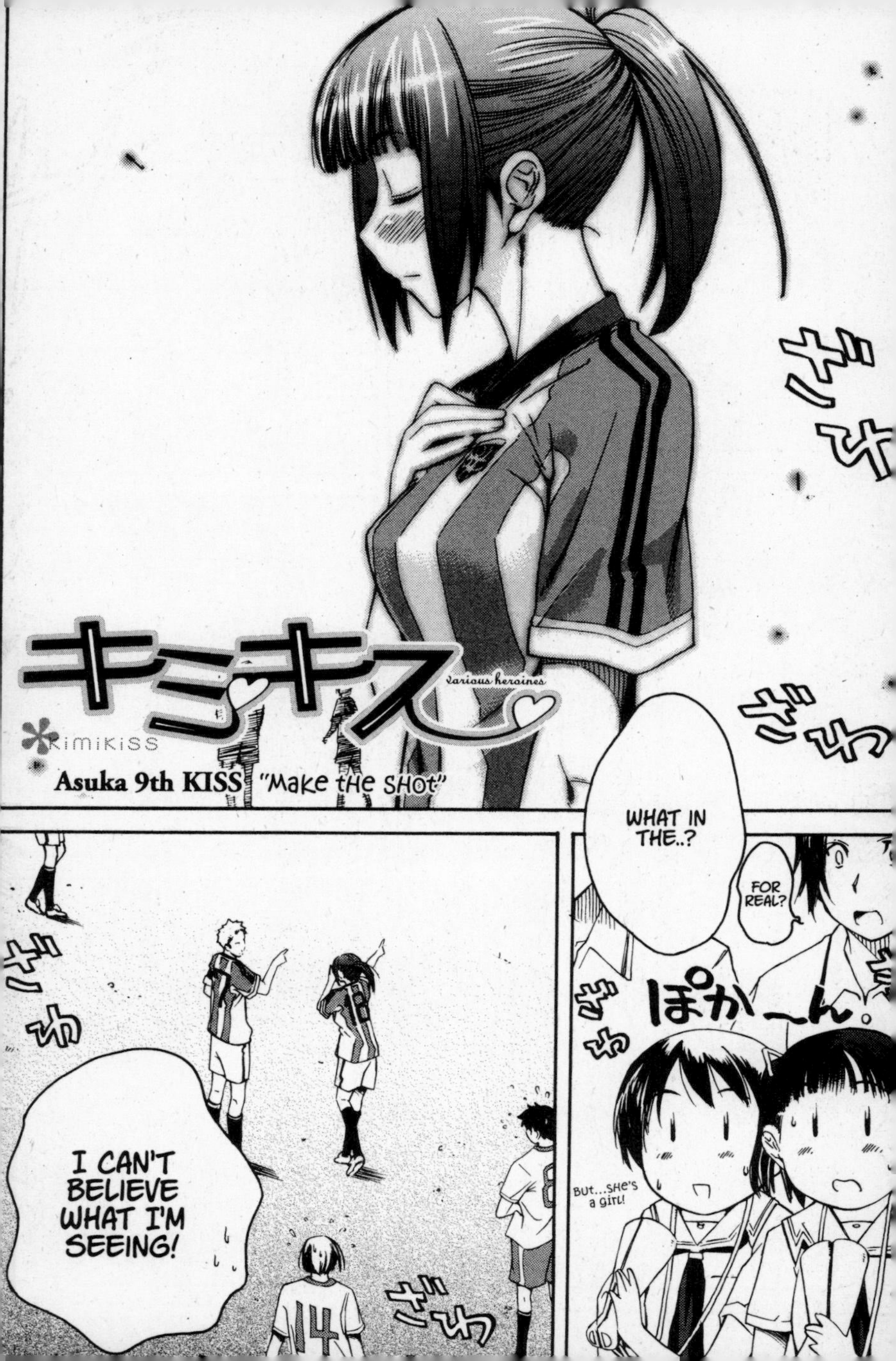
ざわ
ざわ
キミキス
various heroines
kimikiss
Asuka 9th KISS "Make the Shot"
WHAT IN THE..?
FOR REAL?
ざわ
ぽかーん。
But...SHE's a girl!
ざわ
I CAN'T BELIEVE WHAT I'M SEEING!
ざわ

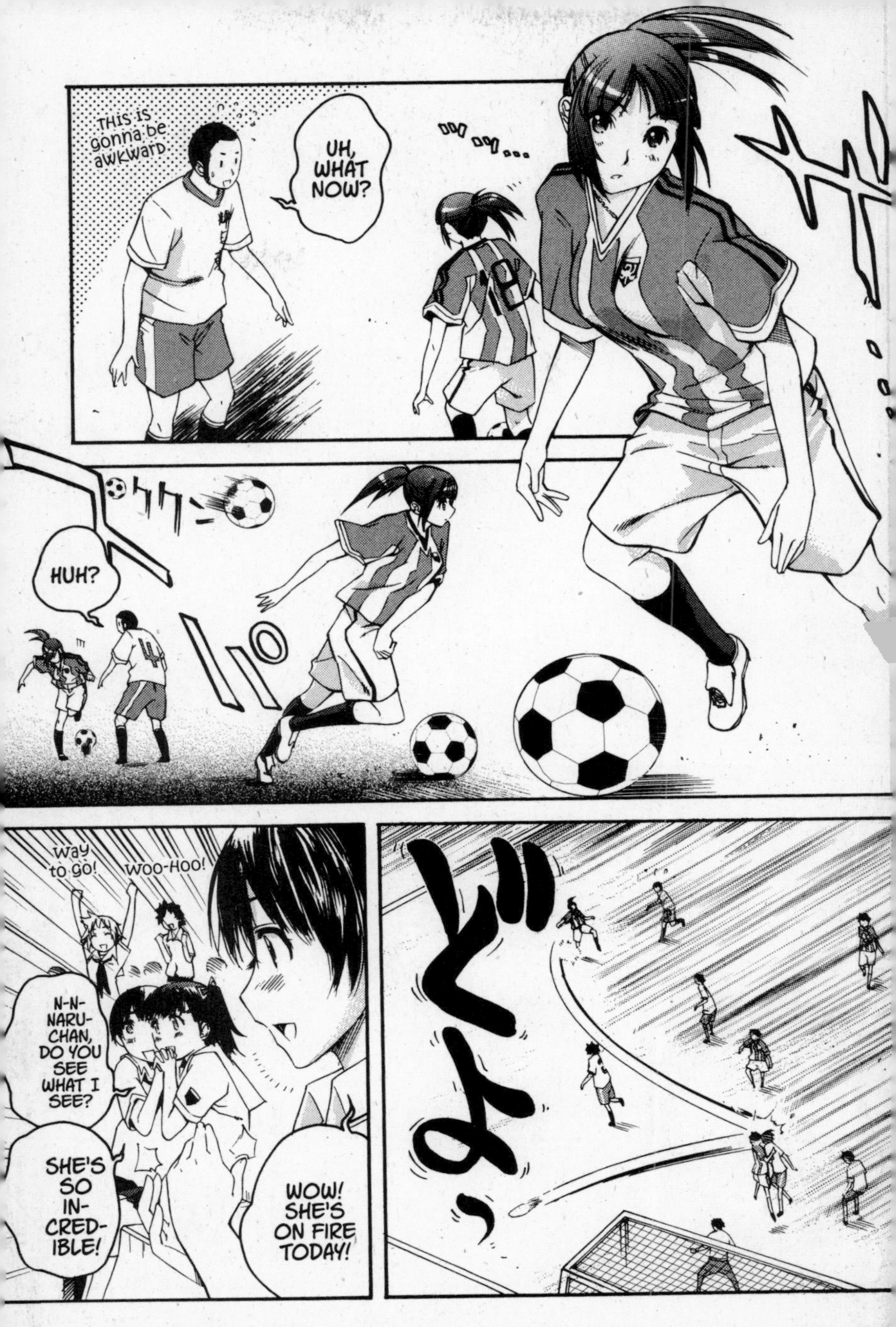
UH, WHAT NOW?
THIS IS gonna be awkward
HUH?
WOO-HOO!
Way to go!
N-N-NARU-CHAN, DO YOU SEE WHAT I SEE?
WOW! SHE'S ON FIRE TODAY!
SHE'S SO IN-CRED-IBLE!

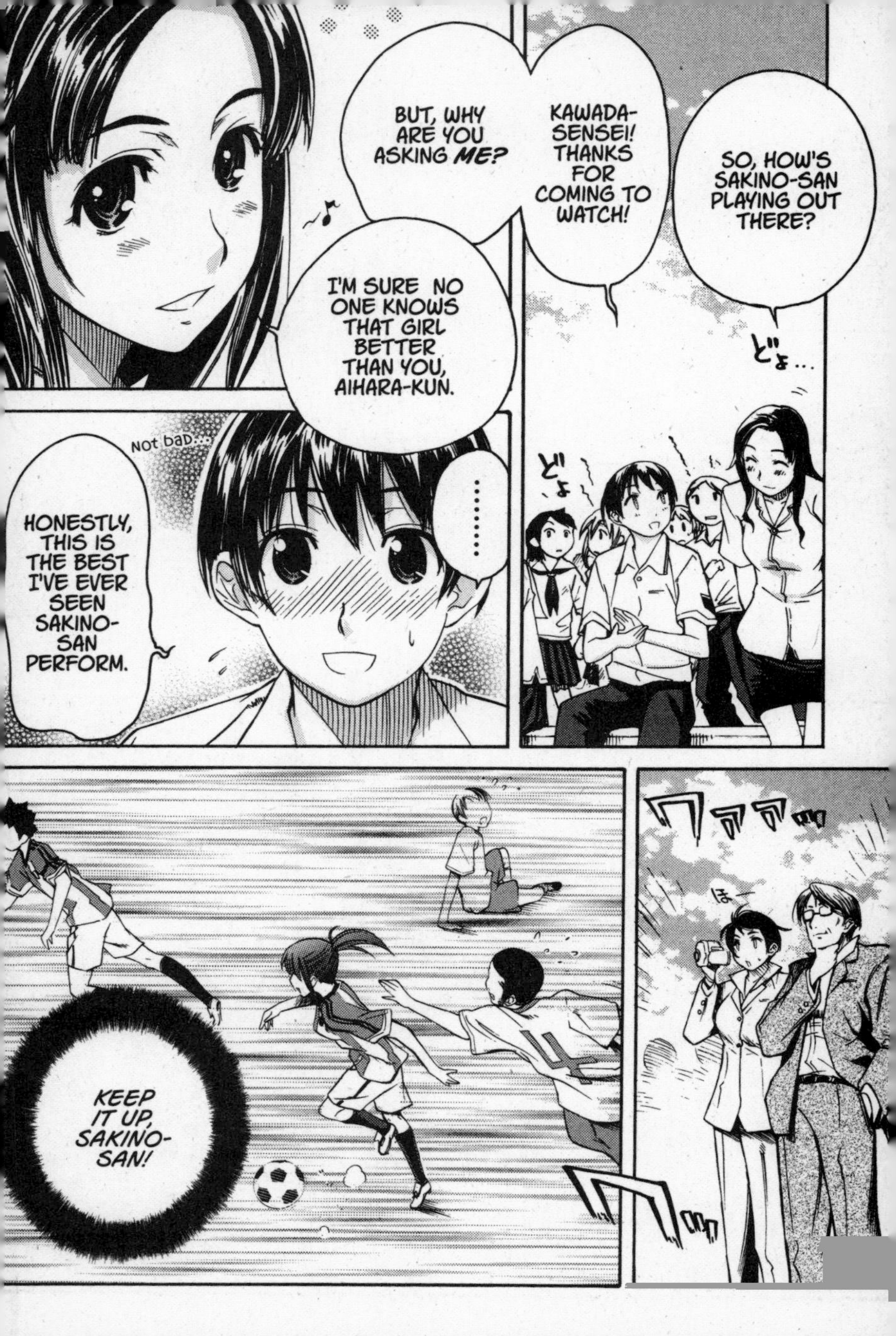

SO, HOW'S SAKINO-SAN PLAYING OUT THERE?
どよ…
KAWADA-SENSEI! THANKS FOR COMING TO WATCH!
どよ
BUT, WHY ARE YOU ASKING *ME*?
I'M SURE NO ONE KNOWS THAT GIRL BETTER THAN YOU, AIHARA-KUN.
......
Not bad...
HONESTLY, THIS IS THE BEST I'VE EVER SEEN SAKINO-SAN PERFORM.
KEEP IT UP, SAKINO-SAN!

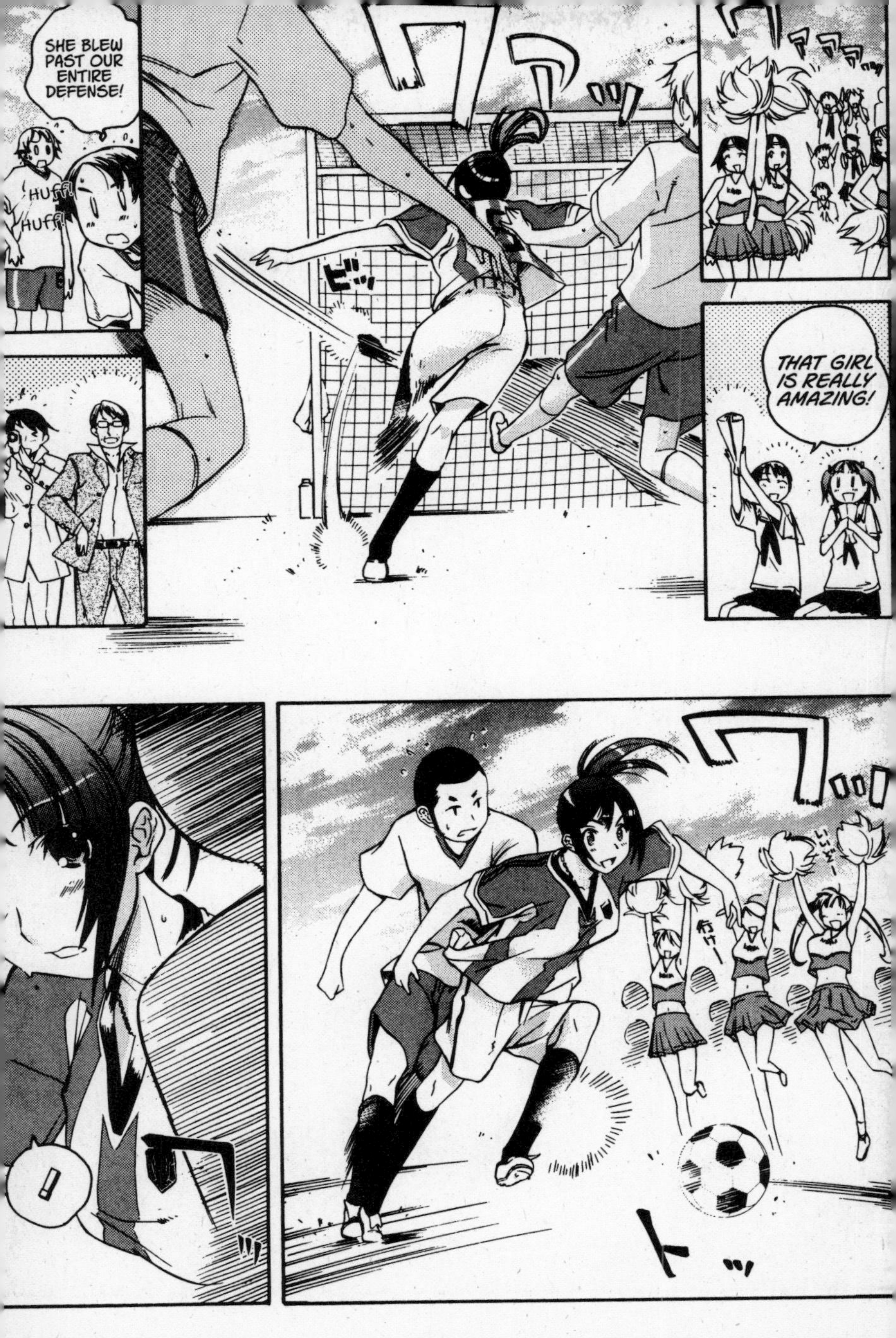

THAT GIRL IS REALLY AMAZING!
SHE BLEW PAST OUR ENTIRE DEFENSE!
HUFF
HUFF
!

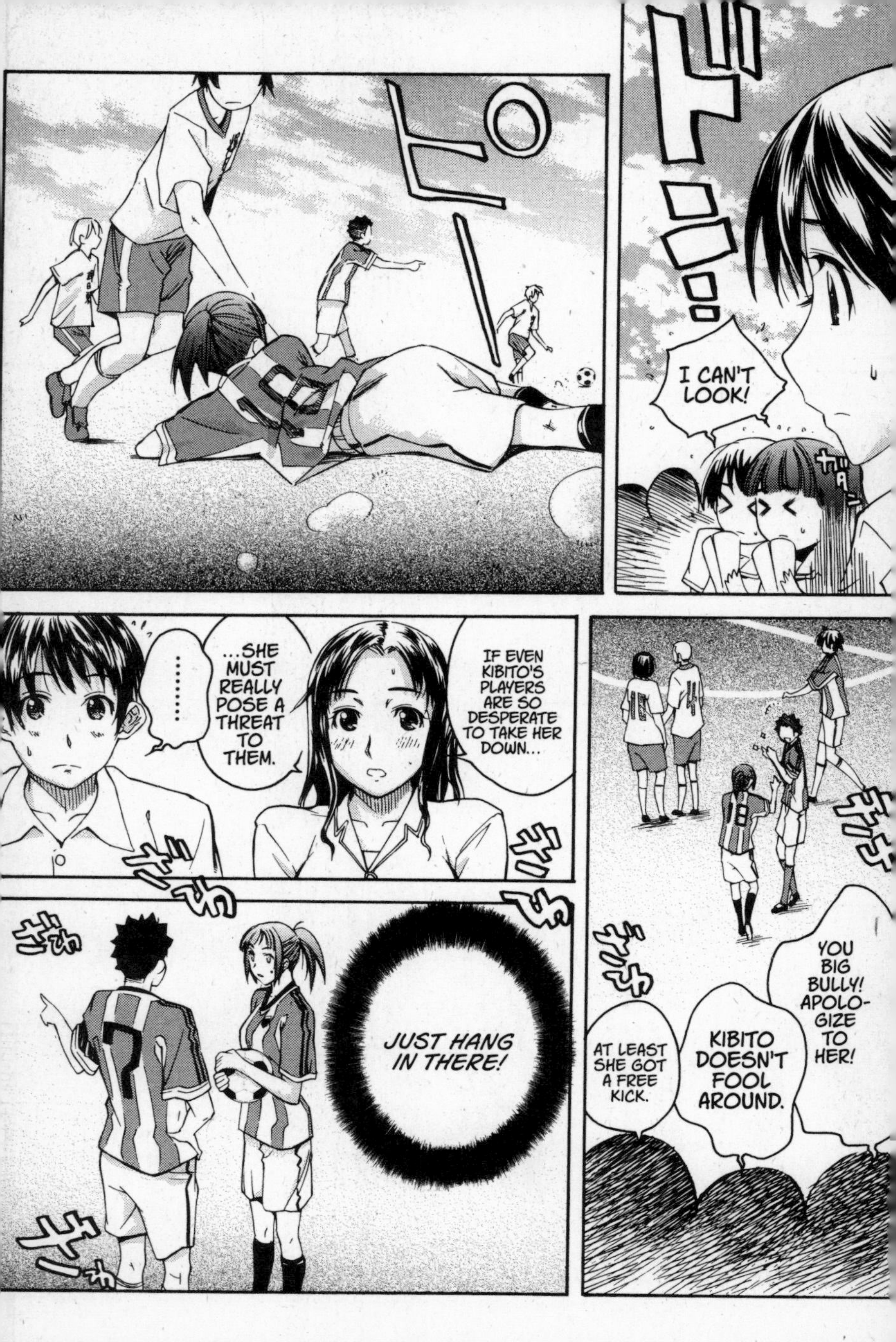
I CAN'T LOOK!
YOU BIG BULLY! APOLOGIZE TO HER!
KIBITO DOESN'T FOOL AROUND.
AT LEAST SHE GOT A FREE KICK.
IF EVEN KIBITO'S PLAYERS ARE SO DESPERATE TO TAKE HER DOWN...
...SHE MUST REALLY POSE A THREAT TO THEM.
......
JUST HANG IN THERE!

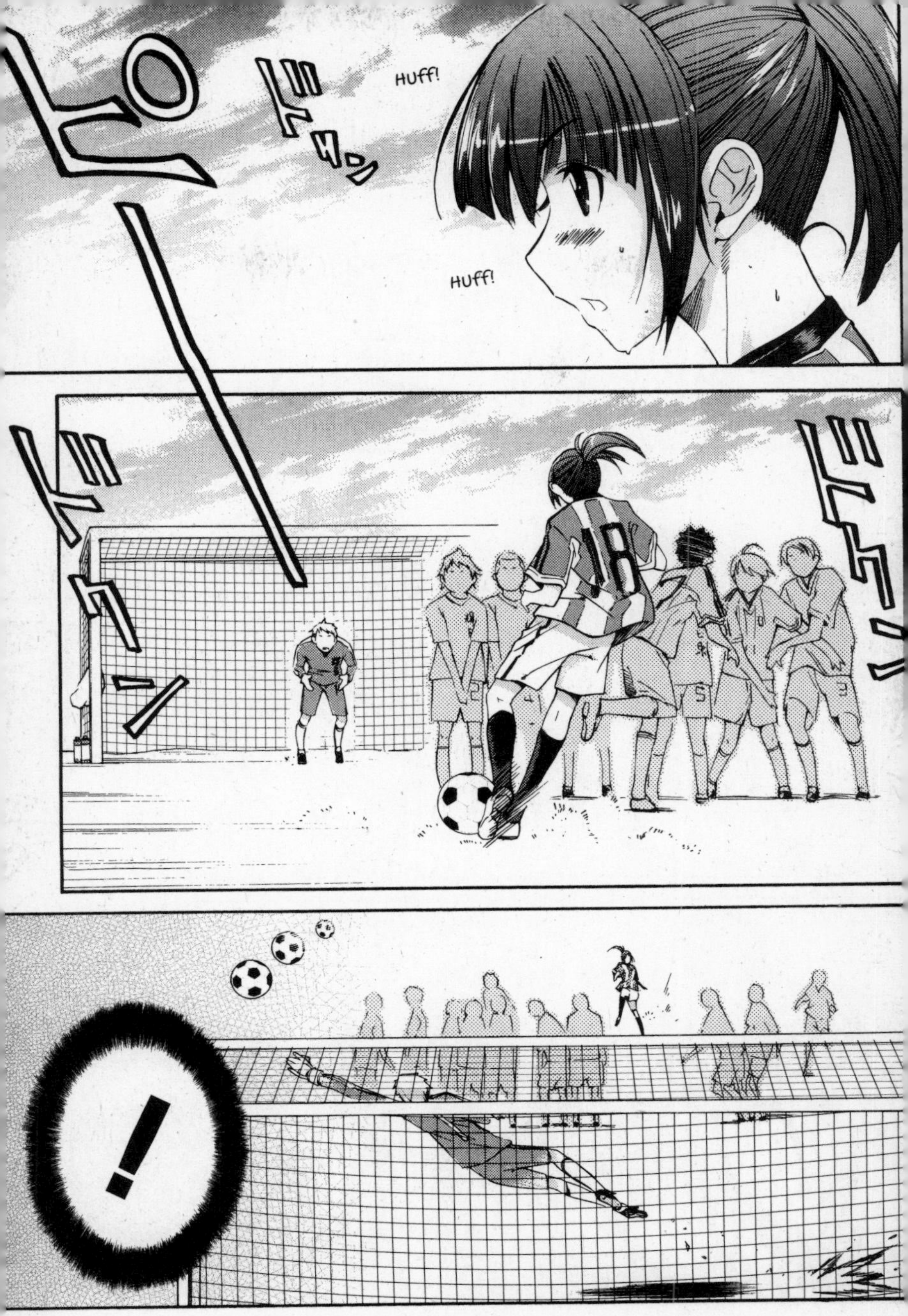
HUFF!
HUFF!
!

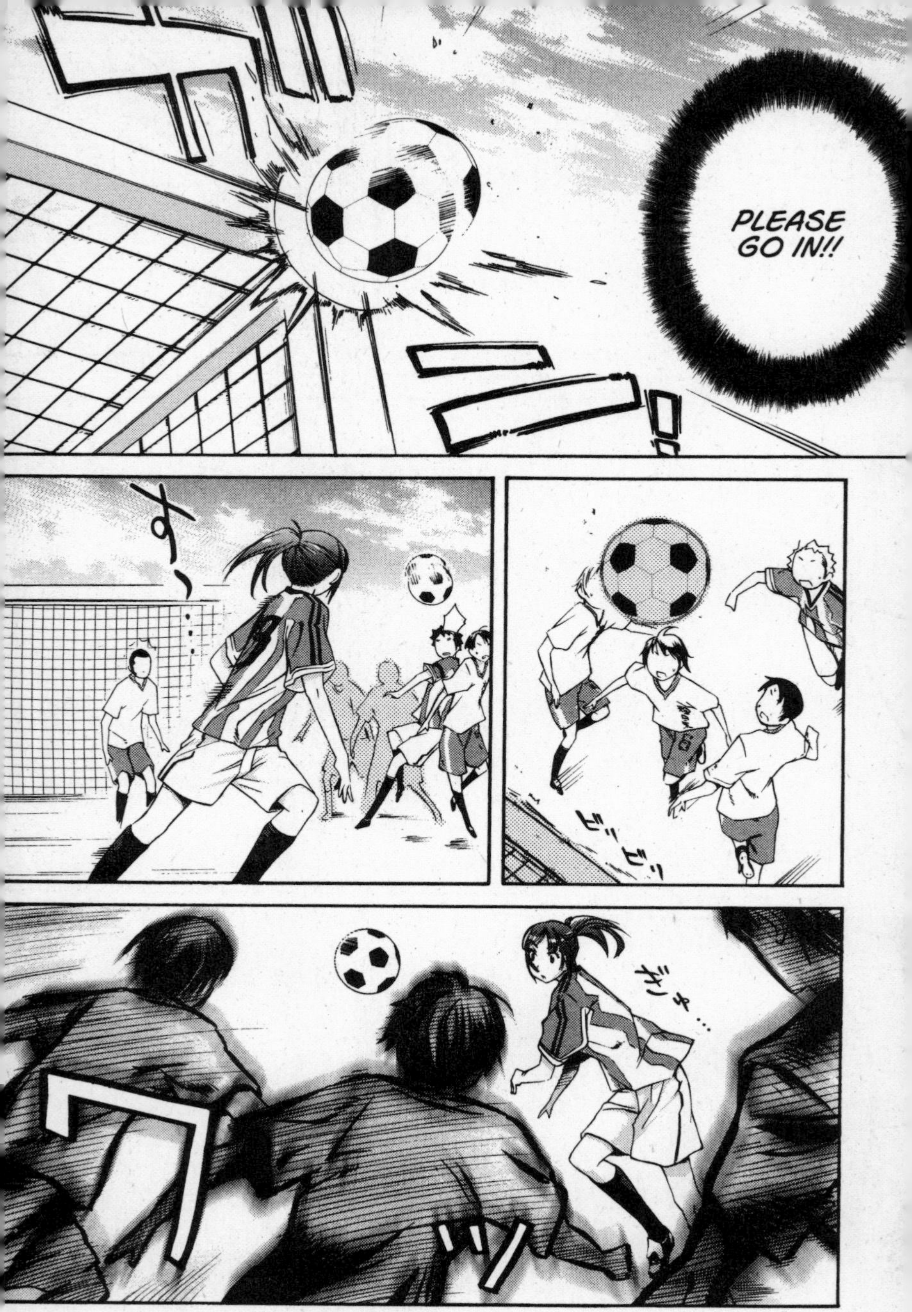
PLEASE GO IN!!
ビッ ビッ
す
ぎゅ…

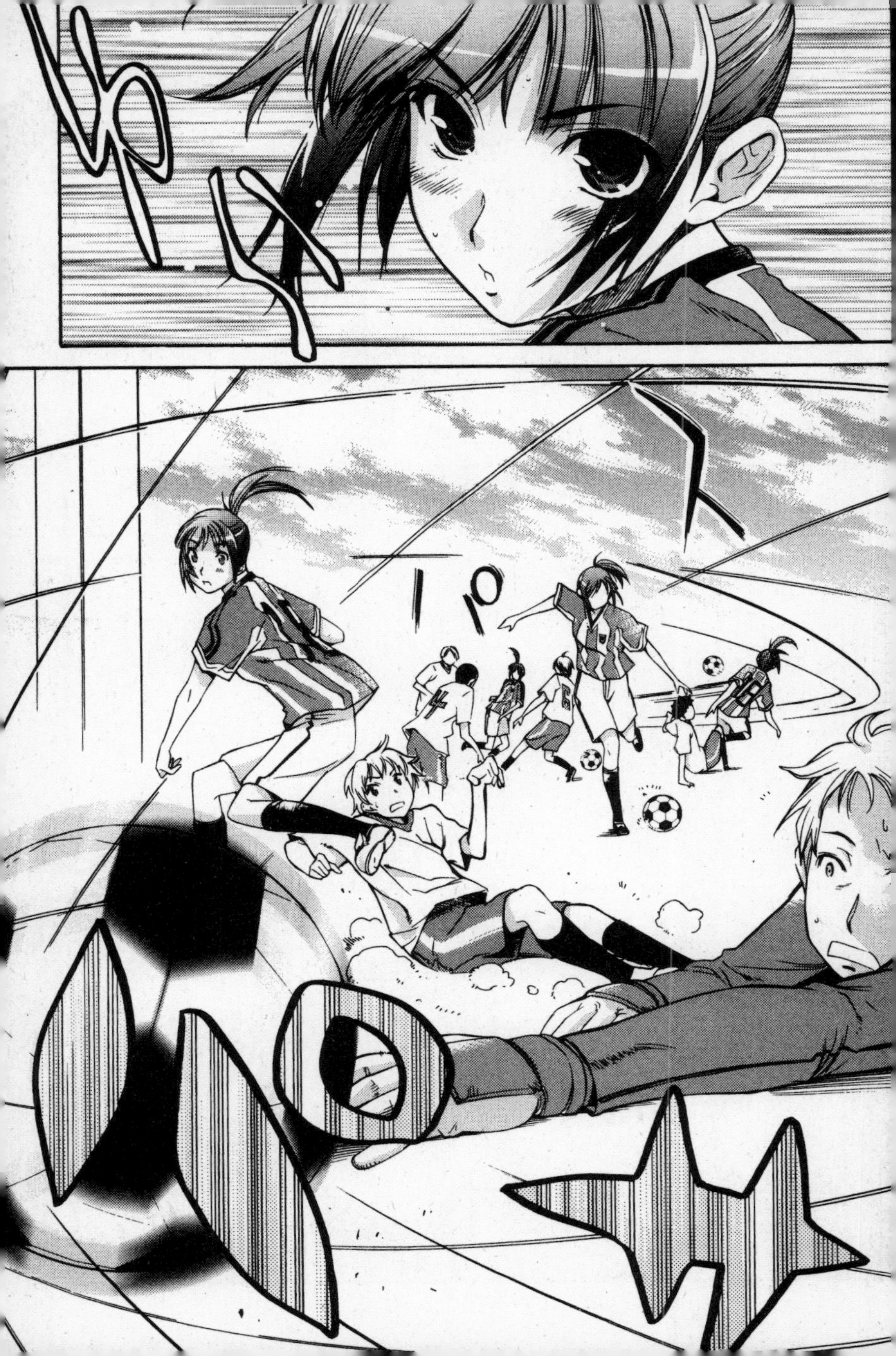

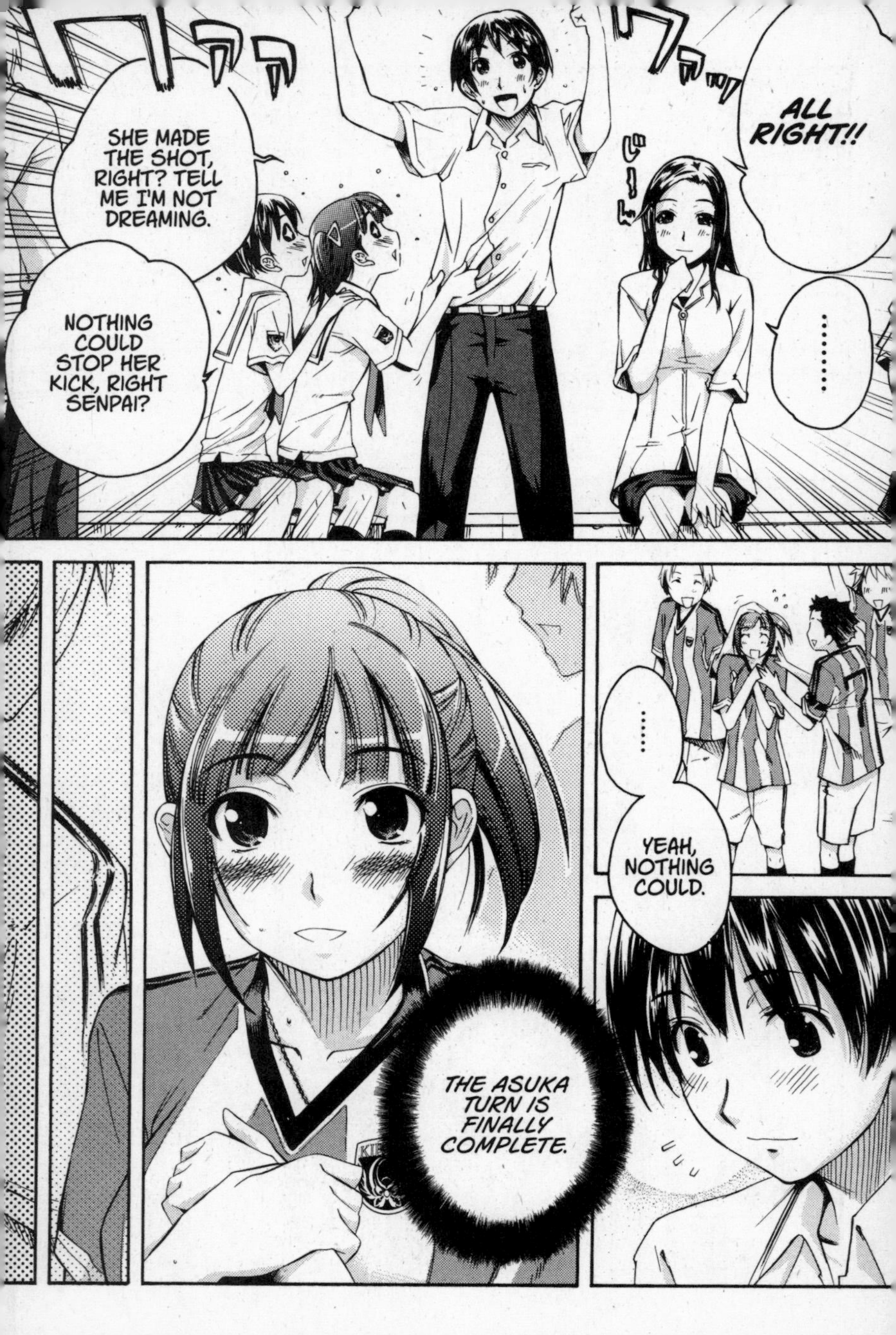
ALL RIGHT!!
......
SHE MADE THE SHOT, RIGHT? TELL ME I'M NOT DREAMING.
NOTHING COULD STOP HER KICK, RIGHT SENPAI?
......
YEAH, NOTHING COULD.
THE ASUKA TURN IS FINALLY COMPLETE.

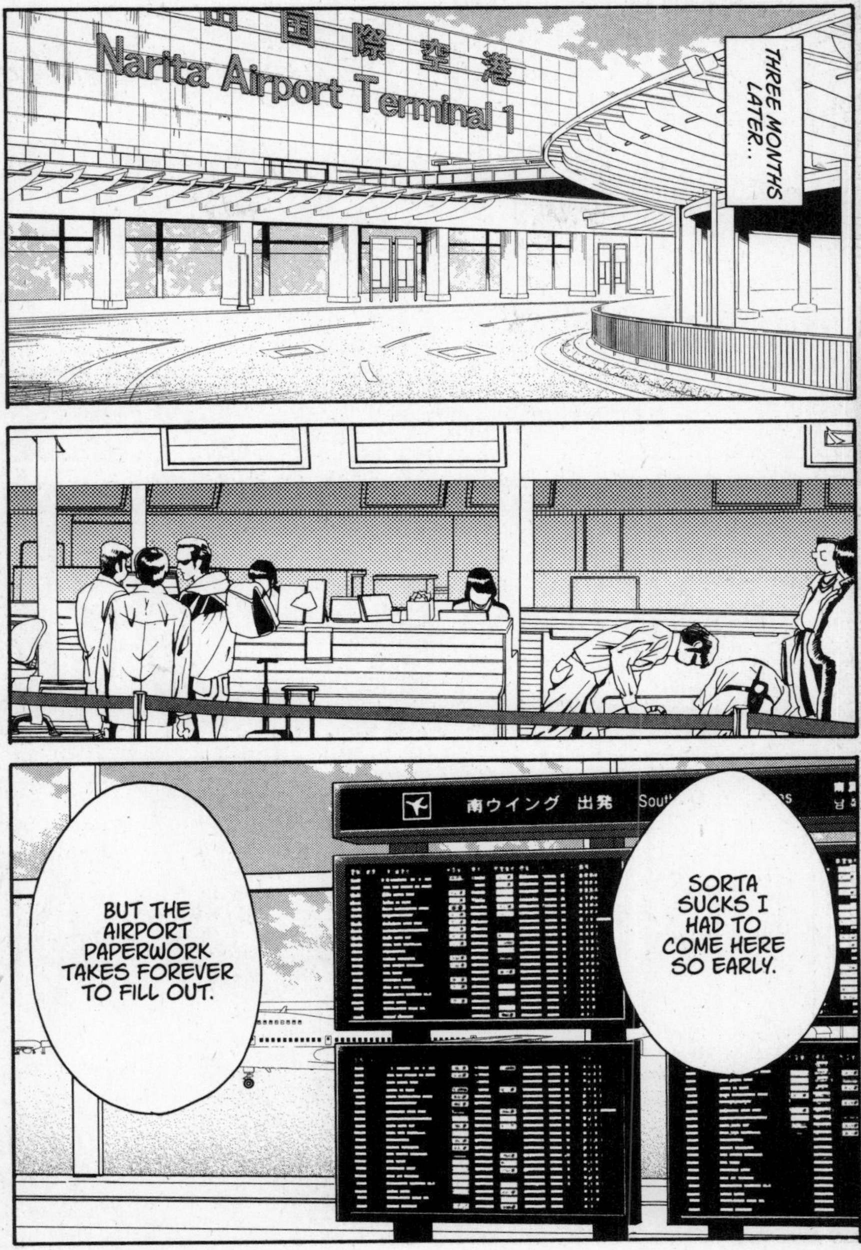
国際空港
Narita Airport Terminal 1
THREE MONTHS LATER...
南ウイング 出発
SORTA SUCKS I HAD TO COME HERE SO EARLY.
BUT THE AIRPORT PAPERWORK TAKES FOREVER TO FILL OUT.

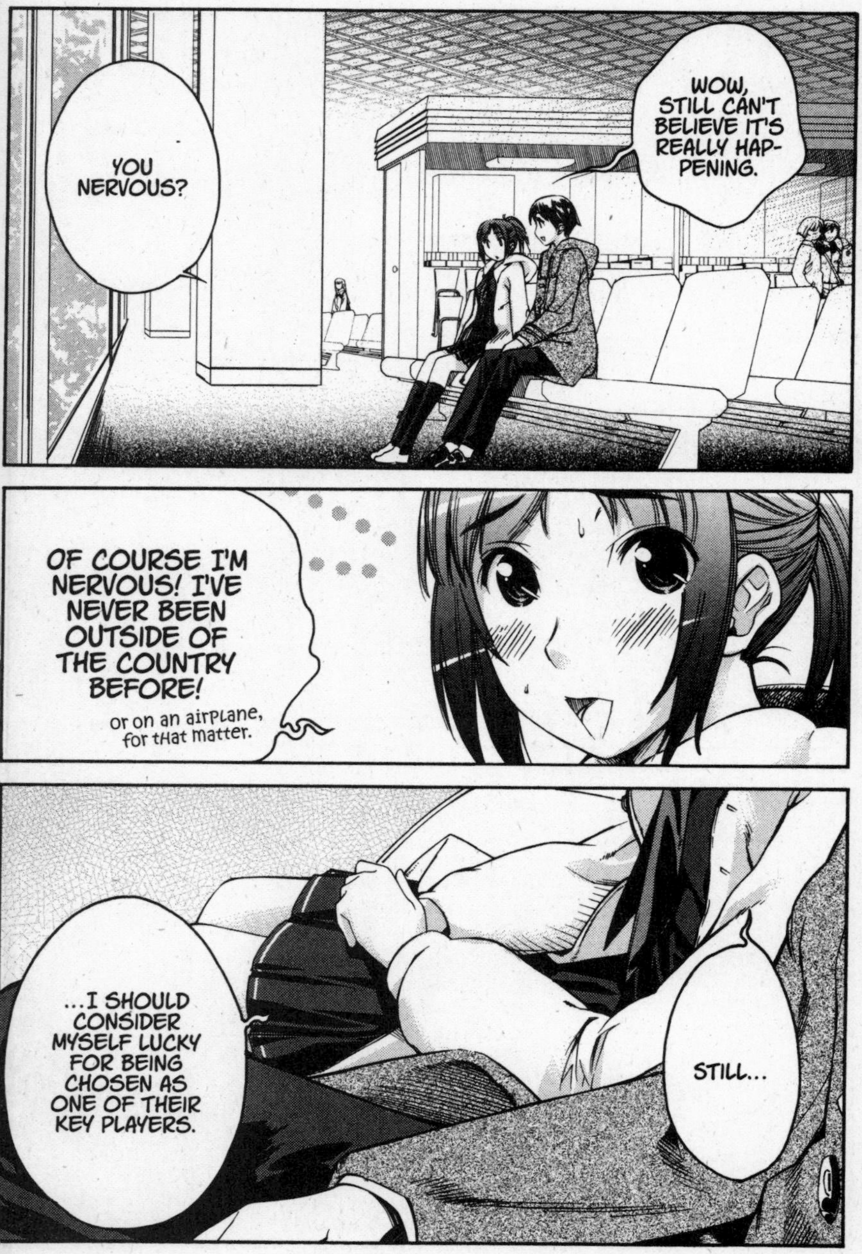

WOW, STILL CAN'T BELIEVE IT'S REALLY HAP-PENING.
YOU NERVOUS?
OF COURSE I'M NERVOUS! I'VE NEVER BEEN OUTSIDE OF THE COUNTRY BEFORE!
or on an airplane, for that matter.
STILL...
...I SHOULD CONSIDER MYSELF LUCKY FOR BEING CHOSEN AS ONE OF THEIR KEY PLAYERS.

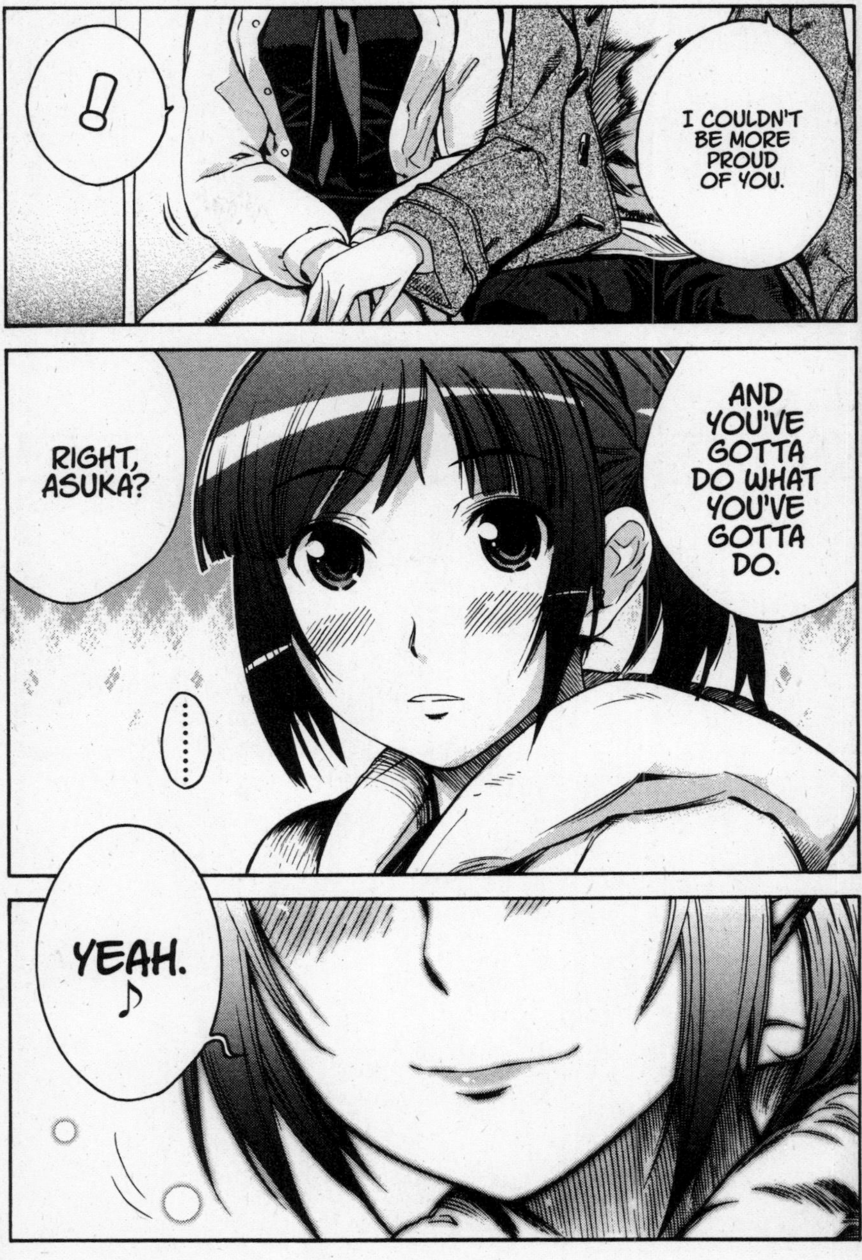
I COULDN'T BE MORE PROUD OF YOU.
!
AND YOU'VE GOTTA DO WHAT YOU'VE GOTTA DO.
RIGHT, ASUKA?
......
YEAH. ♪

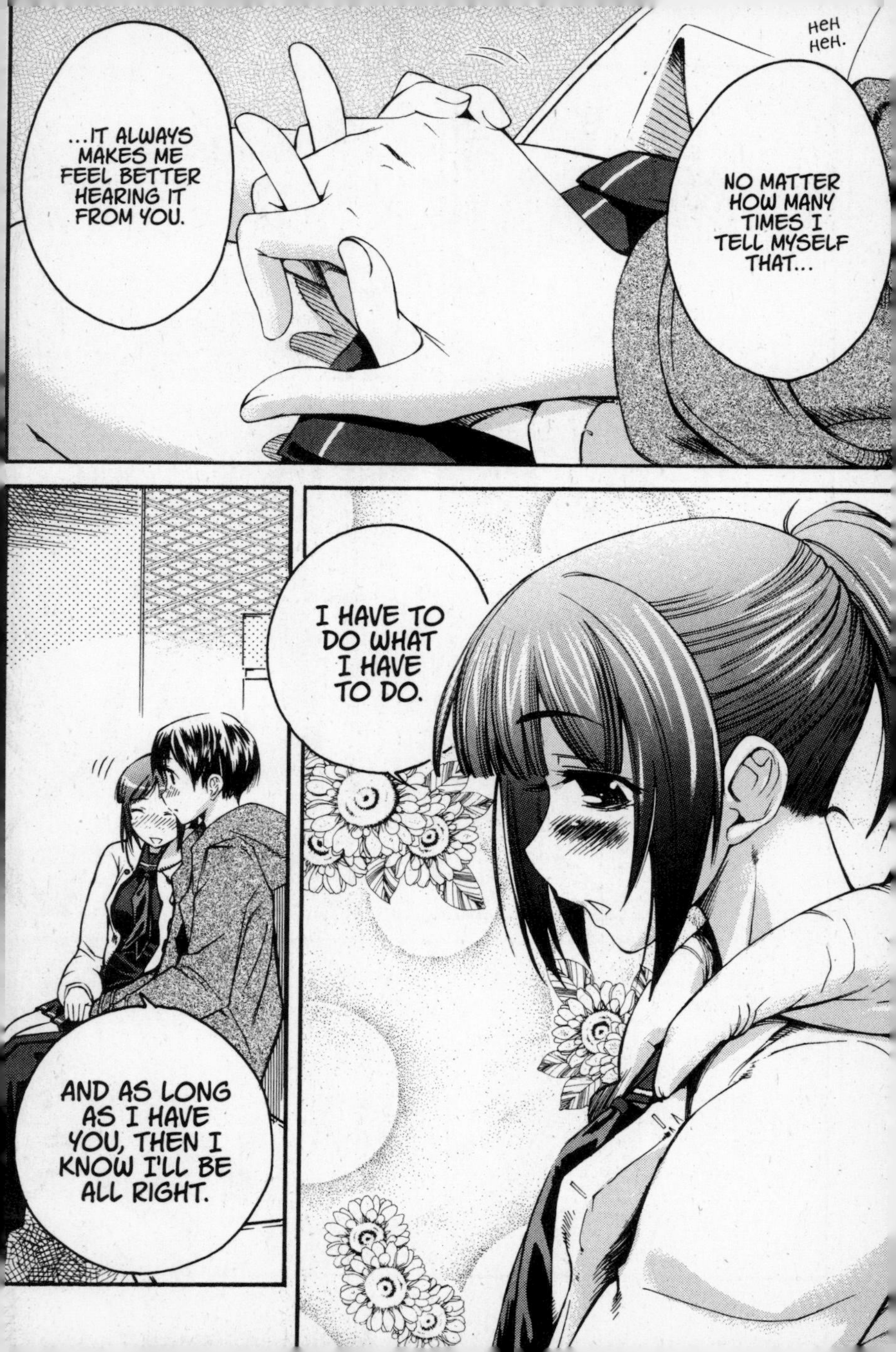
HEH HEH.
NO MATTER HOW MANY TIMES I TELL MYSELF THAT...
...IT ALWAYS MAKES ME FEEL BETTER HEARING IT FROM YOU.
I HAVE TO DO WHAT I HAVE TO DO.
AND AS LONG AS I HAVE YOU, THEN I KNOW I'LL BE ALL RIGHT.

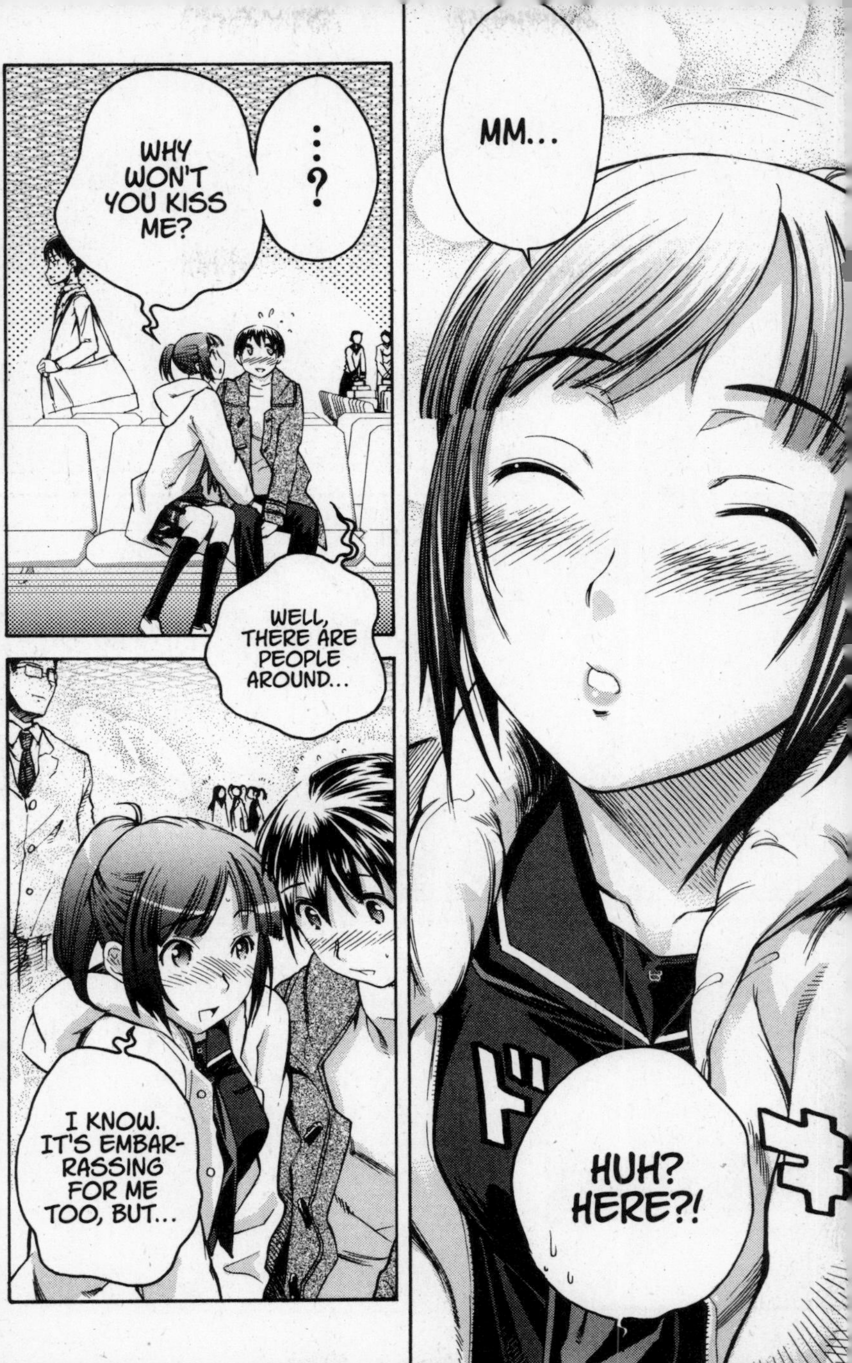
MM...
ド
HUH? HERE?!
...?
WHY WON'T YOU KISS ME?
WELL, THERE ARE PEOPLE AROUND...
I KNOW. IT'S EMBARRASSING FOR ME TOO, BUT...

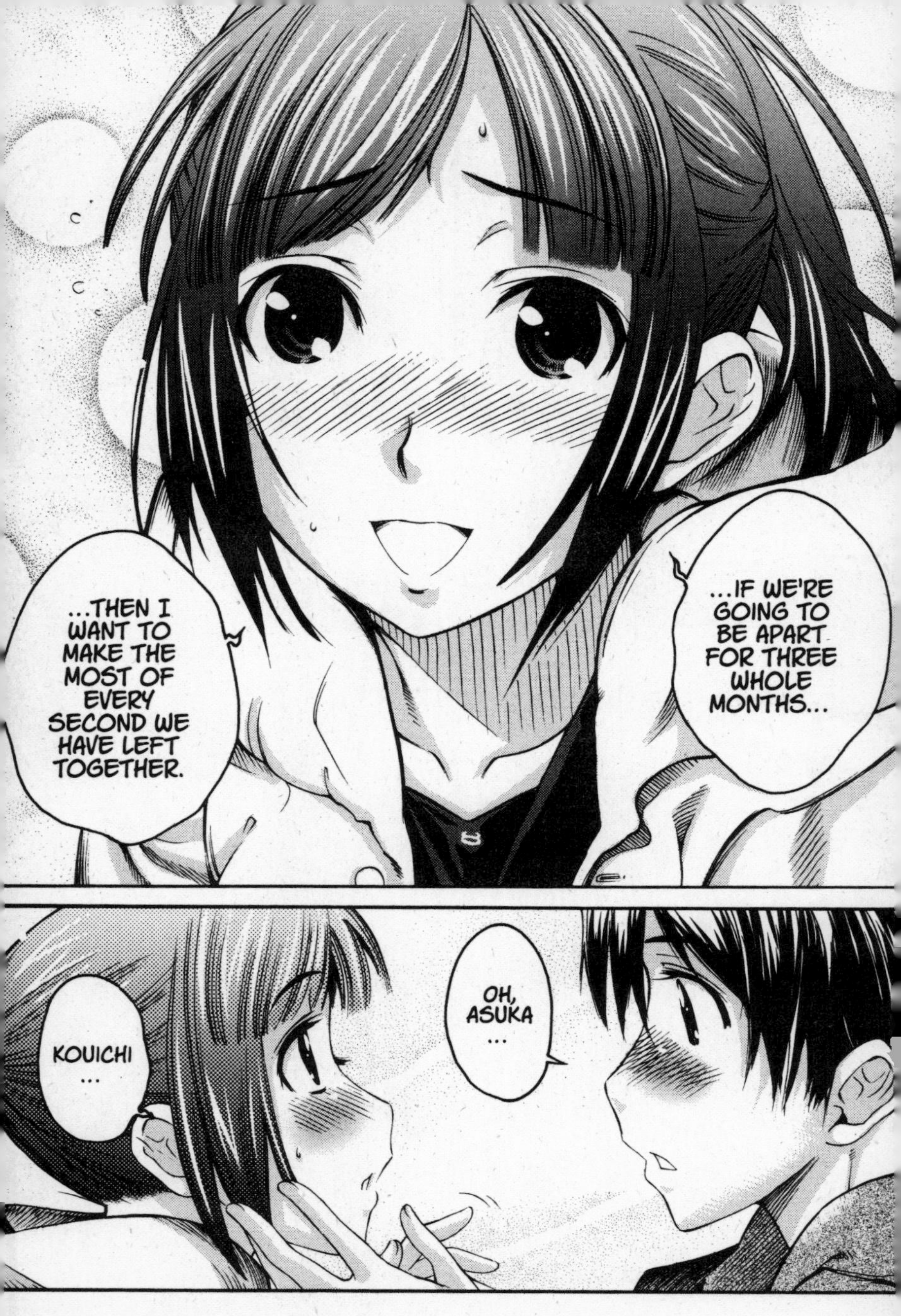
...IF WE'RE GOING TO BE APART FOR THREE WHOLE MONTHS...
...THEN I WANT TO MAKE THE MOST OF EVERY SECOND WE HAVE LEFT TOGETHER.
OH, ASUKA ...
KOUICHI ...

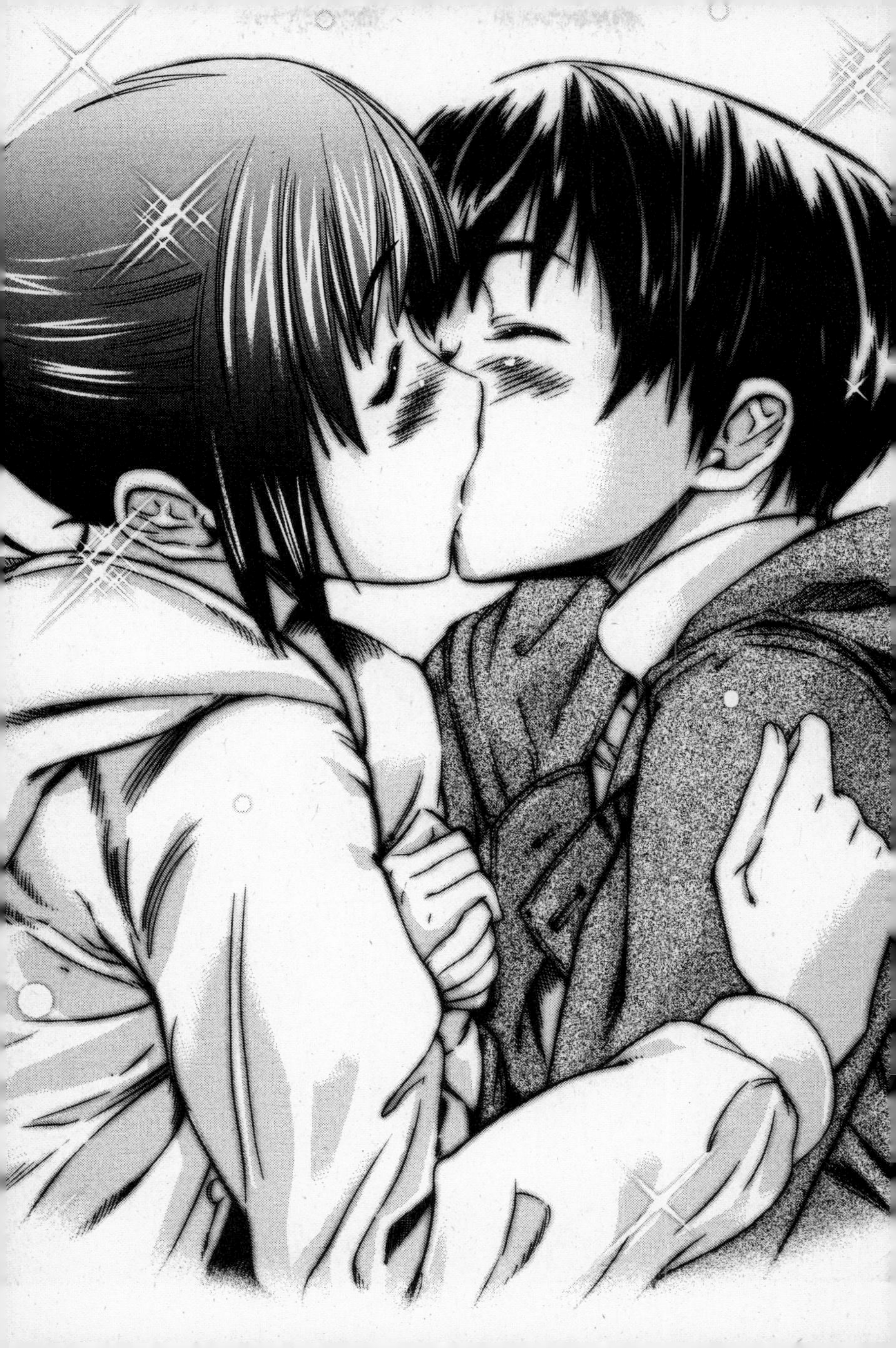

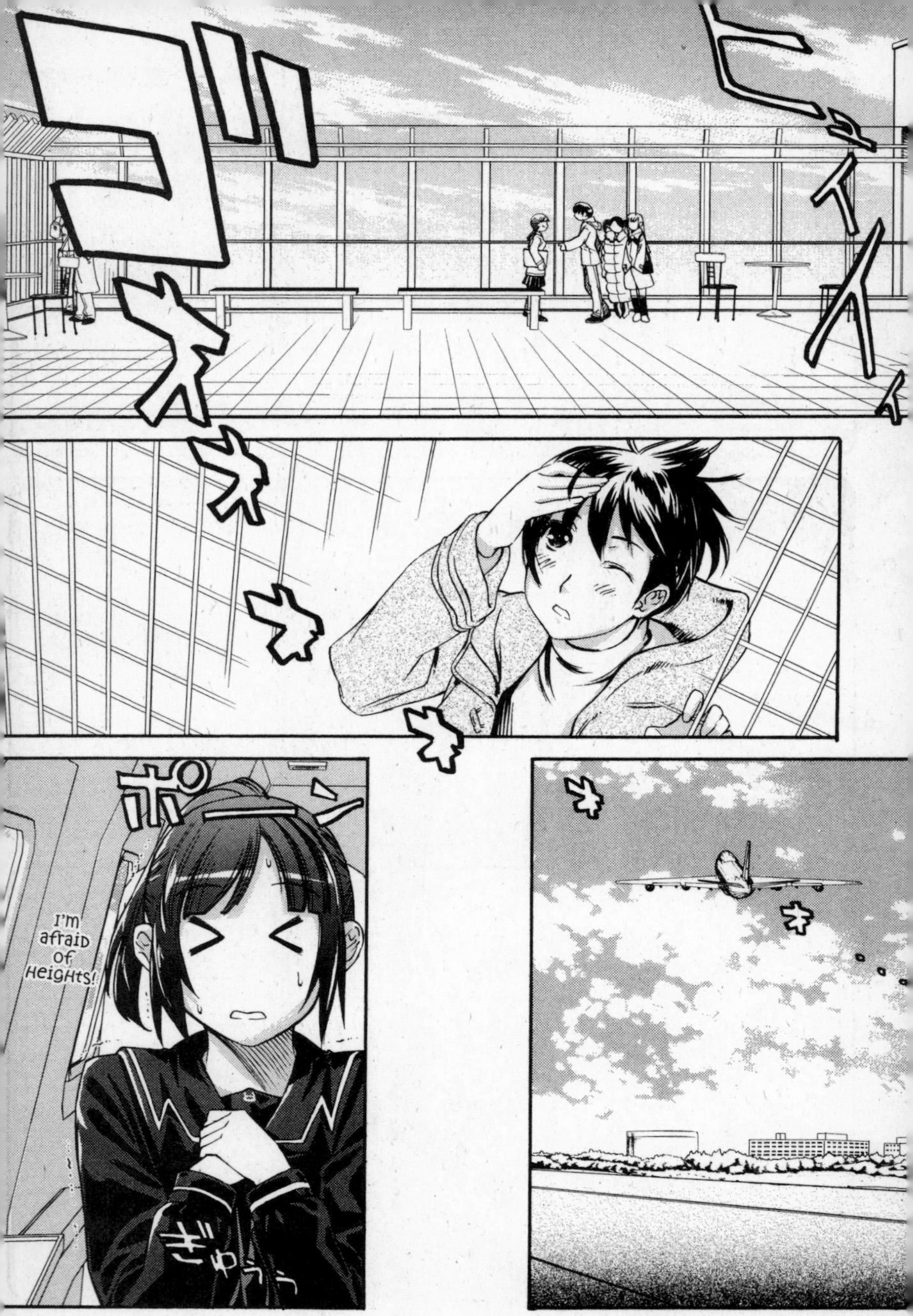

ヒュイイイィ
ゴオオオオ
ポーン
I'm afraid of heights!
ぎゅうう

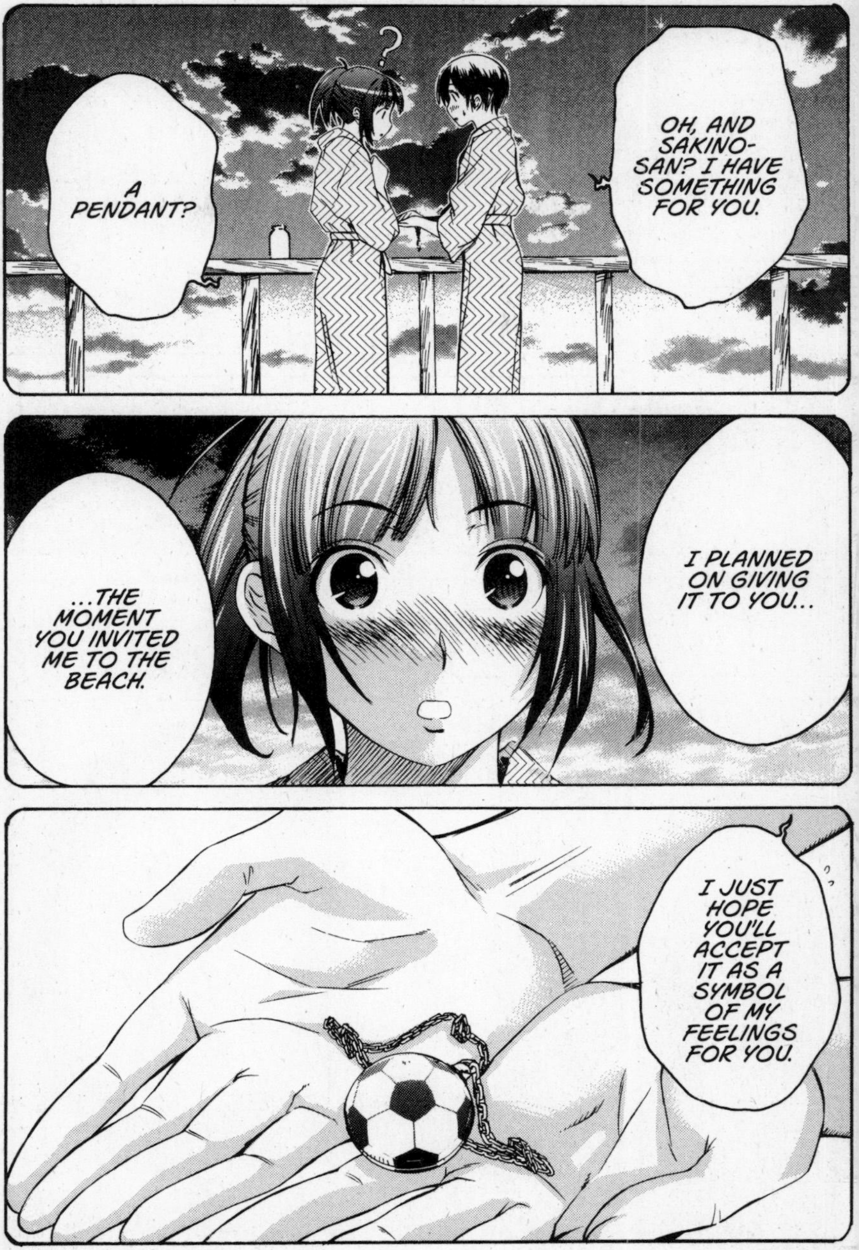
OH, AND SAKINO-SAN? I HAVE SOMETHING FOR YOU.
A PENDANT?
I PLANNED ON GIVING IT TO YOU...
...THE MOMENT YOU INVITED ME TO THE BEACH.
I JUST HOPE YOU'LL ACCEPT IT AS A SYMBOL OF MY FEELINGS FOR YOU.

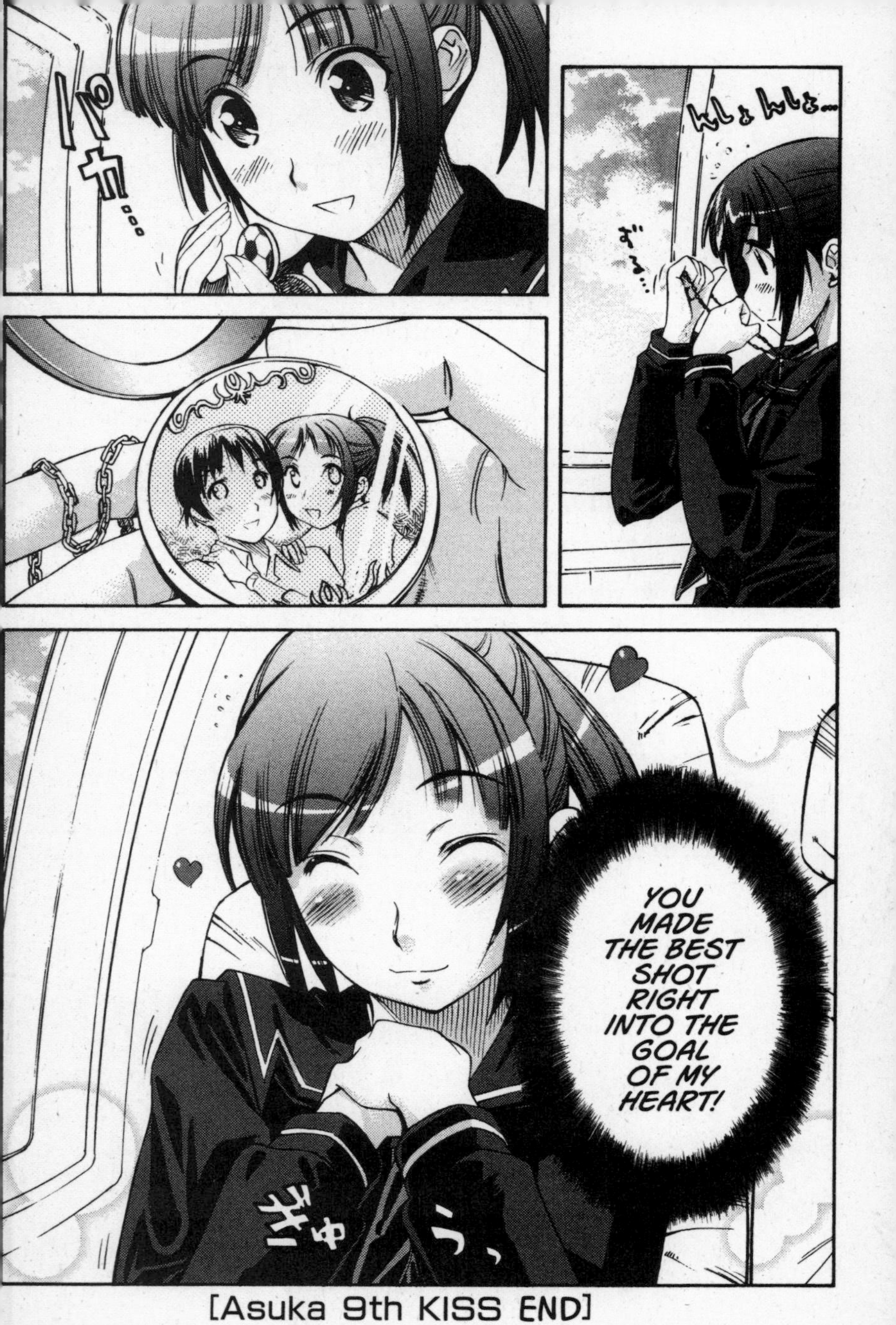

んしょんしょ…
ずる…
パカ…
YOU MADE THE BEST SHOT RIGHT INTO THE GOAL OF MY HEART!
ぎゅう

[Asuka 9th KISS END]

✩Postscript✩

Hey, everyone! Long time no see. I'm proud to announce that with your support, volume 2 of this series can now be found at your local bookstore! It's a joy to be able to draw each of these types of "heroines", and I can't thank you all enough for reading the series! I just hope you enjoy reading future volumes that feature new types of heroines.

Taro Shinonome

Assistants: Mitsuru Yamazaki, Shizuku Amano, LEE

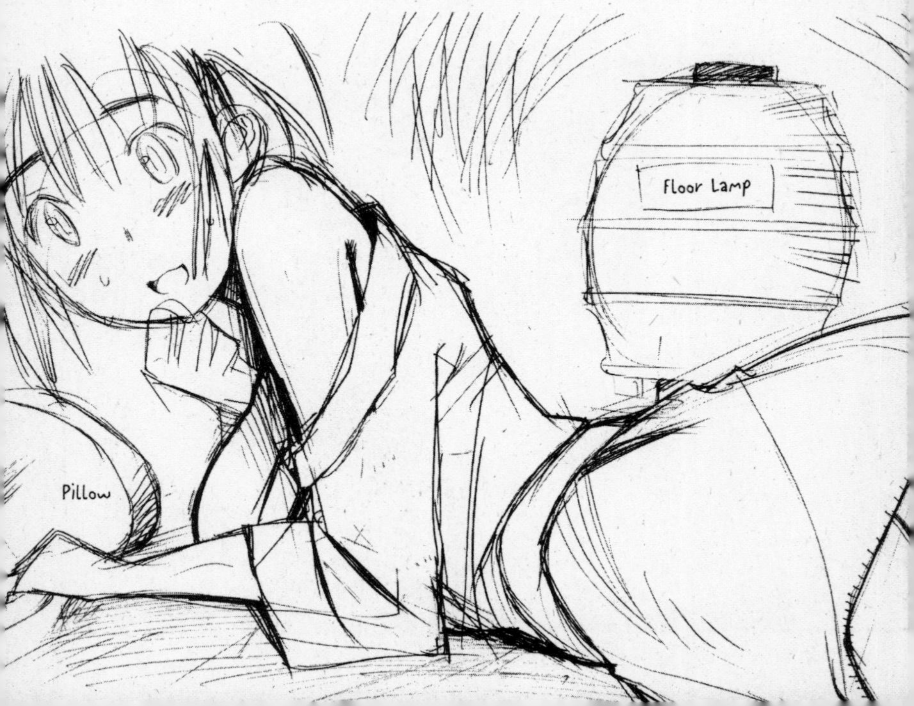
Floor Lamp
Pillow

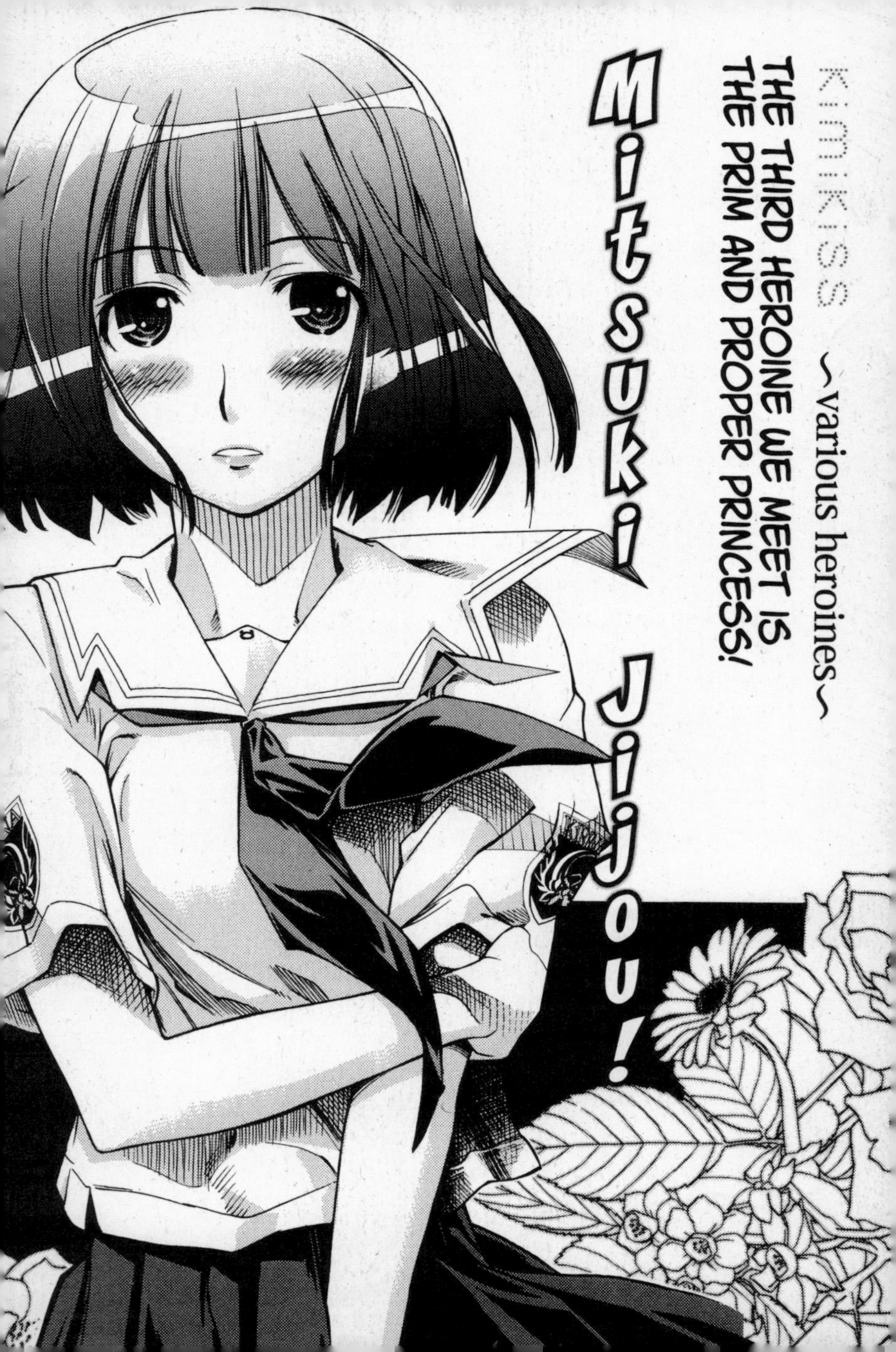
KIMIKISS
~various heroines~
THE THIRD HEROINE WE MEET IS THE PRIM AND PROPER PRINCESS!
Mitsuki Nijou!

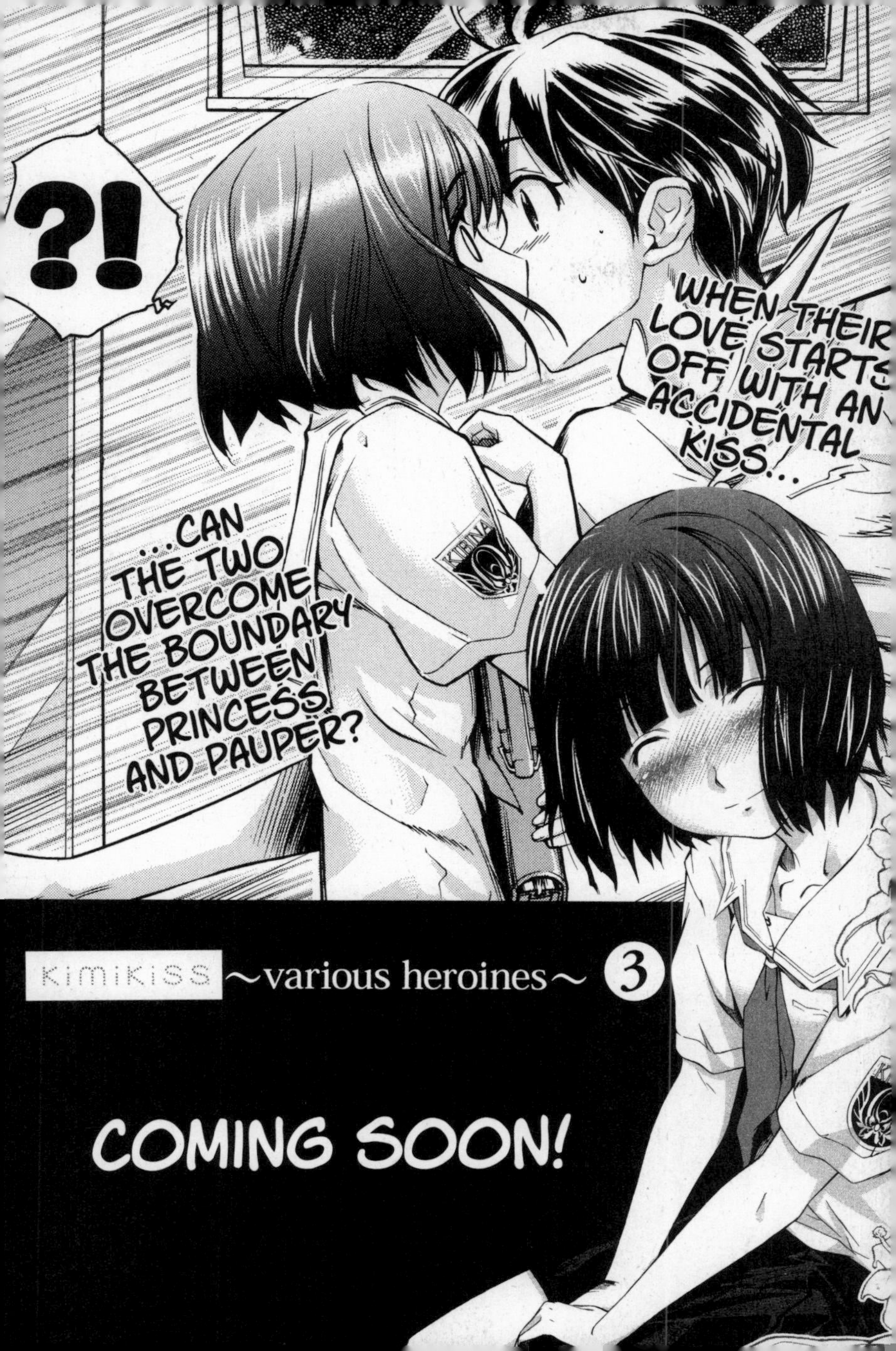
?!
WHEN THEIR LOVE STARTS OFF WITH AN ACCIDENTAL KISS...
...CAN THE TWO OVERCOME THE BOUNDARY BETWEEN PRINCESS AND PAUPER?
KimiKiSS ~various heroines~ 3
COMING SOON!

キミキス various heroines
KimiKiss

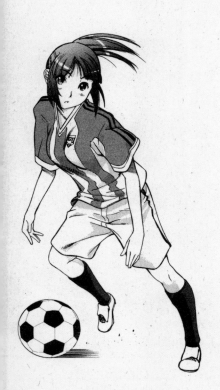

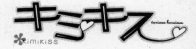

Maria Holic
TOKYOPOP
From the creator of Dazzle
Minari ENDOU
Book ONE

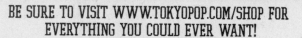

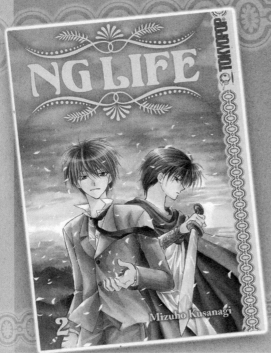

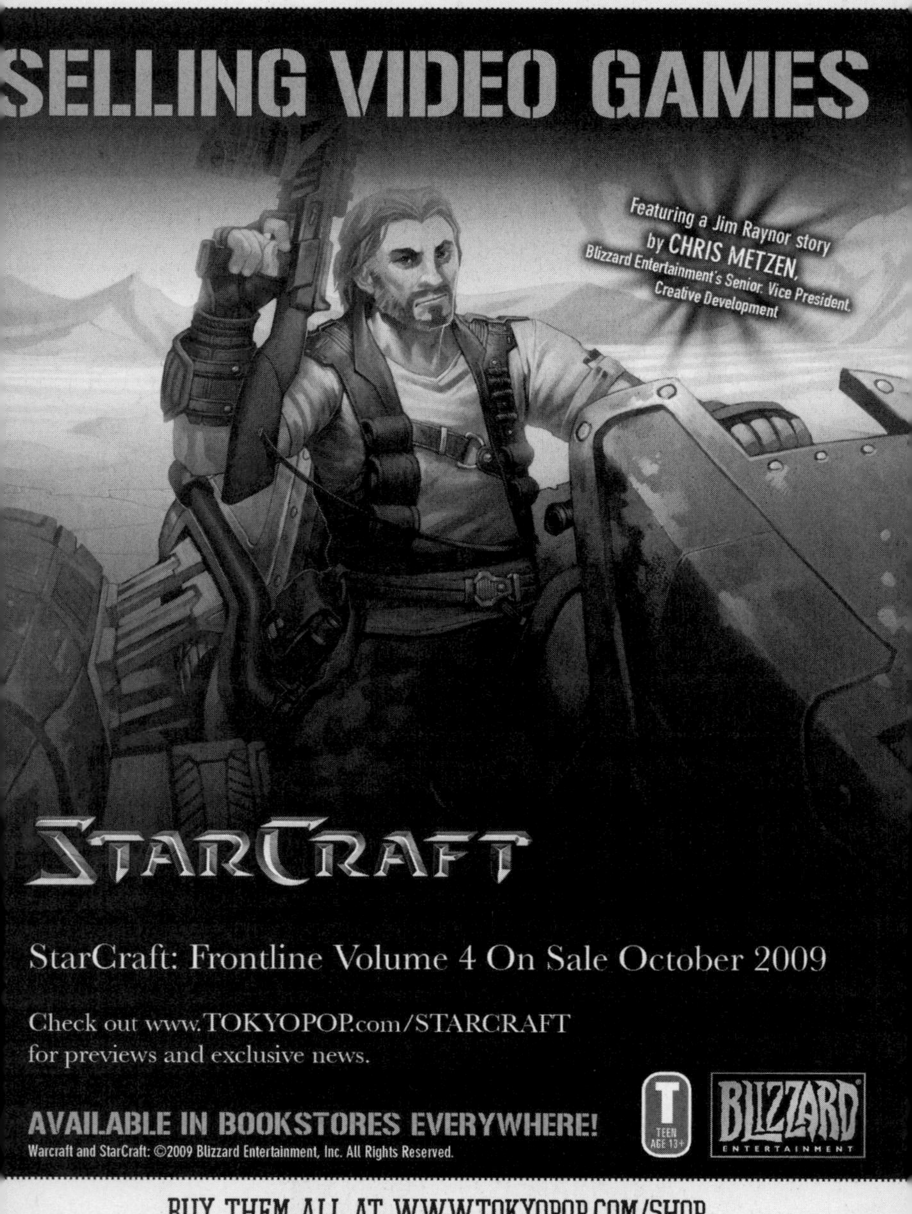
SELLING VIDEO GAMES
Featuring a Jim Raynor story by CHRIS METZEN, Blizzard Entertainment's Senior Vice President, Creative Development
STARCRAFT
StarCraft: Frontline Volume 4 On Sale October 2009
Check out www.TOKYOPOP.com/STARCRAFT for previews and exclusive news.
AVAILABLE IN BOOKSTORES EVERYWHERE!
Warcraft and StarCraft: ©2009 Blizzard Entertainment, Inc. All Rights Reserved.
T TEEN AGE 13+
BLIZZARD ENTERTAINMENT

STOP!

This is the back of the book.
You wouldn't want to spoil a great ending!

This book is printed "manga-style," in the authentic Japanese right-to-left format. Since none of the artwork has been flipped or altered, readers get to experience the story just as the creator intended. You've been asking for it, so TOKYOPOP® delivered: authentic, hot-off-the-press, and far more fun!

1
2
3
4
5
6
7
8
9
10

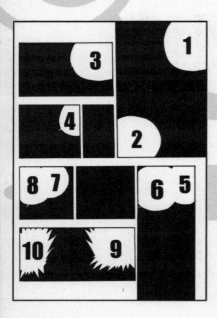

DIRECTIONS

If this is your first time reading manga-style, here's a quick guide to help you understand how it works.

It's easy... just start in the top right panel and follow the numbers. Have fun, and look for more 100% authentic manga from TOKYOPOP®!

THE MANGA REVOLUTION • LEADING
漫画革命
LEADING • THE MANGA REVOLUTION